Foreign Aid Reconsidered

Roger C. Riddell

THE JOHNS HOPKINS UNIVERSITY PRESS

BALTIMORE

JAMES CURREY

LONDON

James Currey Ltd
54b Thornhill Square, Islington
London N1 1BE

Overseas Development Institute
Regent's College, Regent's Park
London NW1 4NS

Book trade orders for edition published by
James Currey Ltd:
J.M. Dent & Sons (Distribution) Ltd
Dunhams Lane, Letchworth, Herts SG6 1LF
or Third World Publications (Co-op) Ltd
151 Stratford Road, Birmingham B11 1RD

© Roger C. Riddell 1987
First published 1987

British Library Cataloguing in Publication Data

Riddell, Roger, *1947–*
    Foreign aid reconsidered.
    1. Economic assistance – Developing
    countries   2. Developing countries –
    Economic conditions
    I. Title
    330.9172'4   HC59.7

ISBN 0-85255-103-7
ISBN 0-85255-104-5

Typeset in 10/11 pt Times by Colset Pte Ltd, Singapore
Printed in Great Britain

Contents

Part II   Theoretical Debates   79

Preface

This book is primarily a study of the ideas about aid (more specifically about official aid). It traces the fundamental ethical and theoretical questions raised in the aid debate and systematically evaluates the arguments of those in favour of official aid and those, from the right and the left, who are critical of such intervention. Considerable space is devoted to the evidence of what aid has achieved in practice, but this is set in the context of the underlying reasons for providing (and not providing) it and of the range and quality of the data that are available. It is thus in many ways a different type of book from those which are available.

The origins of the book lie, on the one hand in the superficial and rhetorical manner in which the aid debate has been conducted in recent years and, on the other, in the impact and influence upon policy-makers that political rightist and economic *laisser faire* ideas about aid and its interventionist role in the development process have had in the 1980s. Until politicians began to take an interest in and indeed implement policies influenced by these criticisms it remained true that aid administrators and the bulk of development professionals concerned with aid questions took little notice of these views. No rigorous analysis of the different rightist criticisms of aid had yet been carried out. Likewise, although of less immediate political interest, the leftist critics have continued their assaults on foreign aid without their arguments being subject to formal assessment even though their influence, if not formally acknowledged, has been important. Perhaps most surprising, however, is the fact that aid donors and their supporters in the churches and aid agencies have proceeded over the past 30 years or so to proclaim that the provision of aid to the Third World is a moral issue, without analysing in any depth the basis for this assertion or its validity vis-à-vis alternative moral beliefs and opposing ethical viewpoints.

The book comprises four distinct, although interrelated, parts. Part I, 'Ethical Foundations', considers the moral questions raised in the aid debate. Part II, 'Theoretical Debates', discusses the various largely macro-theories put forward to support or challenge the view that aid can assist in the development process of Third World countries and examines the cross-country evidence available to support the differing theoretical viewpoints. Part III, 'Assessing the Evidence', examines first the methods used to evaluate aid's impact at the micro-level and then discusses the project and country-specific evidence available for making overall judgements about it. The final part, 'Retaking the Middle Ground', brings together the major threads from the preceding chapters and comes to some overall conclusions about the case for aid and the arguments of its critics. Although it rejects many of the criticisms and argues that there remains a good case for governments to provide aid, the book concludes that the evidence upon which this view is based is far less robust than many advocates of aid have maintained. Ironically, too, the case for aid would be considerably strengthened by the injection of far more honesty into the debate: acknowledging both the data inadequacies that exist and the force of a number of criticisms made as well as recognising that the case for aid is frequently over-stated.

In common with many books on development and in keeping with the breadth of the subject under consideration, this study is interdisciplinary in scope. However, the incorporation of questions of ethics and political philosophy in Part I leads readers into academic disciplines not frequently discussed in such depth in the development literature. On the other hand, some of the more technical theoretical debates of macroeconomics contained in Part II may prove rather detailed for the less specialised reader. A judicious use of the contents pages and a reading of the introductory and concluding chapters of each Part should enable one to pass over the more technical aspects of the book without losing the overall flow of the argument. If ethical or economic theories dominate certain parts of the book, it should not be thought that political questions are thereby underplayed. Although political issues do not feature as such in the contents pages, they constitute a recurring theme throughout the book and receive more detailed treatment in Part III and, also in chapters 11 and 13 in Part II.

The considerable work that has gone into producing this book has involved the input of many hands. Within the ODI, critically important background work and the production of discussion papers and bibliographies have been undertaken by Nick Chisholm, Adam Fforde, Desmond Gasper and Sheila Page. A reference group of scholars and technicians in the field of foreign aid has provided both encouragement and critical comment on the various chapters as they have been produced. In this context I would like to thank especially Basil Cracknell, Charles Elliot, Paul Mosley, Sir Peter Preston, Sir Austin Robinson, John White and ODI colleagues, Adrian Hewitt and the Director, Tony Killick, for their help and assistance. Beyond this group, the following people have also greatly aided the project's evolution with their comments and suggestions: Bob Berg, Nigel Dower, Geoff Harcourt, Gerard Hughes, Peter McCaffery, Roger Plant, Vernon Ruttan, Keith Smith and Paul Spray. A special word of thanks must go to ODI's librarians, Andrea Siemsen and Gill Wilcox, for their help in tracking down documents, to Margaret Cornell for editing the book, and, not least, to Ramila Mistry and Barbara Tilbury for typing numerous drafts. Finally, and importantly, I would like to record my thanks to the Leverhulme Trust for funding the study, to my wife, Abby, for her continual encouragement, and to Eliza for her delightful distractions. None of the above, as they say, can be held responsible for the views expressed in the book, for which I alone take the blame.

PART I
Ethical Foundations

1 Introduction

Governments have appealed in the past, and appeal today, to a variety of explanations to legitimise their granting or withholding of foreign aid to the Third World. National self-interest, commercial considerations, historical links, political goals and the straightforward desire simply to accelerate economic growth in less developed countries are all motives that have been acknowledged as directly affecting policies governing aid flows over the last 25 years or so.

What concerns us here, however, is the claim made by governments, commentators and supporters of aid that it should be given for *moral* reasons. Since its inception, official development assistance (oda) has been continuously provided on the grounds of morality, with governments asserting that there is a moral obligation to grant aid and the general public in donor countries supporting official programmes on that basis. In some instances, for example Sweden in the early 1960s, countries have maintained that morality provides the exclusive reason for an aid programme; in others the moral justification for providing aid is set alongside other reasons. This is, for example, still the current view of the British Government: 'It is both right from a moral point of view and in our long-term interest to promote economic and social development in the poor countries of the world, particularly those with which Britain is closely associated' (ODA, 1983). It is a view which is supported by the British public. For example, a national opinion poll in 1983 found 71 per cent of people in favour of helping poorer countries, and, of these, 78 per cent gave some sort of moral explanation for their positive attitude, citing specifically humanitarian reasons, conscience, duty, Christian duty and the needs of the poor as the underlying reason for their support.[1] More generally, a 1983 EEC-wide opinion survey found strong support for the statement 'We have a moral duty to help them', referring to the Third World.[2] For the 'aid lobby' in particular, the moral basis for having an official aid programme is the fundamental starting-point for all their activities.

Nevertheless, very little systematic analysis has been undertaken either to justify these claims or to counter the views of the different critics whose ethical starting-points and methods of approach lead to very different conclusions. All too often the moral case for aid has been stated boldly but with little or no reasoning to explain it. The tautological statements of the 1960s, which frequently based the moral legitimacy for aid on the fact that it was 'right to give it', sound hollow in the 1980s.

With the benefit of hindsight, this is perhaps understandable. There have always been writers who have challenged the conventional view that there is an essentially moral dimension to the official provision of foreign aid. Yet their views remained, until around the end of the 1970s, both peripheral to mainstream thinking and, more importantly, largely without influence in government decision-making circles. There was little need to spell out the moral case for aid as so few people or groups appeared to challenge the conventionally accepted view.

3

What the swing to the right of the 1980s brought, however, was not only a challenge to widely held beliefs about intervention and planning in development and the giving of greater prominence to the beneficial role of market forces, but also a challenge to the assertions made in support of the ethical case for official aid. The two are of course interrelated. That British aid has declined by 3.7 per cent each year in real terms in the period 1979/80–1984/5 (OECD, 1986:8) is in part due to the government's overall approach to public spending, but it is almost certainly also attributable to less conviction in influential circles about the force of the moral argument. For example, the moral case for aid now seems to have little influence for *The Times*, which commented editorially in 1984: 'Aid is a transfer of taxpayers' money from one government to another . . . such transfers are thus a wholly political matter at both ends of the spectrum'.[3] Across the Atlantic, the Under Secretary for Economic Affairs specifically referred to the influence of Peter Bauer and his colleague Basil Yamey in a speech to the Heritage Foundation in 1983. *Inter alia* he commented:[4]

> It is not news to anyone here that Bauer and Yamey make a powerful case against official development assistance. . . . They have done an important job in demolishing many of the 'economic' arguments often cited in favour of official development assistance. Personally I am persuaded by the major thrusts of their arguments.

Recent conclusions by Singer are profoundly disturbing (1984:1–2):

> My own guess is that perhaps 20 per cent of all aid is morally supportable, about 20 per cent is clearly not moral and 60 per cent belongs to one or other of the mixed cases. Whether or not such a record justifies aid at the present or increased level is a matter of judgement, according to what weight we attach to the moral case for aid as against other justifications. What is clear is that those making a moral case for aid should be concerned to change the mixture so that more aid is clearly morally justifiable both as to motives and as to effects; and perhaps more important, that in the big bag of mixed cases the morally desirable element becomes stronger.

The 'new orthodoxy' of the 1980s highlights a shift in the manner in which aid is viewed. It has found its most fertile ground in Britain, the USA and West Germany. The moral case does not appear to have been challenged in official circles in Italy or in the Scandinavian countries. In the 1960s the central question in the aid debate revolved around whether aid contributed to aggregate growth. In the 1970s the question hinged upon whether aid has a direct impact on the poor. On these bases it was evaluated. Today, however, for a number of critics the debate appears to have shifted back to the assumptions upon which aid is given. If the vigorous promotion and expansion of market forces lead to more rapid development than can be achieved by aid intervention which is said to inhibit such expansion, then analysing the impact and effects of aid would appear to be irrelevant. Equally, if aid is viewed solely as a political matter, then moral arguments will also be irrelevant. Or, to take a central argument of some critics, if it is accepted that the needs of the poor in developing countries provide no or few moral imperatives for donor countries to address those needs, then it matters little whether aid goes to the poorest or not. To run tests on the relationship between aid, savings and growth or to produce expensive analyses of aid effectiveness does little to convince those whose anti-aid – and influential – perspective is based on different *a priori* starting-points.

For those who believe that there is a strong moral case for official aid, or, in the words of Singer, for those 'concerned to change the mixture so that more aid is morally justifiable both as to motives and as to effects,' it would appear essential to put forward a comprehensive defence of the ethical case which both incorporates all the elements of the different arguments making up the total moral view and addresses the opposing perspectives of the critics. The other option is to disregard the criticisms completely or to ignore them by continuing to assert alternative beliefs without addressing the counter-assertions or theories upon which they are based. This is what has tended to happen in practice and it is probably a contributory factor to the influence that the criticisms from the right, especially, have increasingly had in Britain and the USA.

To some extent, too, the phenomenon of Band Aid/Live Aid/Sports Aid etc. has also, albeit indirectly, assisted the critics of the moral case by giving greater prominence to the individual response, thus eclipsing the collective moral response of governments.[5]

This first part of the book explores the crucial ethical dimensions of foreign aid. It highlights, first, the complexities of the apparently simple view that there is a moral case and then focuses particular attention on those critics who have sought to attack the moral argument. While the discussion will conclude that many of the criticisms can be convincingly challenged, it also reveals that at least a part of the moral case is dependent upon an evaluation of the effects of aid. These will be analysed in Parts II and III of the book.

The next chapter examines the manner in which appeals to morality have been used by governments and international agencies to justify their aid programmes. This is followed by an outline of the various elements making up the complete moral case. Chapters 4 to 6 discuss the main challenges to the moral argument: those that reject the notion of obligation, those that argue that because aid does not achieve its objectives any obligation to provide it falls away, and those that argue that the debate about aid and morality is irrelevant as a basis for government decision- and policy-making.

A preliminary caveat needs to be mentioned here. Debate about the ethics of foreign aid can and often does become confused because of carelessness in the use of terms. We are concerned here solely with official development assistance, or economic aid from donor governments and multilateral agencies, and not with military aid or voluntary contributions by individuals to charities or voluntary associations concerned with Third World development. In this discussion, our interest in individual ethical beliefs and theories will be confined only to those which throw light on the general moral questions raised in official aid transfers.

Notes

1. Social Surveys (Gallup Poll), 'Overseas Aid 7–11 January 1983', conducted on behalf of Office of Population Censuses and Surveys, London 1983, CQ848/848A (mimeo).
2. *The Courier*, No. 88, 1984, pp. 39–43.
3. *The Times*, 27 November 1984.
4. A Wallis, *Economics and Politics: The Quandary of Foreign Aid*, US Department of State, Bureau of Public Affairs, Current Policy No. 461, March 1983.
5. For instance, when news of the Ethiopian famine first hit the television screens in 1984 and the question of sending increased quantities of official aid to the victims arose in Parliament, Mr Rifkind, the Minister of State at the Foreign and Commonwealth Office with responsibility for Africa, resisted pleas for more government aid to Ethiopia arguing that the best form of help was through charities like Oxfam and Save The Children Fund (*The Guardian*, 28 October 1984).

2 The Unquestioned Consensus

There can be few informed observers of international relations and professionals concerned with aid and development today who are unaware that the appeal to morality as a justification for governments of rich countries to provide development aid is contentious and controversial. It is all the more surprising therefore to find that when reference to morality as a reason for donor aid programmes began to appear regularly in official statements in the late 1950s and early 1960s, the moral case was stated boldly, repeatedly and usually without any explanation. In short, there would appear to have arisen fairly rapidly an unquestioned consensus that donor governments had a moral obligation to provide aid. That said, however, it has been rare in the past as today to find governments appealing *solely* to morality as the basis for their aid programmes. One of those rare exceptions has been Sweden. In 1962, the Swedish Government first outlined the justification for its recently initiated foreign aid programme thus (quoted in Myrdal, 1970:382):

> The concept of human dignity and the claims to social equality, that have marked development in the majority of Western countries during the past century, no longer halt at the frontiers of nationality or race. . . . The growing feeling of international solidarity and responsibility reflects a deeper insight into the facts that peace, freedom and welfare are not an exclusively national concern, but something increasingly universal and indivisible. The idealistic motives behind assistance are thus at the same time highly realistic . . . No other kind of motive is needed for the extension of assistance by Sweden to underdeveloped countries.

It was two years previously, in 1960, that President Kennedy had (at least in theory) steered US policy on aid away from criteria based on anti-communism and towards an underlying moral basis. In his inauguration speech he declared in characteristic style (quoted in Higgins, 1968:576).

> To those people in the huts and villages of half the globe struggling to break the bonds of mass misery, we pledge our best efforts to help them to help themselves, for whatever period is required – not because the Communists may be doing it, not because we seek their votes, but because it is right. If a free society cannot help the many who are poor, it cannot save the few who are rich.[1]

In 1963 in France the influential Jeanneney Commission Report stated 'The first reason, sufficient in itself, for a French policy of co-operation with the Third World is the feeling which France has of her duties towards humanity'. (ODI, 1964:20). And it was in this same year that the White Paper *Aid to Developing Countries* was published in the UK. This White Paper is significant in British government aid thinking because it indicates the shift in policy to an acceptance that development assistance should be provided not only for countries for which Britain had colonial responsibility but also for independent poor countries.[2] The

1965 White Paper is also a significant document because it spells out what were to become thereafter the twin issues providing at different times and with different emphases the moral justification for official UK aid: human need in situations of extreme poverty, and growing inequality between the industrialised and developing countries. Paras. 2 and 3 of *Aid to Developing Countries* state:[3]

> During the last three years the need for aid has become no less. The difference between the standards of living in the industrialised and in the developing nations has not diminished – on the contrary it has increased. . . . Over a large part of the world poverty and malnutrition still persist; disease and illiteracy are still widespread; and the increase in population exerts a remorseless pressure on resources.

Once the various leading donor countries had raised and accepted moral grounds as a justification for their aid efforts, the moral basis for aid became part of general conventional wisdom. This is illustrated by the influential 1969 report, *Partners in Development*, under the Chairmanship of Lester Pearson, which could answer the question it posed: 'Why Aid?' with the following statement, although adding later that the morality did not provide the whole case for aid (Commission on International Development 1969:8):

> The simplest answer to the question is the moral one: that it is only right for those who have to share with those who have not.
> Moral obligations, however, are usually felt with particular force inside national groups to which people belong and with which they identify. Concern with the needs of other and poorer nations is the expression of a new and fundamental aspect of the modern age – the awareness that we live in a village world, that we belong to a world community.
> It is this which makes the desire to help into more than a moral impulse felt by an individual; makes it into a political and social imperative for governments, which now accept at least a degree of accountability in their relations with each other.
> It is a recognition that concern with improvement of the human condition is no longer divisible. If the rich countries try to make it so, if they concentrate on the elimination of poverty and backwardness at home and ignore them abroad, what would happen to the principles by which they seek to live? Could the moral and social foundations of their own societies remain firm and steady if they washed their hands of the plight of others?

While appeals to morality were becoming commonplace in official documents on aid by the end of the first development decade – and similar quotations from other donor governments could easily be assembled – a careful reading of the above quotations reveals that the general appeal to morality is in reality an appeal to different sorts of moral arguments. For example, the Jeanneney and the SIDA Report appeal to 'human dignity' and the 'duty of human solidarity' which raises the question of what such terms mean and imply. Kennedy's argument is that the alleviation of human misery places a duty on his government to act, while both the Swedish and UK quotations also appeal to egalitarian motives. The Pearson statement implies initially that the moral imperative is based on egalitarian principles, but then it switches to needs and ends up by appealing to logical consistency in government action by arguing that governments have (equal?) responsibility to eliminate poverty at home and abroad because of a new awareness of a world community. Thus the moral basis for aid appears to be based on different types of criteria: on human solidarity, on alleviation of misery, on need, on a sense of equality and on the recognition of a newly created international community.

Of all these different arguments, the belief that the rich have a duty to help the poor has been a dominant theme in the 1970s and early 1980s, influenced significantly by the emphasis in the development literature on addressing first the basic needs of the poor. For example, in its publication *Employment, Growth and Basic Needs, A One-World Problem*, the International Labour Office wrote in 1976 (1976:105 and 107):

> Once the commitment to pursue a basic needs strategy has been firmly established and the necessary structural changes set in motion, the inflows of external capital under appropriate forms and conditions can materially assist in the acceleration of the attainment of basic needs targets. . . . In order to assist in the provision of basic needs, official development assistance would have to be directed to the poorest countries and to poverty groups in other developing countries.

In Britain and other countries this focus was crystallised in the slogan 'aid to the poorest', institutionalised, in the British case, in the 1975 White Paper *The Changing Emphasis in British Aid Policies, More Help for the Poorest*. Dame Judith Hart, who as Minister of Overseas Development in the mid-1970s played a leading role in changing the emphasis in thinking about British aid, attempted more than any other government spokesperson before or since to expand upon the precise nature of the moral obligation to provide aid and to integrate it into other broad government objectives. Taking up the point made in the Pearson Report on the duties of government, she argued that there is and can be an overlap between short-term moral imperatives and long-term political interests (1975:2):

> Every department of the British Government must exercise its efforts and its talents to protect and to further the British interest. That is and must be the primary concern of all of us. But there is a large area of policies and programmes in which the definition of British interest is wide open to discussion and debate. There are times when it can pay too much regard to the short term and too little to the long term. There are times when the understanding of the economic and human situation of two-thirds of the world's population is not only relevant but essential to the definition of long-term interest. There are times when the moral responsibility of the British people – remembering that all the Commonwealth developing countries were part of our history of imperialism, which was an unusual mix of exploitation and paternalism – towards a high proportion of the poor of the world must be exercised if Government is to represent in its own actions and policies the essential morality of political philosophies in Britain.

Three years later, in pointing to the seemingly all-powerful moral case for aid argued 18 years previously by President Kennedy that it is our duty to help the poor, Mrs Hart shifted the moral argument by explaining that this duty is not only based on the compulsion to meet the *needs* of the poor but also that the fulfilment of these needs creates basic human *rights* which to be respected demand action. She said (1978:12):

> When the peoples of the Third World, for the first time, can meet their basic needs – and let me slightly re-formulate that familiar phrase by saying 'when their basic human rights are met' – then, for the first time, they will have the opportunity for full participation within their own societies. They will have the opportunity to determine for themselves how best to create a legal and political structure which protects and advances their rights.

Since the change of government in Britain in 1979, the appeal to morality is still made officially as a basis for providing aid. However, recent statements tend to parallel the bold assertions of the 1960s more than the attempts in the 1970s to explain in more detail how and in what way morality enters into aid-giving and how the moral case for aid can be harmonised with other objectives. For example, in his November 1980 policy statement on overseas aid, the then Minister, Sir Neil Marten stated: 'The Government believes there are powerful moral, economic and political reasons for providing aid to the developing countries, especially for the poorest' (ODA, 1980). Three years later his successor, Timothy Raison, said 'It is both right from a moral point of view and in our long-term interest to promote economic development in the poor countries of the world, particularly those with which Britain is closely associated' (ODA, 1983). No explanation was offered to explain the basis upon which the moral claim was made.[4]

The blending of appeals to morality and the long-term interests of donor countries, referred to by former Minister Raison, is a particular feature emerging in official pronouncements in the late 1970s and 1980s. Note, for example, the change in emphasis in justification for Swedish aid today compared with the solely altruistic arguments of the early 1960s. Why does Sweden give aid?

> The main reason is that we regard solidarity with the under-privileged as a moral responsibility. This is a reflection of what we do in our own country. We allocate resources to those who are in difficulty, either temporarily or more permanently, people like the unemployed, the ill and the elderly. But our motives are not entirely disinterested. If the gap between the developing and the rich countries continues to grow, tensions in the world will go on increasing, with adverse effects for all nations. The promotion of equality and development is thus an integral part of our general endeavours to promote peace in the world. A third reason is the interdependence of all countries, rich and poor. . . . (SIDA 1983:2; see also Palmlund in Fruhling (1986).)

This merging of morality and national interest is developed and expanded upon in the two reports of the Brandt Commission under the term 'mutual interests'. The Commission argues both that a world community (à la Pearson) carries with it moral implications and also that additional moral education has to take place. It states (1980:77):

> All the lessons of reform within national societies confirm the gains for all in a process of change that makes the world a less unequal and a more just and habitable place. The great moral imperatives that underpinned such reforms are as valid internationally as they were and are nationally; but experience confirms that there are other imperatives also, rooted in the hard-headed self-interest of all countries and people, that reinforce the claim of human solidarity. World society now recognises more clearly than ever before its mutual needs; it must accept a shared responsibility for meeting them.
>
> Citizens of rich countries must be brought to understand that the problems of the world must be tackled too, and that a vigorous aid policy would in the end not be a burden but an investment in a healthier world economy as well as in a safer world community. International development issues must be given the attention at a high political level that their urgency entitles them to.

However, it too returns to the general moral imperatives implied by a shared humanity as the key justification for aid. In the opening paragraphs of its chapter on mutual interests it states (1980:64):

> We do not believe that mutual interests alone provide an adequate basis for all the changes that are needed. Especially as far as the poorest people and the poorest countries are concerned, the principal motives for our proposals are human solidarity and a commitment to international social justice. There must be an end to deprivation and suffering. It cannot be accepted that in one part of the world most people live relatively comfortably, while in another they struggle for sheer survival. As we shall argue, there are material reasons for trying to end this state of affairs – international political stability, expanding export markets, the preservation of the biological environment, the limitation of population growth. But we speak of solidarity as something that goes beyond mutual interests.

The unquestioning moral assertions that characterise the language of Brandt and Pearson and most official pronouncements of donor governments contrast sharply with the often hard-hitting criticisms which will be discussed in subsequent chapters. A bridge between the two can, in part, be found in recent reports of the Chairman of the Development Assistance Committee (DAC) of the Organisation for Economic Co-operation and Development. These exhibit an awareness of the need to find the best possible rationale for development assistance but also that the unexplained assertions found in official national statements and in international reports are more open to question than the bold statements would suggest. For example, in his 1981 Review, the then Chairman of the DAC, the American John Lewis, recognised that moral claims within and between states are substantially different and require different sorts of justification. He wrote (DAC 1981:26):

> According to most political thought and practice, the same norms of resource-sharing do not apply between nation states as apply within states. In the latter case, concessional transfers, mediated by the central government, typically flow from richer to poorer areas as a matter of right and routine, just as they do from richer to poorer classes. In the between states case, however, the responsibility to which national governments normally are held accountable is serving the interests of their own constituents, not doing good to outsiders. Seen from the perspective of donor governments, therefore, promotion of Third World development is not quite plausible as an ultimate or basic national purpose; it is an intermediate objective upon which donors bring to bear various aid and other policy instruments as a means of furthering certain of their ultimate ends that they believe development promotion serves.

Clearly, the moral case for aid is a more complex issue than official statements would seem to imply. As Lewis also points out, there are often unstated rationales lying behind justifications for aid made on the basis of human solidarity. With striking honesty he argues (*ibid*.:26):

> Why some governments give development assistance to other governments is a vexed question. The impulse of development professionals, mindful of the philosophical quagmire into which it can lead, often is to suppress the question. Thus in this Report two years ago note simply was made of the fact that all DAC Members (whatever their differences in the priority assigned) have adopted the promotion of Third World development as one of their serious and demonstrated national objectives. Implicitly the plea was: let us not delve behind this overt consensus into the diverse, partially conflicted, rationales motivating us; let us, just as we do when we sign an International Development Strategy or participate in the World Bank, accept development promotion as a *per se* objective and concentrate instead on the operational problems we share.

For the critics, however, and for the growing numbers of sceptics in the 1980s, the fundamental questions that are concealed in the statements which imply a consensus that aid is a moral issue are precisely those issues which need to be debated. But before examining in more detail the arguments of the critics, we now turn from the language of officialdom and, as we have seen, the different sorts of claims that are made under the umbrella term 'moral' to consider the different assumptions that lie behind the seemingly simple claim that aid is a moral issue.

Notes

1. It is not being argued here that for Kennedy, as for President Truman before him or for President Nixon subsequently, the moral principle for providing aid was the sole criterion, nor that quite soon afterwards other statements were made to contradict this particular perspective. The whole thrust of US aid policy is discussed further in Chapter 6 below.
2. This position had been rejected in the 1957 White Paper, *The United Kingdom's Role in Commonwealth Development* Cmnd 237, except 'in very special circumstances'.
3. *Aid to Developing Countries*, Cmnd 2147, HMSO, London, September 1963.
4. At much the same time, the former Minister, Sir Neil Marten confirming this view, stated 'our foremost aim must be to encourage faster economic growth in the poorest countries of the world and help raise living standards. As resources are scarce, we must concentrate on areas where help is most needed.' (Marten, 1983:113).

3 The Moral Case for Aid

Building up the moral case

The moral case for governments to provide foreign aid has been under attack for many years, although attacks in the past were confined largely to the pages of academic journals. A feature of many of today's criticisms is that they are frequently produced in the national press and so are becoming more familiar to a wider public. In practice there has been not one, but a variety of assaults. Some are based on different theories of development, others on different theories of moral philosophy; some on analysing the evidence of what aid has done in practice, others on *a priori* principles, for which the evidence of what aid has achieved in practice is irrelevant; some reject outright all moral obligations, and again others seek to show that the moral imperative for aid is outweighed by other competing moral obligations.

This range of assaults suggests that the view that governments have a moral obligation to provide foreign aid is, in fact, a highly complex claim. This is not only because the proposition contains three distinct elements – moral obligation, governments, and foreign aid – but also because foreign aid is not an end in itself. Development assistance, as it is technically known, is provided for the purpose of achieving secondary objectives. At its most general level, it is provided to promote or to assist the achievement of development, a term itself open to a variety of interpretations.

Examining the different criticisms that have been and are made, it appears that a series of distinct steps is required to build up the complete moral case. The first step is to show that there is a moral basis for policy-oriented action. That there is such a basis itself rests on the belief that some explicit circumstances create the moral obligation to act. Most commonly, these circumstances relate to three particular issues: the needs of extremely poor people in extremely poor countries; large (and growing) inequalities between those with excess resources and those with insufficient; and thirdly, historical relationships evaluated as unjust and requiring restitution and/or compensation. Many arguing the moral case appeal to each of these three starting-points; yet it is not necessary to accept all of them – to accept just one is sufficient to form the basis for building up the total moral case. The following section of this chapter describes the various approaches to the nature of the moral obligation commonly used to justify this claim.

However, the belief that there is a general obligation for something to be done is frequently taken by aid lobbyists and others to imply that therefore governments should provide foreign aid. While this proposition is certainly a necessary basis for arriving at that conclusion, indeed it is a crucial starting-point, it is by no means sufficient to clinch the argument. It is also necessary to show the following: that direct intervention in general and external assistance in particular will help to achieve Third World development and poverty alleviation; that government-to-government action is an appropriate method of intervention; that governments themselves have moral obligations to intervene; that these obligations are more important than other moral claims on their resources; and, finally, that the aid funds allocated by governments either do help the poor in Third World countries in practice or, in the case of failure, are likely to do so in the future.

It would appear, then, that there are some seven steps in the argument necessary to conclude that governments have a moral obligation to provide aid to the Third World. We shall now go through them and their criticisms in more detail.

The first proposition, and the one which is frequently, although incorrectly, viewed as a sufficient condition for official aid's moral justification is this:

1. Comparing domestic living standards with those of others and contrasting domestic development with the lack of development in other countries and among certain groups in other societies, the potential donor accepts that there are problems out of which arise a moral basis for action.

As we have seen, the specific circumstances which invoke the moral response vary from government to government. But widely accepted reasons for action include broad concepts of poverty and inequality in comparison with the absolute and/or relative wealth in donor countries. One major group of criticisms questions whether the facts do indeed, or should, evoke the response that there *is* a duty to act. Is there, the critics ask, a duty to reduce inequalities, to relieve poverty and to meet human needs, especially when action to address these circumstances conflicts with people's other rights? Those who reject this proposition would answer no. Some critics, too, would challenge the view that past historical relationships between industrialised and Third World countries were unjust, and some whether, even if they were, restitution is now required. Nevertheless, even if one does accept that the facts and the ethical beliefs of people in donor countries do provide the moral basis for action, there is still a long way to go before agreeing that therefore *governments* have a moral duty to provide development assistance. Before this conclusion is reached governments would need to agree to six more propositions.

The second proposition, strongly contested by those critics who believe that policies to encourage the expansion and penetration of free market forces provide the best solution to development problems, can be stated as follows:

2. The potential donor government accepts that direct intervention can help to solve the problems that have been recognised as providing a moral basis for action.

Critics accepting proposition 1 and rejecting proposition 2 might argue as follows: yes, the poor in developing countries lack the basic necessities required for them to live a human life, but these people will have their basic needs met quickly and more efficiently by providing the conditions necessary for wealth creation through market expansion rather than by direct intervention which, of its nature, frustrates the rapid development of markets.

3. The potential donor government believes not only that direct intervention in general can further the development objectives that it wishes to see achieved but that external financial and/or technical assistance to assist present development strategies will help in the achievement of its development objectives.

This proposition will, of course, be rejected by those who believe that non-intervention is the better policy (those who reject proposition 2). But it will also be rejected by those, especially on the political left, who view current strategies of development as wholly inappropriate to achieving its goals. One form of the criticism would go like this. The present acute problems of development in Third

World countries are caused by the world capitalist system into which Third World countries have become inserted. While substantial intervention is needed in the world economy to restructure it to achieve development (hence proposition 2 is accepted), the increased flow of financial assistance from industrialised countries can only further the penetration of those market forces which, they argue, are frustrating the fulfilment of the genuine goals of development.

4. The potential donor government accepts that government-to-government aid and/or donor government funds channelled multilaterally to the recipient government can assist in solving the problems which it has identified as creating the moral imperative to provide the aid.

Besides those critics who have rejected one or all of the first three propositions, Proposition 4 is challenged by critics whose focus of criticism is the nature of the state in recipient countries. These critics reject the notion that the recipient government can use aid to further the goals of development. One important reason for rejecting government-to-government aid is, it is argued, that the recipient government acts to further its own elite-oriented interests and not the interests of those marginalised groups upon whose life improvement the moral basis for the aid is rooted. Those non-interventionists who rejected proposition 2 will also be vigorous in their rejection of proposition 4 but for a different reason. They will argue that to give a recipient government development assistance is to encourage that government to play a more direct interventionist role in the economy and this, they claim, can only frustrate the more rapid extension and deepening of the market and thereby slow down the achievement of the objectives of development and the solution to those problems that moral judgement determines are in need of solution.

5. The potential donor government accepts that it has a moral obligation to aid the development of defined categories of countries and through their governments defined groups within foreign countries.

This proposition takes us back again to the donor government and argues that as well as accepting that there is a general moral imperative to act (proposition 1) and that aid granted by governments can achieve the ends desired (propositions 3 and 4) there is also a moral obligation for the potential donor to provide funds from its own resources to help solve problems of non-citizens abroad. One criticism directed at this proposition is simply that governments have responsibility for their own citizens and them only, a variation being that the overriding basis of government action is to further the interests of one's own citizens. To the extent that foreign aid assists in cementing the world community by providing for greater world stability it indirectly helps the citizens of the donor country. But in this case it is not the moral imperative to help foreign citizens that is the principle invoked for government action, but the more basic concern to secure the long-term interests of its own citizens. Another major criticism is simply that governments do not have moral obligations; only individuals can act morally. Hence whatever duties arise from the situation of poverty in the Third World, these duties cannot be government duties but only duties applicable to individual citizens. This leads to the view that aid is correctly placed in the realm of individual charity rather than a matter of communal justice.

6. Weighing the claims for other uses of government funds, the potential donor government accepts that the moral claim to assist in the development of identified countries legitimises its using funds for foreign aid.

It is, however, by no means obvious that a moral claim to provide development assistance for citizens of foreign countries should necessarily lead to the actual provision of aid funds. This is because there are other claims with moral implications on a government's financial resources. Hence to constitute a moral justification for providing aid the potential donor not only has to accept the moral obligation to provide the aid but also has to agree that in comparison with the obligations it has to its citizens and to its own country, foreign aid expenditure is a legitimate use of its financial resources. One common criticism against this proposition is that there are poor people in rich countries and that governments should work to alleviate the poverty of their *own* citizens before attempting to help relieve the poverty of those outside their borders. Hence the moral obligation to provide foreign aid is overridden in practice by greater moral obligations at home.

The preceding six propositions have been based largely on establishing the principles and theories under which the moral claim for governments to provide foreign aid is justified. The final proposition moves more specifically into the real world and the use of aid monies in practice. Whatever the *a priori* moral reasons one can muster for providing aid, there is in addition the necessity to monitor whether the aid provided does indeed achieve its objectives or not. A considerable number of critics contend that aid simply does not help the poor, in which case the moral argument for providing it is called into question. One criticism is that if the aid provided does not achieve the objectives upon which the moral obligation to provide it is based, then the moral question falls away. However, others argue that this criticism is itself inadequate. This is because the moral obligation for governments to provide aid carries with it the additional obligation to attempt to ensure that the aid *is* used to achieve these objectives. In this instance, as long as there is a good possibility that the aid could, even in part, achieve the ends desired by the donor government, then the moral basis for action still remains. However, there are critics who doubt whether even this condition is fulfilled in practice.

These sorts of criticism highlight the need to distinguish carefully between need and obligation and between moral starting-points and moral consequences. Whether aid achieves the objectives for which it is given or not, the moral basis on which it is given – the needs of the poorest or widening inequalities between rich and poor – remains. In other words, the ends are not somehow altered because the means are found to be inadequate, or, in the case of aid, the needs of the poorest still remain needs even if the donor finds it difficult or impossible to assist in meeting them. Those who have come this far but reject the moral argument for aid do so on the assumption that the failure to achieve the objectives removes (or at least reduces) the obligation to provide *aid*. But for most critics this would not remove the obligation to do something. In other words, rejecting the moral argument for *aid* does not have to lead to rejecting the moral argument for *help*. Incorporating these ideas, proposition 7 is as follows:

7. *With its belief in an interventionist theory of development and its conviction that there is a sound moral basis for it to provide aid, the potential donor government becomes a donor government in practice. The moral basis for maintaining aid flows is legitimised either because it is convinced that its aid funds do in practice help to promote the development it desires or because it is convinced that in future, and based on the experience of past mistakes, its aid will help to promote that development.*

Much of the debate about the moral case for aid eventually centres around the discussion of what aid achieves in practice. As a result, many of the critics of the first six propositions listed above will tend to use their interpretation of the evidence or their selection of some evidence to support their particular criticism of the moral case for aid. For example, those criticising proposition 3, because of the belief that recipient states do not channel the aid they receive to the poorest or neediest in their countries, will be eager to provide evidence to support their view. To point this out is, of course, to do little more than to make the fairly obvious statement that there is tension (hopefully constructive) between theory and fact in the social sciences in general and in development studies in particular. Theory is supported by fact and facts provide the basis for many theories. But the implication of this for the discussion here is important. The *total moral case* for governments to provide development aid would seem to be dependent upon a blend of three interrelated factors: narrow ethical beliefs (the basis for action), theories of development (constructs of how the world works) and an assessment of the performance of aid in practice.

However compelling are the individual ethical beliefs of the citizens of donor countries to create the obligation to help, these do not on their own provide a sufficient moral justification for governments to channel foreign aid in the real world. Individual ethical beliefs concerning, for example, the felt need to alleviate extreme poverty in Third World countries do not provide sufficient moral justification for governments to provide foreign aid without further question. However strong the moral imperatives for giving aid are, the balance will be upset when equally pressing moral claims arise nearer to home. For instance, if the donor country is hit by a widespread national disaster, then the moral basis for granting aid to the Third World would need to be weighed against moral obligation to provide basic necessities at home. On the other hand, the *a priori* belief that aid of its nature cannot help provide the needs of the poor in the Third World will be challenged if it can be shown that aid in practice did achieve precisely these objectives.

One final comment will not be out of place at this stage. While we have argued that there are a number of steps necessary before governments and supporters of official aid can provide a consistent and complete moral case, it would be wrong to conclude that governments find it hard to justify each step in the argument. Most donor governments, as already noted, do believe they have a moral obligation to provide foreign aid, indeed many have done so for more than 25 years, and would readily accept each of the different propositions outlined above to reach their conclusion.

The nature of moral obligation

Most writing concerned to argue the moral case for official aid has been confined to providing a justification for the obligation to help, and a large part has taken as its starting-point the needs of the Third World poor. The most interesting, for our purposes, are the arguments which have additionally claimed that governments have an obligation to help the Third World. In this section the main theories are outlined. While all of these are rejected by those critics challenging the very notion of there being any obligation to help, it is useful first to separate out the different sorts of arguments made, highlighting their differences and similarities and the manner in which the different theories are built up.

Outlining the basis for moral obligation is not an occupation universally favoured. Many people are content to state that they believe things are right or are wrong and are uneasy about having to justify their beliefs. Indeed, civil servants and, as we have seen, politicians are particularly reluctant to provide a rigorous justification for official moral positions. However, if pressed, many of those believing that there is an obligation to assist would be prepared to agree that their belief rests on their understanding of what it is to be human – a shared humanity – or on the brotherhood of man. For this group, the following quotation from Streeten in a 1976 article entitled 'It is a Moral Issue' would provide a good starting-point (quoted in Streeten 1981:233):

> In my view, the most fundamental argument for international co-operation in development is that human beings, wherever born, should be able to develop to the fullest extent their capacities, both in order to fulfil themselves and in order to contribute to the common heritage of civilisation. The simple argument for making sacrifices in order to assist development is this: we, the rich, are partly (though only partly and arguably) responsible for the poverty of the poor; we can do something about it: it follows that we ought to. The argument rests only partly (and controversially) on our responsibility. Even if we had no share at all in the responsibility, the Christian and humanist belief in the brotherhood of man imposes certain obligations to alleviate misery and to aid in the full development of others where we can.

Christian faith and theology

For some, it is Christianity or the ethical implications derived from Christianity that provide the basis for the obligation – with the ethical underpinnings sustained even when the faith lies dormant or has been rejected. For this group, Scriptural texts are a powerful force in confirming obligation. Two quotations, selected from among many, would appear to provide the proof for these believers and remove any doubt among the the sceptics. 'If one of your brothers or one of your sisters is in need of clothes and has not enough food to live on and one of you says to them, "I wish you well; keep yourself warm and eat plenty", without giving them the bare necessities of life, then what good is that? Faith is like that: if good works do not go with it, it is quite dead.' (James, 2:15–16). 'In this way we distinguish the children of God from the children of the devil: anybody not living a holy life and not loving his brother is no child of God's. . . . If a man who was rich enough in this world's goods saw that one of his brothers was in need, but closed his heart to him, how could the love of God be living in him?' (First Epistle of John, 3: 10 and 17).

From Scripture and reflection on the Christian faith have arisen learned and widely accepted Christian writings sustaining the notion of obligation. For example, over 700 years ago Thomas Aquinas wrote (*Summa Theologica* II–II, quoted in Singer, 1971:31):

> Now according to the natural order instituted by divine providence, material goods are provided for the satisfaction of human needs. Therefore the division and appropriation of property, which proceeds from human law, must not hinder the satisfaction of man's necessity for such goods. Equally, whatever a man has in superabundance is owed, of natural right, the poor for their sustenance.

It has been, however, within the tradition of the Catholic Church, especially since the time of Pope Leo XIII in the 1890s, that more specific implications of this general grounding of obligation in faith and Scripture have been spelt out in detail, especially in papal pronouncements and in the teaching of the second Vatican Council in the 1960s. For example, *Populorum Progressio* explicitly outlines the obligation of states to help to relieve the problems of underdevelopment (1967:Nos. 43, 44 and 48):

Man must meet man, nation meet nation, as brothers and sisters, as children of God. In this mutual understanding and friendship, in this sacred communion, we must all begin to work together to build the common future of the human race. . . . This duty is the concern especially of the better-off nations. Their obligations stem from a brotherhood that is at once human and supernatural . . .

The same duty of solidarity that rests on individuals exists also for nations: 'It is the very serious duty of the developed nations to help the underdeveloped'. . . .

Given the increasing needs of the underdeveloped countries, it should be considered quite normal for an advanced country to devote a part of its production to meet their needs, and to train teachers, engineers, technicians and scholars prepared to put their knowledge and their skill at the disposal of less fortunate peoples.

We can see here the movement from theology to more philosophical bases for helping: an explanation of what is entailed in the brotherhood of man, the appeal to social justice and, finally, the belief that, in certain circumstances, the needs of some in contrast with the affluence of others compel the wealthy to share their goods and knowledge with the poor. It is to the distinctively philosophical theories on which the notion of obligation rests that we now turn.

The human good
One writer with strong parallels to Streeten's view that being human creates certain types of obligation is Nigel Dower, who bases his philosophical theory of assisting on the concept of the *human good*. What, he asks, makes extreme poverty an evil which ought not to be tolerated and points to the need for those in one country to be concerned with removing evils in other countries? The answer, he contends, lies in accepting as fundamental the principle of promoting the human good, this being 'wherever it may be achieved or maintained, something that ought to be promoted by those who can do so. In particular it is especially important that the conditions which most seriously mar human existence should be removed by those able to do so; for the worse a person's condition, the more pressing is action to improve it' (1983:3).

This fundamental principle of the human good is based on an understanding of being human and what is needed for human well-being. There is a 'basic moral "right to life" and the conditions necessary for it', Dower argues and he then uses this belief to argue the case for official aid. If one accepts the principle of the human good, no distinction is to be made between different people in different countries. While admitting that in the real world there are complexities, Dower argues that the extremes of poverty in the Third World compared with a proper appreciation of our own affluence will lead to a general attitude of concern for the Third World poor. Developing this attitude will lead to a wider sense of private commitment in people and then influence their electoral preferences, so making 'possible or necessary' much greater commitment to the Third World in the form, *inter alia*, of aid programmes.

Dower also makes a case for helping based on the principle of caring. One feature. of living in a community or society, he contends, is that a society or community should *care* for those who fall into desperate need. The fact that society has a collective responsibility for meeting basic needs is, he argues, commonly accepted. He maintains that (1983:5):

Given the fact that developing countries are not in a position to deal with poverty adequately themselves, it is a requirement of international social justice that we should assist in the process of development. If we look at matters in this light, we can see Government Aid, not as an act of charity, but as part of the 'tax' paid by richer countries to be used to alleviate poverty in poorer countries – just as the rich pay taxes which are used to finance the welfare services within Western countries.

Needs

Streeten, Dower and *Populorum Progressio* all have a common underlying thread: the notion of need. The appeals to humanity and to the brotherhood of man carry with them the idea that human beings have needs that have to be fulfilled in order to be human. Thus it is not surprising to find that advocates of aid and those who believe that there is an obligation to provide it have frequently based those claims on a principle of justice captured in the phrase 'to each according to his needs'. Many needs-based theories of justice have been expounded throughout history; here we shall consider just one, as expounded by David Miller in his book *Social Justice*.

For Miller, an account of the theory of justice based on need begins with thinking of the harm that people will suffer through not having, or being provided with, what they need. Hence a sound concept of need is the following:

A needs X = A will suffer harm if he lacks X.

From this follows the necessity of specifying the concept of harm. For Miller, what constitutes harm are actions that hinder the development of a person's 'plan for life'. This plan for life is important because 'a person's identity is established by the aims and activities which constitute his plan for life, and without such an identity he could hardly be regarded as a person in the full sense, rather as an organism of a certain type which was potentially a person' (1979:133). Two types of activity for fulfilling life plans can be established: essential and non-essential. Essential activities include those which actually make up the plan of life and are necessary to support them, such as eating food. Thus, in order to decide what a person's needs are, we must first identify his plan for life, then establish what activities are essential to that plan, and finally investigate the conditions which enable those activities to be carried out.

This may be all well and good, but how does such an idea of need help to tell us which needs should be satisfied if there is conflict in attempting to satisfy the needs of all? Miller takes the situation where a surplus exists after all the needs of members of a society have been satisfied. In this case, he argues, the surplus should be distributed so as to achieve an equal level of well-being for everyone through the proportionate satisfaction of wants. In other words (144):

> the logical extension of the principle of need is the principle of equality, interpreted as the claim that every man should enjoy an equal level of well-being. Equality is achieved by giving first priority to the satisfaction of needs and then by satisfying as large a proportion of each person's further desires as resources will allow – it being assumed that resources are not sufficiently abundant to gratify every wish.

Thus for Miller, the satisfaction of need precedes the notion of bringing about a state in which equal levels of well-being are enjoyed. Need-satisfaction itself can be viewed in two different ways: as a matter of justice or as a matter of humanity. If it is a matter of humanity, then the underlying premise is simply that human suffering should be avoided. This is widely accepted and for many is self-evident. For example, Robinson writes 'official aid is vital to the cause of humanity to relieve suffering and to raise up some societies to the minimum standards of life and health tolerable in a humanistic world' (1971:268). But if it is a matter of justice, then a different premise is required. For the development of a theory of justice based on need, the premise is as follows (Miller, 1979:146-7):

Every man is as worthy of respect as every other. That is to say, although men plainly differ in moral virtue, in merit, in personal success, in usefulness to society, there is an underlying equality which consists in the fact that each man is a unique individual with his own aims, ideals, and outlook on the world, and that consequently he must be treated as such. . . . Unless this premise is granted, we cannot show why it is *unjust* (and not merely inhumane) to satisfy one man's needs and not the needs of another.

It is this link between respect, needs and equality which explains why those who base their argument for helping on fulfilling needs also require some concept of equality upon which to argue the obligation to fulfil needs, including, of course, basic needs.

However, Miller is careful not to equate completely the notion of justice based on need and the concept of equality. He states that the two concepts stand in a peculiarly intimate relationship to one another. To show the difference he makes the following point (149):

It is certainly true that to satisfy everyone's needs it is necessary to mete out different physical resources to different people. This, however, is not inegalitarian, because the principle of equality does not demand that each person should receive the same physical treatment, rather that each person should be treated in such a way that he achieves the same level of well-being as every other. Because people have varied needs and wants, physical resources such as food, medicine, and education should not be assigned in equal quantities to each man, but in different proportions to different people, according to their peculiar characteristics. No serious egalitarian has thought otherwise.

In summary then, the duty to help those in the Third World is based on an understanding of what the essential needs of the mass of people in the Third World are and the obligation to provide them incumbent on those who have resources in excess of their own basic requirements. It is immaterial to ask whether individuals or governments have a greater obligation to provide help; to the extent that both have the ability to help, then both should do so.

Utilitarianism

While some advocates of the moral obligation to help may find comfort in the theory of justice based on need, it is a quite different theory of obligation which is most frequently used by development specialists, namely that of utilitarianism. For example in the 1980 DAC Review, the then Chairman, wrote that 'the core rationale of development assistance remains the profound intuition most people have that unrequited transfers from the averagely richer people of rich areas to the averagely poorer people of poor areas usually add more utility to the latter than they inflict disutility on the former' (DAC, 1980:63). More recently Streeten commented (1983:380): 'The distributional arguments (for aid) can be justified on a variety of philosophical grounds. Perhaps the most common is the utilitarian argument that a dollar redistributed from a rich man to a poor man detracts less utility than it adds, and therefore increases the sum total of utility.'

One attraction of utilitarianism is that it puts forward a single moral principle to guide us in assessing the correctness of action or in assessing that the absence of action is morally wrong. This is a powerful advantage over the theory of justice based on need, because while needs can be seen to demand action for their fulfilment there are in addition other claims to be made; people have rights as well as needs and the theory of justice based on needs is silent about such claims. Another attraction of utilitarianism is its seemingly self-evident appeal. It is, observes Dower (1983:15), the argument that if we think rationally about morality we shall see the appropriateness of utilitarianism and reject other views as muddle-headedness, tradition or sheer rule-worship followed in the absence of any underlying justification.

In very general terms (to be qualified in a moment), utilitarianism rests on the view that the ultimate justification of any action over and against any other action is that it produces the greatest amount of happiness. This becomes a distributive principle because of the necessary link between happiness and the resources required for achieving it; hence a given distribution of *resources* is justified by the total amount of *happiness* which it produces. From the utilitarian point of view, argues Miller (1979:32), the principles of justice become rules for distributing resources which are vindicated by the beneficial results of their application.

In his seminal work on utilitarianism, Lyons (1965) distinguishes between some five variations of the general concept, of which two in particular are of interest to us here. One is *Act Utilitarianism* which states that an act is right if, and only if, it produces a greater amount of happiness than any alternative. The other is *Rule Utilitarianism* which states that an act is right if, and only if, it conforms to a rule whose general acceptance would produce a greater amount of happiness than the general acceptance of any alternative.

A moment's reflection will indicate the implication these principles have for helping the Third World. The implication of *act* utilitarianism is that it is morally right to help the Third World because helping those in need necessarily creates happiness that would be absent without the help. However, the point can be made more forcefully. The moral imperative to help, because it is based on general happiness (including the needs of those to be helped) rather than exclusively on needs, assesses both the happiness of those in the Third World and those in the donor country. It recognises the obligation to help because of an assessment that more happiness will be created overall by providing resources to those in need rather than providing those resources to people whose basic needs have already been met. The implication of *rule* utilitarianism is that specific provision is made for exceptions. For the rule utilitarian, the fact that exceptions can and do arise does not destroy the basic thrust of the argument, provided that in general there is a reallocation of resources away from those with fewer unfulfilled needs to those with more unfulfilled needs and that in general this increases overall happiness. The similarity of the utilitarian arguments for helping and many of those rooted in theology is particularly striking.

Rawls' contractual theory of justice

For the American philosopher John Rawls, utilitarianism is troublesome since it does not appear to go far enough. This is because in his view there is insufficient recognition that certain human basic needs *have* to be satisfied prior to any other consideration, even if that consideration is a greater sum of satisfactions of the many. Or, as Miller concludes, 'utilitarians can show that justice is generally beneficial to society, but they cannot explain why, in particular cases, the distinctive claim of justice should be weighed separately from considerations of utility' (1979:39).

In contrast to utilitarianism, Rawls constructs his own contractual theory of justice.[1] Any moral theory, he believes, has to accord with our intuitive moral judgements or at least with those intuitive judgements which we are not prepared to abandon. He also argues that a moral theory has to be objectively correct, that is, it has to be a theory that would be adopted by rational people who are placed in a situation in which they are unaware of their actual place in society, of whether they are rich or poor and of their particular personal qualities. For Rawls, a theory of social justice is absolutely critical because it provides the fundamental basis for the operation of essential institutions and for the rules and rights of society.

The fundamental principles of Rawls' theory, which is called justice as fairness, are as follows (1973:302–3):

> First Principle. Each person is to have an equal right to the most extensive total system of equal basic liberties compatible with a similar system of liberty for all (principle of equal liberty).

> Second Principle. Social and economic inequalities are to be arranged so that they are both: (a) to the greatest benefit of the least advantaged, consistent with the just savings principle, (difference principle) and (b) attached to offices and positions open to all under conditions of fair equality of opportunity (principle of fair equality of opportunity).

> First Priority Rule (The Priority of Liberty). The principles of justice are to be ranked in lexical order and therefore liberty can be restricted only for the sake of liberty. There are two cases: (a) a less extensive liberty must strengthen the total system of liberty shared by all; (b) a less than equal liberty must be acceptable to those with the lesser liberty.

> Second Priority Rule (The Priority of Justice over Efficiency and Welfare). The second principle of justice is lexically prior to the principle of efficiency and to that of maximizing the sum of advantages; and fair opportunity is prior to the difference principle. There are two cases: (a) an inequality of opportunity must enhance the opportunities of those with the lesser opportunity; (b) an excessive rate of saving must on balance mitigate the burden of those bearing this hardship.

> General Conception (of justice). All social primary goods – liberty and opportunity, income and wealth, and the bases of self-respect – are to be distributed equally unless an unequal distribution of any or all of these goods is to the advantage of the least favoured.

Why, it needs to be asked, would people choose this particular theory of justice over and against any other? Because, argues Rawls, these are precisely the principles that would be accepted by people in a certain hypothetical situation, called the 'original position'. According to Dower's interpretation of Rawls' theory (1983:46):

> In this position each person is a rational self-interested agent who wants to choose principles which are to govern the society in which he is to live. But – and this is the dramatic qualification – each person is behind what Rawls calls the 'veil of ignorance', in that he knows nothing of his personal circumstances. He knows nothing about whether he is rich or poor, or whether he is intelligent and endowed with abilities or not, or about what his own conception of the good is, i.e. what sort of life he wants to lead. This veil of ignorance guarantees lack of bias, and Rawls claims that, under such conditions, parties in the original position would agree on a set of principles, and that these principles constitute the principles of justice which are applicable and acceptable to us real agents who live in real societies in the real world.

If Rawls is right that his theory is both intuitively and objectively attractive, and even correct, then it is forceful indeed because, although making liberty prior to all else, it implies (in the difference principle) that it is morally justifiable for the state to extract resources from some so as to benefit the least advantaged in society. In other words, we have here a theory of justice legitimising the provision of assistance for the specific relief of poverty and, in the general conception of justice, the equal distribution of all social primary goods *unless* 'an unequal distribution is to the advantage of the least favoured'. Only on this basis, argues Rawls, is society deemed legitimate. In short, Rawls' theory of justice accepts and recognises not only that people have rights to life but also that they have rights to the resources necessary to create the conditions for a basic life, even if acquiring these resources entails the extraction of these resources acquired otherwise legitimately by others. Whereas utilitarian theory argued that the poorest should receive resources because providing the poorest with them rather than the affluent would increase the stock of happiness, Rawls argues that they should receive them by right, regardless of the effect on the happiness of those whose resources are taken away from them. And whereas those accepting a theory of justice based on need usually balance need-based requirements with obligations based on rights and deserts, Rawls integrates all these aspects into a single theory.

Hirsch (1977) goes further and contends that Rawls' contribution is even more significant than this because it challenges the view, held among others by Keynes, that economics, political action and morality are separate concepts. The great significance of Rawls' work, states Hirsch (1977:134):

> rests on its attempt to face the problem of political obligation within the context of a liberal market economy, and its acceptance that the basis of such obligation must be the justice of the politico-economic system, in the sense of fairness. The principles of justice that Rawls extracts have been challenged by critics from left, right, and centre; yet all are agreed on the importance of the undertaking itself. Rawls has brought the moral issue back to a system that had earlier hived off the issue as belonging to a separate and higher sphere. Morality of the minimum order necessary for the functioning of a market system was assumed, nearly always implicitly, to be a kind of permanent free good, a natural resource of a non-depleting kind. Beyond this, morality was a luxury not obtainable in the humdrum economic department. The position was neatly put in a much quoted aphorism by a specifically Keynesian prime minister, 'If people want morality let them get it from their Archbishops'.

Rights, deserts and entitlements

The arguments used and the theories expounded above do not quite cover all the arguments put forward to justify the claim that there is a moral obligation to help those disadvantaged economically in the Third World. A further view is that the Third World should be helped because the poorest in these countries have *rights* which demand fulfilment. In particular, it is argued that if people have the right to life, then equally they also have the right to those things required for life to continue. Hence just as the right to life carries with it the obligation of others not to kill, so too the right to continue living carries with it the obligation to provide the wherewithal for that life to continue. The more essential are the instruments necessary to continue life, the greater the obligation on those with the resources available to provide them. If Third World countries are not able to provide these resources for all their inhabitants and other states can do so, then the obligation of the latter becomes paramount.

While there is no doubt that these sorts of arguments are made, there is less certainty that their claims are substantially different from those made on the basis of need; indeed the fact that it is also frequently claimed that the poor have 'rights to basic needs' indicates the close relationship between the two concepts. It would thus appear, following Miller, that 'what makes this class of human rights relevant to social justice is that they are claims based upon need, and moreover of a universal and urgent kind' (1979:79). But this does raise the question of why the language of 'rights' is used at all when it is 'needs' that are at the core of the argument. This, states Miller, is comprehensible as a political device. He quotes Feinberg thus (79–80):

> I accept the moral principle that to have an unfulfilled need is to have a kind of claim against the world, even if against no one in particular. . . . Such claims, based on need alone, are 'permanent possibilities of rights', the natural seed from which rights grow. When manifesto writers speak of them as if already actual rights, they are easily for-given, for this is but a powerful way of expressing the conviction that they ought to be recognised by states here and now as potential rights and consequently as determinants of present aspirations and guides to present policies. That usage, I think, is a valid exercise of rhetorical licence.

There are others, however, who would disagree with the rigidity of the Miller/ Feinberg perspective and argue in favour of the distinct nature of individual rights. This, for example, would appear to be the considered view of some 50 jurists who held a symposium on development and human rights issues in 1981. Indeed, they went further and argued that because of these rights, governments have an obliga-tion to assist other less fortunate states in the promotion of development (Sieghart, 1983:98):

> Development should be understood as a process designed progressively to create condi-tions in which every person can enjoy, exercise and utilise under the Rule of Law all his human rights, whether economic, social, cultural, civil or political.
> Every person has the right to participate in, and benefit from, development in the sense of a progressive improvement in the standard and quality of life.
> The primary obligation to promote development, in such a way as to satisfy this right, rests upon each State for its own territory and for the persons under its jurisdiction. As the development process is a necessary condition for peace and friendship between nations, it is a matter of international concern, imposing responsibilities upon all States.
> A State promoting its own development within its available resources is entitled to the support of other States in the implementation of its policies.

There is, finally, the claim that help should be given to the Third World because of infringements of a widely-held criterion of justice, namely justice as desert. According to justice-as-desert, individuals or groups have a claim to resources in relation to the contribution made and the effort exerted and it is this which entitles them to claim the results of their respective contributions and efforts. How-ever, it is argued, the poverty of the Third World and/or the inability of people in the Third World to fulfil their needs is, in part at least, due to the undeserved gain or acquisition of others and to the fact that this undeserved gain has, again at least in part, led to the comparative affluence of the industrialised world. Clearly this argument will depend crucially on the evidence of past dealings; and the extent of the obligation to help will be related to the degree of past transgressions.

The argument from entitlement is, in theory, quite distinct from the argument based on need, for even if basic needs were satisfied the transgression of acquisi-tion or transfer would still remain and lead to the obligation to right this particular wrong. However, in practice, this argument is frequently used in conjunction with the one based on need to provide an additional justification for the necessity to help.

Knocking down the moral case for aid

Many people, particularly those involved in the 'aid business', find the moral case for aid compelling and persuasive, especially that aspect of the argument which points to donor governments having an obligation to help address the needs of the Third World poor and work to alleviate that poverty. For others, however, the moral case is far from convincing and there are influential writers from within development studies and from other disciplines who argue that there is no moral case for official aid, that it is far less clear than the advocates claim or, alternatively, that a discussion of morality and foreign aid is totally irrelevant. It is these different assaults on the moral case that will be discussed in the next three chapters of this book.

Although there is (perhaps inevitably) a hazy middle ground, the critics have tended to fall into three groups. First, those who question the very objectives for which government aid is or could be given. For them, even a discussion of the impact of aid is irrelevant because there is no moral obligation for governments to provide it or even to assist in the process of development. Indeed within this perspective, arguments are assembled to deduce that there is a moral obligation *not* to help. For some critics within this group the fact that people have needs – be they people at home or abroad – in no way creates an obligation for others, individuals or governments, to work to satisfy those needs. For others there is, in addition, no obligation to share resources or to reduce inequalities, again either at the national or international level. Secondly, there is a group of critics who, while accepting that there is some obligation to help solve the problems of the Third World, reject the notion that government aid can and does help achieve the objectives of development, either for *a priori* reasons or because of their analysis of the evidence. Thirdly, there are critics for whom narrow moral questions – of alleviating poverty, redistributing income, reducing development gaps or whatever – are irrelevant because other principles are claimed as the only legitimate ones upon which governments should base their aid programmes. For this third group, to ask whether foreigners have needs that could be met with external donor assistance or whether that assistance can and does help to alleviate suffering and promote development is of no or very little importance in deciding whether governments should give aid. Also within this group are those critics who challenge the view that moral judgements can be made about nations beyond their national boundaries.

The first group of critics is dominated by philosophers, especially those located within an increasingly influential school of political philosophy, based particularly on the writings of John Locke and, to a lesser extent, David Hume. The greatest recent influence on this perspective comes from the writings of Robert Nozick, although Hayek's and Bauer's arguments have also been important in this context. The arguments of these critics and an assessment of them is the subject of the next chapter.

The second group is dominated by economists and writers concerned with Third World development, and embraces those commonly classified as having both a 'leftist' and a 'rightist' perspective; they include Friedman, Bauer, Krauss, Hayter, Seers, Myrdal and Lappé *et al*. It is their criticisms that we shall be examining in Chapter 5.

The third group is located within a particular school of political science, especially prominent in the United States, and their arguments feature prominently within US official and semi-official documents. Examples here would include writers such as Sumberg, Huntington and, more recently, prominent members of the Reagan Administration. In addition, the British economist Ian Little's views on the nature of moral obligation beyond national boundaries are considered. Discussion of this third area of criticism against the moral case for official aid is contained in Chapter 6.

Notes

1. John Rawls is given such prominence here because of the profound influence his theory of justice has had in discourse about social justice over the past ten years. The reason for this influence is summarised well by one of his most persistent critics, Robert Nozick (1974:183):

   A Theory of Justice is a powerful, deep, subtle, wide-ranging, systematic work in political and moral philosophy which has not seen its like since the writings of John Stuart Mill, if then. It is a fountain of illuminating ideas, integrated together into a lovely whole. Political philosophers now must either work within Rawls' theory or explain why not. The considerations and distinctions we have developed are illuminated by, and help illuminate, Rawls' masterful presentation of an alternative conception. Even those who remain unconvinced after wrestling with Rawls' systematic vision will learn much from closely studying it.

4 Critics of the Moral Case
No Moral Obligation

The most fundamental challenge to the moral case for official aid to Third World countries comes from those critics who reject the notion that states have any obligation to intervene at all, be it to relieve suffering, to meet basic needs, to reduce inequalities or to compensate for past or present wrongdoing. For many people, this criticism is profoundly shocking and distasteful because of deeply held beliefs, learnt in the home and at school about humanity, human conduct, social justice and the very foundation of ethics. For most people in industrialised countries and especially those with a strong Christian tradition, it sounds odd that human beings could, in their view, be so callous as to suggest that helping one's fellow man is immaterial, irrelevant or indeed wrong. Thus the criticism that there is no obligation to help will frequently be dismissed as self-evidently without justification. However, the criticisms considered here are not that an individual should not help, if that is her wish – she is quite at liberty to do so. The criticism is that states should not help, governments should not provide aid based on the needs of recipients because it is not right for *them* to do so – indeed, some critics argue, it is wrong for them to believe that they should help. Yet even this qualification will not satisfy most who believe, and often vehemently, that governments, like individuals, have obligations to help.

There is no moral obligation

In challenging the theories of justice from which need-based action is derived or the general assumptions made by those who argue that there is a moral basis for granting aid, the critics use two approaches. One is to show that the specific arguments pointing to the moral obligation are invalid; the second is to show that other alternative claims lessen or remove the moral claim made or provide the only basis upon which the appeal to morality may legitimately be made. The reason these challenges raise such fundamental issues is that they question the very basis of development studies. As Toye recently put it, 'at the heart of development studies lies an intellectual commitment to find the causes of the persistence of inequality and poverty on a world-wide scale' (1984:17). For the critics whose views will be described here, this whole venture is both fruitless and misguided.

Bauer
It will be no surprise to find that Peter Bauer's comprehensive attack on the various aspects of foreign aid includes a challenge to the theories of justice that are used to argue the moral case. Bauer adopts a number of distinct yet interrelated

approaches to challenge the moral arguments for official aid based on need, egalitarianism and history. For Bauer, economic differences are deserved and are based largely upon the individual differences of people, not on resource availability; the differences that do exist cannot be unjust because they have arisen out of just procedures; even if arguments can be mustered to advocate redistribution, attempts to redistribute will involve coercion and will therefore themselves be unjust because they will conflict with individual liberty; and finally the appeal to history for Bauer does not reveal unjust processes of acquisition, rather the opposite.

Needs cannot provide a basis for granting aid, he states, because there are no common needs. The idea 'that people's requirements are fundamentally the same everywhere' is to him obviously unfounded (1981:118). Yet even if poor people did have needs that required meeting, this is in Bauer's view an insufficient basis for external agencies to provide assistance because it ignores the crucial question of why some people have unmet needs and others do not. For him, economic differences are deserved (19 and 20):

> Economic differences are largely the result of people's capacities and motivations. This is evident in open societies, and also where societies are not open, nor yet completely closed or caste-bound. A disproportionate number of the poor lack the capabilities and inclination for economic achievement and often for cultural achievement as well.

However, he does go on to state that 'weak members of society do need to be helped', although adding that to assist them will impair the prospects of society.

Not only are economic differences deserved because of different personal attributes, but the process by which income differences arise is also just. Bauer maintains that (12):

> Incomes, including those of the relatively prosperous or the owners of property, are not taken from other people. Normally they are produced by their recipients and the resources they own; they are not misappropriated from others; they do not deprive other people of what they had or might have had.

As for the argument that resources upon which progress and development are built are distributed unevenly and so this 'natural' distribution needs to be corrected, Bauer states that 'lack of natural resources, including land, has little or nothing to do with the poverty of individuals or of societies' (1984b:82) and thus is irrelevant.

Finally comes the rejection of redistribution because to redistribute will cause injustice by conflicting with liberty (quoted in Sen 1982b:3):

> In an open and free society, political action which deliberately aimed to minimize or even remove economic differences (i.e. differences in income and wealth) would entail such extensive coercion that the society would cease to be open and free.

and (Bauer 1981:19):

> . . . policies designed to equalize . . . living standards would require world government with totalitarian powers. Such a government, to be equal to its ambitions, would be even more coercive and brutal than the totalitarian governments of individual countries.

Hayek

An equally persistent critic of theories of social justice which would imply moral obligations to provide aid is Friedrich Hayek, although his attacks are not directed specifically at the aid lobby. Hayek's first complaint is over the very debate about social justice which, he believes, is not only misplaced but a threat to society. In his book *The Mirage of Social Justice* he states that 'the prevailing belief in social justice is at present probably the gravest threat to most other values of a free society' (1976:66). He comes to this conclusion because he maintains that to attempt to secure social justice mistakes in a critical way the nature of economic relations between individuals. For Hayek, coercion and injustice can only arise from deliberate action, but, as market transactions cannot have intentionality ascribed to them, their outcome cannot be unjust. If the procedure by which distributive shares arise is just, then the outcome necessarily has to be just and there is thus no moral obligation to intervene to change a distribution caused by a just process. Indeed, he argues, 'to single out some people in such a society as entitled to a particular share (is) evidently unjust' (64).

It is additionally unjust because active and interventionist distribution restricts freedom and individual choice. It is only markets that allow the complete range of choice to individuals and so only markets which provide the means of allocation compatible with the freedom of citizens. Thus whereas for *laisser faire* theorists markets are more highly valued than state intervention because of their greater efficiency in achieving desired goals, for Hayek markets are preferred because they provide the best guarantee of the most extensive access to liberty.

There is, for Hayek, no way that external observers are able to judge the justice or injustice of particular distributive shares. Thus any attempt to create a more just and equal society has no moral legitimacy, in fact worse is in store as Plant (1984), explaining Hayek's perspective, puts it:

> insofar as the state seeks to pursue a goal which is illusory and cannot be achieved it will become prey to the resentment of individuals and groups whose distributive share does not match their own subjective view of what they deserve. The pursuit of equality and social justice will create expectations which cannot possibly be met and this is bound to create a crisis of legitimacy and authority. The only solution is for the government to opt out of the distributive arena altogether and leave the outcomes of the economic market intact.

Nozick

For both Bauer and Hayek, a powerful strand in their arguments against intervention based on moral claims is that situations cannot be unjust – and hence demand action to correct that injustice – if the procedures by which outcomes arise are themselves just. This line of thinking has been developed and expanded by Robert Nozick in his book *Anarchy, State and Utopia* into a comprehensive theory of justice based on *entitlements*, the upshot of which is to lead to a rejection of any theory of justice based on needs or egalitarian principles. According to the economist Deepak Lal, Nozick's book is 'profoundly disturbing to the egalitarian preconceptions of social democrats about distributive justice' (1976:731).

The importance of this perspective on justice and its implications for the world of political decision-making is apparent from similar arguments used by British Cabinet Ministers. Sir Keith Joseph, for instance, writes as follows (Joseph and Sumption 1979:83 and 79):

> At the root of our present preoccupation with equality is the instinctive notion that differences somehow need to be explained and justified. But although this is very frequently asserted there is no obvious reason (or obscure reason) why it should be.
>
> What renders a particular distribution of wealth 'fair' or 'unfair' is not the distribution itself but the manner in which it arose. Since inequality arises from the operation of innumerable individual preferences it cannot be evil unless these preferences are themselves evil.

These words could have come directly from Nozick's book. In the first page of the Preface, Nozick points out a conclusion derived from his theory of justice, namely that the state may not use its powers for the purpose of persuading some citizens to aid others. He comments that many people will reject this instantly because they do not *want* to believe anything so apparently callous towards the needs and sufferings of others; he knows this reaction for it was once his as well, but he has now been convinced of the libertarian view which he goes on to expound.

Nozick's theory of justice is based on individual rights which, *inter alia*, permit only minimal rights for the state. He begins thus (1974:ix):

> Individuals have rights, and there are things no persons or groups may do to them (without violating their rights). So strong and far-reaching are these rights that they raise the question of what, if anything, the state and its officials may do. How much room do individual rights leave for the state . . .? Our main conclusions about the state are that a minimal state, limited to the narrow functions of protection against force, theft, fraud, enforcement of contracts, and so on is justified; that any more extensive state will violate persons' rights not to be forced to do certain things, and is unjustified; and that the minimal state is inspiring and right.

Within the context of individual rights, he draws up his theory of justice which he calls the entitlement theory, developed, he argues, as a challenge to the commonly held belief that a more extensive state is justified because it is necessary to achieve distributive justice (149). A distribution is just if everyone is entitled to the holdings they possess under the distribution, and if it arises from any just distribution by legitimate means. For all societies and at all times, a person's holdings are just and uninfringeable if they are obtained through just original acquisition, through a just transfer, or in redress of a previously unjust acquisition.

All this appears, at first sight, to be clear and even compellingly obvious. However, questions quickly arise when one begins to examine what the theory excludes. Nozick's theory is historical: whether a distribution is just depends upon how it came about. This is very different from a theory dependent upon assessing how things are distributed *now*, i.e. who has what, called by Nozick a current time-slice principle of justice or, better, an end-result principle of justice. Equally disturbing for the moral argument for aid, Nozick's theory is very different from a theory of justice based on need for which the question of what is produced and who should receive what is produced are separable. For the entitlement theory, 'whoever makes something, having bought or contracted for all other held resources used in the process (transferring some of his holdings for those cooperating factors), is entitled to it' (160). Surely, it might be argued, these different theories should be seen as complementary rather than competing. One can see the validity of some arguments favouring entitlement, but are there not also needs of people which demand that at least the very basic human needs should be met? No, argues Nozick, entitlement provides the *only* basis for justice.[1]

In the real world, however, how can one be sure that the original acquisition of holdings is just or, if not, whether correct restitution was paid to counter an original injustice? From Nozick's perspective this is critical because, as we have seen, he does conclude that in the real world the state is not permitted to transfer resources to aid certain citizens.

Nozick answers this question by considering Locke's attempt to specify a principle of justice in acquisition as a fundamental part of his view of the origins of property rights. For Locke, a property entitlement arises when a person mixes his labour with an unowned object. But what happens if mixing one's labour with objects that are unowned worsens the situation of others? For Locke, there is a proviso that there be 'enough and as good left in common for others', which is meant to ensure that the situation of others is not thereby worsened. In a complex discussion, Nozick points out that Locke's proviso can be interpreted in a weaker or stronger sense and he concludes that 'a process normally giving rise to a permanent bequeathable property right in a previously unowned thing will not do so if the position of others no longer at liberty to use the thing is thereby worsened' (1974:178).

After further discussion of extreme or unique circumstances, Nozick stresses that the question of the Lockean proviso being violated arises only in cases of catastrophe (or in a desert-island situation). He argues: 'The fact that someone owns the total supply of something necessary for others to stay alive does *not* entail that his (or anyone's) appropriation of anything left some people (immediately or later) in a situation worse off than the baseline one' (181). Even though he spends some time discussing the origin of property rights in order to throw light on problems of original acquisition, he does not believe that in the real world these exceptional cases are very relevant or that they put an obstacle in the way of his conclusion about the role of the minimalist state. He continues (182):

> I believe that the free operation of a market system will not actually run foul of the Lockean proviso . . . if this is correct, the proviso will not play a very important role in the activities of protective agencies and will not provide a significant opportunity for future state action. Indeed, were it not for the effects of previous illegitimate state action, people would not think the possibility of the proviso's being violated as of more interest than any other logical possibility.

But in practice, he goes even further to eliminate restitution as a ground for previous unjust acquisition by considering net gains and net losses. He argues thus (178 and 179n):

> Fourier held that since the process of civilization had deprived the members of society of certain liberties (to gather, pasture, engage in the chase) a socially guaranteed minimum provision for persons was justified as compensation for the loss. But this puts the point too strongly. This compensation would be due those persons, if any, for whom the process of civilization was a *net loss*, for whom the benefits of civilization did not counterbalance being deprived of these particular liberties.

And, finally, a theory of justice based on need is specifically rejected by Nozick because, if needs require resources for these needs to be met, resources do not come unattached to people and, at bottom, no one has a right to someone else's property (179n):

> But a right to life is not a right to whatever one needs to live; other people may have rights over these things. At most, a right to life would be a right to have or to strive for whatever one needs to live, provided that having it does not violate anyone else's rights. With regard to material things, the question is whether having it does violate any right of others. . . . Since special considerations (such as the Lockean proviso) may enter with regards to material property, one *first* needs a theory of property rights before one can apply any supposed right to life (as amended above). Therefore the right to life cannot provide the foundation for a theory of property rights.

To sum up, the implications of Nozick's theory for our present discussion on moral arguments for aid lead to the following conclusions. For Nozick, state activity is not legitimate when extended beyond certain minimal actions and these exclude those directed at redistribution, because his all-pervasive entitlement theory of justice leads to the rejection of any other. Thus theories based on need, on feelings of a shared humanity, or on sharing are *a priori* rejected. Historical arguments providing a moral case for giving aid are relevant to Nozick insofar as entitlements were acquired unjustly. However, he concludes, this has little practical applicability. Hence his ultimate conclusion that 'the state may not use its coercive apparatus for the purpose of getting some citizens to aid others, or in order to prohibit activities to people for their *own* good or protection' (ix). Thus for Nozick it does not matter if people in the Third World are poor or if their governments are corrupt, it does not matter if aid reaches the goals for which it is intended, because the imperative upon which the desire to help is based is rejected. There is therefore no moral basis for donor governments to provide foreign aid, for to do so would infringe the more basic rights of those whose assets are taken away from them to provide for their distribution to others.

Evaluating the assaults

Problems with Nozick
There is no doubt that Nozick's entitlement theory provides a powerful counter-view to the 'unquestioned consensus' concerning aid as moral obligation. Thus it is important to consider it in some detail.

As Nozick's theory of justice is based on the pre-eminence he gives to individual rights and especially to the absolute nature of property rights, it is appropriate to begin an evaluation by considering his detailed views on rights and the obligations arising from them. But this, surprisingly, cannot be done. Nozick does not provide a theory of individual rights, nor even of property rights. While he states that there is an absolute entitlement to property justly acquired he fails to explain why this is or should be so. Indeed, he comments (1974:171) that we lack a complete theory of property rights. But, as O'Neill points out, this does not deter him from stating that 'individual property rights are rights to control resources in all ways, to dispose of them however and to whoever the owner wishes or to accumulate them without limit' (O'Neill 1982:309).

Yet it is also apparent that Nozick is in some circumstances willing to accept certain constraints on the absoluteness of property rights. He states that 'property rights in my knife allow me to leave it where I will, but not in your chest' (1974:171). However, once exceptions are made, then the basis for such constraints becomes all-important, but Nozick attempts to steer clear of this sort of problem. For example, he makes the surprising statement that the question of whether 'side constraints are absolute, or whether they may be violated in order to avoid catastrophic moral horror, and if the latter, what the resulting structure might look like, is one I hope largely to avoid' (30n). Surely, though, the question is all-important and cannot be avoided. If the taking of a small piece of property that is unnecessary for your survival or well-being can save the life of a child, then the infringement of your property rights would be done for the sustenance of life. Can one object to this basis for overriding absolute property rights, and if not where *does* one draw the line? As Thompson comments (1982:137), Nozick is:

> unclear what degree of stringency should be assigned to rights (and hopes to avoid having to take a stand on the matter), but by the time he gets to government, all is forgotten, and rights – at any rate property rights – are infinitely stringent. It is my impression that his argument for his thesis rests entirely on the supposition that they are.

As well as the conflict between property and life, there is, too, a problem between the rights to property and to liberty. In Nozick's view, liberty is threatened primarily through the imposition of obligations to which one has not con-sented. But liberty can equally be threatened in other ways. As Scanlon points out, the enforcement of absolute property rights for some could well lead to those with property having such power over others that their liberty is severely restricted. 'Why should the loss of liberty caused by enforcement of absolute property rights and contract rights of some not be more important than those rights lost by loss of liberty?' (Scanlon, 1982:123). Nozick does not provide an answer.

These potential conflicts between different individual rights suggest strongly that it is necessary to have a moral basis for judging the strength of these different rights. Nozick, at one point, recognises this need and, while not being explicit, suggests that the moral basis for rights has to do with the capacity to live a meaningful life (50). But does not this bring us back, in some way, to the concept of justice as need? As Scheffler argues: 'Now whatever a meaningful life may turn out to be, it seems reasonable enough to suggest that any distributable good necessary to have a reasonable chance of living a decent and fulfilling life (such as food) will also be necessary for having a meaningful life' (1982:159). Mack extends the argument further, contending that human beings are essentially social beings who can only experience a full and meaningful life in community. 'It should be unnecessary (but it is not) to say that living well involves having, psychologically, a direct interest in the well-being of others' (1982:286). There is, then, no obvious reason why Nozick's views on property and individual rights should be seen as correct; they do conflict with intuitive ideas and, in the absence of a more substan-tial justification for their absolute nature, they remain unproven.

We move now specifically to Nozick's theory of justice and consider first his views on just acquisition and just transfer, which provide the foundation for his entitlement theory. As we have seen, Nozick's theory is historical: whether a distribution is just or not is dependent upon how it came about. There can, then, be no doubt that the starting-point is all-important to his theory and the inferences one can draw from it. There are for Nozick two ways that original acquisition can arise: either by acquiring what is freely available on its own, or by acquiring what is freely available by mixing one's labour with it. Nozick, like Locke before him, is concerned to ascertain whether goods in the pre-society order are or are not freely available, and he accepts Locke's view, or a modification of it, that goods can be acquired provided there is 'enough and as good left over'. Indeed, he goes further to point out instances where acquisition is not allowed because the Lockean pro-viso is not met. He states (1974:180):

> Thus a person may not appropriate the only water-hole in a desert and charge what he will if he possesses one and unfortunately it happens that all the water-holes in the desert dry up, except for his. This unfortunate circumstance, admittedly no fault of his, brings into operation the Lockean proviso and limits his property rights. Similarly, an owner's property right in the only island in an area does not allow him to order a castaway from a shipwreck off his island as a trespasser, for this would violate the Lockean proviso.

What these examples provided by Nozick suggest is that the freedom to acquire property can be constricted; and the reason is surely because the freedom of *others* is thereby restricted. And one reason why the freedom of others is restricted is that the needs of others are considered relevant in *these* instances. But once an excep-tion has been made, the question of where to draw the line between just and unjust acquisition becomes essential. Nozick makes a huge leap from original acquisition in a 'state of nature' situation to present-day society by stating: 'I believe that the free operation of a market situation will not actually run foul of the Lockean proviso . . . If this is correct, the proviso will not play a very important role in the activities of protective agencies and will not provide a significant opportunity for future state action' (182).

This, however, is an opinion heavily laden with value judgements: it is not an argument that is developed. The further one moves from perfect competition and towards monopoly ownership and the more resources there are which are scarce, then the greater the force of the Lockean proviso. The real world is not one of perfect competition, but one of large corporations; there are today few if any free resources, so the vast majority must have been acquired at some point in time without there being 'enough and as good left over'; and, in any case, the world prior to individual ownership was in practice more often common ownership rather than non-ownership and thus Nozick's belief that the mythical past can be used to justify the present would need to be proved to sustain his point.

But even if Nozick's views on just acquisition were found to be convincing, there is doubt about his description of what constitutes justice in transfer, especially as applying to market transactions. It will, by now, come as no surprise that Nozick does not attempt to specify in detail the principles of justice in transfer. However, as Kirzner points out, the basic and appealing notion is that justice in transfer occurs if transactions are voluntary. Now a necessary condition for market equilibrium is a world free from error: decisions could be considered voluntary if they are made with complete awareness of market conditions. Yet the real world is characterised by imperfect information and, argues Kirzner, 'it is further the case that insight into the equilibrating forces of the market generated by the conditions of disequilibrium reveals them to operate through entrepreneurial discovery (and exploitation) of the *very errors which are characteristic* of disequilibrium' (1982:386). Kirzner concludes thus (387):

> If the market depends heavily on the exploitation of profit opportunities made possible only by the errors of others, and *if* goods purchased from sellers who sold only as a result of error be considered unjustly acquired then surely the justice of the market has been unsalvageably compromised.

There are, too, an array of different problems which arise when moving to the real world situation of people mixing their labour with resources to change products and to produce new ones. If, as Arrow (1978:278) points out, there are large gains to social interaction above and beyond what individuals and subgroups could achieve on their own, then just acquisition from labour inputs becomes extremely problematic. In addition, the value of goods a person can produce depends on a mix of inherent ability and learnt techniques and skills, thus raising again the question of a just reward when the good is transferred. Furthermore, as Sen (1982b:3-4) explains, when incomes generated by the production of *different* goods are compared, relative incomes depend on relative prices of products.

> You and I may continue to produce the same goods in unchanged amounts in exactly the same way but a change in the relative prices of our respective products (caused, say, by changing demand conditions having nothing to do with the functioning of the rest of the economy) can make our relative incomes change without any change of anything that you and I are, in fact, doing or producing.

If these problems with justice in acquisition and justice in transfer lead us to doubt the strength of the entitlement theory, we can, with Nozick, revert to the theory of rectification which specifies a procedure to wipe out the effects of past injustices. While he says very little about the rectification principle, the following passage gives the main thrust of its force and implications (Nozick, 1974:152–3):

> Idealizing greatly, let us suppose theoretical investigation will produce a principle of rectification. This principle uses historical information about previous situations and injustices done in them . . . and information about the actual course of events that flowed from these injustices, until the present, and it yields a description (or descriptions) of holdings in the society. The principle of rectification presumably will make use of its best estimate of subjective information about what would have occurred (or a probability distribution over what might have occurred, using the expected value) if the injustice had not taken place. If the actual description of holding turns out not to be one of the descriptions yielded by the principle, then one of the descriptions yielded must be realized.

Only a little thought is needed to see that there are insurmountable difficulties with applying the principle of rectification, especially if, and this may well be the case, the principles of just acquisition and just transfer are continuously being violated. If, in the past, certain injustices drastically altered the subsequent chain of events, then it will be practically impossible to trace through all the different theoretical scenarios resulting in a just outcome. Interestingly, Nozick gets himself out of this cul-de-sac by proposing that if a choice is to be made between different distributions to rectify past injustices, then 'considerations of distributive justice and equality that I argue against play a legitimate role in *this* subsidiary choice' (153). This may be theoretically appealing but it does not get us over the practical problems of working out and agreeing what the situation would have been like without the original injustice. If, for example, in the case of Zimbabwe one agreed that the Rudd Concession granting land rights to the white settlers through the British South Africa Company was unjust, then how does one go about rectifying that injustice today? The law courts continually assess and make judgements on cases of injustice based on corruption, fraud and theft. However, when people are found guilty, nowhere is the suggestion made that rectification of the injustice be assessed through theorising about different outcomes and reappropriating property unjustly acquired. Monetary fines and/or prison sentences are imposed as *practical* methods of coping with recognised injustice. To attempt to apply Nozick's rectification principles is a wholly impractical task, as the legal system recognises.

It should be noted that Nozick himself is worried about the violations of his principles of acquisition and transfer, that there are practical problems about applying his principle of rectification, and also, importantly, that applying the principle of rectification by no means excludes direct state intervention. Indeed, it is of more than passing interest to note the final sentence in his extensive chapter on distributive justice which ends as follows: 'past injustices might be so great as to make necessary in the short run a more extensive state in order to rectify them' (231). Even for Nozick, then, there could well be circumstances in which aid could be legitimate because of past injustice. He does not, however, expand upon this statement or, alas, give any indication for how long the short run might last.[2]

We are now in a position to draw some more specific conclusions about Nozick's views for the ethics of aid. Nozick's theory, if sustainable, would remove completely the obligation of governments to provide aid to Third World countries because it leads to the view that governments have no obligation to act except to preserve and maintain the minimal state, and this excludes any intervention in the form of economic distribution. It also makes entitlement principles the beginning and end of distributive justice, excluding all other theories, be they based on a narrow view of need or on broader principles, like Rawls' theory of justice.

Whatever appeal different aspects of Nozick's theory may have, there is no doubt that it fails in its overall venture, and for a number of reasons. First, it is based on a number of key assumptions about individual rights and property relations that are unexplained; alternative views indicating potential conflict between different rights and their less than absolute quality have still to be refuted by Nozick. Secondly, his entitlement theory, while having a certain intuitive attraction, can certainly not lay claim to exclusivity at the theoretical level both because so much is still vague and also because, at bottom, other concepts of justice, such as that based on need and welfarism, do creep in. Thirdly, a serious question can be raised about the practical application of his theory to the real world and to market arrangements that are not based on the world of perfect competition and probably were – as Nozick himself at one point agrees – derived through unjust means. Nozick himself admits (ix) that his views lack precision, while others such as Thompson would maintain that, even on his own terms, his theory gives us no practical moral lessons in the world today. Because his theory lays claim to exclusivity, one would only have to accept one particular criticism of it as valid to challenge its comprehensive assault on alternative theories of justice which do accept the moral obligation to help. The final word, then, has to be that Nozick fails to convince that there is no obligation to help.

Bauer and Hayek

The views of Peter Bauer, on desert and just processes have already been covered in the earlier discussion on entitlement. While it is probably accepted that in general people do deserve to receive the fruits of their labour and that procedures for creating income and wealth are taken to be just, this is by no means the whole story. As Nozick clearly recognises, there is little justice involved if processes are just and acquisition is not, and there are serious questions to be asked about desert in monopolistic or near-monopolistic situations.[3] The fact that Bauer can state that incomes are 'normally' produced by people from their own resources and that economic differences are 'largely' the result of people's capacities and motivations suggests that he is making not so much moral and sufficient points as factual and qualified ones. These would need to be proved and in any case one would additionally have to show that the resources are always available to produce food, clothing, shelter etc. so that basic needs can be met when the motivational ingredient is there. But can they be proved? It is by no means clear that hard work and motivation are the crucial ingredients in determining income; if this were true there would have been no debate in the 1984 miners' dispute over uneconomic pits. As for the motivation of poor people, Lipton (1977:82–6) convincingly argues that this results from a mix of poverty and policy so that motivation by no means provides sufficient evidence for action. But more fundamentally, there is, in this view, little acknowledgement of the interrelationship in the real world not only of people to motives and resources but also between people in producing resources. As Sen writes (1982b:3):

> Production is based on the joint use of different resources, possibly provided by different people, and it is not in general possible to separate out who – or even which – resource produced how much of the total output. There is no obvious way of deciding that 'this much' of the output is owing to labour, 'that much' to raw materials, 'that much' to machinery and so on.

In addition, Sen adds, incomes are derived from prices which are altered by changes in demand, and one also needs to distinguish between productivity increases and those increases in output related to resource ownership.

A third assertion made by Bauer is that there are no common needs. This is self-evidently false. People, like animals, have basic common needs such as air, food and water, to which should be added shelter and clothing. There is, indeed, controversy over what other needs are basic to different communities and over, for example, the mix of calories, proteins and vitamins needed to sustain life. However, *contra* Bauer, there are common needs which have to be met for people to live in a basic state of physical health and social decency. And even Bauer admits that the weak people in society should be helped (1981:20).

Bauer's next criticism concerns coercion. This brings us back to the minimal state, in fact beyond it to a state of anarchy. There is a distinction, which Bauer chooses not to look at, between the minimal and the totalitarian state. True, there is controversy over where to draw the line, but on Bauer's view of coercion not even a minimal state should be allowed because it restricts the freedom of some for the common good. What should be at issue is the way the freedom of some limits that of others. As few people in the UK, USA or Sweden, nations which do redistribute income from the wealthy to the poor, would argue that their governments are totalitarian, the onus is on Bauer to show, and not simply state, that helping the Third World brings in a distinctly totalitarian dimension to redistribution. He seems to suggest that the advocates of aid argue that it should be provided for the purpose of equalising living standards. While this might be one reason advanced by some advocates of aid, it is certainly not a common argument and not one used by any donor government. Hence to draw general conclusions about coercion from criticising the notion of equalising incomes is an exercise in shooting down not straw men but fairies.

Finally, Bauer challenges the obligation to help based on the need to provide compensation for historical injustices. One view he holds (1984b:57) is that colonialism helped rather than harmed the Third World, presumably by extending market forces to these countries. The stronger view he appears to adhere to, however, is that, even if there were past injustices, 'except over very short periods historical wrongs cannot be put right' (1981:121). Besides the fact that his first point cannot be held universally if he also believes in his second, there is a question to be raised about the short term. Even if Nozick's strong belief that the justice of present entitlements has to be based on just acquisition is laid to one side, one needs to ask whether present transfers in the real world are automatically to be conceived of as just. If, as Bauer believes, the goal of economic development for Third World countries is legitimate and, as he also believes, 'the West can best promote this by the reduction of its own severe barriers to imports from poor countries' (1984b:62), then is it not also true that the inhibitions to development caused by deliberate protectionist policies are unjust and that *this* provides a moral basis for helping? The point is well put and developed by Singer (1984:5–6):

> there is more in the restitution argument than Lord Bauer admits. There are elements in the international economic system which work to the advantage of the rich and the disadvantage of the poor. To have a near-monopoly of technological capacity, of R and D capacity, of know-how, of financial power (at least up to the emergence of OPEC), of investment resources, of entrepreneurial capacity, of information, briefing and negotiating techniques will give the richer industrial countries an edge in trade, investment, growth capacity and indeed in all the bargaining and negotiations relating to economic contacts. It is a matter of terminology whether such built-in advantages

represent 'exploitation' or not – I myself would avoid such terminology as misleading; I prefer to stick to 'built-in advantages'. I would also readily admit that the developing countries and their governments could do a lot more to reduce and cope with the built-in disadvantages by more effective domestic policies and also by better co-operation with each other. Yet the built-in disequilibrium in advantages *does* constitute a *prima facie* moral (or perhaps also economic) case for compensatory action, i.e. aid in one form or another. Such aid in the broader sense – 'in one form or another' – may, of course, take the form of tariff preferences, better prices for their export commodities, liberalised migration etc. rather than aid in the narrower direct sense, but it remains aid in the sense of unilateral concessionary action.

What we have in Bauer's criticisms therefore is not so much a theoretical justification for rejecting the obligation to help but rather a number of objections to a view which is put forward by few people, that there is an exclusive obligation to help and provide aid even when this leads to extreme contradictions and impractical conclusions. In short, Bauer fails to convince.

The first thing to be said about Hayek's views is that he is ready to consider exceptions based on need. He admits that there *is* a state obligation to provide basic needs because there is 'the duty of preventing destitution' (1976:303). He also considers the now familiar example of the owner of the only water-hole in the desert who charges an extravagant price to potential water-users, and is prepared to admit that this exchange is potentially coercive because of the severe deprivation that arises if the exchange fails to occur. In other words, needs-based criteria are a factor recognised by Hayek. They are also recognised by Sir Keith Joseph who writes: 'if the most basic needs of the poorest, measured by some absolute and not relative standard, cannot be satisfied by the amount of wealth which they have, then it would probably be generally agreed that the richest should help them out' (Joseph and Sumption, 1979:85–6). Once an exception is made based upon need, the crucial question is then where one draws the line between the state's obligation to provide for the needy and the intended goal of individual freedom. As we shall see, there are grounds for believing that the role of the state should be far wider than Hayek would wish it to be.

There are additional worries with Hayek's views and their implications for obligation. One needs to pursue more precisely what he means by liberty. If liberty is an ideal to be valued, then in order to sustain it with widespread appeal does one not have to devise a way to ensure not just liberty for some but as equal an access to liberty for all as possible? While the removal of coercion does secure equal liberty to the extent that it draws the parameters for the conditions for individual action, it does not necessarily secure an equal or even fair *value* of liberty. Plant commenting on Hayek continues thus (1984:6–7):

> The limitations on individual freedom are not just those imposed deliberately by the intentional actions of others and which the liberal tradition rightly wishes to resist and restrict but also those imposed by natural differences of birth and genetic inheritance, together with those which are the result of human action whether deliberate or not, in the field of family background, economic resources, welfare and education. The positive resources which individuals need to be able to live in their own way cannot be secured by a set of negative or procedural rights, important though these are. They require rather the marshalling of economic resources to enable individuals to live the kind of lives they want to live. . . . It is because we value liberty for all that we are concerned to secure a greater equality in the *worth* of liberty.

In other words, concern with freedom has to include not only freedom from constraints on doing what one wishes but also freedom *to do* all that one wishes.

This Hayek appears willing to accept. Once he has admitted that I should have access to those goods and services 'that are crucial to my existence or the preservation of what I value most', then he has to accept the need to provide access to those basic goods necessary to pursue my life plan. Thus the criterion of need has to be incorporated into the idea of providing what I value most, and this has a wide applicability if by liberty one means not only liberty for those in society who are privileged and rich but equal access to liberty for all.

There is no doubt that the power of Hayek's views depends to a large extent upon the free operation of the market. A glance at markets at the international level in the real world today does little to convince one that they are free or that they provide a system ensuring equal access to liberty for all. But we need to move to another part of Hayek's argument which has not yet been discussed, namely that the market is neutral and amoral. He argues that while the market does not reward merit or desert, or any other principle for that matter, most of its political defenders believe that it does and that this is the basis on which market claims are legitimised vis-à-vis the electorate (Plant, 1984:13). Even if this is accepted, however, it by no means closes the debate because people and governments do bring their moral beliefs into play to provide constraints on market outcomes which they find disturbing. For example, the recently published Warnock Report lays down limits on the commercialisation of reproduction, and this view received wide acceptance in government circles. Or, to take another instance, few market advocates would remain agnostic if groups or individuals began to set up brothels or sex-shops outside the gates of our schools. In general, there are limits to how far people are prepared to go in accepting the *outcome* of market freedom, so in this sense morality is not excluded when market relations are discussed. As Plant argues, 'any sensitive defence of markets will make some reference to the general environment within which markets operate' for they do not on their own provide their own legitimacy (14).

Hirsch in his book *Social Limits to Growth* instances an additional worry about the consequence of market procedures: that individual choices can and sometimes do result in circumstances which, if those exercising their choice had anticipated them, would have caused them to choose in a different way. Individual choice does not necessarily lead to overall improvement, and in these cases 'only a collective approach . . . can offer individuals the guidance necessary to achieve the solutions that they themselves would prefer' (Hirsch, 1977:10). There are two conclusions to be drawn about markets even when they are working well: first that moral questions are still important, and second that there is no guarantee that what I value most will be preserved by my free choice.

In conclusion, there are two ways in which one can look at the challenge of Hayek's views. At one level, Hayek is ready to admit that in cases of extreme hardship there is an obligation to help; there is in practice therefore no resistance offered to helping, provided one can show that poverty in the Third World is a situation of extreme hardship. At another level, he would maintain that exceptional cases of hardship do not provide support for a general theory of state obligation because this would challenge the individual freedom sustained by markets. We have seen, however, that there are serious problems with his views at the theoretical level and in transferring his ideas to the real world. Taken as a whole, Hayek fails to counter successfully the notion that there is an obligation to help.

More from Bauer

Perhaps as a postscript we should consider a number of other attacks on the moral argument for official aid from the influential Lord Bauer. In a number of places he explicitly refers to the claim that foreign aid is a moral issue, in all instances to reject the moral imperative for governments to provide aid. In *Dissent on Development*, he comments that 'foreign aid is often advocated as if it were the discharge of a moral duty to help the poor', thereby implying that meeting the needs of the poor does, for some, constitute a moral obligation (1971:126). His response to this is that there *is* a moral obligation if this is understood as 'voluntary charity'. The question simply does not arise for government aid since, it 'is taxpayers' money compulsorily collected' and 'the moral obligation to help the less fortunate cannot be discharged by entities such as governments' (1971:126-7). That governments have no moral responsibility in deciding how to use taxpayers' money clearly goes against common experience and against any normal understanding of the functioning of democracy. The fact that governments do appeal to morality when they argue for or against policies – in the field of foreign aid and in other areas – and that parliamentarians invoke moral principles in voting and debating leads one seriously to question and almost certainly to reject Bauer's argument against moral obligation on the part of governments.

But even if one laid this argument to one side and considered only Bauer's comment about taxpayers, there is still doubt about the validity of his claim for it seems to contradict common experience of how things happen in the real world. Even though government expenditure is based upon compulsory collections from taxpayers, taxpayers can and do exert influence on how that expenditure is allocated. Compulsory collections of tax preclude neither having a moral view on, nor attempting to influence, how the money is spent, as Bauer would appear to suggest.

Another of Bauer's arguments is to suggest that, even if aid did reach the poor (which he doubts), they would not use it properly because they are materially unambitious. The argument develops with explicit reference to morality. Bauer comments that it is commonly asserted that conditions in much of the Third World are so desperate that life is barely tolerable (1981:115). To answer the moral claim for help, Bauer appeals to history, arguing that until recently the whole world population was deprived of the satisfaction of its basic needs because the West itself did not have these facilities until they were created in the nineteenth century. He adds, too, the fact that the lot of the poorest is improving (supposedly without aid, though this crucial point is ignored) in most Third World countries and will continue to improve. However, he goes on, this improvement will not remove wretchedness, which advocates of aid equate with poverty. Wretchedness and contentment, he argues, are not simply matters of income or income differences; he quotes the suicide rate as an objective measure of wretchedness and concludes (1981:115):

> if wretchedness were the appropriate measure of wealth transfer, as many people believe it to be, the transfers should be from the Third World to the West, as this would at least enable the wretched to become even more comfortable.

The other assertions in this particular argument appear to be based on similarly faulty reasoning. One is based on an appeal to history. But does the fact that facilities were unavailable in the past and hence that there was clearly no moral obligation to provide them then imply, as does Bauer's argument, that there is no moral obligation to provide them today? Similarly, even if he is correct in his assertion that in most of the Third World the lot of the poorest has improved in the twentieth century, this 'fact' does not eliminate the moral obligation to satisfy the needs of those whose lot has *not* improved nor to ask the more critical question of whether the *improvement* has led to the *satisfaction* of those needs which created the moral obligation. If the moral obligation is based on need satisfaction, that obligation remains until all needs have been satisfied. In other words, Bauer's response, even if factually correct, is not sufficient to answer the general point. Finally, he states that advocates of aid equate poverty with wretchedness; this he says is wrong, explaining the faulty link between poverty and wretchedness with what he admits is a ludicrous extension of the argument. While one can readily agree with him on this, it is not this point that needs to be analysed, but rather the linking of poverty and wretchedness, and here Bauer chooses to misinterpret the connection made between the two concepts. If advocates of aid equate poverty and wretchedness – and let us take Bauer's word for it that they do – then what precisely are they doing? People equate poverty with wretchedness because poor people are wretched or – to use the correct synonym – because they are miserable or unhappy. Unhappiness or wretchedness is not totally removed by eliminating poverty because it can be caused by other factors besides poverty. In short, it is an incorrect use of words to acknowledge that a link between poverty and wretchedness is commonly made and then infer that the words are synonymous, which they clearly are not, and to go on to deduce that wealth transfers should be based on wretchedness. Enough has surely been said to demonstrate the absurdity of this method of presenting an argument which falls down on logic, consistency and meaning.

Bauer also attacks the egalitarian argument that the richer have an obligation towards the poorer. While he devotes considerable space to a critique of those who advocate total global equality, his more important criticism (because it is more frequently used by governments as a justification for providing aid) concerns those who advocate some, but far from total, egalitarianism. Bauer's first point is to question the statistics upon which comparative indicators of international income and wealth are based. These he argues are flawed with inaccuracies, even though they do appear accurate enough for him to argue that 'many donor tax-payers are far poorer than many people in recipient countries where much aid benefits the powerful and the relatively well-off' (1984b:53). Of course, even if this were true, and the general assertion would need to be weighed against the evidence, it is not the whole story. In donor countries it is not only individual taxpayers who contribute to the fiscus, and in recipient countries richer individuals also pay tax. Whether aid is used by recipient governments to benefit the powerful and well-off or the poor and powerless is again a question that can satisfactorily be answered only by evaluating the evidence.

Some concluding comments

In the previous sections of this chapter we have expressed doubts about the views of those writers who reject the notion that governments have a moral obligation to help. These doubts lead us to the view that *single* theories each in different ways fail to provide a convincing and comprehensive case for concluding that governments *never* have an obligation to help. We should add, however, that some of the arguments made by the critics do have validity and are important: markets can and do enhance freedom, individual rights are important, and desert is a factor in determining rights to resources. Moreover, rejecting single theories which conclude that there is no obligation to help by no means implies that single theories which deduce that there is an obligation to help are thereby proved valid. Nozick himself provides some telling criticisms against Rawls' theory of justice, as do other commentators like Barry and Miller.

Our main purpose in this chapter has been to analyse primarily the opponents of aid, and these criticisms have not therefore been reviewed. However, to the extent that they, too, strike home, they also lead us to the view that justice cannot be narrowed down to single explanations. Following Miller, we would say that there are three strands of social justice that together go to make a complete and comprehensive picture. Justice can be understood as 'to each his due' – the just state of affairs is that in which each individual has exactly those benefits and burdens which are due to him by virtue of his personal characteristics and circumstances (Miller 1979:20). The three elements are: to each according to his rights, to each according to his deserts, and to each according to his needs. The three principles testify to a different yet essential concern for the individual: 'the principle of rights by guaranteeing security of expectation and freedom of choice, the principle of desert by recognizing the distinctive value of each person's actions and qualities, and the principle of need by providing the requisites for individual plans of life' (Miller, 1979:151-2). To attempt to create a theory of justice based on only one element must ultimately fail, either because other elements appear in a disguised form or because the other irreducibly different demands of justice stand out as unmet and yet make essentially moral claims.

The moral obligation to provide aid is based upon the obligation to help or the obligation to correct previous injustices. Sometimes these obligations are based on the notion of rights, sometimes on the unjust distribution of previous or current deserts, but more often on the basis of need. It is not our purpose here to argue that there is an absolute obligation to help, overriding all other obligations arising from considerations of justice. Rather it is to conclude that theories which argue that there is never an obligation to help can never be accepted in their totality, because deliberately or not they exclude some aspects of the complete notion of justice.

Notes

1. Nozick proceeds to use an illustration which leads him to conclude that 'it is not clear how those holding alternative conceptions of distributive justice can reject the entitlement conception of justice in holdings' (160). If, he says, you are worried about the all-pervasiveness of the entitlement theory, then select your own favoured distribution and call it D_1. Perhaps it is one where everyone has an equal share or perhaps where shares are related in some way to incentives so that growth and egalitarian objectives are held in constructive tension; it does not matter what the distribution is as long as you believe it to be just. Now suppose, says Nozick, that (*ibid*.: 161-2):

    Wilt Chamberlain is greatly in demand by basketball teams, being a great gate attraction. (Also suppose contracts run only for a year, with players being free agents.) He signs the following sort of contract with a team: in each home game, twenty-five cents from the price of each ticket of admission goes to him. (We ignore the question of whether he is 'gouging' the owners, letting them look out for themselves.) The season starts, and people cheerfully attend his team's games; they buy their tickets, each time dropping a separate twenty-five cents of their admission price into a special box with Chamberlain's name on it. They are excited about seeing him play; it is worth the total admission price to them. Let us suppose that in one season one million persons attend his home games, and Wilt Chamberlain winds up with $250,000, a much larger sum than the average income and larger even than anyone else has. Is he entitled to this income? Is this new distribution D_2, unjust? If so, why? There is no question about whether each of the people was entitled to the control over the resources they held in D_1; because that was the distribution (your favorite) that (for the purposes of argument) we assumed was acceptable. Each of these persons chose to give twenty-five cents of their money to Chamberlain. They could have spent it on going to the movies, or on candy bars, or on copies of *Dissent* magazine, or of *Monthly Review*. But they all, at least one million of them, converged on giving it to Wilt Chamberlain in exchange for watching him play basketball. If D_1 was a just distribution, and people voluntarily moved from it to D_2, transferring parts of their share they were given under D_1 (what was it for if not to do something with?), isn't D_2 also just? If the people were entitled to dispose of the resources to which they were entitled (under D_1), didn't this include their being entitled to give it to, or exchange it with, Wilt Chamberlain? Can anyone else complain on grounds of justice? Each other person already has his legitimate share under D_1. Under D_1, there is nothing that anyone has that anyone else has a claim of justice against. After someone transfers something to Wilt Chamberlain, third parties still have their legitimate shares; their shares are not changed. By what process could such a transfer among two persons give rise to legitimate claim of distributive justice on a portion of what was transferred by a third party who had no claim of justice on any holding of the other *before* the transfer'.

What this example shows is that if the process is just by which one moves from a position one accepts as just to a second or third position, then the second and third positions are also just. However, the Wilt Chamberlain example is precisely that – an example. We need to move from the world of theory to the real world.

2. How about the Wilt Chamberlain story upon which Nozick sets such store to influence those unconvinced of the truth and exclusivity of his theory of justice? While there is no doubt at all that the argument is intuitively appealing, on examination it is far from totally convincing.

   Choose your own preferred distribution of holding, begins Nozick, and call this D_1. Then allow those with money to spend it freely. One consequence could be that one person receives a massive amount of money from entertaining many different people. Surely, continues Nozick, the person who receives this vast income is entitled to it because the original distribution was just and the money was freely given? The first problem with the example is its unreality and the difficulty of transferring the analogy to the real world. If one's original starting-point is a distribution where everyone has their basic needs met, then immediately and at a stroke the needs of the real world have already been satisfied and the example is dealing with surplus income in an affluent society. But suppose, for the sake of argument, one began with the distribution of holdings currently available in Calcutta. If Wilt were playing basketball in Calcutta it is not immediately self-evident that potential spectators should be completely free to walk past starving Indians lined up at the entrance to the stadium, likely to die for lack of 25 cents, and pay the money for sheer superfluous entertainment.

   But even if one accepted the example as it stands, it does not necessarily have to follow that Wilt Chamberlain is entitled to all his income. Suppose that one's preferred theory of distribution was based on some notion of egalitarianism – for example that incomes exceeding twenty times the minimum should be subject to progressive taxation – then in this instance Wilt Chamberlain would *not* be entitled to all his earnings for the reason that the preferred distribution theory carries with it in-built assumptions about *future* distributions and entitlements arising from them. Indeed, this is not far from beliefs widely held in industrialised societies that have tax systems which incorporate restriction on widening inequalities. The trouble with the way the Chamberlain argument is presented, argues O'Neill, is that it presupposes but fails to demonstrate that it is wrong to interfere to restore disturbed patterns or end-states and that such restorations are always redistributive and violate individuals' property rights. But it is precisely *these* property rights which have yet to be established. Another problem of the starting-point has been observed by Arrow, who states that if the just allocation were Pareto-efficient at the outset, then the example could not even occur, for any exchange would indicate that the first distribution was not Pareto-optimal (Arrow, 1978:269).

   There is an additional issue raised by Nozick's example. His theory assumes that all holdings come under the rights of private ownership, that is, that all holdings are private property; and the implication drawn from the Wilt Chamberlain example is that if any holding is justly acquired it can be justly transferred and lead to just entitlement. But, as Ryan correctly shows, not all holdings can have those attributes. Individuals are by no means always free to give away or exchange all their holdings (Ryan, 1982:328ff). People who pass examinations or have jobs are entitled to them and the incomes derived from employment. They are not, however, entitled to give their 'A' levels or degrees to their friends or to pass on jobs to their children when they retire. This is for the simple reason that one can be entitled to things one does not own. Thus preventing exchange does not necessarily have to be because of coercion, as Nozick would have us believe.

3. Bauer's statement that it is 'by no means obvious why it should be unjust that those who produce more should enjoy higher incomes' has the intuitive appeal of Nozick's Wilt Chamberlain example. The immediate reply derived from the critique of the Chamberlain example is that it is not obvious either why those who produce more should always be entitled to all their income without question while additional questions about ownership of assets and transfer procedures will also need to be looked into.

5 Critics of the Moral Case
Similar Goals and Different Means

The moral case for governments to provide foreign aid is rooted in the belief that there is a moral obligation to act because of perceived or acknowledged injustice originating most commonly in straightforward lack of resources, unequal distribution of resources, or historical exploitation of resources; it is sustained by assurances that the aid provided does or can address these injustices. The previous chapter focused on those critics of the moral case who challenged its starting-point: the obligation to act. In this chapter we shall examine those critics who accept that there is an obligation to help but, in various ways, question the means chosen – the provision of official aid – to achieve these common goals. Thus it is assumed here that the goals of development should be promoted and that policies should be initiated within and between countries to accelerate the development process, leaving aside, initially, the thorny question of how precisely development is defined.

Within the development literature, aid is under attack from both left and right, and more recently from writers within the centre, because of its failure to achieve the objectives for which it is given, be they specific measurable objectives such as relieving poverty, reducing inequalities or meeting basic minimum needs or more general ones such as contributing to overall socio-economic development. What the criticisms of aid described in this chapter have in common is at minimum a radical questioning and at the extreme a rejection of the conventionally accepted view, that aid is a positive force in development. In its strongest form the assault on aid argues that it does not help to achieve its objectives, and never can do so. In milder form, it contends that aid is not helping to achieve the objectives for which it is given but that it could do so to the extent that its composition, method or form of transfer, or the target group to whom it is specifically directed, could be altered.

There are two questions raised by these criticisms that have a direct bearing upon the ethics of aid and which need to be addressed. The first is whether the critics are indeed correct in their analysis of what donor government aid achieves in practice. The second is what the implications would be for the moral case for aid if the criticisms made were found to be valid. If the criticisms are found to be incorrect or at best unsubstantiated, then the moral case for providing aid would appear to be strengthened. But even if there is strong evidence and theoretical backing to support the criticisms levelled against aid, would this necessarily lead to the conclusion that the moral case for aid has to be discarded completely? Before examining this latter question we need to begin to analyse the various criticisms made.

First, a word of warning, however. A large part of the discussion of this chapter will be inconclusive at this stage. This is because the moral conclusions derived from the criticisms discussed here are deduced largely from an evaluation of the evidence of what aid has achieved in practice and/or are based on a particular understanding of the process of development in which aid in its present form is inserted. These issues are so vast and complex as to deserve separate and detailed treatment in Parts II and III, below.

The different criticisms outlined

The view from the right

Nearly 30 years ago the economist Milton Friedman wrote an article entitled 'Foreign economic aid: means and objectives', whose arguments, while never forgotten, appear to have generated fresh appeal in the 1980s. While Friedman sees the objectives of US foreign aid as, at bottom, to further US interests, it is his conclusion about the effect of foreign aid on development that is of prime interest to us here. Friedman explains that he is concerned solely with 'one particular category of US expenditure on foreign aid – economic aid – and with one class of arguments for such expenditure – their value in promoting the economic development of other countries' (1958:64). His opinion is simply stated: that foreign aid 'is likely to retard improvement in the well-being of the masses' (78). This stark conclusion, which carries the forceful implication that governments have no moral obligation to provide aid, indeed rather the opposite, is based on both theory and evidence. First, the theory. 'What is required [for development] is rather an atmosphere of freedom, of maximum opportunity for individuals to experiment, and of incentive for them to do so in an environment in which there are objective tests of success and failure, in short, a vigorous, free capitalistic market' (71). Next, the evidence. 'It thus seems clear that a free market without central planning has, at least to date, been not only the most effective route to economic development but the *only* effective route to a rising standard of life for the masses of the people' (72). Thus for Friedman from both theory and evidence there is no moral obligation for governments to provide foreign aid.

For Peter Bauer, there would seem to be very little that foreign aid can achieve for poor people in poor countries even if these people can be clearly identified, which he also doubts. He states: 'The central argument for foreign aid has remained that without it Third World countries cannot progress at a reasonable rate, if at all (1984:43). But, he contends (44);

> not only is such aid patently not required for development: it has tended to obstruct development more than it has promoted it. External donations have never been necessary for the development of any society anywhere. Economic achievement depends on personal, cultural, social and political factors, that is people's own faculties, motivations, mores, their institutions and the policies of their rulers.

Aid can therefore be rejected for at least these four reasons. Nor is it needed to accelerate the progress of Third World countries, for, as he writes elsewhere (1981:100):

> It might be argued that while aid is not indispensable for progress, it is required to accelerate what would otherwise be very slow progress. This contention differs substantially from the widely canvassed vicious circle but it is still invalid. Official aid played no

part in the progress of the West, nor in the very rapid progress of many Third World countries since the closing decades of the nineteenth century. It is patronizing to suggest that the peoples of the Third World crave for material progress but, unlike people in the West, they cannot progress at a reasonable rate without external donations. This condescension is misplaced.

If, as Bauer argues, aid is not required for development, then how is development achieved? The answer is by extending the range of individual choice in a freely operating market system in which the government plays no direct role (1984b:22, 25 and 26):

Extension of the range of choice of people as consumers and producers is perhaps the most satisfactory criterion of economic development. . . .

Extension of the range of choice is most likely to be promoted by an economic order in which firms and individuals largely determine what is produced and consumed, where they will work, how much they will save and how they will invest their savings. . . .

In a freely operating market system people can decide where they work, what they buy, how much they spend or save and where they invest. For most people freedom of choice in these matters is crucial. . . .

Critics of the market often dispute the reality and significance of the freedom and choices protected by decentralised decision, on the ground that such choices are of little value to many people, notably the poor. This criticism is epitomized in the familiar jibes that the Ritz is open to all, or that the poor are free to starve. It is a criticism which is radically misconceived. The ability to use their resources to their own best advantage, in particular to choose their employment freely and to have different employers competing for their services, is especially important to the poor and to people of humble status. It is well-to-do and established politicians, academics, media men, clerics, writers and artists who are apt to dismiss economic choice as unimportant.

Clearly then, Bauer's views on development provide a fundamental basis for his rejection of the notion that aid is necessary or even desirable for that development to occur. If aid is neither necessary nor desirable, then the moral obligation to provide it falls away.

Even more explicit and extreme in his rejection of foreign aid and its moral underpinnings is New York economics professor, Melvyn Krauss. For Krauss, aid not only fails to achieve the objectives of raising the living standards of the poor, it does positive harm. 'Foreign aid *hurts* not helps the LDCs' (1983a:157 and 190):

Economic development without aid is more than a slogan. It indicates an *essential condition* for economic development. If a less developed country is intent upon rapid growth, it cannot afford to tax the competitive sectors of the economy. Foreign aid and the big government it encourages impose such taxes, thus foreign aid and rapid growth are inconsistent.

But, it might be asked, does rapid growth provide the best method of helping the poor? Krauss has no doubts. 'Even if supply-side policies do foster growth, some argue the poor will benefit only marginally. But this is nonsense. In countries which have followed true supply-side policies, the poor have benefited enormously from economic growth' (1983b:52). Elsewhere (1983a:45) he states that there is incontrovertible evidence to show that the absolute real income of the poor is increased wherever and whenever growth has taken place in the Third World. How about food aid for starving people or for humanitarian reasons? No problem. Rather than going to poor people in real need, food aid often ends up being used by governments in poor countries to subsidise the politically powerful middle class and to keep themselves in power, he argues (150). Food aid critics 'understand how aid given for humanitarian reasons typically winds up being used to aid corrupt governments whose economic policies are not only biased against the starving . . . but destructive to the agricultural base of the economy' (159–60). All government-to-government aid has to be rejected, because 'Foreign aid involves a transfer of income between governments . . . it is part of a strategy of activist and interventionist government' (189). And 'the biggest obstacle to the economic development of the third world is big government' (186). But it is not only government-to-government aid that is to be eliminated; so too is government aid channelled multi-laterally through agencies like the World Bank. 'If the World Bank were to discontinue its poverty program . . . the main beneficiaries would be the third world poor themselves' (167). Or again, 'The World Bank must get out of the poverty business. If economic growth succeeds, poverty will take care of itself' (172).

Is this a callous uncaring conclusion? By no means. As Krauss explains (54 and 45):

> I certainly believe in social justice. The difference between myself and the traditional type of thinking you get in development economics is the way to promote it. I define social justice as increasing the standard of living of poor people. I don't believe you increase people's living standards by redistribution and restrictionist policies that destroy a country's economic base. You foster social justice by permitting growth, and you permit growth through economic freedom. Increased social services follow. . . .
>
> The Third World faces enough problems in achieving the imperative of growth without being distracted by naive concepts of social justice.

For Krauss then, far more than for Peter Bauer, it is crystal clear there is not only no moral obligation whatever to provide aid, but also, by implication, an extremely strong moral imperative *not* to provide aid. To the extent that donor governments continue to give aid they stand morally guilty of frustrating the alleviation of that poverty which they maintain they are trying to solve.

From right to left

One common strand running through these arguments of Friedman, Bauer and Krauss is their belief that unimpeded market forces provide the only or the best basis for development and that official aid of its very nature must frustrate their extension and penetration. At their weakest these views question the moral case for aid and at their strongest reject the moral imperative outright. A different set of arguments, also leading to the same questioning, has come from writers who are deeply sceptical or totally unconvinced of the role that market forces can play in achieving the objectives for which aid is given.

Foreign aid hurts not helps the developing countries, states Krauss. This bold and simple conclusion was also drawn by Lappé and her colleagues in their 1980 book *Aid As Obstacle*. US foreign assistance, they argue, fails to help the poor and by providing it 'instead of helping, we hurt the dispossessed majority' (1980:11). They have two basic arguments to make, both concerning aspects of power relations in developing countries. People (and we would add governments who use the moral argument) are in favour of aid because of the belief that it can reach the poor and this, they argue, it cannot do. Their case is succinctly put (11):

> US foreign assistance fails to help the poor because it is *of necessity* based on one fundamental fallacy: that aid can reach the powerless even though channelled through the powerful. Official foreign assistance necessarily flows through the recipient governments and too often (particularly in those countries to which the United States confines most of its aid) these governments represent narrow, elite economic interests. We have

learned that additional material resources are usually not needed to eliminate hunger. In fact, the influx of such outside resources into those countries where economic control is concentrated in the hands of the few bolsters the local, national and international elites, whose stranglehold over land and other productive resources generates poverty and hunger in the first place.

Thus aid is rejected both because it goes to the powerful and does not trickle down to the poor who are powerless and, perhaps more surprisingly, because even if it did reach the poor they do not really need it to alleviate their hunger. They explain this second point in the following way (11 and 12):

> The prevailing diagnosis of why people are poor and hungry is that they have been 'left out' of the development process. From this diagnosis flows one solution – bring the poor into development. 'Basic needs' aid strategies are conceived as a way to widen the development process to include the poor. But such a diagnosis is simply another version of the fallacious theory that one can reach the poor by expanding a process controlled by the rich. . . .
> The issue, then, is not to bring the poor into the development process, but for the poor to achieve the power they need to direct a development process in their interests.

Where do these conclusions leave the moral obligation to help which Lappé *et al.* believe in so fervently? Does the fact that US foreign assistance does not help the poor mean that Lappé and her colleagues believe, like Krauss although for very different reasons, that there is a moral obligation to work for the ending of aid? Their book leaves this question unresolved: at times they imply that they are of the opinion that all US aid should cease, at others they argue that aid could help countries which are working to solve the problems of the powerlessness of the poor. The ambiguity lies in uncertainty over whether US aid could ever provide help for the ends they see as critical for genuine development. The less extreme position is taken early on (14):

> Once we understand that government to government aid cannot transform power relations but can only reinforce what exists, it becomes clear that we must work to limit such aid to countries where there is already under way a fundamental restructuring of decision-making. . . .
> We are calling for a halt to all economic and military support for governments controlled by narrowly-based elites which use repression to protect their interests and to block the demands of their own people for redistribution of control over productive assets. Such a move would mean cutting off those governments now most favoured by US economic assistance and military aid.

Yet later on, in two different places, they conclude that all official aid should cease (123 and 136):

> . . . . in all cases, our prime responsibility is to work to end support for the enemies of the poor and hungry – beginning by exposing the uses and impact of *all types* of government economic and military aid (emphasis in original).
> We are not saying that direct material help to the poor abroad is completely impossible. But if there is a chance that outside resources will help rather than hurt, it is through voluntary, non-governmental aid agencies, not through official aid. Even then, achieving positive results is far from certain.

For Teresa Hayter, discussing whether governments do or do not have a moral obligation to provide aid would probably appear an odd and almost certainly an irrelevant occupation. Her analysis leads her to conclude that whether 'aid' does or does not help the poor is rather beside the main point. While aid may contribute to *some specific* improvement in the well-being of the Third World, this improvement is incidental to the main purpose for which it is given. She states in the preface to her book *Aid As Imperialism* (1971:9):

> I believe, now, that the existence of aid can be explained only in terms of an attempt to preserve the capitalist system in the Third World. Aid is not a particularly effective instrument for achieving this; hence its current decline.

Insofar as aid is effective in helping to preserve the capitalist system, Hayter concludes that its *general* contribution to the well-being of the Third World is negative. Whatever aid agencies or governments may say about why they give aid is an invalid starting-point for Hayter because for her these statements are irrelevant when one grasps the underlying rationale for providing aid. To assume that 'the well-being of the peoples of the Third World was or at least could become the primary consideration of aid policies' is, she argues, invalid (11).

We can still ask, however, whether she believes that aid should or could help improve the well-being of people of the Third World and whether donor governments should be providing aid to achieve these ends. Her answer to this question would be a resounding 'yes', although the implication of her analysis is that it could only be a relevant question for Western donor governments after their renunciation of the capitalist system. But that it *is* a question of concern to her is implied by the final discussion raised towards the end of her book of whether aid in a changed form could achieve the goals it should have. She states that 'it is necessary to discuss the possibility of such reforms' (184). However, ten years later she still remains extremely pessimistic about its potential success, arguing that 'most of these suggestions (for reform) are, however, unrealistic' (1981:184). 'For the moment, therefore, the realistic alternatives are the present, politically determined policies of the international agencies, or no aid' (91). Thus for Hayter, as for Lappé *et al.*, official aid under its present form is no answer to the problems of the poor and needy in the Third World, indeed this sort of aid has a negative effect. At this level, then, the conclusion has to be that there is a moral obligation for donor governments not to provide this aid. But for Hayter that conclusion by no means closes the debate, and she would certainly agree with the following comment made by Lappé *et al.* (1980:14):

> Many who have called for a halt or a reduction in US foreign aid have actually been saying, 'Cut them off. Let them solve their own problems. We must take care of our own.' This is *not* what we are saying . . . we must work to make our own society truly democratic and self-reliant so that one day it might play a constructive role around the world.

For these writers of the left, then, what is at issue is fundamentally the process of development that official aid is currently attempting to accelerate. The thrust of their analyses leads to the conclusion that one cannot discuss the morality of aid without evaluating the dynamic socio-economic system into which the aid is inserted. Questioning the appropriateness of the development strategies implied in donor country initiatives is the focus of two other substantial studies: the first by Willem Zeylstra, *Aid or Development* and the second by Tibor Mende, *From Aid to Recolonisation: Lessons of A Failure*. Zeylstra ends with a quotation from Mende 'if it is morally inadmissable to be against aid, it is immoral to prolong it when it implies acquiescence in the price it exacts in its present form' (1975:257). For Zeylstra, development aid is a failure. 'It has so far been rarely positive and often decidely negative' (256), because it proceeds from a diagnosis of the phenomenon of underdevelopment based at root on an exaggerated optimism in Western man's power of understanding the nature of social problems in a non-Western environment. It is, he contends, a false approach because (225-6):

> it exaggerates the importance of economic symptoms while neglecting to explain them in historical perspective. The idea that underdevelopment can only be overcome through modernization, that is, through accepting Western civilization as a model for thought and action is itself the fruit of a particular post-war phase of the history of the Western view of life – a phase which is now drawing to an end – in which Western man came close to believing himself capable of replacing his God in controlling the imminent dynamic forces within human society.

Less pretentious in style than Zeylstra and fleshing out what for Hayter and Lappé and her colleagues are often little more than assertions, Tibor Mende's book weaves its way through the evidence of what development policies are achieving to come to the unequivocal conclusion that official aid is damaging to the poor and marginalised people in the poor countries of the world. The main reason is that official aid lubricates a system which, divorced from the rhetoric of what it is supposed to achieve, in practice supports and reinforces structures between rich and poor countries and within the poor countries themselves that lead not to development and to meeting the needs of the poor but to underdevelopment, increased marginalisation, and increased alienation and lack of self-respect among the poor majorities. Agreeing with Lappé *et al.* that it is not a lack of resources that is the root cause of the problems of the poor, Mende (1973:210) pinpoints the mobilisation of domestic resources rather than the greater inflow of external resources as the key to providing the poor with their basic needs. Nevertheless, he argues, the present socio-political structures create a type of economic growth that by-passes genuine development and the rulers of the poor countries are unable/unwilling to address these critical realities. Instead, they turn to external aid which is in practice no solution to the bigger and more fundamental issues (92):

> The new ruling groups represent only small urban elites and lack the means of communicating with the masses. They cannot mobilise their people. Yet to do so is an indispensable prerequisite of the mobilisation of internal resources. Unable to do this, they are deprived of the major instrument of development and so become proportionately more dependent on the other far less important components: exports and aid.

In direct contrast to Krauss, Bauer and Friedman who maintain that aid is preventing development because it inhibits the penetration and expansion of market forces, Mende argues that aid acts as a catalyst for market forces which prevent the achievement of the objectives for which aid is advocated (160 and 202):

> Through the mercenary role of ruling oligarchies and with the catalytic effect of aid, the underdeveloped countries have become even more firmly knit into the pattern of the international market economy with its rules so heavily weighed against their interests.
>   The longer the sovereignty of the market lasts then the more the ruling minorities will support the outsiders in order that their own preferences and options may prevail. In the meantime, the economic surpluses generated remain under their control, and the way they make use of them frustrates development and the satisfaction of essential needs.

If, as these quotations clearly show, aid does not achieve the objectives for which it is given, then does Mende conclude that there is no moral obligation for governments to help? By no means; his whole book could be interpreted as an attempt to provide moral reasons for governments to act, but in a substantially *different* way. He certainly asserts that it is immoral to prolong aid when one realises that it is not achieving the ends upon which the moral case is based. But that does not conclude the moral debate. Mende implies that the moral imperative 'we must do something' has been so intricately bound up with a particular method of doing that the distinctly separate ideas – *we must do something* and *this is what we must do* – have been joined together. As a result, when aid is seen to fail, too often the response is that we are therefore absolved of our obligation to act. The neutralisation of moral indignation, he argues, has become a professional skill. He continues (275–6):

> With racialist and xenophobic pseudotheories providing anesthetics, the ground seems well prepared for the acceptance of the sufferings of the 'underdeveloped' with a moral discrimination which implies that even meriting compassion or indignation indicates inferior status. Uncannily, the whole process begins to resemble the subconscious forging of moral and mental shields in expectation of even greater horrors vaguely felt to be inevitable.

For Mende, the compelling moral imperative to do something and the failure of present methods of achieving the objectives create a moral urgency to find new ways of approaching the problems, even though, as he admits, the complexities of discovering what this new 'something' is should not be underestimated (235):

> It is not, then, the principle of aid one is obliged to question, but rather the probability of any timely and serious change in its present forms. And if it is unlikely that the motivations determining its employment will seriously change, the problem is in what other forms foreign assistance may be provided so as to preclude the possibility of its misuse by the recipients or of its serving mainly the interests of the donors.

He only hints at what precisely should be done – in part because of his conviction that vast differences in circumstances and conditions in different countries and varying degrees of integration of countries into the world system demand different approaches to development. However, he opts for neither the end of old aid nor for the 'horrors of the inevitable' to produce revolutionary change. His ultimate views on morals and action are encapsulated in this final quotation, in which on balance he implies a preference for more aid (247):

> A really serious and systematic policy of economic emancipation would imply an immense effort by rich countries. It would require a massive transfer of really productive resources amounting to several times the present still-unfulfilled target of 1 per cent of their gross national product. It would also demand a radical transformation of their own economic structures to permit the coordination of the poor and rich countries' industrial policies, the creation of entirely new rules and mechanisms of international trade, and an unshakable determination and courage to confront the internal political consequences the indispensable adjustments would entail. And it would also imply the subordination of all political and strategic interests, as well as ideological predilections, to the overriding need to support governments devoted to social and economic change in order to permit optimum mobilization of internal resources.
>
> It would be morally and intellectually untenable to exclude the possibility of all this happening. But it would be morally and intellectually dishonest to sustain illusions regarding its probability.

Surveying the evidence of what aid has achieved over the past decades, and analysing the methods by which official aid is channelled from donor government to recipient government, has led in the 1970s and 1980s to former advocates of aid rethinking the basis of their support for aid and the moral imperative upon which that support was based. Among those who have voiced criticisms of development aid have been two influential writers and advisers on Third World affairs, Gunnar Myrdal and the late Dudley Seers. In the 1950s and 1960s they were both of the view that aid *per se* was good for the South, and therefore the more of it the better. Seeing the poverty in the countries of the South, they believed that aid would in due course help create the economic basis for social welfare and political democracy.

Their more recent questioning is based on three conclusions: that much aid has been frittered away through missed opportunities and corruption; that where economic growth has been rapid it has rarely proved of much benefit to the poor; and, finally, that the aim of the rulers of recipient countries, who in general do not represent their people, 'is not to relieve poverty, rather the contrary, to make sure that the incomes of the masses are kept low and social services restricted' (Seers and Myrdal, 1982). And it is these conclusions, together with the view that aid also failed because of bad advice given, which led both authors to question the moral imperative for governments to provide aid. As a step to answering this question, Seers is clear that the onus is now on those like the members of the Brandt Commission who claim that there are moral grounds for a general and massive increase in aid to the South to show that recipient governments represent the interests of their people (Seers, 1983:37). For Seers and Myrdal (1982) the Brandt Commission stands condemned for exploiting 'as do many others, the double meaning of *aid* – as financial transfer and as help. Taken together, these confusions enable the advocates of aid to argue that the fact that a country's *people* are poor and need *help* automatically justifies financial *transfers* to its *government*. They avoid discussing the internal politics of aid receivers.'

For them, as for Mende, the moral basis for helping remains because the objectives for which help is to be given – relieving the needs of the poor – are still very much there. But the moral argument for providing *aid* is only satisfied when 'the donor is absolutely sure [it] will be used for elementary needs, such as pure water or primary health care in a really poor country'. Thus they see no general moral case for official aid without good reason for expecting it to be used in the interests of the poor. However, they also argue that there is no moral case for abandoning all aid, although they submit that to initiate a very big increase in aid, à la Brandt, would be especially dangerous because of the negative effects this aid is more than likely to bring with it. A total abandonment of aid is not advocated because:

> We cannot ignore the real damage that could be brought about in some oil-importing countries in Africa and South Asia by the sudden and complete elimination of aid to their governments. This would not be wholly at the expense of corrupt officials or big landowners; the blow might fall in part at least on the poor, because their political defences are so weak and the social costs could be exceptionally severe.

Clearly this position is far less extreme than that taken by Hayter who advocates a complete elimination of aid in present circumstances. As Seers argues (1983:39): 'I could not myself take the heavy responsibility of the Marxist position, that greater difficulties for the elites of the Third World would necessarily lead to social revolutions – still less that these would automatically improve the lot of the poor.'

An initial assessment

Mainstream analysis assumes that foreign assistance can help in the development process though quickening the pace of development either by inserting resources that are unavailable, in short supply, or otherwise too costly or by mobilising resources that are available but which lie dormant or which are underutilised. The 'development process' is a catch-all phrase into which is subsumed the notion of economic growth and poverty alleviation and, for some, greater equality. More specifically, the mainstream analysis carries with it assumptions about the market, about the state and about power. It assumes that market forces have a role to play in accelerating the pace of development, that the state is a passive or benevolent actor influencing the process of development, and that, at minimum, the changing power relations following development and benevolent state action will not frustrate the pace of further development and more effective and widespread alleviation of poverty.[1] It is upon these assumptions that donor government aid is given and the moral case for granting aid sustained. And it is the rejection of these assumptions that leads the critics discussed above to challenge, directly or by implication, the moral argument for aid made by governments, international agencies and aid lobbyists.

But it is only in their challenge that these critics find common ground; their reasons for the challenge are often profoundly different. For Friedman and Krauss, and for Bauer to a lesser extent, foreign aid is under attack because it is said to impede the extension and penetration of market forces which they see as an *essential pre-condition* for development to begin and continue. On the other hand, for Lappé *et al.*, Hayter and Mende, aid is under attack because it is said to further the extension and penetration of market forces which they see as the *core of the problem*. For them, intervention in the economy is a *sine qua non* but as foreign aid is regarded as a type of intervention that, in Mende's words, 'lubricates the market', it is in its present form a negative force frustrating the very end for which it is (supposedly) intended.

Both groups of critics assemble evidence to support their respective views of aid and the market: the former to show that development occurs more rapidly without aid, the latter to show that aid has helped a form of growth that frustrates improvements in the living standards of the poor. Frequently the same countries are selected, such as Taiwan, South Korea, Chile or Brazil, to prove their differing viewpoints. On occasions, too, evidence contrary to the perspective taken is not seen as a major challenge. For example, Hayter regards the fact that aid can contribute to some improvement in well-being as incidental. In essence, what is at the centre of debate is the market and the role it plays in the development process. The market optimists believe that aid impedes this process, the market pessimists that the process lubricated by aid cannot achieve the objectives for which it is given. Clearly both arguments cannot be correct, though they could both be wrong. The resolution of these opposing views lies in a critical examination both of the evidence of what aid has achieved and of the theoretical perspectives taken by the opposing critics vis-à-vis that of conventional analysis and this is the heart of the discussion of Parts II and III of this book.

As well as the market, other central concepts that are interpreted radically differently by the critics are the role of the state and power. While there is agreement among them that conventional analysis is incorrect in viewing the state as a benevolent or passive actor, they strongly disagree about the nature of the state in development. For Friedman, Bauer and Krauss, foreign aid enhances the influence and role of the state and thereby increases its size and economic power; this of necessity frustrates more rapid development because, in what is seen as a zero-sum game, it impedes the extension and penetration of market forces and individual freedom. For Hayter, Lappé *et al.* and Mende, aid does indeed strengthen the state and its power but this, they argue, rather than inhibiting the market, accentuates its power and influence. This is because, *contra* the market optimists, they believe the state is a force which channels and develops those very market forces that are frustrating development.[2] Their views are precisely the opposite of the market optimists and clearly they cannot both be correct.

But the state's influence extends beyond its theoretical role in contributing to or inhibiting market forces. More concretely, critics of the left and right are agreed that the state, or more precisely the ruling government, is not concerned with the alleviation of poverty but that it uses its influence directly to frustrate the objectives of development. Both Bauer from the right and Lappé *et al.* and Mende from the left would agree with Seers and Myrdal that the aim of rulers of Third World countries 'is not to relieve poverty, rather the contrary, to make sure that the incomes of the masses are kept low and services restricted'. This is indeed a dramatic claim, for it challenges head-on the conventional view that aid to recipient governments is a positive and progressive tool in assisting the development process. But are the critics correct? The only sure way of finding out is to assess the record of state-initiated policies in Third World countries, to evaluate patterns of development and the influence governments have had on these patterns, and to analyse what the rulers have done with the aid they have been given. Without such an assessment, the claim of the critics that Third World governments frustrate the objectives of development and the counter-claim that they do not remain unanswered. To anticipate, discussion in Parts II and III indicates little general support for either of these viewpoints.

There is another area of common ground over the precise role and influence that external aid has in the development process. Mende and Lappé *et al.* would agree with Bauer (1981:100) that 'insofar as the development prospects of many Third World countries are unfavourable, this has nothing to do with external factors'. But the reasons for reaching this conclusion are poles apart. According to Bauer, it is because development depends most crucially on individual attributes. According to Mende, it is because development depends critically on the mobilisation of domestic resources, which according to Lappé *et al.* entails giving the poor the power to direct the development process in their own interests. If aid is, at bottom, largely irrelevant to achieving development, then again the obligation to provide it is crucially challenged. The validity of this conclusion and of the alternative reasons for it needs to be evaluated. We need to know specifically: if development is determined overwhelmingly by personal attributes (Bauer), by the mobilisation of domestic resources (Mende), by the poor achieving greater absolute and relative power (Lappé *et al.*) or by a combination of factors including crucially the influence of foreign aid (conventional analysis). Anticipating again, one of the conclusions of the discussion in Parts II and III is that the development process is so complex that single and exclusive factors provide an inadequate explanation although the evidence does suggest that resources are a crucial factor in raising income levels across a wide cross-section of countries.

Other examples could be taken from the development literature, but probably enough has been said to indicate that at this level of discussion the debate about the effects of aid in the development process is clearly inconclusive. Aid is being criticised because of its failure to achieve the agreed objectives of development upon which conventional analysis bases the reasons for providing it. The implication for the ethics of aid is this: to the extent that the moral case for aid is dependent upon its helping to achieve the objectives of development – and this is almost always implied when governments draw on moral arguments to justify their aid programmes – its failure to achieve these objectives challenges the moral argument. In some cases the critics make explicit reference to morality in reaching their conclusions about aid; in others the moral force for providing aid is undermined by implication. Ultimately, therefore, an answer to the question of whether this part of the moral argument for aid has validity can only be decided by reference to the real world: the moral case is supported or challenged by evaluating the evidence of what aid does achieve, the evidence of the effects of present patterns of growth and development which aid influences, and the strength and ability of different theories critical of aid to explain what is occurring in the real world.

This does not close this part of the discussion of the ethics of aid entirely, however. We can still ask what effect these criticisms have on the moral argument. Even if they were in part correct, would they nullify the moral case completely? It is to this question that we now turn.

Whatever force there is in the arguments of the critics under discussion, there is also among all of them an expressed concern that their arguments should not be misinterpreted. None of them wishes to be understood as arguing that helping the poor, eliminating starvation, improving life chances, or however they define the objectives to be met, are irrelevant or unimportant issues. Their criticisms are not those of callous, uncaring people. Thus they are not criticisms of the need to help. They are all, to paraphrase the words of Mende, criticisms of the method of helping rather than of the belief that something must be done. It would, therefore, be quite wrong to argue that the critics believe that governments should, as a result of their questioning of aid, abandon their desire to help address the problems of the Third World. If politicians refer to the writings of Bauer, Krauss or Friedman as intellectual backing for abandoning the needs of the Third World, then they are gravely guilty of misinterpreting their arguments. There is common ground between governments claiming that they have a moral obligation to help and the views of the critics discussed here; even if their criticisms are found to be correct, this common starting-point remains untouched. It is this conclusion which would appear to lead these critics to agree with Mende that if there are moral reasons for promoting development and if aid is found to be hindering it, then the correct moral action would be to stop providing aid.

This final comment leads us to consider in more detail the precise criticisms made; are they criticisms of all aid in all circumstances or of something less categorical? On a careful reading, it does seem that Krauss is the only one who comes near to a blanket and absolute criticism of all aid. Friedman's view is that aid is 'likely to retard improvement in the well-being of the masses', thus implying that some forms of aid could help. And Bauer goes so far as to make specific proposals for changing the form of aid: by better identifying its costs and possibly its benefits, by replacing soft loans with outright grants, and by concentrating aid carefully on governments whose policies are most likely to promote the general welfare of their people (1984:61).

The positions adopted by Seers and Myrdal and Mende are of even greater interest. Although Seers and Myrdal argue that much aid is frittered away, that where growth has occurred it has rarely proved of much benefit to the poor, and that the aim of Third World rulers is not to relieve poverty, they do not thereby reach the conclusion that aid should cease. The main reason they give for not dismissing aid altogether is itself based on the moral consequences of the greater harm that they believe would result if all aid was abandoned. The blow, they contend, might fall in part at least on the poor because their political defences are so weak, and the social costs could be exceptionally severe. In similar vein, Mende believes that aid on balance is harmful but also concludes that the moral obligation to help is so strong that it demands from donors 'a massive transfer of really productive resources amounting to several times the present unfulfilled target of one per cent of their gross national product', albeit in parallel with a radical change in present economic and political structures. This is also the implication of the arguments of Lappé *et al.* and of Hayter. So where does this leave the moral argument for aid?

From what has been said so far, it would appear insufficient and superficial to draw the unequivocal conclusion that there is no moral obligation to provide aid because some or even most aid does not achieve the objectives for which it is given. This is largely because the moral implications of withdrawing all aid are not considered and because only part of the moral question is addressed. Rather, the views of the different critics for whom there is no blanket rejection of aid (hence excluding Krauss for the present) would appear to lead to three different conclusions for the ethics of aid – assuming, of course, that their criticisms are found to have validity. First, Seers and Myrdal view aid in its present form as neutral (it does not promote the objectives for which it is given) or as positively harmful (the effect is to make it more difficult to achieve these objectives). However, they also believe that to withdraw all aid even within prevailing structures would inflict harm, and this would be morally wrong. The implication of this for the ethics of aid is that there is a moral obligation to provide aid at present but on a selective basis, and in addition a moral obligation to change existing institutional structures to ensure that economic development, with or without aid but probably with it, is directed more specifically than at present to addressing the socio-economic needs of the Third World poor.

Secondly, according to Hayter and Mende, most aid in its present form is harmful. For Hayter especially, the fact that some aid helps is irrelevant; there is no obligation therefore to continue to provide it in its present form and within existing structures. Yet both critics also believe that not only government intervention, including aid, but also structural change in the world economy and in local Third World economies are *essential* to promote the objectives for which aid in its present (misguided or deliberately misconceived) form is given. The implication of this for the ethics of aid is that there are compelling and parallel moral obligations both to grant aid and to alter existing structures, for only this will provide the conditions necessary for addressing the socio-economic needs of the Third World poor.

The position of Lappé and her colleagues, as already noted, is ambiguous, falling sometimes within the Seers and Myrdal perspective and sometimes within the Hayter perspective. However, for all these critics, if their criticisms are valid it would seem that the moral case for providing aid still remains intact. All not only believe that there is a need to help but also that there is a need to provide aid (development assistance), albeit mostly or entirely in a new form and in a different context. If their criticisms are found wanting, then the moral arguments which are based on conventional analysis would appear strengthened. Thus in either case the moral argument for providing aid is not destroyed. It is true that Seers and Myrdal question directly the moral imperative for governments to grant aid in general, but they themselves provide the conditions for the maintenance of that imperative. They point out that these are satisfied when the donor is absolutely sure that the aid will be used for fundamental needs in a really poor country. The theoretical controversy arises, then, not over the ethics of aid in general but over the morality of providing different sorts of aid in different sorts of circumstances.

According to these critics, the morality of aid can never lie exclusively in the *a priori* obligation to help; this can only be fleshed out in the moral obligation to *provide aid* if there is evidence that the aid granted does indeed help. The practical controversy lies in assessing whether particular forms of aid, given in particular ways and channelled through particular institutions, can be deemed a help or a hindrance. It is ultimately a controversy resolved by assessing the evidence.

This leaves us, finally, to consider the implications for the ethics of aid of the criticisms of the right. Excluding the blanket criticisms of Krauss, the rightist view of aid is that most of it is harmful. For this group of critics, the imperative to help in general is translated in practice into the obligation to remove all obstacles that prevent development, from this particular perspective, from taking place. To the extent that aid is a significant influence in disrupting the market mechanism, the conclusion has therefore to be that there is a moral obligation to work for its cessation. However, in the specific case we are considering (*most* aid is harmful), the criticism of aid is not absolute. Thus some aid *could* possibly assist in accelerating the process of development providing it is aid directed at these ends and these only – hence Bauer's specific proposals for altering the form in which it is given and the institutions through which it is channelled. Indeed, if it could be shown that market forces are promoted better and more rapidly with specific types of aid than without it, then there would be an obligation to provide it.

Let us now consider specifically the arguments put forward by Melvyn Krauss. While his views appear extreme and exclusive, there is reason to doubt whether even he fully believes the complete argument he is putting forward. Is not the view of foreign aid that he portrays the view of those types of foreign aid that he does not like? Does foreign aid have to be part of a strategy of activist and interventionist government, and does foreign aid of its very nature have to have a direct and inverse effect on economic growth? If there is incontrovertible evidence to show that the real incomes of the poor have increased whenever and wherever growth has taken place, is there also evidence to show that these societies do not receive aid? All these questions are open to doubt and are not answered by bold statements asserting their validity.

Krauss fails to distinguish between different dimensions of state policy and action, implying that all government action hinders growth. This is clearly an oversimplification and almost certainly wrong. Would Krauss object to the US Government providing aid for him to go to Third World countries to propound his views or to fund the establishment of supply-side centres of excellence or entrepreneurial institutions in Third World countries? Surely not. Indeed, Krauss would be likely to applaud any donor government action which led to a greater maximisation of economic growth through market expansion, and there is no *a priori* reason why aid cannot be channelled to private-sector organisations in the Third World; this is precisely what the US Government is doing through its Bureau for Private Enterprise. At times, too, Krauss' extreme position leads him to seeming contradictions. His major theme is that the biggest obstacle to development, big government in the South, has constrained economic growth by taxing the dynamic competitive sectors. Then surely aid could help by financing basic services – one suspects he would not object to Third World countries employing police forces – so that business and personal taxes could be reduced and development accelerated? Thus, in spite of his polemical presentation to the contrary, there are sound reasons for concluding that Krauss' position is less absolutist then he maintains and that aid can have a role in promoting development, even if one that is far more circumscribed than at present.

If this conclusion is correct, then Krauss' position would be similar to that of Bauer and Friedman – that most aid currently provided to the Third World is harmful. It would thus appear that he would agree with the conclusion reached above that if it can be shown that market forces are promoted better and more rapidly with specific types of aid than without it, then there would be an obligation to provide it. If this is so, then we have to conclude that for the rightist critics of aid there is no absolute rejection of the view that aid can be a moral issue. As with the leftists, the moral obligation to provide it depends both on the prior acceptance of the need to help and on the types of aid given in specific circumstances. In other words, it is a qualified rather than a blanket acceptance of the moral obligation to provide aid, even though it will be a very different type of aid from that acceptable for the critics of the left, given in a different form and in different circumstances.

None the less, even if there are circumstances when extreme market-oriented critics of present aid flows would agree that there is a moral obligation to provide aid, the acceptance by this group of critics of the morality of giving aid is far less direct and less strong than for the critics of the left or for those accepting the assumptions of conventional analysis. For Friedman, Bauer and, we would now argue, also for Krauss, the accepted obligation to help is dominated in practice by the obligation to promote market expansion and penetration. In the real world aid is assessed as almost exclusively harmful; hence there is in the real world an obligation to work for the *demise* of all that aid that inhibits market expansion and penetration. Of course, to accept this position is also to accept the view that most aid does, or indeed necessarily must, frustrate the improvement of the living standards of the poorest, that the most rapid expansion of market forces and the maximisation of economic freedom are the best way to achieve growth, and that there is incontrovertible evidence that rapid growth without government influence always leads to the most rapid and widespread increase in the absolute real incomes of the poorest. But if that is so, then one would also have to agree with Hayter on the bad will of donors: that it is invalid and misleading to assume that the well-being of the peoples of the Third World is, or at least could become, the primary consideration of why governments give aid.

Conclusions

Criticisms from within the development literature have challenged the belief that governments have a moral obligation to provide foreign aid by questioning, and at times rejecting, the assumption that aid helps to solve the problems identified, on which an agreed general obligation to help is based. These criticisms question key assumptions about the development process and the part played by aid in further- ing it, including the role of markets, of the state, and of external factors in development, and changing power relations. Some of these criticisms, as well as challenging conventional beliefs, are themselves diametrically opposed to each other and mutually exclusive. Ultimately their correctness can be verified only by surveying the evidence of what aid has done, of what present patterns of develop- ment are achieving, and hence of the strength of the different theoretical perspec- tives offered.

Even without a clear answer as to the validity of the criticisms made, it is still possible to derive some conclusions about the status of the moral case for provid- ing aid, on the assumption shared by governments and critics alike that there is an obligation to help in some way to promote the objectives of development in Third World countries. Very few, if any, of the critics hold the view that all aid is harmful in all circumstances. This being so, it is then very difficult if not impossible to conclude that there is never an obligation for governments to provide aid. On the other hand, to the extent that some of the criticisms are found to be valid and on the assumption that aid needs to achieve the ends upon which the moral obligation to provide it is based, one can also conclude that there is never a general moral obligation for governments *to* provide aid. In short, the moral case cannot be sustained indefinitely if aid fails to achieve its moral objectives. Between these two extremes, conclusions about the moral imperative to give aid will vary in relation to an assessment of what aid achieves and an evaluation of the development process into which aid is or could be inserted. For those critics on the left the obligation to provide aid remains strong but usually aid in a different form from that granted at present and always dependent on changing present socio-economic and political structures which they regard as inimical to 'genuine' development. For the critics on the right it would appear that the consequence of their views is that there is an obligation to stop providing (most) aid, which at present they view as destructive of 'genuine' development. But this is not a sufficient understanding of their position on the moral question, for there would also appear to be an obligation for governments to change the type and form of aid provided to that (however small) amount which is conducive to achieving, in their view, the objectives of development.

Notes

1. This brief justification for aid is examined fully in Part II, below.
2. This idea is developed more fully in Wood (1980).

6 Critics of the Moral Case
National Self-Interest

We now shift our attention away from the debate about the role of aid in the development process and its moral implications to the assumption that there are moral obligations for donor governments to assist in solving the problems of development in the Third World, and to two types of criticism made against this. The first is based on the belief that government action beyond national borders should be determined exclusively by considerations of national interest, and the second on the belief that moral obligations do not exist beyond national borders at all. The implication of both is that there is no moral obligation to help the Third World in general or poor people in the Third World in particular; and if there is no moral obligation to help, then there can be no moral obligation to provide aid, whatever the effects of that aid in practice.

The exclusivity of national self-interest

Those arguing the moral case for official aid are convinced that there is a duty to help the needy outside the borders of one's home country, especially when the poorest among them are incapable of achieving even basic living conditions and when the home country has the means to help. In this section we consider a group of critics for whom this type of moral argument – though it frequently elicits sympathy – is, at bottom, irrelevant. They contend that the fundamental basis for government action beyond national boundaries is national self-interest or national security; it is on this criterion that the decision to grant or withhold aid ultimately rests. If national-interest criteria lead to the decision that aid should be provided to assist in the relief of poverty or accelerate the pace of development in a poor country – as frequently happens – so much the better; but these would be subsidiary advantages and not the basis upon which the decision to provide the aid was made. From this perspective there is no particular hierarchy of international activity and no *a priori* assumption which would lead one to select humanitarian aid rather than aid that benefits commercial interests, development aid rather than military aid, or even to provide aid at all. The particular choice made will depend upon particular circumstances based on an assessment of what is best for the national interest of the donor country.

The history of US foreign aid policy indicates that the national self-interest perspective has been a prominent theme from the time of President Truman's Point Four programme in 1949 down to the present day. However, the national self-interest criterion has waxed and waned in importance during various phases of recent US history. Chapter 2 recalled President Kennedy's inaugural speech stating that America was pledged to help the world's poor 'not because the Communists may be doing it but because it is right.' Yet a year later he could say that foreign aid was 'a method by which the United States maintains a position of influence and control around the world and sustains a good many countries which would definitely collapse or pass into the Communist bloc' (quoted in Hayter, 1981:83). Similarly, President Nixon stated in his 1968 Presidential campaign 'let us remember that the main purpose of American aid is not to help other nations but to help ourselves' (*ibid.*:84), yet in his first message to Congress on foreign aid a year later he could add, after listing other reasons for providing aid: 'These are all sound, practical reasons for our foreign aid program. But they do not do justice to our fundamental character and purpose. There is a moral quality in this nation that will not permit us to close our eyes to the want in this world . . .' (quoted in Myrdal, 1970:355).

Various commentators on US aid have argued the national self-interest criterion more systematically. For example, Black in *The Strategy of Foreign Aid* makes the point unequivocally (1968:18):

> The basic, long-range goal of foreign aid is political. It is not economic development *per se*. The primary purpose of foreign aid is to supplement and complement the efforts of the developing nations to enhance their strength and stability and to defend their freedom. Success in these efforts is necessary to counter the spread of Communism. Further, the growth of strong independent nations which are successfully meeting the economic, social, and political needs and demands of their people contributes in many other ways to US interests.

The most closely argued case for placing foreign aid within the wider perspective of US interests has been made by Huntington in two articles published in *Foreign Policy* in 1971. He argues that while the enthusiasts for economic development may be able to make a case for purely economic criteria, 'they clearly cannot hope to persuade political leaders that purely economic criteria should be used in allocating resources among countries' (1971 II:182). He lists five criteria for deciding how aid should be allocated: economic performance, security relevance, political democracy, historical association and global importance. His crucial conclusion, however, is that US interest in the economic development of a country is only one aspect of the overall US interest in that country and must be meshed with the totality of US foreign policy towards it. He rejects the claim that morality should be the basis or indeed a predominant criterion for granting aid, independent of political factors. Illustrating this by an examination of India he sums up thus (181): 'The general point simply is that the US interest in the economic development of India or any other part of the Third World has to be viewed in the context of other US interests in those areas. Economic development cannot be presumed to be the only US interest or even the primary US interest in developing countries'.

In the final analysis, and assessing the reality of global politics, Huntington believes (1971 I:121 and 125):

> the United States has a limited but real interest in the general economic development of the Third World . . . one controversial issue remains. What level of US aid is warranted by the US interest in promoting the economic development of poor foreign countries generally? Any answer necessarily requires a weighing of this interest against other goals which the United States should pursue at home and abroad. Even a narrow definition of the US interest in the economic development of poor countries, however, would seem to argue for more rather than less effort.

In other words, for Huntington there is not only a case for aid, there is even a case for an increase in aid. But this conclusion is based neither on humanitarian or moral concerns nor on any criteria other than the US national interest.

That Huntington's arguments are far from academic is plainly apparent when one analyses the perspective on foreign aid adopted by the present Reagan Administration. Its view is that foreign aid allocations should ultimately be guided by US foreign policy interests, although, in assessing these interests, humanitarian assistance should also have a place. As former Secretary of State Haig implied in his evidence to the 1981 Foreign Relations Committee, these humanitarian concerns, while important, should be considered only in the context of broader national interests:[1]

> development assistance provides the United States with other opportunities to influence economic, social and political change abroad. We remain committed to a strong development assistance program as an integral element toward our international economic and security objectives. US foreign policy interests should guide our allocation of foreign aid. But the humanitarian aspects of the development assistance program should not be overlooked. As a cooperative partner helping to meet the needs of the developing countries we will contribute to the achievement of a variety of key US foreign and economic policy goals.

More recently, when presenting the Administration's Program for International Security and Development Cooperation to Congress in April 1984, his successor provided the *raison d'être* for foreign financial assistance. All assistance, both economic and military, is to be assessed in relation to broad US interests, particularly the need to promote world stability; even food aid under PL480 is now to be allocated in accordance with the effect it has upon the United States. The Program, according to Secretary of State Shultz:[2]

> is, in effect, the foreign policy budget of the United States. It is that portion of the total Federal budget which directly protects and furthers US national interests abroad . . .
> The means available to us to promote and maintain the kind of stable international environment we need are varied, ranging from keeping our market open to developing-country exports to projecting a strong US defence posture to help deter acts of adventurism by our adversaries. Some of the most effective means we have to promote stability are the varied programs of foreign assistance we have developed, ranging from direct military aid to pay for training or weapons, to short-term economic stabilization support, to long-term development assistance. . .
> Effectively protecting and advancing American interests, particularly in the poorer countries, takes considerable resources. . . . Our adversaries will rarely choose to pose their challenges in places where we are strong. But they will challenge us where weak links in the chain exist. It is in our clear national interest to help strengthen those links and to do so requires resources . . .
> *Public Law 480 (Food for Peace)*
> Title I concessional food sales permit a flexible response to the pressing economic needs of recipient countries. Title II provides food on a grant basis. These programs also provide support in times of national disasters, support market development for US agricultural products, and provide leverage for agricultural self-help measures. Greater emphasis is being placed on integrating these humanitarian programs, aimed at serious food-deficit countries, with our overall economic development, market development and other foreign policy objectives . . .

A year previously, the Under-Secretary for Economic Affairs, Allen Wallis, had stressed that aid is not to be allocated on the basis of the needs of the recipients. *Inter alia* he stated 'It is essential that economic assistance, bilateral or multilateral, not become an entitlement program with the spigot open even in the face of inadequate policies'.[3]

Such then is the perspective of present-day US aid policies. Dominated by the overriding aim of furthering US interests, it is a far cry from the needs-based criteria incorporated in the 1973 amendment to the Foreign Assistance Act, ironically still on the statute book (quoted in Morss and Morss, 1982:27):

> United States bilateral assistance should give the highest priority to undertakings submitted by host governments which directly improve the lives of the poorest of their people and their capacity to participate in the development of their countries.

Indications of a similar downgrading of the moral imperative for giving aid and a greater prominence to national interest considerations are also evident in Britain. For example, in a parliamentary debate on overseas aid in March 1985 Baroness Young, a Minister of State at the Foreign and Commonwealth Office, stated: 'In its broadest sense, aid must be seen in the context of our overall foreign policy objectives'.[4]

No moral obligations beyond national borders

A variant of the national self-interest perspective challenges the view that governments can have moral obligations to other than their own citizens. If, it is argued, there is a moral basis for governments to provide aid to other governments, then there has to be a recognised and accepted international moral community into which international obligation is inserted. But no such international moral community exists. There is, it is agreed, an international community of sorts, but it is more a community of intention than of reality for no international structures and institutions that have been created have the right to challenge the basic sovereignty of individual states to determine what will happen within their own national boundaries. Indeed, the very nature of inter-state relations precludes the transfer of moral obligations across boundaries. As Hoffman comments in his book *Duties Beyond Borders*, 'Obligations to other people exist only if they are all part of the same community. We may be interdependent with others but interdependence is a material fact, community is a moral fact' (1981:151–2).

Dismissing the notion of an international moral community leads to a rejection of any moral obligation to provide aid beyond national boundaries. To accept the moral basis for aid, argues Huntington, leads to ridiculous conclusions. Indeed, he states, if the moral case is correct 'then the case for not bothering to do anything becomes overpowering. As Ambassador Edward Korry neatly put it: "by not differentiating our development objectives in accordance with realities, we appear to be engaged in developing virtually the entire less developed world. An undertaking of that kind is simply not credible" ' (1971 II:167–8). But this is precisely what some advocates of the moral argument do contend. For example, Singer compares the £14¾ million Britain gave to the famine in East Bengal with the £440 million allocated to the development costs of Concorde and comments: 'the implication is that the British Government values supersonic transport more than thirty times as highly as it values the lives of 9 million refugees' (1971:22). He concludes:

> the way people in relatively affluent countries react to a situation like that in Bengal cannot be justified. Indeed the whole way we look at moral issues – our moral conceptual scheme – needs to be altered and with it the way of life that comes to be taken for granted in our society. If it is in our power to prevent something bad from happening without thereby sacrificing anything of comparable moral importance then we ought morally to do it.

Surveying this part of the literature, Little comments (1983:49 and 51):

there is a continuous outpouring of books and articles which are essentially trying to arouse the conscience of people in the West towards the appalling poverty of hundreds of millions of people in the developing countries. The appeal of such books and articles is universalistic and in the name of humanity. Many liberals would claim that Western governments have a duty to support basic needs to reduce inequality in the world . . . on the international stage, the meaning and extent of community seems vital. I think the idea of justice requires a moral community. Those who appeal to the community of man seem to be going beyond what exists.

For Little, official aid is to be seen more as charity than as a response to a moral duty. Is there, he asks, a set of imperatives obliging richer states within an international community to help poorer states without questioning their behaviour towards their own citizens, or towards those of other countries? He responds as follows (48):

I can see no moral theory backing up the development of such obligations. Still less can one say that they are now accepted by the richer states. Developed countries have, of course, accepted aid targets, thereby putting themselves in a position in which they can be (rightly) berated for their failure to take their promises seriously. But what sort of obligation have they accepted? Certainly not to give regardless of the recipients' behaviour. The assumed obligation is only to transfer a certain volume of purchasing power to developing countries in general. This is no different from rich men accepting that they ought to give so much to charity, or to charitable organisations whose policies they approve. They are far from accepting any such notion as an international income tax.

The complexities of the real world

Morality and self-interest: a false dichotomy

The national self-interest argument, taken crudely, would tend to suggest two propositions which are necessarily mutually exclusive: either aid should be granted on the basis of moral criteria or it should be granted on the basis of national interest criteria. However, the dichotomy is not so simple: it conceals a variety of different views about the relationship between morality and national interest. Excluding those for whom matters of national interest are of no interest or relevance, there would seem, in general terms, to be five such views as follows:

i)   National interest considerations are important in deciding whether aid should be given, to whom, in what quantities and in what form, but so too are moral considerations and both should be referred to in assessing the basis for providing aid.

ii) National interest considerations are important in aid decisions but the needs of the Third World create such an overriding moral imperative to assist that prior consideration should be given to helping to solve these problems even if this results in conflicts with the broad national interest of the donor.

iii) National interest considerations are fundamental in decisions on aid, but the needs of the Third World provide an important moral perspective and to the extent that the provision of aid on the basis of this moral perspective is in harmony with pursuing the national interest, then aid should be granted; to the extent that it is not, then aid should be withheld.

iv) National interest considerations are fundamental in decisions on aid and all other criteria are quite irrelevant.

v)   National interest considerations are fundamental in foreign policy decisions issues, and the national interest is best served by providing no aid to the Third World.

Statement (i) is probably the most widely held of the five among citizens in donor countries. While this perspective conforms to the view that there is a moral obligation for the government to provide aid, it admits that there are other obligations to be considered, and gives no guidance for action or attitude when there is conflict between them. When pressed, advocates of this view would have to come down off the fence and opt for either statement (ii) or statement (iii), both of which still admit that there is a moral reason for providing aid though they differ in the priority they would give to it. Many aid lobbyists would accept statement (ii); it is the view, we have seen above, which is closely argued by Singer (1971). However, other aid lobbyists would favour statement (iii), which is the viewpoint most commonly accepted by donor governments: the moral basis for helping is accepted, but ultimately it is subservient to broad national interest considerations. Moving from individual views to those of governments, most of them prefer to debate the issue within the framework of statement (i). However, some leading figures within the present Reagan Administration appear willing to opt for statement (iii) explicitly. On the other hand, some, like the present Swedish Government and more particularly its aid agency SIDA, take a statement (ii) position and hope to avoid having to face the implications in practice.[5] But in each case the moral argument for aid is accepted; the critical question turns upon deciding the degree to which it is to be used in assessing action to be taken.

Only in statements (iv) and (v) is the moral case for aid rejected in its entirety. For those agreeing with statement (iv) morality is irrelevant, a common reason being that government action should be guided by political and not by moral considerations. 'In a classical exposition of this argument, Reinhold Niebuhr argued . . . that, given the fundamental difference between the morality of individuals and the morality of collectives, group relations, including international relations must therefore always be predominantly political rather than ethical' (Kim, 1984:242). Statements (iv) and (v) differ crucially on the respective roles that each gives to the state. For those accepting statement (iv) as the principle for action, governments can and probably should act to address needs – be they needs at home or abroad – but the decision to do so is based on factors other than morality. For those advocating statement (v), however, not only are national interests paramount in deciding appropriate action, but any government intervention in the economy is to be rejected as inappropriate.

Thus far we have done little but separate out the different arguments concerning the relationship, if any, between issues of national interest and issues of morality. We now need to ask whether those rejecting the moral argument for providing aid for reasons of national interest are correct. Let us first consider statement (v). This criticism is based on one particular view of the role and nature of the state: that the national interest is best served by having a minimal state which never interferes in the field of economics or development at all, be it at the national or international level, for to do so would be to infringe the rights of citizens, most particularly their right to freedom. There are no obligations for citizens or for governments to meet the needs of other citizens or to alleviate suffering either within national boundaries or abroad. What we have here is the Nozickian position discussed in Chapter 4. As Nozick's perspective on obligation was found to be inadequate, statement (v) can also be rejected as an untenable position.

To respond to statement (iv)'s argument about irrelevance, we begin by delving more deeply into the dichotomy between national interest and morality posited in the different perspectives outlined above. Are the terms morality and national interest totally distinct and separate to the extent that appeal to the national interest excludes all moral considerations? Or, more specifically, is the distinction between politics and political action and morality and moral action a hard and fast one? There would seem to be good reasons for doubting this.

In our discussion of Bauer's rejection of the moral argument for aid in Chapter 4, doubt was expressed about his view that moral questions do not arise when governments decide how to spend taxpayers' money. It was suggested that governments, politicians and citizens in parliamentary democracies would at least be doubtful about this proposition or would reject it. We now need to pursue this point further. When governments explain their reasons for action and in doing so appeal to the national interest, there is an implicit appeal to shared beliefs (shared at least within the ruling elite) about the nation and about the nature of their society. For example, if the British Government states that it is in the national interest to accept US troops and cruise missiles on British soil, it is implying something about preserving British society and about the implications of life under the shadow of the USA and its value systems rather than of the Soviet Union and its value systems. (Whether it is correct in its *interpretation* of the national interest is, of course, a different matter!) As Kim argues, 'Implicit in the debates on world order lie contending images and assumptions about man and society, and different visions of the limits and possibilities of human behaviour' (1984:68).

For the citizens and government of the United States the basis for legitimate action and the correct ordering of society is enshrined in the preamble to the Constitution: 'We hold these truths to be self-evident. That all men are created equal. That they are endowed by their creator with certain unalienable rights. That amongst these are life, liberty and the pursuit of happiness.' Broadly speaking, the national interest is promoted by actions consistent with these shared beliefs. For the purposes of this part of the argument it is immaterial what specific ethical implications could or should be drawn from this appeal to a shared, albeit abstract, view of man and society. The important point is that the appeal is made and that it is grounded in beliefs about man and society which are the foundations of any theory of ethics and social justice. What is more, it is an appeal that is universal, not one that is confined to the boundaries of the nation. It would sound distinctly odd to proclaim that 'all men are created equal provided they were created within the borders of the United States'.[6]

We saw above that Secretary of State Shultz implied in his submission to Congress of the Administration's Program for International Security and Development Co-operation that moral and humanitarian questions raised over aid policy decisions were secondary to foreign policy decisions, which themselves were to be consistent with protecting and furthering national interests. But even for the Reagan Administration the case is far from clear-cut. For example, at the start of his campaign for the 1984 presidential election, President Reagan stated explicitly his belief that politics was grounded in morality. Earlier, the US Ambassador to the United Nations, Jeane Kirkpatrick, made the link between national interest and morality explicit (1984:180):

> Today as in the past, the United States has a powerful proclivity for trying to serve universal goals through its foreign policy. Reluctant to become deeply involved in foreign affairs in the first place, we have always tended to feel our participation is justified only if it is devoted to abstract universal ends like 'making the world safe for democracy', 'abolishing war, hunger, chaos'.

And in 1986, Secretary of State Shultz argued that 'American people believe in our nation's ideals and they want our foreign policy to reflect them' in a speech entitled

'Moral Principles and Strategic Interests: The Worldwide Movement Toward Democracy' (1986). More explicit still was the report of the Carlucci Commission (Commission on Security and Economic Assistance, 1983:42):

> This country has an ethical interest in the long-term economic and social development of these [Third World] countries that springs from our basic national values. The United States – founded on principles of freedom, democracy and humanitarianism – cannot be indifferent to the international neglect of these same principles without imperiling its own future.

Nigel Dower pursues the link between self-interest and morality further by arguing that self-interest is justified as a reason for acting only if it is preceded by there being a moral basis for acting. He explains (1983:75):

> Suppose there is a conflict between self-interest and morality. What does one advocate? It is clear that reasons of morality take precedence over reasons of self-interest: that is, one should only advocate self-interest as a legitimate reason for doing anything provided that doing so is acceptable from one's moral point of view. It is on this condition and with this understood that one advocates policies on the grounds of self-interest. It must not be denied that the fact that something promotes one's interests is one of the considerations which enters one's moral thinking about what to do. But the point remains that, if moral considerations show that not pursuing one's interests is required, then self-interest offers no legitimacy and one cannot advocate it for others in like circumstances.

We can thus conclude that appeals to the national interest do carry with them implicit moral assumptions about society and about humanity. But such a conclusion by no means answers statement (iv)'s objection to the moral case for aid in its totality. We need also to ask whether the moral assumptions underlying the appeal to the national interest carry with them the imperative to help the Third World, on which the moral case for providing aid rests.

Anyone familiar with the arguments propounded in the reports of the Brandt Commission recognises that the term 'help the Third World' can be interpreted in different ways with substantially different implications for assessing the moral basis for action. One could argue that circumstances in the Third World are such as to create a direct moral imperative for donor governments to do something to relieve the hardships analysed. Alternatively, one could argue that circumstances in the Third World are such that their continuation or deterioration will harm the industrialised world. As governments in the industrialised world have a duty to act in the national interest, then the preservation or continued improvement of their own societies demands (that is, provides a moral obligation) that Third World countries should be assisted in their development.

The latter point could be argued even more forcefully. If governments have an obligation to act in the national interest, then do they not equally have an obligation to act in a way that will maximise the national interest? What these examples show is that different moral arguments can be used to provide the basis for stating that there is an obligation to help the Third World. The first case derives the obligation to help from universal moral precepts; the second (the mutual interests argument) derives the obligation to help from a particular understanding of the national interest. However, it must also be noted that a total separation between these two types of argument cannot always be maintained. Thus to the extent that the term national interest carries within it universal values, mutual interest arguments for helping do not have to exclude arguments based specifically on needs beyond borders, as the reports of the Brandt Commission would appear to suggest.

National and international morality: separate or united?

Having cautioned against oversimplification in attempting to isolate different arguments *for* helping, we can now return to the range of criticisms made *against* helping. These revolve around the role that it is assumed the state should play in promoting the national interest. Two main sub-strands to this argument need to be considered. One would argue simply that it is not in the national interest for the state to help the Third World; in this case the mutual interest arguments of the Brandt Commission are not accepted. One reason could be that national stability and development, in the donor as also in the recipient country, are thought to be best achieved without state intervention and that the gains to the potential donor – largely through trade and access to raw materials needed from the Third World – are maximised by allowing free play to market forces. Ultimately the correctness of this view will be dependent upon the evidence and the ability of market forces to achieve the objectives of development. Another reason could be that all relations with the Third World are themselves considered irrelevant to the national interest. To sustain this argument it would also have to be accepted that instability in the Third World, the cessation of trade with Third World countries and the withdrawal of the potential donor nation from world affairs would further its national interest more than maintaining and enhancing the present world system, based as it is on considerable interdependence. It is, in short, an argument for national autarchy with implications far wider than straightforward economic isolation. Given the fact of interdependence, the fact that potential donor countries do trade with Third World countries (presumably to obtain goods they need), and the growing realisation that the demarcation of national boundaries is no guarantee of insulation from environmental pollution, this extreme view would appear to be fundamentally flawed or at minimum open to the most extreme hazards. To paraphrase Dower (1983:103), if nations adopt the siege mentality, if they reject the notion of helping each other, if they continue to arm and engage in deterrence whatever the cost, if they are determined to maintain material standards by belligerent competition for scarce resources, then global breakdown is much more likely than if nations do not do such things. On the premise that no nation stands to gain from global breakdown, it would seem to follow that the national interest is more likely to be enhanced by reducing its probability by helping the Third World and putting more effort rather than less into achieving world stability.

The second strand of the argument is based on the assumption that the morality of state intervention to alleviate suffering, reduce inequalities or in general to promote development ceases at the national border. Thus there can be no moral obligation on donor governments to provide help to the Third World based on its people's needs and hence no moral basis for providing aid. If this assumption is accepted, then there are *never* twin considerations in assessing whether aid should be given – those based on the national interest and those based on the obligation to relieve the suffering of the Third World – but only national interest considerations.

One assumption supporting the view that state morality stops at the national border is that sovereignty is an absolute concept giving each state the right to pursue its own interests. This raises two questions: first, is it true that sovereignty is absolute, and secondly do states have any obligations beyond their borders? As regards the first, there is enough evidence available to put this view in serious doubt. It is true that the present understanding of statehood, which can be traced back to the Peace of Westphalia in 1648, was indeed based on absolute sovereignty but such absolute sovereignty no longer exists. As Hodson (1984:131) puts it:

> The world of nation states has changed radically in respect of international relations since the eighteenth and more rapidly still since the nineteenth centuries. It is now one of a network of bilateral and multilateral treaties or conventions, each compromising in some respect the absolutism of sovereignty.

There have arisen a proliferation of non-state actors, such as transnational corporations, international airlines, international civil servants, international non-governmental organisations and so on as well as highly significant cross-country groupings such as the European Community established under the Treaty of Rome. These institutions, argues Kim, 'have certainly deprived the state of its exclusive status in international law and politics' (1984:53). And the consequence, as the international lawyer Starke points out, is to challenge the absolute nature of state sovereignty in today's world. He writes (quoted in Hodson, 1984:131):

> There is hardly a state which, in the interests of the international community, has not accepted restrictions on its liberty of action . . . Therefore it is probably more accurate today to say that sovereignty of a state means the residuum of power which it possesses within the confines laid down by international law . . . In a practical sense, sovereignty is largely a matter of degree.

But even if the notion of absolute sovereignty is challenged, critics have argued that states have no international *obligations*; rather there are international *norms* and *principles* which may guide states but which do little else. While it is true that adherence to universal declarations would fall within the category of norm-acceptance and that states have shown an extreme reluctance to commit themselves to external obligations, there is also evidence to show that there are considerable and indeed increasing obligations to which nation states are committed. Within the United Nations system, under Article 25 of Chapter V of the Charter member nations agree to accept and carry out the unanimous decisions of the Security Council. There is, too, an observable movement in relation to international declarations from establishing these as norms to ratifying them and finally creating binding obligations in law. Similarly with UN Conventions. None the less critics have also argued that this process is meaningless and that the USSR, for example, has only been willing to ratify those UN Conventions which it perceives are incapable of penetrating the shield of its domestic jurisdiction (Kim, 1984:237).

Perhaps more telling, then, is the voluntary agreement on the part of states to submit reports to international juridical bodies on the progress achieved in complying with agreed norms. Over 40 states have submitted reports to the Human Rights Committee. Of even greater significance is the fact that some states – at least Canada, Sweden and Senegal can be identified – have begun to re-examine their domestic legal systems to ensure that these conform to international law. Moreover 14 states, including the UK, Sweden, Canada and three other EEC member states have taken action under Article 41 of the Covenant on Civil and Political Rights.

One may quibble about particular examples given of states imposing international obligations upon themselves, the degree to which these obligations are real rather than part of a process of political window-dressing or the extent to which international obligations affect more than a handful of countries. However, there seems to be little doubt that developments in international and inter-state relations over the past 40 years have tended towards a greater number of instances of states having accepted particular obligations. We are far away, it is readily admitted, from an agreed, consistent and clear-cut system of international obligation and even further from one which nullifies the power of individual states. But, equally, neither do we live in a world where there are no international obligations backed up in some manner by the force of law.

There is, however, a crucial difference between general obligation, self-imposed obligation, legal obligation and, finally, moral obligation. Do states have moral obligations outside their borders? Little would answer 'No because there is no international moral community'. But is he correct?

We began this particular discussion by accepting the claim that states have obligations to intervene, for example to relieve suffering, *within* their borders. (To reject this assumption is to move quickly to Nozick's minimal state.) Hence, from Little's perspective, this particular claim for distributive justice implies the existence of a *national* moral community. But does it follow that within a nation there is total or near total agreement among citizens or even within the state structure over the precise nature of morality? Clearly not. National morality is fought over, often with extreme vigour: there is no total agreement in Britain over equality, the degree to which wealth should be shared or the poor should be assisted, even though there are laws that reflect a particular interpretation of what is right and just in particular circumstances and, crucially, who is in power to enforce them.

What we have, however, within nations are *dominant* moral views and it is these which tend to be reflected in laws enacted and to have some influence (together with economic and political theory) upon how the state intervenes. And, as already pointed out, these dominant moralities contain universal values and prescriptions concerning man as an individual and in society, concerning for example the obligation to help the poor, feed the starving etc., which do not stop at national borders. This was, as we have seen, the point Judith Hart was making when she stated that there are times when the moral responsibility of the British people towards a high proportion of the poor of the world *must be exercised* if the government is to represent in its own actions and policies the essential morality of political philosophies in Britain. The evolution since 1945 of an increasing international consensus over what constitutes human rights is clear evidence that there is some common ground between nations in the dominant moralities rooted in different national communities. What is more, the process is not all one way; principles and norms that are analysed and debated at the international level are having an increasing influence on domestic moral perceptions. For example, the sharing of ideas on racism at the international level and, in the economic sphere, concern about the behaviour of transnational corporations, have had some influence within individual countries in questioning traditionally held beliefs which are at variance with widely agreed international norms. The influence of such organisations as Amnesty International has also been profound in some societies.

We can probably go further. If we examine the reasons why states have accepted international obligations, particularly those in the human rights field, do we not find that the legal obligations are themselves at least in part based on moral principles? The notion of obligation raises the question of 'obligation to whom?'. When states accept obligations beyond their borders they are accepting obligations to something beyond the nation state. Call this 'God', common morality or the international community; whatever label is used, it implies shared or agreed values upon which the obligation is based. The moral underpinning of obligation is of particular significance in the field of human rights and these obligations, agreed by *states*, are predominantly obligations to *individuals*: against slavery, *apartheid* and torture, and protection for refugees and stateless persons. Dower summarises these two types of criticism that can be levelled against Little thus (1983:106):

> the claim that there is no international point of view from which to derive an inter-national morality is factually mistaken as well. For any candid look at the workings of international institutions, at the establishment of international conventions and cov-enants, or at the vast area of economic transactions, shows quite clearly the existence of international morality. Indeed if one did not know of its existence, one would be bound to assume it, for all the ingredients within a society which make morality necessary and natural are also present in the international sphere – interdependence, the need for agreements, goals pursued effectively only through collaboration, rules for the peaceful settlement of conflicts of interest, and so on. To be sure there is much debate about what the principles of international ethics should be. But the fact that thinkers dispute over the content of international ethics should no more cast doubt on the reality of international morality, than does the fact that there are disagreements about morality within ordinary societies cast doubt on the reality of those moralities.

Little's rejection of international morality appears to be based on a factually incorrect notion of state sovereignty, influenced considerably by world order analyses conducted by Tucker (1977) and Bull (1977). These views have been challenged on both empirical and theoretical grounds by Kim (1984) and Beitz (1979 and 1981). Beitz rejects Tucker's state-of-war image of society with its international moral scepticism, because it no longer accurately describes global reality and because it will lead to a more general scepticism of national morality which even Tucker appears unwilling to embrace. Beitz maintains that if national boundaries are not morally decisive features of the earth's social geography and if international relations are coming more and more to resemble domestic society in terms of developing complex patterns of co-operation and interaction, then the cosmopolitan image of a world of individuals united by transnational interests and universal values into a community of humankind becomes more relevant than other images, even if this community does not yet exist in any complete or recog-nised form.

Finally, it is pertinent to return to the statements that governments themselves make. Clearly some commentators do reject the idea that there is a moral obliga-tion for governments to act and to intervene beyond their borders. Their case would be strengthened considerably if governments were to agree with them. But, as we have seen, even though the precise basis for the obligation differs, Western donor governments have themselves acknowledged that they do have a moral obligation to act. If, as Little maintains, this claim can be made only if there is some sort of international moral community, then these governments are implic-itly acknowledging the existence of such a community.

Conclusions

In this chapter, we have discussed two interrelated sets of criticisms of the ethics of aid, both hinging on the concept of obligation. We have seen that the criticism based upon the notion that there are no obligations beyond national boundaries is at best weak and at worst misplaced. As regards that based on considerations of national interest, different conclusions emerge. The core of the criticism is based on the belief that moral questions, and hence moral obligations, are irrelevant when considering the rationale for state action. We have found, however, that there is reason to believe that when one attempts to define the term national interests more closely, moral questions again become relevant. We have also found that, though the claim is made that governments should and do act on the basis of politics and political benefit, questions of morality are not thereby forgotten or eliminated. It is thus only if the additional assumption is made that the state should never become involved in economic matters, either at home or abroad, that the moral basis for helping has to be rejected. But, as discussed in Chapter 4, this viewpoint has been found to be indefensible.

Notes

1. US Department of State, Bureau of Public Affairs, Current Policy No. 264, 19 March 1981.
2. US Department of State, Special Report No. 116, *International Security and Development Cooperation Program, April 1984*. This perspective was stressed again by Mr Shultz in April 1986 when he stated, *inter alia*, that 'The United States possesses a wide range of instruments for promoting our interests abroad. . . . The first is economic assistance'. 'Moral Principles and Strategic Interests: The Worldwide Movement Toward Democracy'. US Department of State, Bureau of Public Affairs, Current Policy No. 820, April 1986.
3. *Economics and Politics: The Quandary of Foreign Aid*, US Department of State, Bureau of Economic Affairs, Current Policy No. 461, 3 March 1983.
4. *House of Lords Hansard*, 28 March 1985, 1270.
5. A recent example of this particular debate about priorities comes from the Report of the Jackson Committee to Review the Australian Overseas Aid Programme, tabled in the Federal Parliament in June 1974 and comment on it. In its submission to the Committee, Community Aid Abroad (CAA) wrote as follows: 'The only acceptable goal for an Australian development assistance programme is the elimination of chronic poverty amongst the poorest communities within Australia's geo-cultural sphere of concern . . . where conflict does occur between competing policy imperatives, this conflict can and must be resolved in favour of a clear policy commitment to a humanitarian aid programme.' However, argues the *CAA Review*, the writers of the Report disagree. 'While saying that aid policy must reflect public attitudes, and . . . that the majority of Australians expect an aid programme to be used primarily to assist the poor, they then propose a series of recommendations in which Australia's strategic and commercial interests are the determining factor.' *CAA Review*, No. 295, July-August 1984, p. 1.
6. Even if the majority of the US Supreme Court did declare in 1857 that they did not think that blacks were included and were not intended to be included under the term 'citizens' in the constitution (see Kim, 1984:199). Even as vigorous a critic of aid as Robert Nozick would appear to accept the link between ethics and politics. He writes thus: 'Moral philosophy sets the background for, and the boundaries of, political philosophy. What persons may or may not do to one another limits what they may do through the apparatus of a state, or do to establish such an apparatus. The moral prohibitions it is permissible to enforce are the source of whatever legitimacy the state's fundamental coercive power has. This provides a primary arena of state activity, perhaps the only legitimate arena' (1974:6).

7 The Moral Case Reassessed

The first part of this book has set out to examine not the politics, the economics or the foreign policy strategy of aid but the ethics of aid. Its general purpose has been to explore the question of whether – in addition to, in conjunction with, or over-riding other reasons for providing it – there is a moral case for donor governments to provide aid to the Third World. More specifically, the approach adopted here has been to present, discuss and evaluate the arguments of those critics who challenge the view that there is a moral obligation for governments to give such aid.

The reason for this particular approach can be simply stated. For some two and a half decades, governments and aid lobbyists have worked comfortably with the assumption that there is a moral case for official aid, even if there has been debate – heated at times – concerning the emphasis that should be given to the moral dimension and its priority among other reasons for having, maintaining or expanding particular aid programmes. True, criticisms of the moral argument have been made repeatedly but these criticisms failed until recently to threaten what had become the prevailing wisdom, namely that aid is a moral issue. In the late 1970s and early 1980s, however, the ground has shifted. Critics of aid, including critics of the moral argument for aid, are being listened to with more seriousness by Western donor governments, particularly in Britain, the USA and West Germany, and their views are gaining adherents in the media, the establishment and growing numbers of the public. This move is challenging the advocates of aid and donor governments to emerge from what in a number of instances had become unquestioned complacency and to provide an explanation of why their view of the world, of development and of aid should continue to hold the stage. To date, however, the critics appear to be leading the field in the debate, in spite of some efforts being made to rebut the new conventional wisdom, and in these efforts moral questions are again coming to the fore. For example, in Britain, the Independent Group on British Aid (IGBA) has argued that the legitimacy of British official aid rests on the primary impact it has on the productive capacity of poor people (IGBA, 1982:2), while Oxfam began a three-year campaign in late 1984 which opened with the comment 'the current emphasis on increasing food production is no solution; it's not food that is in short supply, but simple justice' (Twose, 1984:1).

Western donor countries have certainly acknowledged moral and humanitarian justifications for their aid programmes, although different stresses have been laid upon this aspect of legitimising aid flows by different governments at different periods of time. However, a review of the literature on official aid reveals the almost complete absence of a systematic and comprehensive defence of the moral case for aid. Analysing the different criticisms reveals that there are a series of stages in the argument which need to be unpacked in order to provide a comprehensive and systematic account of the complete moral case for official aid. Here we have attempted to isolate the different stages in the argument and to pinpoint the varied, although frequently overlapping, reasons why people believe, often vehemently, that donor countries have obligations to the Third World.

There are two distinct and separate steps in the argument: first, that there is an obligation to *help*, and secondly that aid is a mechanism that does or can achieve the objectives upon which the moral obligation to provide it rests.[1] That there is an obligation to help needs to be unpacked. It is necessary to show what the basis of obligation is, why governments have moral obligations, and why obligations of governments extend beyond national boundaries. Once it is accepted that governments do have moral obligations to help the Third World, it is necessary to unpack the reasons why they should help by providing aid. The policies of donor governments presume that aid does help, and this presumption rests on a number of sometimes explicit but more often implicit assumptions: it has to be shown that direct intervention is appropriate to achieving the stated objectives, that aid is an effective tool of intervention, that the process of development which aid funds are inserted to promote is itself conducive to solving the problems identified, and finally that official aid channelled through prevailing recipient government structures does or can effectively help. If the latter arguments cannot be sustained, then the moral case for providing aid in its present form will be in doubt even though the obligation to help probably remains strong. If the moral obligation for governments to help at all is in doubt, then the question of the role of official aid and its effects is no longer a moral question for governments providing it, regardless of its ability to achieve certain (non-moral) objectives.

In turn, each of these different assumptions that go to make up the total moral case for aid has been questioned or rejected by the critics. Three distinct clusters of criticism have been identified. The first claims that there is no obligation for governments to help; the second that aid as such does not help either in its present form or even at all; and the third that moral arguments are irrelevant to government action. Our discussion of the various groups of criticisms has led us in our turn to reject or question them.

The statement that governments have no obligation to help is certainly qualified by a number of critics when extreme deprivation is involved. But even the general theory underlying this claim can be challenged both by questioning its relevance to the real world and by considering other demands of justice that there would appear to be no good reason to lay aside. In short, assertions that morality is irrelevant or that governments have no obligation to help have been found unconvincing.

This brings us to the second group of criticisms which we have examined in two ways; first, by asking if they were correct, and, secondly, by asking what the implications for the moral argument would be if they were correct. On the first question, it is apparent that not all the criticisms can be correct because some are mutually exclusive: some leftist critics argue that aid cannot help because it lubricates market forces which are the major factor inhibiting the alleviation of poverty; while some rightist critics argue that aid of its nature, as a tool of intervention, frustrates the penetration and expansion of market forces which are the most appropriate method of solving the problem of poverty. The fact that both points of view cannot be correct, however, does not necessarily mean that both are therefore wrong. Serious questions have been raised and they demand serious answers. Among these questions are the following: Does aid in practice work towards the alleviation of poverty? Do recipient governments prevent aid from reaching its targets? Does the present process of development into which aid funds are inserted frustrate or enhance the life-chances of the poor? Is unimpeded economic growth the best method of helping the poorest? Are more extensive market forces the answer or the problem? And is foreign aid important in solving poverty problems? Complete answers to these questions have not been provided here; they can only be answered by deeper consideration of aid theory and development theory and an evaluation of what has been happening in the real world. It is these issues that are addressed in the rest of this book.

Even if the critics of aid are correct, however, the moral case is by no means rejected. For those on the extreme left, the view that foreign aid as presently given and disbursed is on balance hindering and not helping the poor in the Third World is not cause for concluding that there is no moral case for providing it. Rather it is the basis for arguing that aid in a different form and in a different context is required for basic needs to be met and for the misery of the majority in the Third World to be eliminated. For these critics, the obligation to help is compelling and intervention forms a constituent part of their theory of progress. Hence the moral case for aid, albeit channelled in a different context, is far from rejected.

For those who, like Seers, Myrdal and Mende, point to institutional constraints which prevent or severely inhibit aid from reaching its targets – particularly the corruption/inefficiency/elitism of recipient governments and state structures within the developing world – the moral case for aid is also not abandoned with their criticisms. Indeed, while they favour structural change they do not go as far as the most radical leftists in concluding that all aid should be halted prior to these changes occurring. Their reason for this is essentially a moral one. They argue that, in spite of the grave problems with present aid, there is no general moral case for its abandonment because of the likely increased hardships that would result. Ethical issues, and particularly the need to alleviate poverty, are central to their critique and indeed lead them to advocate the continuation of what is for them on balance 'perverted' aid because of the moral costs of abandoning it.

The critics from the right provide the greatest challenge to those arguing the moral case for aid, not only because of their belief that aid as currently provided does not help, but more fundamentally because of their theoretical perspective which views any intervention, including aid, as always harmful. They have much to prove, however. They need to show that development can best be achieved and poverty eliminated more rapidly in the absence of aid and with a substantial reduction of state intervention in the economy. They need, in addition, to show that it is both possible and practicable to move from our present world riddled with protectionist policies, intervention in the market and less than fully competitive actors in the market place to a free and unbridled market system, and then to show that such a system does deliver. They need to show that it is possible and practicable not only to get prices right but to make them work effectively and efficiently, and that, until such time as this occurs, aid can never bridge the gap between present market failure and immediate poverty alleviation. Unless they are able to do all this their rejection of the moral case for providing aid will remain unconvincing. As we shall see, there are few grounds either in theory or in practice to support these extreme, though influential, beliefs.

Notes

1. The important distinction between helping and giving aid is not always recognised. For example, in a 1978 publication of the Central Office of Information on behalf of the Ministry of Overseas Development entitled *Survey Attitudes Towards Overseas Development*, answers to survey questions 'How do you feel about richer countries of the world giving help to the poorer countries?' and 'How do you feel about Britain giving help to the poorer countries of the world?' were consistently analysed by the authors as indicating public attitudes towards aid. See Bowles, 1978:46ff.

    Singer makes the distinction by pointing out that those advocating a moral case for aid should be concerned to ensure that aid is clearly morally justifiable both as to its motives and to its effects (1984:2).

PART II
Theoretical Debates

8 Introduction

One of the fundamental assumptions in support of the moral case for aid is that the effect of aid is positive, or more specifically that aid does help to eliminate poverty by promoting development. Even for those advocates of aid who find the debates about the ethics, sterile inconclusive, or irrelevant, the belief that aid is positively linked to more rapid development is central. It is the challenge to or outright rejection of this belief which the critics of aid within the development literature put forward and which will be the principal subject of discussion here.

That aid helps to promote development is the most enduring and widespread reason given by official donors for providing it. Indeed, even if its motives are more political than economic and even if the decisions about which countries are to receive it are based explicitly on political criteria, the giving of aid is always assumed to result in more rapid development. In short, donors provide aid on the assumption that it has a positive (and almost certainly a significant) influence upon the economic growth and development of the recipient. Thus more aid is expected to lead to higher rates of growth or a greater pace of development, and the electorates and politicians in donor countries are well-schooled in accepting this positive link. Cuts in aid votes by a number of Western donor governments in recent years have been used by parliamentary oppositions to accuse them of not caring about Third World development and defended as a necessary evil because of temporary hardship – both arguments based on the assumption that more aid means faster development and less aid slower development.

Not only is the belief in this assumption fundamental, but the very terminology used in the discussion reinforces this belief. The word 'aid' is defined in the Oxford Dictionary by the single positive synonym 'help' and the word 'development' by the phrase 'stage of advancement' – all the terms being value-loaded. But there is more. Official aid is now termed 'development assistance', and the donors' club of OECD member nations is called the Development Assistance Committee (DAC). Not only is the DAC careful to distinguish military aid and commercial transactions from development assistance, thereby implying that it is the latter category of funds that is a cause of or motor in development, but in order to be called 'aid', funds from DAC members have to fulfil certain criteria, one of which is that 'They must be administered with the promotion of economic development and welfare of developing countries as their main objective'. (*DAC Review*, 1984:188). It is thus not hard to understand how readily the general public, politicians and even professionals concerned with Third World issues are lured into drawing the further conclusion that because monies are provided *for* development they are *a necessary ingredient of* the development process.

But does aid contribute to development, as the terminology, the donors, and other aid advocates, including those using moral arguments, would have us believe? For those critics who reject all forms of aid the answer is that aid can never help development; for those who are critical of certain forms of aid or certain patterns of development the answer will be less absolute, although the vigour of their criticism is often greater. Two different types of criticism challenge the conventional pro-aid view and lead to a blanket rejection of all official aid. The first engages in the debate about the relationship between aid and development and concludes that, instead of assisting development, aid in theory and in practice inhibits and prevents further development. At its most radical, this criticism results in the assertion that aid does not and cannot help the development process and in the conclusion that aid flows should cease. The second type of criticism is built upon the assumption that the whole debate about aid and development is misconceived: discussion about the role that aid plays in the development process is for these critics irrelevant. It is, however, irrelevant for different reasons. For writers and commentators on the radical left, the growth and development path that aid is promoting (and most of these critics would argue, is largely successful in promoting) is wholly inappropriate to the needs of the poor in poor countries. Thus in today's world, with the prevailing socio-economic and political structures, they argue that aid is harmful precisely because it reinforces and is successful in promoting and extending present patterns of development. For writers and commentators on the radical right, who advocate a *laisser faire* approach to economic development, aid is rejected because it is, for some, a less efficient and therefore slower way of achieving economic growth and development and, for others, an actual obstacle to it. It is said to frustrate the penetration and expansion of market forces wherein, in their view, lies the key to further development. For these critics, development is best achieved by the cessation of aid, at least as currently transferred, and the encouragement of market signals to determine the pattern of economic activity.

Blanket criticisms, such as those described in the preceding paragraph, receive considerable attention in professional journals and in the media. They do not, however, reflect anything like a majority view in the literature on aid and development and they are entirely absent from the views of any government in the contemporary world, rich or poor, from East or West. But this does not mean that their arguments are also of little importance either to economists and those professionally concerned with development issues or to politicians and policy-makers. Far from it. The blanket criticisms are important because they crystallise the controversies and debates that are taking place in the middle ground over the nature of both aid policy and development strategy and in particular over the type of aid that should be offered. In the debates at both national and international level, the sympathy of those in power to the respective arguments of the free market or the radical structural change perspective has a decisive effect on practical policy and strategy, leading to changes in both the quantity of aid offered and the manner in which it influences the pattern of growth and development in recipient countries.

Widespread consensus in favour of aid conceals profound criticism over different types of aid that has its roots in different views on how to achieve economic growth and development and, in particular today, on the role and place of market forces versus direct intervention in the economy. For the radical market optimists, the role of government is to create the conditions for the contraction of direct intervention in the economy and to remove disincentives which inhibit the expansion of private and profit-motive enterprise. Within this perspective, increasing the quantity of official aid is of low priority and whatever assistance is provided is to be judged as positive and effective to the extent that it directly stimulates market-oriented growth; aid intervention is a prelude to an eventual era of non-intervention. In contrast, for the market pessimists, aid is one among a range of direct tools of intervention seen as essential for the foreseeable future to bring about structural change which is viewed as fundamental for the achievement of further development. Within this perspective, and particularly given the current inequalities in income distribution, the present price system and market forces are viewed as major constraints on potential development.

Given these very different approaches, it can be readily appreciated that critics of aid can and frequently do embrace many who in broad terms are in favour of aid. This is well illustrated by considering briefly the respective policies of the Conservative and Labour parties in Britain. Both parties state that they are in favour of aid and both agree that its basic purpose is to help accelerate development. But there the similarities appear to end. On quantity, Labour is committed to increasing the aid vote to 0.7 per cent of gross national product by the end of its first full period in government; in contrast, the Conservatives have no quantity targets and in practice have reduced aid quantities in real terms at least from 1979 to 1983. On quality, Labour judges aid effectiveness principally on the basis of its direct impact on the poorest people in the poorest countries; in contrast, the Conservatives' main aim for the aid programme 'remains the encouragement of faster economic growth with a related rise in the standard of welfare in the poorest countries of the world'. Indeed, the present Conservative Government suggests that expanding open markets is more effective for development than providing aid. For example, its 1980 aid policy statement made the following point: 'It is arguable that the greatest contribution which Britain could make to the problems of many Third World countries would be to maintain a prosperous and open market here at home'. More recently, in its 1984 Memorandum to the DAC, it stated (ODA, 1984:3):

> the Government continue to believe that the United Kingdom and other developed countries can make an important contribution to the economic conditions of the under-developed world by establishing those conditions which are conducive to sustained global economic recovery. This involves sound domestic economic management and the maintenance of an open trading system. A major element of sound domestic policy has been close control of public expenditure, including overseas aid.

The Reagan Administration has been more explicit still in spelling out the role of aid in accelerating market-oriented development. In September 1984, for instance, the head of USAID listed what he called the aims and successes so far of the new American development aid policy thus:[1]

> Our concern is with policies, institutions, technologies and greater reliance on free market forces and indigenous private sectors. These are the fundamental structures without which development cannot occur and from which broad-based prosperity and stability will arise.

What this discussion indicates is that there is a whole array of criticisms of foreign aid which question its positive role in the development process. They range from a blanket or outright rejection of all types of aid to partial criticisms of different sorts of aid inserted to promote different patterns of economic growth and development. In some instances, aid is under attack because of the claim that it does not contribute to development, in others because the end result is not assessed as development, and in yet others because different means are said to be better able to achieve the desired objectives.

In most cases, the assessment one has of the impact of aid is likely to be profoundly affected by the analysis made of conditions in recipient countries and the importance given to particular variables, and by the understanding one has of the process and dynamics of economic growth and development which aid is being inserted to influence. Many of the controversies over the role of aid are therefore at root controversies over patterns of and strategies for development. Indeed, to the extent that theories of development are mutually exclusive, it will be rare indeed to find anyone uncritical of some form of foreign aid intervention. How, then, does one assess the different criticisms?

The approach adopted in this part of the book is to begin by analysing the evolution and present status of the macro-theories lying behind the conventional assertion that aid does help to promote development (Chapter 9). This is all-important because it provides the intellectual justification for donors to provide development assistance. The strength and weaknesses of these pro-aid theories will be evaluated against the criticisms made of them (Chapter 10). Thereafter, in turn, each of the alternative theories which lead to a rejection of aid in its present form will be evaluated, both in relation to their theoretical completeness and to the cross-country evidence available: the *laisser faire* alternative which rejects any type of direct intervention, including aid, and the Marxian-Dependency alternative which maintains that the development pattern that aid (successfully) promotes is detrimental to the alleviation of poverty in recipient countries (Chapters 11 and 12). The conclusions of these macro-debates will lead into the third Part of the book, which will evaluate the approaches to assessing aid performance at the micro-level and examine the more detailed case-study evidence of what aid has achieved in practice. Together these two parts will enable us to weigh up the differing claims of the advocates and critics of official aid.

Notes

1. Quoted in *Development Cooperation*, No. 6, 1984, p.5.

9 Foreign Aid Theory

Context and origins

Economic aid to developing countries has been traced back in general terms to the colonial links between Western imperial powers and their overseas territories and, in the case of the United States, to the Truman Doctrine of the late 1940s (see Zeylstra, 1975). Whatever its precise origins, aid began to be an important facet of international relations in the 1950s; in the next 30 years it grew in importance both as quantities of aid flows increased and as international attention focused more and more on the economic conditions and especially the poverty of what became known as the developing countries. During this period not only did increasing numbers of countries become donors but colonial and past historical links no longer provided the sole reason for giving aid, as multilateral institutions were created or expanded their operations substantially to receive funds from a range of donors and to provide aid to a range of recipients. That the flow of foreign aid authorised by governments is a recognised characteristic of international relations today should not conceal the fact that it gained universal political acceptance in a remarkably short space of time.

Whether by accident or design, the attention of economists and development analysts to the phenomenon of foreign aid coincided with the growing political acceptability of providing it and the rapid expansion in the quantities that different governments were giving in the mid to late 1950s.[1] Even at this time, however, when the theoretical justification for providing aid was emerging, there were theories being debated in the literature which either directly or indirectly give little or no attention to either aid as a particular form of international transfer, or to additional resources as a crucial factor in promoting economic development. For example, for Schumpeter 'the hero of the development story and the fundamental determinant of growth was neither saving nor capital but the entrepreneur or innovator'. He 'would have had little sympathy for the view that development is limited by the supply of external capital' (Mickesell, 1968:30). Similarly those theories giving pride of place to sociological or cultural factors as the motor for development, for example those propounded by Hagen and McLelland, have little or no place for aid as a critical factor in achieving or accelerating growth.

The importance of these alternative theories lies in the fact that theories of aid and development fulfil two distinct functions. The main function of a pro-aid theory is clearly to put forward an explanation of how aid contributes to development, but it also carries with it an implicit rejection of any theory of development that does not give a role to aid in accelerating development: why aid helps development is thus assumed in the theoretical explanation of how it does so. The arguments of alternative theories concluding either that aid is not necessary or that other means of achieving development could be better are simply not addressed. Two key assumptions are made: that aid constitutes additional resources, and that these are important for accelerating development. Given these assumptions, it is immediately apparent that foreign aid theory has to place strong emphasis on the need for intervention in promoting development and on the belief that more resources lead to greater development. It is therefore, not hard to understand why it should lean so heavily on interventionist theories of development and associate aid so closely with what growth theorists at the time believed to be the critical factor in accelerating growth, namely capital investment.

The fact that these assumptions were so readily accepted is explained in part by the context in which foreign aid became widely accepted among Western donors. It was supremely one of confidence: confidence that the post-war economic expansion among leading Western industrialised nations would continue, confidence that Keynesian economic policies, which were believed to be a cause of this expansion and gave a critical role to direct interventionist policies in these economies, had universal applicability, confidence that the success of Marshall Aid could lead to similar results in the developing world, and confidence, too, that, as in Europe, concentration on accelerating economic growth would lead to economic development in other places and in different circumstances. Given this background and the fact that development economics (that is, economics and economic theory arising directly out of the experience and conditions within developing countries) was in its infancy, it is easy to see how powerful would be the attraction of applying theory currently in use in Western industrialised countries directly to the developing world. It was, as Hirschman has recently argued, the success of the Marshall Plan that led policy-makers and enlightened opinion (to which one could add theoreticians) in the West 'into believing that infusion of capital helped along by investment planning might be able to grind out growth and welfare all over the globe' (1982c:380). It is probably also true that, because the ideas of foreign aid which the theoreticians evolved gave cause for belief that it would only be needed temporarily, the politicians came to highlight the theory so prominently within the political arena.

Conventional aid theory has its origins in Keynesian economics and in particular in the theories of economic growth that writers in the Keynesian tradition applied to industrialised economies. Yet while aid theory used Keynesian growth models, it would be mistaken to argue that the foreign aid theory that evolved was exclusively an economic growth theory. Both Rostow and, more substantially, Chenery and Strout, placed emphasis on the need for structural change to create the conditions necessary for growth to occur, and both highlighted the need for human capital as well as infrastructural investment to achieve more rapid development.

Keynes' own theory hardly discussed questions of dynamic growth, the particular problems of poor countries, or the role of foreign aid in the process of achieving high levels of growth or development. Thus if Keynesianism is to be judged solely on this basis, then it has no relevance to conventional aid theory.[2] It is, however, the challenge that Keynes made to key basic assumptions of neo-classical theory and which led him to recommend a particular form of state intervention which provides the basis for arguing that the first aid theories were influenced by contemporary Keynesian analysis. In particular, his view that savings and investment are not automatically equated through changes in the rate of interest while income levels remain unchanged, but that their levels can be altered by changing levels of aggregate demand, provides the basis for arguing that intervention in the economy can help. It was the extension of this insight which aid theory in particular came to build upon.

There are, argued Keynes, three basic assumptions that *laisser-faire* theory makes, which are profoundly deficient: that economies are stable, that economies left to themselves tend towards a full employment level of output, and that, as a result, there is no case for government intervention to ensure stability and to promote full employment. Economic stability and a full employment level of output occur, he stated, only in very particular circumstances; in general and without state intervention, unemployment will be the rule rather than the exception. Hence, state intervention will be required, in particular to maintain levels of aggregate demand at a volume corresponding to high (full) levels of employment.

It was this conclusion which was to have a profound effect on the attitudes and policies of governments towards economies in industrialised countries in the post-1945 period. They no longer believed they should have a nightwatchman role in economic matters but rather that they should intervene, as suggested by Keynes, to direct and stimulate their economies to higher levels of economic activity. Keynes' own theory was not one of dynamic growth, however, and it was left to Harrod and Domar to extend the basic ideas of Keynesian analysis to the longer term. It was, in particular, their introduction of the concept of the capital-output ratio and the assumption that it remained fixed over a specific time period that enabled them to transform the Keynesian short-run aggregate demand function into a long-term dynamic model. The importance of their work to the aid and development debate lay not so much in highlighting the important place of capital investment for achieving growth – for both classical and neo-classical theory had long before done this – as in establishing a dynamic model susceptible to policy influence. Even economists working in developing countries, like Lewis and Singer, were emphasising the importance of capital for achieving development. What was new in the Keynes/Harrod-Domar model was that it indicated quite specifically how the process could be speeded up.[3]

Foreign aid theory established

We now need to shift our attention directly to the creation of aid theory, the clear beginnings of which can be seen in the mid to late 1950s. One of the first people to make explicit reference to contemporary Keynesian growth theory and to incorporate these ideas into the economic purpose of providing aid was the American, Walt Rostow. In many ways Rostow can be seen as the bridge between the politics and economics of aid, for his economic reasoning was clearly placed within a specific political ideology. Indeed, his lasting place in the creation of orthodox aid theory lies not so much in the analytical rigour with which he spelt out the relationship between foreign aid and economic development, nor in the acclaim (or lack of it) that his ideas received in economic circles, but rather because the terminology and general concepts he used have become an integral and influential part of the conventional view of Third World development and how to accelerate the development process.[4]

Writing in the mid-1950s Rostow made a number of judgements about the world economy, the most influential of which were to be the following: the industrialised countries are in many important respects 'developed' – they have reached what Rostow termed 'the era of high mass consumption'; this they achieved by going through a number of stages of growth; the most important phase in achieving this developed state was the process of *take-off* into self-sustaining growth'; the take-off stage is a relatively short period that is prepared by creating the social and economic conditions for self-sustaining growth. Having laid down these different stages, one question arises with urgency: how can the poorer countries of the world achieve the take-off to self-sustaining growth and join the community of fully-fledged developed and industrialised countries? It was in providing an answer to this question that Rostow leaned heavily on the Harrod-Domar model of long-term economic growth. For the take-off to occur, Rostow defines three necessary conditions. First, there has to be a significant increase in the rate of net investment in the economies of poor countries, say from 5 per cent to 10 per cent. Secondly, one or more of the manufacturing sectors of the economy has to exhibit a high rate of growth. Thirdly, there needs to be an institutionally favourable environment to ensure that the impulses derived from growth are transmitted throughout the economy. With the achievement of the third condition, the growth process will be self-sustaining.

It is in increasing the investment rate to accelerate the process of economic growth and achieve the take-off that Rostow gives a critical role to economic aid. Within the Harrod-Domar paradigm, the investment rate of the developing countries is raised by injections of foreign capital, so augmenting the domestic savings rate without reducing the level of domestic consumption. While aid is not absolutely necessary to raise the level of investment, it speeds up the historical process of reaching the stage of self-sustaining growth, particularly by providing the means to expand and deepen social overhead capital. Yet, for Rostow, aid is not only to be directed at achieving higher levels of economic growth. It is to be used to address social constraints inhibiting structural transformation as well as (more than 20 years before the Brandt Report was written) to promote the mutual interests of industrialised and developing countries. In 1957, with fellow economist Max Millikan, Rostow summarised his view of the economic role of aid in development thus (Millikan and Rostow, 1957: 49–50; 65):

> The assistance which countries need from outside if they are to develop is of two kinds. In the first place they need capital, both to establish the preconditions of growth and to make sure during the second stage that growth is maintained until they reach a point where they can be reasonably sure of maintaining it out of their own increasing output. Underdeveloped countries may require two sorts of capital. They will need from outside some of the equipment and supplies required to construct particular development projects. They will also frequently need a certain volume of food and consumer goods to permit them to divert their own labor and other resources from output for consumption to development. But in addition to capital they will also need a great deal of technical assistance, a transfer of knowledge and skills from other parts of the world, to permit them to make effective use both of their own meagre supplies of capital and of whatever capital is made available from abroad. The strictly economic purposes of the program (for world economic growth) would be: first, to make available sufficient capital to permit the low-income countries to launch an ultimately self-sustaining process of economic development; second, to stimulate and assist the underdeveloped countries to overcome obstacles to their own development other than lack of capital; and third, to create a climate of international economic activity in which the economies of the industrialised countries of Europe and Japan, as well as the United States, could continue to grow.

Rostow's theory, however, goes beyond the explanation of how aid assists development to provide the justification for arguing why, in time, it will no longer be necessary. Aid is needed only in the period prior to take-off. This period, he says, will last between ten and fifteen years (although he gives no good analytical reason for this specific period) after which 'the supplying countries can look forward to a time when extraordinary measures to obtain capital from outside can be discontinued. It is not that external capital is then no longer required but rather that at this stage the normal channels of international capital supply can be relied on to take over the burden of any net capital inflow still required' (ibid.:54).

Whatever political message he intended to convey, Rostow certainly did provide in addition an economic explanation for the role of aid in accelerating the pace of development in Third World countries. It was left to others, however, to spell out in detail how specific and quantifiable amounts of aid would affect this process and in what precise manner. The writer who has provided the most detailed theoretical explanation of the role of aid is Hollis Chenery. It is his theory, especially as expounded with Alan Strout, which gives us the classical theoretical justification for providing economic aid for development – an approach still taught to economics students to this day, over 20 years since its original publication in the *American Economic Review*.

Acknowledging their debt to Rostow and Lewis, among others, Chenery and Strout pose the question of the role of aid within the context of theories of economic development which 'investigate the process by which a poor, stagnant economy can be transformed into one whose normal condition is sustained growth' (1966:680). The changes needed for such transformation are listed as: an increase in human skills, a rise in the level of investment and saving, the adoption of more productive technology, changes in the composition of output and employment, and the development of new institutions. The framework for their analysis, spelt out explicitly, is 'the possibility of accelerating these changes through the use of significant amounts of external resources over a limited period of time' (*ibid.*). In other words, detailing *how* economic aid will act to accelerate the development process. Aid contributes, according to Chenery and Strout, by relieving certain specific bottlenecks inhibiting domestic growth and development, and in fulfilling this role it increases the efficiency of the domestic resource base. Descriptively the theory of aid is summarised thus (680–1):

> A country setting out to transform its economy without external assistance must provide for all of the requirements of accelerated growth from its own resources or from imports paid by exports. Success thus requires a simultaneous increase in skills, domestic saving, and export earnings as well as an allocation of these increased resources in such a way as to satisfy the changing demands resulting from rising levels of income. The attempt to increase output can be frustrated by failure in any one of these attempts, even when the others have been quite successful. When growth is limited in this way by a few bottlenecks, there is likely to be under-utilization of other factors such as labor, natural resources, and specific types of productive capacity.
>
> By relieving these constraints, foreign assistance can make possible fuller use of domestic resources and hence accelerate growth. Some of the potential bottlenecks – of skills, savings, or foreign exchange – can be temporarily relaxed by adding external resources for which current payment is not required. More efficient use can be made of other resources, so that the growth of total output may be substantially higher than would be permitted by the rate of increase of the most restrictive domestic factor.

Within this perspective, an economic theoretical model is constructed. This is based on Harrod-Domar and therefore Keynesian growth theory in the short run (five to seven years), where the pattern of growth is determined by a set of linear relations under certain given assumptions as to government policy. However, in the longer run it is based on the neo-classical view that domestic resources can be substituted for imports 'to the extent required by changing demands, although with diminishing productivity', the upshot being that in time, and consistent with the Rostovian view, aid requirements will be reduced (682).

Under the Chenery and Strout model, different types of bottleneck constrain the economic development of recipient countries at different stages of development. Three types need to be addressed at different times: shortages of skills and organisational ability, constraints on achieving required levels of domestic saving, and limits arising from inadequate supplies of imported commodities and services. Chenery and Strout's model is characterised by two different sort of gaps in domestic resources that can be filled by external assistance. In the first, called investment-limited growth, skills and savings are in short supply. In the second, trade-limited growth, foreign exchange is in short supply because export earnings are lower than import needs. What they suggest is that foreign aid can help to bridge each of these gaps at the different stages of development, thereby fulfilling the overall function of assisting the acceleration of the growth rate until the self-sustaining stage is achieved.

More specifically, self-sustaining growth occurs after the developing economy passes in turn through each of three phases. In Phase I there is a skill limit in the economy but no balance-of-payments constraints that directly affect the achievement of specified target growth rates. The skill-limit prevents potential investment levels reaching the level required for the target growth rate to be achieved. To address these problems, foreign aid during Phase I fills the gap between the increment in investment and that in domestic saving until such time as the rate of investment is high enough to sustain the target growth rate, namely, when the domestic saving ratio rises to the level of the target (and actual) investment level. For the model to operate, it is assumed that aid is sufficiently limited or expensive to make the recipient unwilling or unable to use it merely to increase consumption without also securing some rise in aggregate output, or to increase consumption by reducing domestic savings. This period Chenery and Strout judge to last for between five and ten years, if the rate of investment settles at around the level of 10–12 per cent of gross output.

Phase II is essentially a transitionary phase. In this period foreign aid is no longer required to sustain the target rate of growth through raising the level of investment; however, it will probably still be needed to help raise the rate of increase of investment, because the skills constraint will continue to maintain the marginal saving rate below its necessary target level. In addition, it is also likely that structural rigidities in the economy and the likelihood of over-valued exchange rates will be causing a critical trade gap to arise which can at this stage also be filled by foreign aid. The trade gap arises because at this stage the economy is not able to adjust rapidly enough to the loss of foreign exchange arising from the drop in aid that had been targeted at bridging the saving gap: hence in this phase, although foreign aid will still be needed, its function will have changed.

In Phase III the savings constraints will have been successfully overcome, and so in this period it is only the trade gap which, primarily because of structural rigidities, provides the prime constraint to self-sustaining growth and hence the need for aid. Phase III ends when the economy adjusts and grows in response to changing price and market conditions. However, Chenery and Strout do admit that Phase III is likely to persist not only because of internal structural rigidities but also because the 'efforts of the underdeveloped countries to increase their exports are frustrated' (691).

It would be a profound mistake to assume that in practice the model is expected to work mechanistically or automatically. Chenery and Strout lay great emphasis on the operation of domestic policy within which external flows are inserted, and in particular on the speed with which adjustments can be made in the structure of the economy to ensure the more efficient use of resources and an adequate response to changes in aggregate demand. While explaining that their analysis shows 'the conditions under which external assistance *may* make possible a substantial acceleration in the process of economic development' (723 with emphasis added), they also state explicitly that the contribution of external resources 'may be large or small depending upon the response of the recipient country' (703). And in projecting external resource needs into the future, they add that 'perhaps the most notable feature of this analysis is the sensitivity of aid requirements to variations in internal performance' (721). Indeed, they caution against concentrating too much on measuring aid effectiveness in the longer run, emphasising the adjustments made to the recipient economy subsequent to achieving higher growth levels (724 and 726):

> The critical elements in the development sequence are getting the initial increase in the rate of growth, channelling the increments in income into increased saving and allocating investments so as to avoid balance of payments bottlenecks. These long run aspects are likely to be considerably more important than the efficiency with which external capital is used in the short run.
>
> It is the need for rapid structural change which sets the lower limit to the time required to complete the transition to self-sustaining growth. Even though the simplified model underlying Figure 3 suggests the possibility of completing this transition in less than 20 years starting from typical Asian or African conditions, it is very unlikely that any such country can meet all the requirements of skills formation, institution building, investment allocation, etc. in less than one generation.

In emphasising the conditions within the recipient country necessary for aid funds to accelerate the pace of economic development effectively, Chenery and Strout were echoing the words of Rosenstein-Rodan who in 1961 was among the first economists to provide theoretical justification for giving economic aid. Rosenstein-Rodan specified the purpose of aid to underdeveloped countries as 'to accelerate their economic development up to a point where a satisfactory rate of growth can be achieved on a self-sustaining basis'. But he equally emphasised that the principal element in the transition to self-sustaining economic growth 'must be the efforts that the citizens of the recipient countries themselves make to bring it about', adding that 'capital aid should be offered wherever there is reasonable assurance that it will be effectively used' (1961:107).

Caution in assuming aid will necessarily be effective is paralleled in Rosenstein-Rodan's approach with caution in assuming that all aid should be classified as capital inflow and that all additional capital will necessarily be used to raise domestic investment levels. He states that foreign capital inflow and aid are not synonymous, adding that 'aid, properly speaking, refers only to those parts of capital inflow which normal market incentives do not provide' (109). In particular, he says that technical assistance should not be included in capital inflow figures even though he considers it 'a most important part of aid to underdeveloped countries' (110).

On the investment issue, he sees the additional resources provided by foreign capital achieving an increase in production but adds that not all will necessarily be channelled into savings and hence contribute to raising the aggregate investment level. The amount that will raise total savings is determined by the marginal saving rate being higher than the average saving rate, and this differential, he argues, should be a specific condition for providing capital aid. The size of this differential is itself dependent upon the absorptive capacity of the recipient economy. While this cannot be measured with strict accuracy, it can be judged, according to Rosenstein-Rodan, within broad parameters sufficient to ascertain capital inflow levels that can be utilised effectively by considering three elements: levels of investment over the previous few years, past differences between average and marginal savings rates, and the level and degree of the country's overall administrative and developmental organisation.

Thus, while Rosenstein-Rodan provides an explanation for the role of aid in the development process, and goes to considerable lengths to specify the quantities of aid required on a country by country basis, he is equally concerned to point out that there are major constraints inhibiting the successful injection of capital aid to accelerate the pace of economic development. Indeed, if these inhibiting factors predominate, his theoretical perspective would lead to a rejection of the view that more aid will mean more development. Finally, it should be noted that he also rejects the provision of aid specifically to raise income levels in poor countries. Aid, he argues, 'should continue not until a certain income level is reached in underdeveloped countries but only until those countries can mobilise a level of capital formation sufficient for self-sustaining growth' (107).

Shifts in emphasis in the 1970s and 1980s

The 1960s proved, in retrospect, to be the decade when most work was done by theoreticians in the development of an economic theory of foreign aid. Besides Rostow, Rosenstein-Rodan, Chenery and Strout, contributions were made by others such as Lewis, Ranis, Fei and Paauw.[5] While these differed somewhat in detail and in the degree of analytical rigour with which they were presented (and the three views outlined above encompass the main differences), they shared a substantial common ground: that aid as a tool of direct intervention can, on the basis of certain conditions, help to accelerate a development process already in progress by filling critical gaps preventing further growth, including structural inhibitions, predominantly by raising investment levels and increasing absorptive capacity such that after a certain time aid will no longer be required.

After the publication in 1966 of Chenery and Strout's important contribution, a spate of articles appeared in the technical journals on aid and development issues. Their concern, however, was not so much to develop the conventional theory as to debate it in the light of the evidence available of what aid had achieved at the macro-level, concentrating in particular on the question of additionality and on whether aid was directly linked with increases in saving in recipient countries and with changes in rates of economic growth.

Throughout the intervening period it has been the Chenery and Strout two-gap model which has received most attention, both from the critics of the theory and those concerned to test its validity in the real world. No other substantial contribution detailing the theoretical case for aid at the macro-level has been published and the Chenery-Strout contribution is still the core theory to which reference is made. Indeed, in a World Bank publication of 1979, *Structural Changes and Development Policy*, the 1966 article was reprinted, indicating both its continued relevance and importance. In the 1979 reprint, however, Chenery added a postscript in which he addresses two of the criticisms made in the intervening period, one of which he contests and one which he accepts. The criticism he challenges is one made by Bruton (1969) from a neo-classical perspective which maintains that 'the trade limit is unlikely to occur in a well-managed economy and . . . that basing aid policy on this hypothesis provides the wrong incentives to developing countries' (Chenery, 1979:444). Chenery's reply is that the assertion is correct but the conclusion wrong: while in a well-managed economy a trade limit will not occur, it will do so in practice in the real world. Thus, he argues, the neo-classical challenge to the

Keynesian basis for aid intervention in the first part of the two-gap model is in practice irrelevant.[6] The criticism he takes more note of is the possibility that inflows of external resources can lead to increases in consumption as well as savings, thereby affecting negatively the direct one-to-one relationship between capital inflow and increases in domestic savings levels. As a result, Chenery alters the basic model to allow for a reduction in the savings function by subtracting the amount of the net inflow of foreign capital that is directly consumed. Thus the up-dated version incorporates the notion that aid can be directed towards raising levels of consumption (either directly or indirectly), although Chenery makes explicit one of the theory's main policy implications – that 'an effective development policy is one that channels a high proportion of external resources into investment when savings constitute the binding constraint' (448).

While conventional aid theory as developed in the 1960s, and especially the Chenery-Strout version of it, has survived without being replaced, it would be profoundly incorrect to conclude that its relevance to development, and hence the manner in which it has been applied, has remained unchanged. The Chenery-Strout model is a 'stages' theory – and is provided to explain how different sorts of bottlenecks at different times can be relieved within a process that ends with a self-sustaining path of development – and one in which aid's positive effect on development is intricately related to certain assumptions being met. As perceptions of the prospects for development in the 1970s and 1980s have altered, as certain bottlenecks have become more severe rather than being progressively eliminated, and as the assumptions upon which aid's positive contribution to development was predicated have been questioned, so shifts have become discernible in the way that aid's function has been understood which pose questions for the theory put forward in the 1950s and 1960s to explain its role.

A number of factors have been at work and can be identified. On the world economy front, the earlier optimism was jolted in the mid-1970s and reversed in the early 1980s, especially for the least developed countries, and this led to a shift in emphasis from questions centred around how economic growth rates could be accelerated to questions of how it could be re-started. Also in the late 1960s to early 1970s, the assumption that the effects of economic growth would necessarily trickle down to the poorest groups within developing countries came increasingly under question; this led to more emphasis being put on the distinction between economic growth and economic development, to distribution questions being added to the agenda for development policy, and to the drawing up of needs-based and welfare-specific targets as well as, or in some instances in place of, growth targets. Relief of poverty was always a central reason for providing aid. It was disillusion with the assumed method of alleviating poverty – indirectly through accelerating the growth rate – that led to an increasing emphasis on direct action through targeting aid to the poor. At the same time, the optimism that foreign-exchange bottlenecks could quickly be eliminated was increasingly shaken when more and more developing countries incurred large and growing balance-of-payments deficits, as world trade contracted and Third World debt grew.

But all was not gloom and doom, especially in the 1970s. Concern to find examples of success led to particular attention being focused on the newly industrialised countries (NICs) which, on a wide variety of criteria, seemed to have achieved self-sustaining growth. What was more, they were no longer dependent upon concessional aid flows, having made increasing use of private capital markets. It was the belief that the success of their economic development strategies had been profoundly affected not so much by levels of aid (although aid was not viewed as unimportant) as by the manner in which they had responded to changing economic signals by adjusting their productive structures to internal and external constraints that was to provide the basis for shifts in the way economists working in the aid and development field perceived the role of aid in the development process. To understand the importance of these shifts we need to return to the underlying assumptions upon which the aid theories of the 1950s and 1960s were based.

One fundamental and optimistic assumption of all the different theories reviewed above was that recipient countries would adjust their economic structures to make maximum use of aid and other resources towards the achievement of self-sustaining growth. Aid, argued Rosenstein-Rodan, would provide 'a positive incentive for maximum national effort to increase its rate of growth' and 'knowledge that capital will be available over a decade or more up to the limits of the capacity to absorb it will act in many cases as an incentive to greater effort' (1961:107). Chenery and Strout based their model on the assumption that the injection of aid would enable more efficient use of other resources 'so that growth of total output may be substantially higher than would be permitted by the rate of increase of the most restrictive domestic factor' (1966:681). While acknowledging that accelerated growth may be limited by a country's inability to change its productive structure to meet the changing patterns of internal and external demand, Chenery and Strout expressed the view that 'this problem is not likely to be serious in a slowly developing economy' (682). Likewise, Rostow stated that 'it is a fundamental assumption of this program that the development of capacity to use capital effectively to promote growth is a job mainly for the underdeveloped countries themselves', and that knowledge that aid would be available 'would be a powerful force pushing countries to take steps needed for their own growth' (Millikan and Rostow, 1957: 60–61).

In the 1970s and 1980s these assumptions have been increasingly and more widely questioned. For many developing countries, particularly the poorest, development was not occurring or the pace was slowing down. Structural changes were not occurring automatically: at the level of the domestic economy, structures were not being altered in response to changes in resource allocation and production was not diversifying, while there was also little sign of changes in external economic conditions leading to market-led responses occurring internally. All these different constraints were resulting in large and growing balance-of-payments deficits. And this appeared to challenge basic tenets of the aid theory that had been developed. According to the theory, aid was supposed to speed up a development process that was already taking place; but development was slowing down. Aid was supposed to encourage structural flexibility and adaptability; but structural rigidity appeared to be the norm and recipient economies were not adapting to market and price changes. And aid was supposed to relieve certain specific bottlenecks; instead, the foreign-exchange gap was widening and investment levels were not rising.

These seeming anomalies led to the focusing of attention on the concept of development that economists had been working with in the late 1950s and 1960s. The earlier optimism had been shattered. Two types of response can be identified, the first associated with the late 1970s and the second with the early to mid-1980s. The first could be characterised as disillusion with development strategies as put forward by mainstream development economists and utilised by politicians as justification for providing aid, and, as a result, a growing concern to deal directly with the seemingly ever-increasing problems of poverty. The second, while accepting that development had not worked as expected, sought ways to start the engine again, in part by rebuilding it. Both responses were to change in ideas of how aid could assist in these processes.

In the 1970s the attention of policy-makers and official aid agencies was directed away from the growth models upon which the theoretical role of aid was based to a direct concern with poverty and its alleviation and to policies concerned specifically with redistribution. Redistribution with growth and basic-needs approaches to development took the centre of the stage, commonly shifting attention away from macro-questions and towards micro-interventionist policies and projects. This led to political assertions that aid should be given directly for poverty alleviation. To the extent that this became the predominant and lasting economic basis for giving aid, it would have challenged and indeed replaced the 1960s theories based on growth stimulation and an optimistic view of trickle down. However, the *dominance* of basic-needs approaches was, in the event, relatively short-lived. By 1979 a new (or reassertion of the old) consensus among leading donors had emerged, focusing attention again on questions of aggregate growth and development. However, micro-directed or welfare-targeted aid by no means disappeared from the donors' agenda, as Chenery's adaptation of the two-gap model to allow for consumption aid clearly illustrates. Furthermore, while some donors, the largest and most influential, reasserted their belief in the growth route to poverty alleviation, some did continue to base their aid policies on direct targeting of aid funds to the poor.

Yet the widespread setting aside of poverty-specific targeted aid within the framework of a basic human needs development strategy by no means led to a blind return to the 1960s in either development or aid thinking. The questioning of assumptions had if anything intensified as the 1980s began and the world recession deepened. But whereas, in the 1970s, slow growth and continued widespread poverty in Third World countries had led to the question 'how can the poor be assisted more rapidly?' in the 1980s an even more fundamental question was asked: 'how can the pre-conditions be altered so that economic development can get started again?'

The answer was to lie in what has become known as the *adjustment process*. The belief grew and gained widespread although not complete acceptance that the successes and failures of most developing countries were due to policies executed (or not executed) within developing economies which had responded to (or ignored) market changes and price signals domestically and in the international economy. And as adjustment came to be seen as a pre-condition for development, so the role and place of aid underwent an apparent change. Whereas in the 1960s the basic question addressed by the aid theory was how aid could assist in the development process, in the 1980s it is in furthering the adjustment process that aid is perceived as central. The 1984 DAC Review (p. 49) states the new position clearly and explicitly:

> all concerned with development cooperation should set aside business-as-usual administrative and programming habits and grasp the fresh opportunities created by the economic adjustment process to make aid more relevant and effective.

Structural adjustment and conventional aid theory

The present chapter's primary concern is not to examine the rationale presented by donors in providing aid but the theoretical justification for providing it. Of particular interest to us here therefore is the theoretical basis for providing aid for adjustment, and more specifically whether and to what extent the conventional aid theories of the 1960s are consistent with or challenged by the apparently new rationale. Any answers to these questions must, of course, remain tentative, for no systematic treatment of the adjustment rationale has as yet been provided in the literature.

If, as appears to be the case, aid is now commonly being given at the macro-level within the general context of assisting recipient countries to adjust, then a number of specific questions for aid theory arise. What is the adjustment process and how does it differ from the development process? What role is aid supposed to fulfil in the process of adjustment as distinct from its role in the process of development? The first problem to face in attempting to answer these questions concerns the very definition of adjustment. As Killick (1985) points out, there is no agreed definition, and as a result adjustment policies vary considerably depending upon the concept being used. For the purposes of the present discussion, however, we can begin with Killick's own definition (1985a:13):

> Adjustment is a gradual, non-temporary response of the economy to the existence of an unviable BoP deficit, involving the reallocation of resources between sectors, between factors and between categories of expenditure (including savings). Such reallocations may occur automatically in response to changing monetary conditions and price relativities but governments will often judge it necessary to reinforce any automatic tendencies with the introduction of discretionary policy changes.

The adjustment process is essentially a transition from what is perceived as an unviable process to a sustainable one. Seen in this light, interventionist adjustment policies aim to alter structures within an economy so that self-sustaining and expansive development will occur. Hence the adjustment concept can be understood as part of a 'stages' concept of growth and development, with adjustment policies canvassed as a necessary condition for economic development to become self-sustaining. The importance of the adjustment process as a pre-condition for development is argued by Please, when explaining the new function of the World Bank in the changed conditions of the 1980s (1984:26):

> It is now widely recognized that distorted policy frameworks that were undesirable in the 1960s and 1970s are unsustainable in the 1980s and beyond, given the deteriorated global economic environment in prospect for developing countries including meeting their debt servicing obligations. Domestic policy reform for most developing countries has now become essential and urgent if these countries are to be able to maintain a reasonable rate of growth of incomes and to achieve their other development objectives of human resource development and the provision for basic needs. For Sub-Saharan Africa, as the Bank's Report 'Accelerated Development in Sub-Saharan Africa: An Agenda for Action' has emphasized, domestic policy reform of major proportions is required simply to stop per capita incomes from continuing to fall and then, hopefully, increasing them by the late 1980s and into the 1990s.

If (as the less than fully developed or even agreed theory suggests) successful adjustment is a necessary prelude to self-sustaining growth, then even at this level of abstraction it would seem that aid given for adjustment is provided to fulfil different functions from those of aid inserted to accelerate the development process through its traditional gap-filling role. This becomes even more evident when it is recognised that adjustment policies are intricately related to short-term economic *contraction* – the specific type of adjustment determining the type of contraction envisaged. As Killick points out, 'It is almost inevitable that a programme that has to achieve large results over a brief period will have to concentrate on the repression of demand and the compression of imports' (1985a:17), and he cites the work of Khan and Knight that such programmes are likely to have significant detrimental effects on output, employment and factor incomes. The implication for aid theory is clear. Adjustment policies are quite likely to lead to a lowering of investment levels, falls in the saving ratio, and even an overall decline in the level of national expenditure. As such, the justification for giving aid to provide additional resources to raise saving ratios and investment levels becomes less critical.[7] What then *is* the role of aid, if given as part of an adjustment strategy package?

At a general level, the answer is simple: to provide some slack to cushion the often severe negative effects resulting from the contraction that takes place during the adjustment process. As adjustment policies focus specifically upon balance-of-payments difficulties, that cushion is provided by giving balance-of-payments support, for example by contributing to debt-service payments, or by raising import levels to maintain consumption or investment levels higher than would have been possible without the aid inflow. Within the context of the World Bank's structural adjustment programme, one basic objective appears to be that of raising the level of economic efficiency. Please, for example, argues that adjustment programmes ask the question 'How, through changing policies and institutional arrangements in a country, can existing productive capacity be more efficiently used?' (1984:18).

Yet in fulfilling these particular functions there would appear to be parallels with the function of aid in accelerating the development process under conventional aid theory. Within the context of that theory, aid was seen to be neither necessary nor sufficient for development to take place; its role was to speed up the development process. Likewise, aid is not viewed as either necessary or sufficient to achieve adjustment, but its insertion into an economy that is adjusting is provided to speed up the necessary process of structural change. But there are also differences as well. In the theories of Rostow, Rosenstein-Rodan and Chenery, aid's effectiveness and impact were judged in part in relation to the level of development attained. Within the context of conventional aid theories there is little point in pumping in aid in excess of its absorptive capacity, or its efficient usage in raising investment levels. Within the aid for adjustment perspective, however, the reverse would seem to be true. In this instance, *more* aid would appear to be required the *lower* the level of development, because here the capacity to adjust will be less. This point is clearly argued by Killick (1985a: 19–20):

In a mixed economy the capacity to adjust will be determined by the efficacy of the market mechanism and the quality of decision-making and execution in the organs of the state. It is suggested that the efficiency of the market system (and of the information flows upon which it depends) is likely to be at its lowest in the least developed countries. Poor communications and transport; low levels of education and literacy; social and other obstacles to the mobility of labour; dualistic capital markets; heavy concentrations of monopoly and monopsony power; as well as the often malign influence of state interventions all conspire to make it so. Moreover, the least developed countries are the more heavily dependent on the export of minerals and agricultural commodities, which are often subject to particularly long gestation lags. In a rough and ready way, it is also plausible to think of the efficacy of the state as being positively correlated with economic development, including the government's capacity to achieve its objectives by means of the policy instruments available to it. For example, the government's ability to regulate aggregate demand is likely to be at its lowest in an economy still largely based on primary production, with a limited monetisation of economic activity, with poorly developed banking and other financial institutions, with a narrow tax base and with a probably inefficient public administration. Demand management should at least become a little less difficult as development proceeds.

The above discussion has indicated some differences between adjustment and development policies and in the role of aid in assisting the achievement of the two objectives. But this is still a far cry from the creation of a new theoretical justification for providing aid. To establish such a theory it would be necessary to be able to indicate and to predict, with some attempt at quantification, how a given amount of aid 'x' was expected to contribute positively to the economy into which it was inserted and as it was adjusting. But this requires a far greater precision than at present exists in the prediction of the quantifiable results to be expected from implementing adjustment policies. For, as Killick explains, not only is there no consensus over the definition of adjustment, but the determination of adjustment targets cannot readily be reduced to one or two simple statistical targets. And even if, as is usually the case, adjustment policies are proposed because of severe balance-of-payments problems, the effect of 'successful' adjustment policies on 'the current account may be ambiguous – both tending to strengthen it and yet to permit a larger current deficit to be financed' (6-7).

But beyond these statistically-related problems there are others, some substantial, which inhibit the development of a new theory of aid based on its role in the adjustment process. One reason for scepticism is that the longer-term success of adjustment policies is dependent not only upon domestic policy within aid-recipient countries but also upon the continued and progressive expansion of the international economy. For example, an aid-recipient country's balance-of-payments position is likely to be affected substantially by changes in world-wide commodity prices, the level of world trade and, at present, the strength of the US dollar. Thus whereas conventional aid theory, based on bottlenecks and gap-filling, is specific to the aid-recipient economy, adjustment theory has a wider international dimension. Hence any comprehensive aid theory for adjustment would have to be international in scope, so lessening its predictive value for particular developing countries.

A second problem concerns causality. The link between aid and adjustment is far removed from the slot-machine analogy – you put the money in and adjustment policies result. The insertion of more aid by no means ensures more or better adjustment because, far more than with the aid/development link of, say, the two-gap model, the very success of adjustment is fundamentally dependent upon structural changes occurring. There is, however, a new twist in the link in the mid-1980s, namely the growing requirements that aid provision be conditional on an adjustment strategy being carried out or agreed upon. To the extent that the strategy adopted will lead to successful adjustment occurring, the conditionality attached to the aid being granted at all will then provide the basis for asserting its effective use.

Thirdly, one dominant reason (as Please indicated above) for implementing adjustment policies is to raise the level of efficiency of already available domestic resources and to increase the responsiveness of resource allocation to price changes and market forces; thus the changes in aggregate figures resulting from successful adjustment are likely to be due more to the increasingly efficient utilisation of existing resources than to the provision of additional resources including the aid provided. It would be wrong therefore, on this basis, even to expect a direct link between aid inflows and a higher level of economic activity, for aid is given here primarily to cushion the negative effects of economic contraction resulting from the first phase of the adjustment process. Aid's positive contribution would thus be indirect and lagged.

But perhaps the most fundamental challenge to the creation of a theory of aid for adjustment separate and distinct from a theory of aid for development arises because the distinction between adjustment and development is far from clear-cut. To maintain that there is a distinct adjustment phase and then a development phase in the history of the economic progress of aid-recipient countries is to attempt to isolate stages in a process that is in practice continuous, as the critics of Rostow convincingly argued over 20 years ago. In other words, creating the conditions for economic growth to occur is intricately bound up with creating the conditions for it to continue. In a very important sense, as the economies of many industrialised and Latin American countries illustrate clearly, adjustment is a continuous process.

This was stressed by Tom Clausen in one of his last speeches as World Bank President in early 1986:[8]

> The issue is not new, and never has been, whether adjustment is necessary for development. The two are inseparably linked. Development has always implied adjustment . . . It is the nature of the adjustment which is the issue: its scope; its pace; who pays the costs and who reaps the benefits.

The changing manner in which adjustment and development are at one point seen as distinct and separate and at another as critically interrelated is illustrated in Please's recent discussion of the World Bank's structural adjustment programmes. At one point Please states that 'Adjustment programs can be differentiated from development programs in terms of time horizons' but a few paragraphs on he makes the following point (1984: 19–20):

> the structural adjustment component of adjustment programs is fundamental because it embodies policy changes that are also central to development. Structural adjustment programs include policy and institutional changes in the directly productive sectors of industry and agriculture, in energy, and in macro aggregates, such as the size and composition of the public investment program and of recurrent expenditure on development services. Thus, medium term structural adjustment programs cover many, but not all, of the elements of a long-term development program. Consequently, the World Bank has seen the need for greater emphasis on these components of adjustment programs not only because they are important for meeting the needs of short- and medium-term balance of payments adjustment, but also because they further the achievement of a country's long-term development objectives. The longer-term development programs of population policy, policy towards human resource development, agricultural research, and so on, can be assisted through the implementation of well-formulated structural adjustment programs.

These then are some of the reasons why one is unlikely to see a distinct *theory* of aid's role in the adjustment process emerging, even though the precise role of aid during a substantial period of 'adjustment' is evidently different from its role in the broader 'development' process. Reflecting on these obstacles to the creation of a new theory raises the question of whether the evidently new role for aid in fact *requires* a new theory or whether the conventional theory is able to incorporate the new role into its original perspective.

The answer would appear to be neither that conventional theory needs to be abandoned nor that it needs to be replaced, but rather that it needs to be adapted. One reason for abandoning conventional aid theory would be if it were no longer seen as relevant. But the dominant concern in the mid-1980s with providing aid for adjustment has not led to a rejection of the notion that aid has a role in accelerating the development process. What the aid/adjustment debate appears to have done is to provide an *additional* justification for providing aid, by shifting attention away from how the aid/development models are predicted to operate to the assumptions upon which the models are based. What has been rejected is the optimism that the transformation of aid-recipient economies would occur during the process of achieving self-sustaining growth, to be replaced by the belief that structural changes have to be implemented by direct policy intervention prior to the establishment (or re-establishment) of the conditions in which aid can contribute in a specific and quantifiable manner to the development process. What is new is giving a specific role to aid in the period prior to its more traditional gap-filling role. And it is because this period is commonly characterised by sharp structural, institutional and qualitative changes that the precise contribution of aid funds to the adjustment process cannot easily be quantified.

In one respect, this adaptation of conventional aid theory can be seen as little more than a shift of emphasis. As was pointed out above, Chenery and Strout, Rostow and Rosenstein-Rodan were all careful to qualify their views on how aid could contribute to the development process with cautionary words about the commitment needed within recipient countries to use resources efficiently and the need for an environment suitable for sustaining higher levels of growth.

But, in other respects, the questioning and revising of these optimistic pre-conditions of conventional aid theory do have far-reaching implications, if not for the core of the theory itself at least for the manner in which it can be tested. Once it is acknowledged that the adjustment and development to self-sustaining growth periods of an economy's evolution are in some ways distinct, if only because aid will contribute in a different manner in each, then it is no longer justified to reject conventional aid theory because aid is not positively correlated to increases in investment, savings ratio rises or the aggregate growth rate of the economy. Where aid is being used to promote adjustment policies there is a strong assumption that markets are inefficient, resources are underutilised, exchange rates are not reflective of market forces, etc. Hence aid would not, in the adapted theory, be expected to have the direct positive and specific effect on macroeconomic aggregates that the unadapted theory would suggest. And to the extent that adjustment is necessary over a long period, the predictive value of conventional theory will be lessened. Thus while changes·in the world economy and a heightened awareness of the importance of structural change in the process of achieving long-lasting economic development have by no means replaced the conventional economic arguments for providing aid, they have certainly decreased the possibility of empirical evidence being able to prove conventional theory right or wrong.

Notes

1. It is not only aid critics who accept the view that theories of foreign aid followed the practice of giving aid. For example, Benjamin Higgins writes: 'The truth is that foreign aid programs developed first on an *ad hoc* basis and the effort to provide a logically consistent rationale came afterwards'. (Higgins, 1968:575).
2. For an examination of the ways that Keynes' *General Theory of Employment, Interest and Money* was drawn into discussing longer-term aspects of growth, see Kurihara, 1959.
3. As Singer later observed (1970:4) 'the influence of these ideas was to be profound; it is a fact that Keynesian concepts have now become the traditional basis for development planning, for measuring the force of economic progress in the under-developed countries, and they have become the basis of international approaches to the problems posed by the past and coming development decades.'

4. A critique of Rostow's theory of the stages of economic growth is contained in Yotopoulos and Nugent, 1976: 28–40.
5. A good summary of the different contributions of these and other authors is contained in the first 90 pages of Mickesell, 1968.
6. It is not entirely clear why Chenery should have agreed with Bruton's assertion that even in a well-managed economy a trade limit will not occur. As Professor Sir Austin Robinson points out, 'if one thinks about the problems of developing a small economy with no machine-building industry and depending upon one or two products only for its exports, it is less easy than seems to be supposed to create the balance of payments while importing most of the machinery that is required. That apart, some of the machinery requires very large-scale production. The bottleneck in India at one stage was energy. India has now learnt how to build a power station. But the same is not true of most African developing countries or some smaller Asian countries' (Personal communication, February 1986.)
7. But not irrelevant because the absence of aid in the adjustment process could result in even further falls in investment levels.
8. In an address at the Commonwealth Secretariat, London, in March 1986 – 'Adjustment with growth in developing countries: a challenge for the international community' (mimeo).

10 Aid, Savings and Economic Growth

Aid as necessary and sufficient

From both the left and the right, critics have attacked foreign aid because, they argue, it is neither necessary nor sufficient for the development of recipient countries and the alleviation of poverty there. This attack implies that the defenders of aid claim that aid *is* necessary and sufficient for such development to occur.

From the left, Byres (1972:130) follows a section heading 'Is aid really necessary?' with the statement: 'Until fairly recently only a very few economists, of extreme laisser-faire views, questioned the desirability, the necessity or the positive contribution to growth and development of foreign aid. These were, notably, P.T. Bauer, Milton Friedman and B.R. Shenoy'. For his part, from the right Bauer wrote, in 1981, that the most familiar arguments (for aid) were that aid is indispensable for development' (1981:97). In his 1984 book, the chapter on foreign aid begins thus (1984b:38):

> 'Foreign aid is the central component of world development'. So in 1981 said Professor Hollis B. Chenery, then Vice President of the World Bank in charge of economic research. How can he have been right? Large-scale development occurs in many places without foreign aid and did so long before foreign aid was invented.

Reading these comments might convince the unwary that conventional pro-aid theory maintains that aid is a necessary condition for development. However, this is quite simply untrue. Foreign aid theory, in all its different manifestations, asserts only that aid will, under certain specified conditions, *accelerate* the growth and/or development process or within the basic-needs perspective assist in the direct or indirect fulfilment of certain basic requirements. There is all the difference in the world between accelerating a process and providing an ingredient without which a process can never start. Foreign aid theory nowhere asserts that aid is a necessary or a sufficient condition for development to begin or to continue.

But if that is true, then how can such an eminent authority as Hollis Chenery make such a statement as that attributed to him by Bauer indicating that aid is necessary and fundamental to world development? Three initial points are of relevance. The first is that the quotation attributed to Chenery is taken from an interview recorded by a newspaper reporter and not from his direct writings. The second is that even in that particular interview Chenery is also quoted as saying 'I wouldn't argue that aid is the sufficient condition. There are no single sufficient conditions' (*New York Times*, 1 March 1981). And thirdly, as Chenery's technical writings reveal, his view on the importance of aid and its role in development is highly qualified. Thus for Bauer to use this quotation in an attempt to make orthodox aid theory look foolish is at best regrettable and at worst dishonest.[1]

It would, however, be equally dishonest to suggest that the critics are involved exclusively in putting up a straw man to knock down. While aid theory is not itself based on the assumption that aid is necessary or sufficient for development, there is no doubt that many aid advocates *do* maintain that aid is a necessary condition. In the same *New York Times* interview, Chenery is also quoted as saying that 'for poor countries, aid is crucial, even though it is small', a sentiment with which most pro-aid advocates would agree.

But this imperative for providing aid comes not from foreign aid theory but from particular value judgements distinct from the exclusively economic argument. Most commonly it originates in a moral judgement: for example, that the poverty of the Third World calls for urgent alleviation or that for poverty to be reduced or eliminated economic development needs to be speeded up. (It could, however, equally well come from an assessment of national or international security or stability.)

Whatever its origins, the common view is that there is a necessity to speed up or accelerate the process of poverty alleviation and/or economic development. And to the extent that aid is believed to assist in this process, *then* aid is seen as necessary and crucial. In short, the claim that aid is necessary is a two-tiered claim based not on the belief that it is necessary for development to occur but on the belief that the speeding up of the development process faster than could be expected without aid is necessary. For those basing their belief on moral criteria, the necessity for aid is grounded in the conviction that in present circumstances the process of poverty alleviation and/or economic development without aid would be slower than the moral imperative demands. Seen in this light, two conclusions follow. The first is that the fact that countries have developed or are developing without aid does not have to lead to the conclusion that aid is unnecessary or that those believing in the necessity for aid hold views at variance with historical fact, as Bauer would imply. The second is that the necessity for providing aid is crucially linked to its having the positive accelerating impact that the theory maintains. This itself indicates how crucial it is to evaluate those criticisms which maintain that, contrary to foreign aid theory, aid does not lead to the positive outcome predicted.

Aid and macroeconomic growth

An overview of the debate
Of the wide variety of issues raised in the aid debate the one that has received most attention in the technical literature is the relationship between aid and domestic savings in recipient countries and aid and economic growth performance. This is hardly surprising because one of the core tenets of foreign aid theory, particularly as encapsulated in the two-gap model, is that the insertion of aid funds into a recipient economy sets in motion a causal chain of positive influences in the following broad manner:

aid ---> increase in domestic investible resources ---> increase in domestic investment ---> more rapid rate of economic growth.

If this assertion is correct, then, *prima facie*, one would expect increased aid flows to be positively associated with a rise in domestic investment, and more aid to lead to higher rates of economic growth in the recipient country. What could be apparently simpler than to move out into the real world, quantify the variables and test the validity of the theory and draw the conclusion that aid either does or does not make a positive contribution to the economic performance of recipient countries?

From the late 1950s to the mid-1980s the literature records well over 20 major statistical exercises that have been undertaken to test these relationships in the attempt to resolve the question of the contribution of aid to raising economic growth rates.[2]

There can be little doubt that the results of these tests provide a far from reassuring picture. Many studies record a negative relationship between aid and domestic savings, some reveal an inverse relationship between aid flows and current-account deficits on the balance of payments, while others fail to provide a statistically significant and positive relationship between aid inflows and economic growth.

The debate about the relationship between aid, savings and growth can be divided up historically into a number of distinct phases. In the 1960s the assertion that aid accelerated economic growth through raising the level of domestic saving and/or providing necessary and scarce foreign exchange became part of accepted conventional wisdom. Spirited and specific challenges to this view came particularly from Griffin (1970), Griffin and Enos (1970) and Weisskopf (1972b and 1973), supported in part by a number of broad literature reviews, for example, by Bornschier, Chase-Dunn and Rubinson (1978) and earlier by Mickesell and Zinser (1973). These studies strongly suggested that the available evidence pointed to a negative relationship between aid and domestic savings and that an increase in development aid most commonly does not result in proportionate increases in investment and sometimes leads to a fall. Griffin and Enos and Weisskopf, in particular, pointed to evidence, largely based on cross-sectional data, showing that there was, in addition, reason to conclude that there is a negative relationship between aid and economic growth.

Next came a defence of the positive relationship derived from traditional foreign aid theory by Papanek (1972 and 1973). Papanek's criticism of the attacks consisted of a number of elements: that correlation and causality have been muddled up (the fact that aid is related to a fall in domestic saving does not have to mean that it is the only or dominant cause of the savings decline); that in many studies aid has been included with all other capital inflows or the deficit on current account so that its particular effect is not isolated, and hence conclusions about its specific influence cannot be deduced; and that assumptions made to calculate savings ratios were incorrect and thus distorted the data used. Papanek went on to argue that a series of exogenous factors such as political unrest, changes in the terms of trade, the weather, and the tendencies of particular countries to be 'low or high saving societies' could well influence the variables being measured so as to swamp the expected positive relationships between aid, savings and growth and lead to the negative relationships found. He proceeded to rework the data from a number of studies, most notably those from which Griffin derived his adverse conclusions, and found a positive relationship between aid and economic growth. However, as he later stated (1983:171) his principal conclusion was a negative one: that is was unjustified to rely on simple negative correlations between aid and savings to substantiate the conclusion that aid did not contribute significantly to growth.

A third stage in the debate has been marked not by the critics of aid questioning the conventional view but by aid advocates expressing even greater scepticism about finding a strong and consistent correlation. For example, Mosley (1980), taking up a criticism of the statistical methodology of testing eloquently discussed by Lipton (1972), pointed out that 'none of the estimated equations offers any kind of lag structure relating the independent and dependent variables'. Mosley also questioned Papanek's use of a single equation model using ordinary least squares, which he argued was inappropriate if the right-hand side of the equation contained variables which were endogenous to the process being examined. Using a lagged response of GNP to aid, a two-stage least squares regression analysis, and testing the relationships for the 1970s and for the 1960s, Mosley found that the overall positive effect of aid on growth adduced by Papanek for the 1960s had by and large vanished in the 1970s. For 83 less-developed countries, he found a weak and insignificant but negative correlation between aid and growth and, supporting Griffin's contention, a strong and significant negative relationship between aid and saving. However, his conclusions on causality were similar to those of Papanek rather than Griffin, namely that the negative link between aid and saving was likely to be 'little more than a reflection of the fact that the poorest countries attract the most aid in proportion to their income and that the poorest countries save least' (1980:90) But he did find a significant and positive relationship between aid and growth for the 30 poorest groups in his sample.

By 1984, Mosley's conclusions had become even more gloomy for orthodox foreign aid theory. With Hudson he expanded the single equation derived from the Harrod-Domar growth model, where economic growth is related to aid inflows, domestic saving and inflows of private capital from overseas, to include the influence of estimates for changes in the stock of human capital (measured by the rate of growth of literacy) and in export volumes and prices (measured by the rate of growth of export values). Their results show that aid was not a significant influence on growth *either* in the 1960s *or* in the 1970s. Their best conclusion is that 'aid *in the aggregate* has no demonstrable effect on economic growth in recipient countries in either period' (1984:25), thus throwing into doubt Papanek's positive view of the aid/growth relationship in the 1960s. Even Mosley's favourable view of the relationship for the poorest group of countries from his 1980 results is altered: now it is shown that for the poorest 23 countries aid is negatively correlated with growth in the 1970–1980 period (25–6).

This discussion of the attempts and, by and large, the failures to provide conclusive evidence of a positive relationship between aid, saving and economic growth raises a fundamental question. Can the whole approach, debated in the literature, of attempting to derive a quantitative link between aid, savings and economic growth for a range of different aid-recipient countries at different periods of time be expected to prove or disprove the validity of the assertions of foreign aid theory? If the answer is 'no', then those criticisms of foreign aid that have been based on this sort of evidence cannot be taken as convincing proof that aid's insertion is misplaced. The rest of this chapter attempts to delve deeper into the aid, savings and growth controversy by examining three central questions: the quality of the data used in testing the relationships, the various theoretical perspectives that seek to explain different expected outcomes, and the methodology and quality of the tests used. As will become clear, there are major problems with the quality of the data used, little cause for believing the theoretical differences can be resolved without reference to the evidence but, finally, no assurance that, even if the data were reliable, the results of testing would ever be able to resolve unambiguously the effects that aid will have on recipient economies.

The quality of the data base

To test the relationship between foreign aid and saving and growth it is clearly essential to use accurate quantifiable data. The early attempts to test the effects of aid on economic growth were largely inadequate because it was not *aid* that was being quantified but proxies such as the current account of the balance of payments or aggregate capital inflows. Not only is aid different from the current account deficit but it does not even approximate to capital inflow as Stewart (1971) has shown. The mistake of equating aid with all capital inflows is a criticism which applies to the work of Griffin and Weisskopf, as indeed to much of the early work of Chenery. The inaccuracy arising from this can be seen by examining trends in the proportion of total capital inflows to developing countries attributable to official development assistance. Table 10.1 shows that oda has until very recently accounted for a decreasing amount of total inflows and in the early 1980s accounted for only between one half and one third of all such resource receipts of aid-recipient countries. Hence to lump aid flows with other financial flows and to use these figures as a basis for commenting on the effects of official aid is likely to be highly suspect.

For particular categories of recipient countries the gap between aid resources and other external flows is narrower than the aggregate figures shown in Table 10.1. For example, for all low-income countries, oda accounted for 69 per cent of all external resources between 1980 and 1982, and for Africa south of the Sahara, for 56 per cent of total external receipts between 1981 and 1982. However, for both groups, over $7 billion of resource flows is attributable to non-oda flows, a sizeable amount. The only category of countries for which aid funds are an overwhelmingly high proportion of total external receipts is the 'least developed countries'; in 1981–2, oda accounted for 92 per cent of all financial receipts flowing to them.

Recognition of the substantial potential error involved in attempting to derive conclusions about aid effectiveness from examining the effects of all inflows led in the 1970s and 1980s to researchers isolating official aid flows and examining the relationship between this figure and other economic aggregates. This has been done, for example, by Papanek (1972), Mosley (1980), Dowling and Hiemenz (1982), Crosswell (1981), Gupta and Islam (1983) and Mosley and Hudson (1984). Almost exclusively, the figures selected for aid flows are those provided by the OECD's Development Assistance Committee. There are, however, major conceptual and analytical problems with using even the DAC's oda data many of which are either ignored or not specifically discussed in the literature.

The first problem to arise in using oda figures is to ensure that the 'aid' quantified consists only of the grant element of total aid flows. Thus there is a need to subtract both the non-grant parts of gross oda from the aggregate oda figures and to make an allowance for the repayment of the concessional part of previous loan-aid funds channelled to particular countries. While this requirement is allowed for in the DAC's data on net flows, a number of additional problems occur for which there are no satisfactory or agreed solutions. One concerns whether aid inflows are measured in constant or current prices, another concerns the exchange rate used in determining cross-country comparability, and yet another concerns the variation in repayments caused by high and varying interest rates. As Beenstock (1980:138), Papanek (1983:172–6) and the DAC Review (1984:67) convincingly point out, differing assumptions here can and do lead to huge differences in the aid figures used, and in certain circumstances cross-country comparability will not be possible.[3] The DAC readily admits that there is no agreed methodology for ironing out all the potential errors: it states that the figures it uses for international comparison are only an 'estimate', but without specifying the magnitude of the potential error involved. Independent verifiability of data thus becomes exceedingly difficult.

Table 10.1:   Official Development Assistance and Total Financial Receipts of Less Developed Countries, 1970–1983 ($b)

Type of flow to all developing countries	1970	1975	1976	1977	1978	1979	1980	1981	1982	1983	1984	1985
Oda	8.08	20.07	19.99	20.72	27.71	31.67	37.50	37.28	34.74	33.65	34.60	35.20
Total receipts	9.89	55.72	59.19	66.64	86.51	85.78	99.15	109.76	97.41	99.75	83.00	80.00
Oda as % of total	82	36	34	35	32	37	38	34	36	34	42	44

Source: DAC *Review* 1984: 64–65 and 1986:13.

A second area of sizeable potential error concerns what is termed the 'lag' factor. One would not expect aid, especially aid directed to projects which take months or years to be completed, to be effective at once. Nor would one expect all aid to be effective in a single time period. Programme aid would be expected to have a more rapid impact than infrastructural aid and infrastructural aid to have a more rapid impact than human resource aid directed at raising the level of human skills. A number of implications follow. First, to measure the effect of aid inflows with aggregate economic variables in the *same year* as the aid enters the recipient economy would be likely seriously to underestimate the effect of aid flows. But secondly, to allow for this error by applying an arbitrary period of, say, three or four years for aid's impact to be felt, would be likely to be equally inaccurate when aid is given to different areas of economic activity in different proportions in different recipient countries. Hence cross-country averages of an assumed lag-factor are likely to contain substantial error, while time series averages using the same proportionate lag structures are also likely to mis-specify the relationship one is attempting to examine.

A third and interrelated distortion will arise to the extent that official aid is tied to purchases from the donor country. Tying will affect both the price used in determining the 'true' value of the resource flow and the length of time it is expected to take for the aid received to have its expected outcome. The effect of tying will be related to the type of aid tied, for example whether it is tied to general commodity purchases, to purchases of specific products or to specific engineering contracts, *and* the relative costs of the donor package vis à vis alternative costs of purchases either from other donors or from non-donors. DAC figures for 1983 aid flows suggest that over 40 per cent of all bilateral aid from DAC donors consists of tied aid. The general point to be emphasised is that aid tying distorts prices and lag effects and that these distortions would need to be allowed for when testing the impact of aid on recipient countries.

These general types of problems have been discussed in the literature for some considerable time. For example, Lipton (1972:165-7) discusses each in turn after raising the question 'Before lots more regressions are run, it is worth asking just what relationship between aid and growth we are seeking to measure'. As most statistical tests of aid effectiveness at the country level since 1972 have been based on DAC statistics, it is worth adapting Lipton's question thus: before a lot more regressions are run based on the DAC statistics, are we sure that these figures can provide an accurate enough data-base for testing the effects of aid?

There are a number of more specific difficulties with using the DAC's figures of net disbursements of donor assistance to recipient countries as a measure of the aid available to them and used by them. The most immediate concerns the accuracy of the data themselves. A number of questions arise here to add to those already highlighted. First, the DAC data flows to recipient countries contain a substantial financial category termed 'unspecified' – suggesting that the precise destination of financial flows has not been traced. For example, between 1979 and 1982 the DAC figures recorded an annual average of 15 per cent of all aid flows to recipient countries as unspecified, and for DAC donors between 1980 and 1982 an average of over $900m. of net disbursements to individual recipients was categorised as 'unspecified' each year. Secondly, while the figures for DAC aid flows may well be reasonably accurate, the data for aid flows from other donors are not nearly so accurate and vary, at least according to DAC estimates, often quite substantially from year to year. For instance, total net DAC aid disbursements (bilateral and multilateral) accounted for 63 per cent of all official aid in 1975-6 and for 77 per cent in 1983-4 (DAC, 1985:93); and in 1984, OPEC sources of aid consisted of in excess of 10 per cent of all bilateral aid in 13 sub-Saharan African countries and for over 60 per cent in the cases of Sierra Leone and Guinea, according to the World Bank (1986a:84). An indication of the errors contained in the published data – or the controversy surrounding them – is illustrated by the wide divergence of opinion between the DAC and individual Comecon countries concerning aid flows. According to DAC data, Soviet aid to developing countries in 1982-3 accounted for some $2.5 billion and 0.19 per cent of GNP; according to the Soviet Union it amounted to $17 billion and 1.3 per cent of GNP.[4] Moreover, the DAC data of 'net disbursements of ODA from all sources combined to individual recipients' specifically exclude *all* bilateral aid from non-DAC donors, indicating serious inaccuracy in this particular data source, even though it has been frequently used as the basis for testing the aid relationship.[5]

Perhaps of most importance is the fact that the DAC figures are based on data from donor countries and agencies and on DAC-agreed definitions of what should or should not be included. It cannot be assumed that the quantity of funds which donors specify as aid flows are the same as the quantity of funds which either arrive in or are utilised by recipient countries. Nor can it be assumed that the distinction made by donor countries between development assistance funds and other flows is a distinction that recipient countries are able to make in identifying the different types of funds they utilise, or that the DAC distinction is relevant to analysing the impact of different types of financial and financially-linked inflows from abroad. If the quantities of aid monies received and utilised by recipient countries are widely at variance with the quantities that the donors state are flowing to them, then the methodology of using DAC statistics of aid flows as a basis for analysing the influence of aid funds on growth, saving and other economic indicators of recipient economies is thrown into question. Some examples will highlight this methodological problem.

The first is the issue of administrative costs. DAC definitions state that 'ODA is measured to include both the resources reaching developing countries (or multilateral organisations) and the corresponding administrative costs' (DAC Review, 1984:188). While it can certainly be argued that the costs of providing aid to recipient countries are a legitimate aid-related expense for the donor (and hence should be met by aid funds), the finance devoted to aid administration is neither seen nor utilised by recipients. For the DAC countries, $900m. or 5 per cent of all bilateral aid consisted of administrative costs in 1983, with proportions varying between different donors. To the extent that aid statistics include donor-based administrative costs these figures inflate the aid monies available to recipients.

A second difficulty is the fact that country of destination figures exclude all non-official development assistance. However, from the point of view of the recipient, the nature, the purpose and the utilisation of aid from private agencies are very often identical to those provided by official aid; there is no *a priori* reason for assuming that grant aid from non-official sources will have a different influence on domestic savings, the balance of payments or the savings effort from that of official aid. In 1983, private aid amounted to $2.3 billion, according to DAC statistics, accounting for 8.5 per cent of all official aid from DAC members (DAC Review, 1984:202). Since then, and with the publicity given to the African famine, private aid donations have risen dramatically. But in a year or two this trend could again be reversed. For the Federal Republic of Germany, in 1984 private aid totalled DM 1.1m., 20 per cent of total bilateral official aid.[6] This particular type of anomaly is well illustrated by the example of the cost accounting for providing volunteers under the British Volunteer Programme. Under the official volunteer scheme, the government currently pays for 90 per cent of the costs of placing volunteers in aid-recipient countries, the voluntary sending agency providing the balance. DAC statistics of aid to recipient countries include the government's financial contribution but not the private funds raised. For some countries, like Haiti, the private aid contribution is large in both absolute and relative terms.

More substantial still in aggregate financial terms is the official aid provided under supplier or mixed credit schemes. While these funds are readily allocated by donors to those countries to which the money is directed, they do not reach recipient countries in a manner clearly distinguishable from commercial and/or trade finance. For example, under British aid statistics, the money provided to private British companies through the Aid and Trade Provision (ATP) to enable them to sell their goods to aid-recipient countries is counted as part of the aid receipts of those countries. In 1982 this amounted to £63m., 10 per cent of gross bilateral aid flows.[7] As the purpose of this form of official assistance is to enable British firms to supply products at the same price as international competitors, the money provides no addition to similar products or services which could have been supplied from elsewhere and, in addition, it does not appear on the balance-of-payments figures of recipient countries as a foreign-exchange credit. This type of accounting convention is therefore likely to create a differential between aid flows from donor countries and aid receipts by recipient countries of many hundreds of millions of dollars. Moreover, recent debate among DAC members indicates considerable definitional problems within the donor community over the aid component of these sorts of commercially-directed uses of official development assistance. In many respects aid is being defined in terms of an accounting convention consensus.

Defining what counts as development assistance highlights further questions about separating out different types of official flows. DAC statistics on official aid are distinguished from other flows as they refer only to flows 'with promotion of economic development and welfare as their main objectives'.[8] Thus the statistics are, in part at least, classified in terms of *intentionality*. However, associations between economic variables within a recipient country will be more likely to be related to the effects of aggregate flows than to the interpretation given by donors of the reasons for providing different forms of finance, particularly if these effects cannot be separated out with ease by the recipient.

This general point can be illustrated by considering US assistance. In 1983, the US provided $14.3 billion in government assistance programmes. Of this, $5.5 billion was termed military assistance, including $1.6 billion provided on varying concessional terms. According to DAC definitions, $8.7 billion of the $14.3 billion was termed 'development assistance' and this $8.7 billion included $3 billion of what the US Government calls its 'Economic Support Fund' assistance. This latter item, accounting for 34 per cent of DAC-defined development assistance, is, according to the US Foreign Assistance Act, 'Economic support for countries in amounts which could not be justified solely under development assistance criteria'.[9] Now while it is perfectly understandable why the DAC makes a distinction between 'development' and 'other' assistance and isolates the flow of development assistance to recipient countries and calls this official aid, it is far from clear why these different sorts of assistance should have markedly different and distinguishable *macroeconomic* effects on the recipient economy. Military assistance will, like development assistance, have certain recognisable economic characteristics. Military grants will have a beneficial effect on the balance of payments of recipient countries and also on the tax and saving effort of the recipient state in a manner, in aggregate, very similar to that of development assistance and especially tied aid, on the assumption that at least some and perhaps most military equipment would have been purchased in the absence of donations from donor governments. Indeed, there would appear to be as strong a likelihood that concessional military aid will have a more substantial and positive effect on investment and saving aggregates in the recipient country than food aid directed to immediate consumption needs. From the point of view of *monitoring the effects of external funding on the dynamics of recipient economies*, if it is accepted that Economic Support Fund financing is included in aid flows because its effects are economic, even though the motivation for providing the assistance is in part based on politico-military factors, then this argument should be applied to all assistance which has an economic effect on the recipient, however the donors choose to define the different concessional flows they allocate to different countries.

The whole area of food aid in particular and consumption-oriented aid in general raises yet another crucial question. Aid targeted specifically to raising immediate consumption levels should surely be subtracted from total aid flows if one's purpose in examining aid flows is to test the relationship between aid and investment.[10] The quantities involved here are quite considerable. In 1983, over 15 per cent of US development assistance was food aid, supplied under the PL480 provision, and total food aid from DAC countries amounted to $937m., 5 per cent of all bilateral aid provided by DAC donors (DAC Review, 1984:259). However, no tests that have been run on the impact of aid have taken account of this particular and influential dimension.

If the DAC statistics on aid flows are an unreliable source for capturing the quantities of aid available to and used by recipient countries, what other sources are available? The answer – if there is one – surely lies in examining the national accounts and balance-of-payments data of individual aid-recipient countries. But there are also problems here. A major one is that for most of these countries the available data do not separate out aid funds and aid flows from other flows. It is also apparent that to attempt to use national recipient-country accounts to extract aid flow data would be an immensely time-consuming process requiring, as Lipton suggests, 'several man-years of sustained effort' (1972:168). And even then the conceptual problems of lags, price differentials, exchange rates and what to define as aid would still remain to be addressed. No cross-country tests of aid's effectiveness on recipient economies have yet been based on recipient-based aid data.

Questions about the accuracy of data are by no means confined to the reliability of the statistics on aid: they apply, too, to other aggregates like growth rates, savings and investment schedules. As statisticians and national accounts experts continually stress, the less developed a country the more likely it will be that national economic aggregates will be incorrectly calculated or estimated.[11] National accounts can only provide a 'guestimate' of non-monetary GDP, and as a country develops the mix between monetary and non-monetary GDP will clearly change. But once estimates of growth rates are made, a further characteristic of international statistics is the wide range of estimates used by different organisations. One example, from among many, illustrates the problem. The World Bank's report, *Accelerated Development in Sub-Saharan Africa*, reveals (1981:187) that different estimates of Mali's annual GDP growth for the decade of the 1970s have varied from 0.5 per cent to 6.6 per cent, a thirteenfold discrepancy; for all Sahelian countries the smallest range of estimates for the same country, Mauritania, is 23 per cent, from a low of 6.5 per cent to a high of 7.7 per cent.

As regards the savings function, data inaccuracy and volatility in estimates are likely to be particularly marked. This has led Mickesell to comment 'it is my contention that the behaviour of savings in developing countries has been far too erratic to provide a basis for a foreign aid model in which the marginal savings ratio constitutes a critical variable' (1968:96). In a comprehensive review of the literature on the nature of the savings function in developing countries, Mickesell and Zinser comment on the data inadequacies and lack of comparability of savings data across developing countries. Most savings functions, they argue, are in practice derived as residuals following a process of deducting the current-account deficit from gross capital formation, while data on gross capital formation are themselves open to biases and serious discrepancies. Concluding that aggregate savings estimates are subject 'to a rather wide margin of error' – even in the USA – they draw together a number of implications of this data inadequacy: that great caution needs to be exercised in evaluating the results of cross-sectional savings behaviour based on aggregate savings data; that *ex-post* savings, as it is a statistical residual, does not provide a true measure of savings effort; and that year to year changes in marginal savings ratios are subject to such a high degree of error as to make their usefulness questionable (1973:2–3).

It is an old adage that conclusions drawn from quantitative data will only be as good as the quality of the data upon which they are based. The upshot of this discussion on the data which have been used to test the effects of aid on recipient economies is to question seriously whether the sources used have been accurate enough to produce any reliable conclusions at the aggregate and cross-country level, particularly because quantitative levels of aid as between DAC and non-DAC donors and in the respective levels of official and non-official, military and non-military and consumption and non-consumption targeted aid have all been subject to significant fluctuations of a non-random, non-predictable and complex character. This suggests that those critics of aid who have arrived at the view that aid hinders growth, or those advocates of aid who are concerned that with the data they have used no proof of aid's positive impact has been found, have both placed too much faith on the accuracy of the data to come to their respective conclusions.

The theoretical debate·
Data accuracy is only one area of controversy surrounding criticism of that aspect of foreign aid theory which implies a positive relationship between aid and economic growth. Another major area of controversy concerns the theoretical link to be expected between aid, savings and growth.

The unadapted Chenery-Strout model makes the assumption that capital inflows, including aid, provide an addition to the recipient country's total investible resources, that this increase leads to a rise in the level of investment, and that a higher investment-to-GDP ratio raises the growth rate of the recipient economy. The adapted model is less extreme. It takes on board the view of much conventional economic analysis that additional resources are used in part to increase aggregate consumption and in part to raise aggregate investment; however, it asserts that the loss to consumption is minimal and that the dominant effect of providing additional resources is positively to increase domestic savings levels. Hence the positive link of aid to more growth is maintained, although in a less absolutist manner.

Three sorts of counter-assertions have appeared in the literature. The strongest is that capital inflows in general and aid in particular *necessarily* lead to a direct fall in domestic saving levels, so setting in motion a vicious rather than a virtuous circle, causing a decline in saving and hence in investment, thus leading to a lower growth rate. A second view asserts that no particular and necessarily predictable effect on domestic savings is to be expected from a capital resource inflow. A third is that capital and in particular aid inflows create the circumstances for a decline in domestic savings to result, albeit indirectly. In addition, critics have attacked other aspects of the general pro-aid models. These criticisms have included the following: the separation and distinction between the saving and foreign-exchange gap, whether foreign-exchange shortages constitute a binding constraint on potential growth, and whether the optimism built into the models which concludes that aid will soon no longer be required can be sustained.

Challenging the assumed positive relationship between aid and domestic savings, Haavelmo (1965) argued that investment is a function of income including what is obtained from abroad, the implication being that, if the capital inflow is large, then domestic saving could be negative because the inflow could be used to substitute for domestic saving as well as for augmenting investment. Rahman (1968) slightly adapted the Haavelmo view and drew the conclusion that governments in developing countries may 'voluntarily relax domestic saving efforts when more foreign aid is available than otherwise' (1968:317).

This general point has been pursued and extended by Griffin (1978). He challenges the Keynesian-derived models (including under this categorisation both the Harrod-Domar and the Chenery-Strout paradigms) which are based on the belief that the investment ratio will rise if capital imports increase. The first part of his attack, allowed for in the adapted Chenery-Strout model, is based 'on the possibility of capital imports supplementing consumption' (1978:59). As this assumption is incorporated in the adapted Chenery-Strout model, controversy over this particular issue is no longer one of principle. (However, it does remain a matter of degree, with Griffin maintaining that in practice the consumption-leakage effect is highly significant, Chenery that it is far less important.) Griffin's 'alternative view . . . is that aid is essentially a substitute for saving and that a large fraction of foreign capital is used to increase consumption rather than investment'(61). In other words, with a given level of income, the larger the inflow of capital the lower the *level* of domestic saving.

However, he also stresses that his view is not deterministic, his belief that aid inflows will be accompanied by a decline in domestic savings depends crucially on the actions of the recipient governments. Whereas the Chenery-Strout model assumes the government will be *growth-maximising* and hence will attempt to utilise any additional funds to raise investment levels, Griffin assumes that it is not, hence the likelihood that a part of the aid inflow (substantial for Griffin) is channelled into raising consumption either directly, or more likely, through shifting resources currently allocated to investment expenditure. Various pointers are suggested. Public savings could fall through tax receipts falling or through a change in the composition of government expenditure. Foreign capital could lower private domestic savings or foreign imports could reduce domestic saving by stimulating the consumption of importables and exportables.

The second part of the Griffin attack moves beyond the consumption-diverting aspect of aid, which would lead to *some* increase in domestic saving and hence of domestic investment, to the negation of this slight positive effect through changes that he asserts will occur in the output–capital ratio. Griffin correctly states that the Chenery-Strout model is based on there being a fixed output–capital ratio. However, he continues, it is more likely that there will be a loose negative association between the incremental output–capital ratio and aid inflow which will result in 'the slight positive effect of foreign capital in raising investment [being] . . . more than offset by a decline in the output–capital ratio, so that the growth rate actually falls' (67). Various explanations are given for this: donors' propensity to channel funds into prestigious and large projects will lower investment effectiveness; donors' bias against productive and in favour of infrastructural projects; tied aid and project selection biased in favour of foreign-exchange-intensive activities.[12]

Moving from the saving-specific question, Griffin argues that *ex post* the saving and foreign-exchange gaps must be equal but that in any case the foreign-exchange gap is illusory because, especially over the longer term, it can be filled by altering domestic policies in the recipient country. In a more rigorous analysis, Joshi maintains that, whatever theoretical constructs are erected for recipient economies, in practice the saving and foreign-exchange gaps cannot be distinguished because resources are so underutilised in poor countries that 'the identification of constraints . . . becomes a matter of judgement' (1970:119). Much of Joshi's criticisms are a challenge to the assumptions of the pro-aid models. He writes (127–8):

> The pseudo-mathematical certainty of the two-gap models conceals important judgements about domestic objectives and the technological and institutional restrictions on their attainment. . . . Theoretically it is based on very extreme assumptions which reduce its value as a classification of reality.

The fundamental controversy between these criticisms and the pro-aid models revolves around the question of the nature of the impact of the additional capital inserted (as aid) on key variables in the recipient economy. In many ways this debate turns out *not* to be a debate about pure theory; rather it is focused on the assumptions of the different models and their relevance to the real world and thus on what are the most likely effects to result from providing aid. There is, in fact, considerable common ground between foreign-aid theory and the theory lying behind these particular criticisms. It is agreed, for example, that income consists of consumption and saving, that investment is furthered by increasing savings, and that economic growth is positively expanded by raising the level of investment. What is at issue is how the insertion of foreign aid affects these relationships and whether the effects result in a positive or negative outcome. For, as Griffin is only too ready to accept, 'the pattern of development is complex and the effect upon it of foreign assistance is undetermined' Griffin and Enos (1970:325).

The chain of cause and effect assumed by the critics to result from aid inflow is based on a series of assumptions deemed to be more relevant to the real world than those which the critics assert are part and parcel of foreign-aid theory. That this *is* a central element in the theoretical debate is well illustrated by the exchange between Griffin and Eshag in the *Bulletin of the Oxford University Institute of Economics and Statistics* following Griffin's 1970 article. Eshag points out that Griffin's conclusion that aid inflows have a negative impact on domestic savings is based upon the assumption of a zero elasticity of supply of labour and of goods and services, i.e. productive resources are fully utilised prior to the receipt of aid (1971:149). Once this assumption is removed, he continues (150):

> There will be no theoretical reason to expect a foreign capital inflow to reduce domestic savings as claimed by Griffin. There is in fact every reason to expect that domestic savings will increase on the assumptions that some domestic savings which would otherwise have remained unemployed are used in conjunction with foreign resources on the new investment projects, and that the growth in public consumption does not exceed the

rise in government revenue plus the rise in private savings generated by the increase in domestic income.

Eshag goes on to demonstrate the thrust of this point with a simple mathematical model. In his comment on this point, Griffin states that his dispute is over the 'economics' not the algebra. By economics Griffin is referring to the evidence of what happens in practice, not to pure theory. It is Griffin's assessment of the *evidence* which leads him to his view of aid's negative macro-economic impact on recipient countries. His assessment is based on two assumptions at variance with specific assumptions contained in foreign-aid theory. The first is that much aid is channelled directly or indirectly into consumption, the second that aid inflow causes a fall in the output-capital ratio. Together these assumptions provide the 'economic' conclusion that aid leads to a lower level of domestic saving and to either a neutral or negative impact on recipient economies.

Of course, there is no *a priori* reason why, even if these assumptions are correct, one *necessarily* has to conclude that aid has to have a negative impact. This is the gist of much of Joshi's work. Indeed, much of the literature attacking what has been termed the 'displacement' theory critique of aid has revolved around producing arguments to indicate either that the assumptions do not *always* hold or that different outcomes are possible. For example, Stewart (1971) argues both that an increase in consumption is not only a welfare gain to recipient countries but can also have a positive effect on investment over the longer term and that Griffin's conclusion on output–capital ratios is based on very partial analysis. She was also one of the first to point out that correlation does not necessarily or always mean causality: in other words, the fact that aid is associated with a lower than 'anticipated' rise in saving does not have to mean that it was the aid inflow that was the direct cause of the saving effect. Both Gupta and Islam (1983) and Nelson (1964) have gone further to stress that many key quantitative variables are interrelated and interdependent, revealing a complex relationship of cause and effect. Dacy (1975) has argued that one needs to distinguish between the short-term and long-term impact of aid on recipient countries. He has introduced yet another assumption into the debate: if aid does lead to an increase in consumption but when it is withdrawn consumption does not fall back to its original level, then the overall effect of aid will be to lead to an increase in domestic saving and hence be positive (1975:557).

The importance of this debate for our present discussion is that it highlights the crucial links not only between formal theoretical statements and evidence (referred to by Griffin) but also between assumptions surrounding different theories and the real world. It is no accident that the literature concentrates predominantly on testing the various relationships expected by the aid theory or its critical alternative models to pertain, since testing relationships in the real world holds out the possibility of arriving at firm conclusions about the different theoretical propositions outlined by the defenders or critics of aid which debate at the theoretical level cannot hope to achieve.

The debate about assumptions concerns not only the realism of the assumptions upon which the formal propositions of the theory captured in quantitative terms are based, but also a judgement about the way the real world functions. Thus, for example, Chenery-Strout's technical model is built upon various assumptions embodied principally in Keynesian dynamic growth models, which, *if* they reflect correctly what happens in the real world, would lead to a positive impact on the recipient economy of capital (and aid) inflows. The Griffin-type model contains

key alternative assumptions which his reading of the evidence leads him to conclude are more appropriate because they accord more closely with reality.

The prime importance of the evidence for clinching the argument about both the
appropriateness of the theory and the relevance of the assumptions is brought out
well by Papanek, who explains that there are various plausible savings functions
which could produce alternatively a rise or a fall in savings and a rise or a fall in
investment; *both* are crucially affected by what happens in the real world. As
Papanek explains, the Griffin model is crucially affected by the assumptions made
about the government response to capital inflow: if one assumes that savings are a
function of government effort or policies, that governments have a fixed growth
rate as their objective, that achievement of this growth rate requires a given
investment, then, if any resources for investment come from abroad, a government will change its policies and programmes to reduce domestic savings by an
equivalent amount' (1972:936–7). Yet, he continues, an alternative view could (in
the absence of *evidence*) be equally plausible (938):

> If savings are a function of income and the Government has no effective mechanism for
> achieving a reduction in the savings function . . . to compensate for any increase in
> investment directly financed by foreign capital, the net effect of foreign inflows on
> investment will depend on the proportion of inflows allocated to investment. When
> foreign resources first flow into a country a large share is directly invested – almost all of
> aid and of foreign private investment – and aid donors exert pressure for increases in
> domestically financed investment: the resulting extra income will lead to an initial
> increase in saving. The question then is whether in a second round the Government can
> and will make compensatory adjustments in domestic savings and consumption in order
> to meet its specified objective function (if it has one of the kind postulated).

The thrust of this part of the discussion would seem to lead us to the conclusion
that the 'correctness' of these different perspectives can only be conclusively
proved or disproved by examining and evaluating the evidence. These summary
remarks from Eshag would therefore appear to be correct (1971:156):

> On the basis of the foregoing observations, it is clear that the net balance of cost or
> benefit of foreign aid will depend on the type of aid received (its direct and indirect costs)
> and on the use made of it (its direct and indirect benefits). Both the costs and benefits of
> aid will in turn depend largely on the character and policies of the governments in the
> donor and recipient countries which can vary considerably from one country to another
> and, for the same countries, from one situation to another. It would, therefore, be
> impossible to postulate a general proposition claiming that foreign aid is invariably
> beneficial or harmful; each case has to be studied separately and judged on its merits.

This itself highlights weaknesses in the attempts made to build quantitative
models to explain the expected aid/growth/savings/investment/foreign exchange
relationships of foreign aid theory. The fact that evidence is brought forward to
conclude that the expected relationships have not resulted and, indeed, that the
same data have been worked to produce conflicting conclusions indicates that the
models are without doubt poor predictors of aid's actual performance.[13] The point
can be developed even more strongly. Key predictions emerging from foreign aid
theory have simply not resulted as expected; for most countries, and especially for
the poorer ones, the era of self-sustaining growth without aid has simply not arrived
and foreign-exchange gaps have, if anything, widened rather than narrowed. Part
of the reason for this lies in the nature of the assumptions on which the models are
expected to operate. For example, they assume either that resources are fully utilised or that the greater utilisation of resources is brought about only as a result of

the capital inflow, that no other internal or external influences will affect the recipient economy, that cyclical variations do not arise, and that the effects of technology, politics, income distribution and structural change are all neutral. This is a world that no recipient country, its government or its population, inhabits.

There is, however, a crucial difference between arguing that the models will be poor predictors of aid's effects in the real world and arguing that therefore aid theory is wrong. To clinch the case it would be necessary for the critics not only to show that aid does not have the positive effects predicted by the models but also that the factors, including government policies, that are causing the adverse effects cannot be altered to bring about the results which the theory expects. Two points need to be made here. The first is that the criticisms of aid theory made in the literature have concentrated almost exclusively on discussing or testing the technical relationships of the models to the exclusion of the context in which they are placed. One of the purposes of describing in some detail in Chapter 9 the evolution and context of aid theory was to emphasise the caution with which the proponents presented their technical models. They were well aware that certain conditions had to be fulfilled for the models to operate and that the models presented were *only* valid on the assumption that these conditions did hold. It is important in this context to note that it is Chenery and not Griffin who wrote the following: 'It is the need for rapid structural change which sets the lower limit to the time required to complete the transition to self-sustaining growth . . . it is very unlikely that any (typical Asian or African) country can meet all the requirements of skill formation, institution building, investment allocation, and so forth in less than one generation' (1966:726). And it is Griffin and not Chenery who wrote that 'if capital imports . . . enable the poor to improve their diet, enjoy better health and have smaller families, they may make a significant contribution' (1971:159). Thus to launch into an attack on the theory because it is unrealistic or likely to be untrue in the real world is in many respects to erect a straw man by confusing theory with policy. As Grinols and Bhagwati observed some time ago but which has been frequently forgotten or ignored (1976:416):

> To be fair to the economists (such as Rosenstein-Rodan) who used the approach being criticised, they thought of the Keynesian domestic savings function as one which the economy would adhere to (via tax effort, for example) as part of its 'matching effort' while receiving the capital inflow, so that it was a 'policy' function rather than a 'behavioural' function as implied by the radical writings.

The second point concerns the manner in which discussion within the pro-aid camp has shifted in recent years away from the technical relationships of the models constructed in the 1960s to the assumptions upon which the models' successful outcome is dependent. The rationale for providing aid has moved away from that of accelerating the growth and transformation of the recipient economy, on the assumption that policies would be executed to effect the maximum utilisation of the aid inflow, and towards the alteration of the policy environment itself through structural adjustment initiatives. In many ways this change in the role given to aid is an implicit acceptance of the thrust of the criticism discussed in this section: that the assumptions of the traditional models were both too optimistic and at variance with the realities of conditions in recipient countries. Significantly, however, this has not led to any new attacks on aid theory (taken in its broadest sense) – possibly because of the far less specific outcome expected from *aid* in its structural adjustment phase.

Summarising this sub-section, it would thus appear that the controversies surrounding the theory of aid, savings and growth turn out to be overwhelmingly concerned with the appropriateness and relevance of different assumptions. Ironically, perhaps, the views of the critics have made two major and positive contributions to aid theory. First, they have helped to explain why the optimism inherent in early versions of the theory was misplaced. Secondly, and relatedly, they have led to a questioning of the optimistic assumptions and a shift away from predicting the pattern of the technical relationships to attempting to alter the policy environment so that the assumptions could hold better. As a result, there is little interest today in debating the skeleton of the theory, for the flesh of the policy environment is now widely recognised as holding the key to aid's effectiveness. But the shift has itself removed much of the force of this sort of criticism. The debate at the theoretical level has a hope of being resolved only by examining what does happen in the real world.

Macro-models and the evidence

Setting aside for the moment the (often fundamental) difficulties in quantifying the variables, we now examine the cross-country statistical analyses that have been carried out and the various models constructed to attempt to throw light on the aid, savings and growth debate. The discussion will indicate serious inadequacies in most of the tests carried out and the consequent ambiguity of many of the published results.

The main cross-country analyses which have led to a negative view of aid's impact on recipient economies are those of Rahman, Areskong, Griffin, Griffin and Enos, and Weisskopf, all published over ten years ago. Characteristic of the thrust of these studies is the claim made by Griffin and Enos that increased foreign aid actually leads to a decrease in domestic savings and hence that foreign aid has a negligible or even a detrimental effect on the growth rate of the recipient country. The method of testing common to all the studies is multiple regression analysis. There is, however, no unanimity of method among the different approaches. For example, Weisskopf argues that the Griffin and Enos and Rahman results can only be taken as suggestive rather than conclusive, because their analyses fail to exclude countries where there was a net outflow of capital and because the savings functions used in the tests were *ex-post* accounting relationships and not *ex-ante* behavioural relationships (1972b:26).

The variables to be tested have varied both between studies and within them. The most frequently run tests have been of the domestic savings to national income ratio as the independent variable and of the current-account deficit as the dependent variable. However, the Griffin and Enos study discusses the estimated relationship between the foreign aid to GNP ratio as the independent variable and the growth of GNP as the dependent variable first for 15 African and Asian countries and then for 12 Latin American countries. The one common conclusion from these studies is that there is a negative relationship between domestic savings and foreign inflow (as measured by the current-account deficit) and, in the case of the Griffin and Enos study, a significant negative relationship of aid/GNP to GNP growth for the Latin American countries selected. This negative relationship between capital inflow and domestic savings was confirmed by Landau (1966) for 18 Latin American countries. However, Gupta's 1970 results for 31 countries indicate that foreign capital inflow has had little effect on domestic saving ratios. Nevertheless, in an article in 1975, he suggests that aid does contribute to growth, and his 1983 book with Islam challenges his original conclusions (1983:43). As for the effect of foreign capital inflow on domestic saving, Gupta and Islam's rigorous analysis leads to the conclusion that its negative impact cannot be unambiguously stated (132). This appears to contradict the literature review ten years previously by Mickesell and Zinser which concluded: 'we found substantial agreement among the investigators that saving in developing countries is negatively related to net capital imports' (1973:19).

Moving from the anti-aid to the pro-aid camp, it is of considerable interest to find that Papanek finds a negative correlation between aid flows and domestic savings (1972:939). However, his results also indicate a strong and significant impact of aid on growth in the 1960s. For the 1970s, Mosley (1980) finds that between 4 per cent and 25 per cent of growth in aid-recipient countries is explained by domestic saving and capital flows from abroad. He comments thus: 'the overall positive effect of aid on growth which Papanek found in the 1960s has in large part vanished: what is apparent if one takes the sample as a whole, rather, is a weak and insignificant but *negative* correlation between aid and growth' (1980:82). However, his results indicate that for the 30 poorest countries out of his sample of 83, aid is *positively* correlated with growth and significantly so if it is lagged five years. But then, in his 1984 publication with Hudson, Mosley reworks Papanek's 1960s data and finds that his conclusions were incorrect. Thus, 'aid was a significant influence on growth neither in the 1960s nor in the 1970s' (1984:25). Moreover Mosley and Hudson contradict a conclusion of Mosley (1980), stating that in the 1970s middle-income recipient countries achieved a higher aid effectiveness than did the poorest countries (1984:25). Yet Dowling and Hiemenz's regression results for 52 countries in the Asian region for the 1970s support the Papanek and contradict the Mosley conclusions. They 'strongly support the hypothesis that foreign aid contributes to economic growth' (1983:11), while results by different country-groupings indicate that aid's contribution is more significant for high-growth Asian countries. This particular finding is confirmed by Gupta and Islam (1983:34). Finally, Stoneman finds support in his regression results for both the Papanek and Griffin views. His results show that aid is a major contributor to growth (far more so in Latin America than Papanek's figures reveal), but also that growth is negatively correlated with overall capital inflow when account is taken of foreign capital stock accumulation (1975:17).

If this brief summary of the conclusions of some of the major studies carried out to test the relationship between aid, savings and growth reveals anything, it is surely the ambiguous nature of the results. The cross-country evidence would thus appear to provide no firm resolution of the theoretical debates about aid's overall impact on recipient economies. But it would be premature to conclude that this ambiguity provides equal support for the views of the critics and advocates of aid, or that the issue of aid effectiveness at the macroeconomic level can be resolved by totting up and balancing the results of the different analyses revealing positive, negative or neutral consequences. Indeed, delving deeper into the issues indicates the partial nature of the statistical models used, and hence their serious inadequacies for testing the impact of foreign aid.

Setting aside the (major) problem of data quality, there are three crucial difficulties with using these studies to prove or disprove aid effectiveness at the macro-level. All three have been raised in the literature: they centre around causality, verifiability and comparability. The comparability issue concerns what precisely one is comparing the effects of aid with: if one is trying to examine the contribution that aid makes to a recipient economy, then the crucial comparison would be the performance of that economy with aid and its performance in the absence of aid flows over the same period. Comparing the performance of economies that use aid with those that do not, or comparing the performance of the same economies with aid at one period of time and without aid at another, is but a proxy for knowing the circumstances of specific economies in the same time periods with or without aid. Clearly what we would wish to test cannot be tested in practice; yet the fact that the crucially important test cannot be made is far too frequently overlooked in the debates that ensue on aid effectiveness. In practice, therefore, any test that is constructed to deduce the impact of aid at the macro-level will always be an inaccurate assessment of aid effectiveness.

The issue of verifiability relates to the quality of the data available and the nature of the tests conducted. Mention has already been made of contradictory results achieved by researchers attempting to rework the data of other researchers and frequently coming up with different results. Papanek, for example, compares the results of tests on capital inflow and savings for the same countries in the same time period carried out by Weisskopf, Chenery, Griffin and Areskong and shows that the impact of foreign inflows on investment varies among these studies from 11 per cent to 77 per cent (1972:940–1). The fact that these sorts of problems have occurred with such frequency in the aid/growth/savings literature (I have found references to at least ten data reworkings that have produced contradictory results) throws open the question of the scientific rigour of the conclusions drawn. For as Lipton observed over ten years ago (though few appear to have responded to his remarks), if, as happens, secondary sources specify data and primary sources incompletely, then quantitative results cannot be interpersonally falsified – the only criterion for their scientific validity (1972:159).

The major difficulty with deducing particular conclusions from the results of the various regression analyses that have been carried out revolves, however, around the question of *causality*. As both Lipton and Papanek have convincingly argued (and their arguments have not been refuted), the fact that a relationship is found to exist between measured variables provides no *a priori* reason for deducing that a linked association is necessarily proof of causality or of the direction of the supposed causality. In short, to show that aid inflows are associated with stagnant growth or with a declining savings ratio is no proof that it was aid that on its own and unambiguously caused the observed resulting effects. In characteristic style, Lipton makes the following point (1972:168):

> Merely to reiterate correlations, before the direction of causation or even the definition of variables has been clarified, is . . . to risk 'falsisms'. There is little difference between 'coffee puts you to sleep because (since one observes that it is taken when people feel sleepy) it has a *virtus dormitiva*' and 'foreign capital retards growth because, suitably defined, it flows in while saving and growth are low'.

Indeed, recent work on Kenya by Duncan and Mosley (1985) suggests that donors put more aid into the country as a consequence of poor economic performance.

For Papanek, the results of analyses showing that greater foreign resource inflow occurs at the same time as lower savings ratios and lower aggregate growth are achieved prove nothing. He explains that a deteriorating economic and political environment may well be the cause, pinpointing four influences that will set off these sorts of results: wars and political disturbances, variations in the terms of trade, the effects of the weather and other exogenous variables, and finally whether recipients are high-saving or low-saving societies. The argument is of course two-edged. Papanek has put forward a strong case for concluding that the negative effects found by the critics to be associated with aid inflow do not prove that aid's impact is detrimental to recipients. However, the same general perspective could, equally well, be utilised by the critics to argue that Papanek's data could in the same way be affected by other factors which influence the virtuous results that these data and their associations reveal, or simply that, if the macro-conditions are so adverse, why give aid at all – a point recently highlighted in the debate about aid and structural adjustment.

The debate about causality has been fruitful in one general respect, in that it has led to a far more hard-headed reflection on the whole nature of the methodology of quantitative testing through multiple regression analysis. As even Papanek is ready to admit, not only could statistically significant relationships be quite unrelated to causality, but they could also be due to a mis-specification of the model used, and correlations could be the result of excluding variables from the regression equation (1973:129). More recent studies have indicated that the model-building implicit in the earlier analyses was crude in the extreme, as revealed particularly in the Gupta and Islam (1983) study.

One problem, highlighted first by Heller, is that aid recipients are almost certainly not growth-maximisers to the exclusion of all other goals. This insight has been extended by Mosley and Hudson, who have argued that, in common with their counterparts in advanced countries, aid-recipient governments have complex welfare objectives which include growth maximisation but not to the exclusion of other goals. This has led to extending the number of independent variables in the multiple regression equation so as to capture the influences of additional variables which are now seen as crucial. The effects on analysis are twofold: to the extent that other variables are influential in affecting growth, then aid's influence becomes thereby reduced; secondly the coefficients of the simpler models (with fewer variables) will have tended to be biased. But one can only go on adding variables at a price, and one price is the assumption of linearity. Multiple regression analysis established to test the aid/savings/growth relationship has assumed (but not proved) that the relationship to be tested is a straight-lined one. Another problem, always present with two or more 'independent variables', is whether one can be certain that there is no interrelationship between them; if there is, then the multi-collinearity resulting will again bias the results produced.

It is more serious still for these simple models if there is, in addition, an interrelationship between the dependent and independent variables, for this cannot easily be captured in a simple multiple regression equation. Mosley (1980) suggests that using a single equation model by ordinary least squares is inappropriate because such a model assumes that the variables in the right-hand side of the equation are not endogenous to the process under examination. He argues, on the contrary, that aid both influences and is influenced by the recipient country's level of income, which is why he opts for a two-stage least squares method.

But even this approach is not without its own problems. Mosley's statistical testing, in common with all pre-1980 work, concentrates solely on the direct effects of the independent variables on the dependent variables. For Gupta and Islam, these models are unsatisfactory because second-round indirect effects are also seen to be crucial in affecting changes in the variables. The fact that their use of simultaneous equations (to attempt to capture these indirect effects) produces a relationship *twice* as significant as single equation models does indicate that the point they are making could well be important. Finally, the saving ---> investment ---> growth link is itself built on the assumption of a smooth progressive relationship between these variables. However, work by Matthews, for example, indicates that significant increases in output can arise not only by increasing the quantities of inputs but also by improving their quality such that growth needs to be measured in terms of total factor productivity as well as total factor incomes. And Nelson has shown that, with increasing rates of unemployment, capital inputs have operated at less than the rate assumed at higher levels of employment (1964:595). To the extent that these influences are significant the simple links between the variables assumed in most models will be incorrectly specified.

The complexity of the various economic variables and their potential inter-relationship is illustrated by a summary conclusion at the end of the study by Gupta and Islam (1983:129):

> Using the simultaneous equations model, we have shown that foreign capital affects saving and growth both directly, as shown in the single equation models, but also indirectly, because of the interdependence between savings and growth. We have further shown that the total effect, which consists of both the direct and the indirect effects, may be different from the direct effect both in terms of the magnitude, and sometimes even more significant, in terms of the direction (that is, the sign of the *total* and the *direct* effects may be opposite).

However, for some analysts even this attempt to widen the influence of the different variables is still incomplete. For example, Stoneman (1975:12) and Seers (1963:84) argue that both the independent and dependent variables are themselves crucially affected by trends in the world economy, thus implying that ignoring world cyclical changes, for example, will fail to capture crucial factors in the variables to be measured. Indeed, there would be few who would challenge the World Bank's view that the 1979–82 world recession, deepened by policies in the industrialised countries to reverse the trend of rising inflation levels, has had a profound effect on Third World growth rates.

Most of these questions raised about the simple models constructed to attempt to test the relationship between aid, savings and growth concern the types of variables that are central to mainstream economic theory. But there are others which focus on social, political and structural variables which can affect the economic variables and how they might change over time. Dowling and Hiemenz (1983) add four variables to the multiple regression equation in the attempt to capture the influence of different aspects of government policy in each country: the degree of openness of the economy, the role of government in domestic resource mobilisation, the share of the public sector in economic activities, and the degree of financial repression. Gupta and Islam include the following variables to attempt to capture aspects of the whole development process that are thought to be influential in affecting the growth-specific variables: the dependency rate; the birth rate; female labour force participation; the infant mortality rate; per capita energy consumption; total labour force participation; population density; the literacy rate; the proportion of the labour force engaged in agriculture; the number of persons per hospital bed; and the growth rate of the labour force (1983:65).

More radical still in its implications for testing the effects of aid on macro-economic variables is the work of Venieris and Gupta (1983), which sets out to examine the effects of socio-political influences on developing economies and finds them to be profound and far-reaching. Their study indicates that there are substantial differences in growth rates between developing countries due to various degrees of political instability and these can lead to a 40-year variation between countries achieving a $20 per capita increase in GDP. The implication is that without capturing the influence of socio-political influences, changes in economic variables will remain seriously incomplete. It is Reynolds, however, who provides the most radical critique of economic modelling and variable testing. In an article reviewing the spread of economic growth in Third World countries in the past 130 years, he concludes that the single most important indicator of variations in growth among less developed countries is 'political organisation and the adminis-trative competence of government' (1983:976). One need not, however, go to this extreme to question the ability of models to explain the complete pattern of cause and effect among different variables. For, as Robert Lucas argues, any change in government policy can alter the entire structure of an economic model, not just those bits where the policy features explicitly.[14]

Moving from the specification of the models used to the results of the tests carried out, what is striking is that in a large majority of cases – and including those that have been influential in the literature – the degree to which aid and other 'independent' variables inserted in the models have been able to explain changes in economic growth has been far from comprehensive. This weak associa-tion has been derived by both critics and advocates of aid. For example, Griffin and Enos base their conclusions on three tests. The first shows a *positive* aid–growth link for 15 African and Asian countries, significant at the 10 per cent level (r^2 = 0.33). The second shows a *negative* correlation for 12 Latin American countries, but not even significant at the 10 per cent level (r^2 = 0.13). The third gives the implausible result that in Turkey from 1957 to 1964 deprivation of aid would have produced 12.5 per cent annual growth. Reviewing 17 pre-1972 tests, Lipton concludes that 'the only quantitative links remotely credible in respect of overall growth indicated and significant statistically . . . show a positive, though weak, association between growth and aid'. However, he is, correctly, sceptical of the results proving anything: 'Given the small aid/GNP ratios of most poor countries, the weakness of the indicators chosen for the regression, and the fami-liar deficiencies of the GNP data, the capacity of regressions to suggest even this is rather surprising' (1972:164).

Results from straightforward multiple regression tests carried out subsequently provide little more assurance of firm and incontestable conclusions. Papanek's equations for the 1950s and 1960s covering 85 observations indicate aid having a coefficient nearly twice that of other independent variables (0.39 to 0.47 in differ-ent equations), although his r^2 values for the growth equations range from 0.02 to a high of only 0.46. Clearly there is a significant element of growth which is unexplained, and whose influence on aid or other variables is not discussed. Yet not even Papanek is convinced his aggregate results prove too much, for he recently commented that 'there is no simple relationship between aid and growth' (1983:177). Even in Asia where a number of studies have indicated a firmer rela-tionship between aid and growth, the results that have been published still leave substantial gaps. For example, Dowling and Hiemenz's analysis of 52 Asian countries using their extended growth equation reveals that the variables employed explain only about 50 per cent of the changes in growth. Here again far too much is left unexplained to draw firm and conclusive implications for the causes of growth, let alone the precise influence that aid has in the overall growth process.

A far more rigorous approach, although one that ignores lags in the direct influence of aid and capital inflows, is that carried out by Gupta and Islam. In contrast with most straightforward multiple regression tests, the Gupta and Islam method incorporates direct and indirect consequences of foreign capital inflow, allows for interdependence of the variables, incorporates a wide variety of social and structural variables, treats savings and growth as jointly dependent variables,

Table 10.2:   *Direct and Total Effect of Capital Inflows on the Savings Rate – Gupta and Islam's Results (1983)*

Sample	Direct Effect			Total Effect		
	AID	FPI	RFI	AID	FPI	RFI
Total Sample (n = 52)	–0.6851	–0.1912	–1.3019	–0.4681	–0.0069	–1.1204
Income Groups						
I	–0.3433	–0.1590	0.1594	0.6942	1.3078	0.9408
II	1.4213	–0.1146	–1.4620	1.5390	–0.2148	–1.3368
III	–0.2428	0.0067	–0.1795	–2.2163	0.1761	–1.7722
Regional Groups						
Asia	–2.5920	–0.6104	–1.3580	–2.0051	1.2066	–0.1299
Africa	–0.4415	–0.1032	–1.7148	–0.3606	–6.6967	–1.2605
Latin America	0.2865	0.0457	–0.4360	0.3280	0.0840	0.3583

Notes: AID = net transfers received by governments, plus official long-term borrowing as a percentage of GNP.

FPI = Foreign private investment, including private long-term borrowing plus net private direct investment as a percentage of GNP.

RFI = Other foreign inflows, which include net private transfers, net short-term borrowing, other capital (net) and errors and omissions in the balance of payments as a percentage of GNP.

Income Group I = *per capita* annual income less than $300.
II = *per capita* annual income from $301 to $600.
III = *per capita* annual income greater than $600.

Source: Gupta and Islam, 1983: 91.

introduces an error term to account for omitted variables, uses a growth model that takes explicit account of the stage of economic development achieved, divides capital inflow into three components – aid, foreign private investment and other foreign inflows (à la Papanek), and splits up the (small) grouping of 52 countries into three different income groups and regionally, treating Africa, Asia and Latin America separately. While the general problems of data reliability apply equally to the Gupta and Islam results, the methodology used is a significant improvement on past tests and, in passing, highlights the oversimplified nature of many of the previous tests. Of the many results of Gupta and Islam's tests which are of considerable interest, the two most important summary tables are reproduced here. Table 10.2 shows the results for capital inflows on domestic savings and Table 10.3 the results for different types of capital inflow on the growth rate of recipient countries. The tables record both the direct results (derived from nine multiple regression equations) and the indirect results (derived from solving the various equations simultaneously). Not without importance, too, is the fact that the r^2 value for their growth equation for the complete sample is 0.49, ranging from 0.25 for Latin America to 0.93 for Africa. For different income groups their model explains more than twice the variation captured, for example, by Papanek's equation (1983:52).

The results shown in the tables are of major interest to the debate about the effect of aid and other capital inflows on domestic saving and economic growth. They

Table 10.3:   *Direct and Total Effect of Capital Inflows on the Growth Rate of Developing*
Countries – Gupta and Islam's Results (1983)

Sample	Direct Effect			Total Effect		
	AID	FPI	RFI	AID	FPI	RFI
Total Sample	0.3001	0.1604	0.4417	0.1776	0.1622	1.1486
Income Groups						
I	0.3974	0.4784	0.1851	0.5691	0.8018	0.4089
II	–0.1790	–0.1483	0.6260	0.2435	–0.2073	0.2590
III	0.9916	0.1091	0.6448	0.2144	0.1709	0.0233
Regional Groups						
Asia	1.0338	0.6004	0.3563	0.3306	1.0236	–0.0581
Africa	0.1380	0.0380	0.5430	0.0285	–1.9968	0.1601
Latin America	0.1338	0.1302	0.2796	0.1435	0.1327	0.2690

Source: *Ibid.*

reveal the degree of complexity of the interrelationships of the variables: as one moves from direct to indirect effects, not only do the co-ordinates change in value but not infrequently there is a sign change. Thus, isolating particular results, one could find support for the following contradictory conclusions: that capital inflows have a negative or a positive effect on saving; that aid has a negative or a positive effect on domestic saving; that aid has a positive or a negative effect on economic growth; that aid has a greater or smaller effect on economic growth than other inflows of capital. In general, Gupta and Islam observe that the results one obtains from quantitative testing are very sensitive to the form of equation used, and the level and type of sample disaggregation. In addition, they find that the savings function component is structurally far more unstable than the growth function.

Gupta and Islam's work analyses not only the influence of external factors on domestic growth but also those internal to recipient economies, including social and structural factors, in part by examining various elasticity multipliers. Of considerable interest is what they term 'the most important policy conclusion' derived from their study, because it gives support to *both* the Chenery/Papanek and the Griffin view. They write thus (1983:134):

> Although foreign capital has a positive role to play, capital accumulation from internal sources remains by far the most significant determinant of growth in developing countries. Consequently if these countries wish to achieve rapid economic growth, maximum efforts will have to be directed towards domestic saving rates. This may involve difficult choices and necessitate tough and even unpleasant policies, but there is no escaping the implication that reliance on foreign capital does not offer the solution for high and rapid growth.

Concluding remarks
At the theoretical level, there are a variety of different scenarios one can outline which suggest that the effect of aid on domestic saving could range from positive and highly significant to negative and highly significant, dependent upon the different assumptions made. Hence, without assessing the appropriateness of these assumptions to conditions in the real world, no *a priori* judgement can be made about the nature of the contribution that aid will make to domestic savings

levels. That additional foreign resources, including aid, make a positive contribution to a recipient economy (if only by raising levels of consumption) and hence have a positive effect on economic growth has not been seriously disputed by the critics at the theoretical level, although even here it is possible to make assumptions which could lead to a negative outcome. Thus, in general the strength of foreign aid theory and the opposing views of the different critics depends upon the appropriateness of the assumptions made.

The debate about assumptions, however, has led to changes in the context within which foreign aid theory has been put forward. Two significant changes need to be mentioned: one, the incorporation of possible consumption-leakage into the original Chenery-Strout model; the other, the recognition that assumptions about the role of recipient governments acting to maximise growth need to be questioned, if not revised. Both considerably weaken traditional theory as a predictor of a particular positive outcome and highlight the need to assess the evidence to resolve the theoretical controversies and the different assumptions upon which they are built.

The cross-country tests run to analyse the impact of aid at the macro-level have to date provided no series of consistent results to resolve the theoretical debate. Some show that aid leads to a significant increase in domestic savings levels and to higher rates of economic growth and others show the opposite effects – at different time periods for different groups of countries divided geographically and by income-group classification.

The ambiguity of these results raises two fundamental questions. First, whether the tests have been accurate enough to deduce firm conclusions and whether they are ever likely to do so. Second, whether accurate testing will itself provide the results necessary to clinch the argument. There are strong grounds for doubt in both cases. All the early cross-country studies – and particularly those used as a basis for defending or attacking aid flows – are open to serious criticisms that question their accuracy and reliability. These criticisms centre around widespread data inaccuracy, model mis-specification, inappropriate isolation of interrelated variables, particularly due to exclusion of critical variables that there is no good reason for omitting, and the need to consider the important and often crucial influences that social, political and structural factors have on the expected relationship between economic variables. The more recent and more complex models suffer from almost all the past problems of data inaccuracy, which alone throws doubt on their conclusions. But, in addition, they reveal the complexity of the relationship between aid inflow and economic growth and the difficulty of tracing through particular causal relationships when other internal and external variables (often interrelated) can have a decisive effect on the variables one is attempting to isolate. Most importantly, however, these recent studies highlight the fact that different *policy choices* are highly likely to alter the variables being measured and their relationship to one another. This indicates that, even if the data were sufficiently accurate to run sophisticated tests, the fact that it could be shown that aid did or did not raise domestic saving levels or did or did not contribute to growth would not provide the evidence required to conclude that aid *necessarily* contributed to the growth of recipient economies. Indeed, the fact that the most technically satisfactory tests by Gupta and Islam pointed to different outcomes in different circumstances and highlighted the crucial nature of policy changes in effecting different outcomes suggests that to attempt to *prove* that aid does or does not assist recipient economies is akin to trying to locate the end of the rainbow.

But this conclusion by no means has to be a cause for grave concern for the donor community, as, for example, Mosley and Hudson believe, having found it 'impossible to establish a statistically significant correlation between aid and growth of GNP, the presence of published results to the contrary notwithstanding' (1984:31). What the evolution of more intricate (and hence mostly more satisfactory) models of aid and economic growth have achieved over the past 20-30 years is an appreciation of the great complexity of the relationships involved and the key role of policy variables within recipient countries for affecting an improved use of resources, domestic and foreign, and the constraints inhibiting such changes. And this should lead to a greater understanding of how external and internal circumstances can change or be changed either to further aid effectiveness or to pinpoint why particular aid to particular countries at particular times is contributing very little if anything to the recipient country's economic growth.

It has already been stressed, at the beginning of this chapter, that foreign aid theory asserts neither that aid is necessary for economic growth nor that it is a sufficient condition. What this discussion of the debate about aid theory and the cross-country tests has attempted is to pinpoint with greater accuracy those constraints inhibiting aid's favourable impact in raising growth rates in recipient countries. And to the extent that Griffin *et al* or Mosley are correct in pointing out the circumstances in which aid leads to a fall in domestic savings ratio, and why this outcome occurs, their studies, too, contribute to our understanding of aid effectiveness at the macro-level.

There are, however, critics for whom the whole aid/savings/growth debate is irrelevant either because of the belief that economic growth, with or without aid, does not result in economic development and the alleviation of poverty or because of the belief that aid intervention inhibits more rapid growth in poor countries. It is to these debates that we now turn.

Notes

1. Bauer's ridiculing of the case for aid is illustrated in his 1984 book *Reality and Rhetoric*. He writes '. . . new arguments for aid sprout with regularity . . . since 1980, yet another argument for foreign aid has become prominent. According to this, without continuing or additional aid, Third World debtors would default on their obligations to Western banks, which would lead to financial crisis or even collapse. . . . This argument is the latest in a long line of rationalisations for foreign aid. It will not be the last' (1984:59–60). He continues in a footnote thus: 'Professor Harold Rose has suggested that prediction of prospective new arguments for aid would make an interesting quasi-academic parlour game' (*ibid*:168).

2. Major non-country-specific statistical testing of the variables has been carried out or reviewed in the following publications: Griffin (1970), Griffin and Enos (1971), Weisskopf (1972), Papanek (1972), (1973), (1983), Heller (1975), Dacy (1975), Mosley (1980), Mosley and Hudson (1984), Lipton (1972), Dowling and Hiemenz (1983), Gualti (1978), Gupta (1975), Gupta and Islam (1983), World Bank (1968), Stoneman (1975), Mickesell and Zinser (1973), Crosswell (1981), Kraska and Taira (1974), Rahman (1968), Robinson (1971), Bornschier, Chase-Dunn and Rubinson (1978), Grinols and Bhagwati (1976), Krueger and Ruttan (1983), Massell, Pearson and Fitch (1975), Reynolds (1983), Landau (1966), Chenery (1979).

3. Beenstock comments thus: 'ODA does not take account of the grant element that is brought about when inflation lowers the real value of developing-country indebtedness. In any year, inflation will reduce the real value of the repayment stream on existing loans; indeed, it is most probably the case that inflation has greatly eased the debt burden of developing countries in recent years. Thus, loans outstanding from the past which might not even have been considered as ODA at the time of their inception would become concessionary if inflation grew sufficiently. For example a 2 year loan at

8 per cent incurred in 1966 would not have counted as ODA in 1966 because the grant element was not sufficiently high. If, however, by, say, 1973, the rate of inflation has risen by six annual points, the real grant element on the balance of the loan will have risen; it would be as if the rate of interest had been reduced from 8 to 12 per cent, which would be sufficient to generate a sufficiently large grant element. However, the present ODA formula does not reflect such inflation accounting.' (1980:138).

4. See, for example, *Financial Times*, 10 July 1985.

5. In the DAC publication *Geographical Distribution of Financial Flows to Developing Countries* (1984) the table on p. 4 is entitled 'Net Disbursements of ODA from All Sources Combined To Individual Recipients'. Yet the data for this table are derived from those recorded in the series of individual country tables which provide bilateral aid from DAC countries.

6. Kreditanstalt für Wiederaufbau, *Annual Report For The Year 1984*, Frankfurt am Main, June 1984, p. 67.

7. Overseas Development Administration, *British Aid Statistics 1979–1983*, ODA, London, Table 18.

8. The full definition is as follows:
   AID: The word 'aid' or 'assistance' refers only to flows which qualify as official development assistance (ODA), i.e. grants or loans:
   – undertaken by the official sector;
   –with promotion of economic development and welfare as main objectives;
   – at concessional financial terms (if a loan, at least 25 per cent grant element).
   In addition to financial flows, technical co-operation is included in aid. It comprises grants (and a very small volume of loans) to nationals of developing countries receiving education or training at home or abroad, and to defray the costs of teachers, administrators, advisers and similar personnel serving in developing countries.' (OECD, 1984:188).

9. Quoted in *The Commission on Security and Economic Assistance, A Report To The Secretary of State*, (The Carlucci Commission), Washington, November 1983, p. 21.

10. But even this point is oversimplified. Aid channelled to direct consumption end-use could, in part, release other domestic resources to raise domestic savings and investment levels. The extent to which different outcomes result in practice in particular countries is frequently eclipsed in broad cross-country analyses.

11. The classic text on data errors and unreliability remains O. Morgenstern, *On the Accuracy of Economic Observations*, Princeton University Press, Princeton, 1963. Recent discussion of inaccurate biases in GDP estimates especially of low-income countries includes I.B. Kravis, 'Comparative Studies of National Income and Prices', and R. Marris, 'Comparing the Incomes of Nations', *Journal of Economic Literature*, Vol. XXII, No. 1, March 1984, pp. 1–57.

12. Griffin does state in passing that 'increased investment is neither necessary nor sufficient to achieve a high rate of growth in an underdeveloped country' (100). However, this comment is not central to the main thrust of his article and so will not be discussed here. It will be taken up later.

13. For example, Mosley and Hudson (1984) reworked Papanek's 1972 data and obtained different, and less favourable, results.

14. *The Economist*, 15 December 1984.

11 Criticisms from the Radical Left

We now shift our attention away from the narrowly-focused debate about aid and its effects on levels of saving and aggregate economic growth to those criticisms of foreign aid for which this debate fails to address what are seen as more fundamental issues. For the radical critics on the left, it is not growth *per se* which is the problem to be analysed but the type of growth that is achieved or attempted. Because, it is argued, the pattern of growth that the insertion of aid into the recipient economy attempts to promote does not lead to recognisable benefits in economic development – and particularly highlighted are the effects on poverty alleviation and income and asset distribution – its positive value is undermined, no matter if aid leads to an addition to national saving, an increase in foreign exchange or a rise in the growth rate. For some critics, the outcome is judged to be so detrimental to the poor in recipient countries that foreign aid inserted into recipient economies within the present environment cannot be viewed as a beneficial force at all. For others, this absolute conclusion is rejected, because it is acknowledged that some benefits may result; however, for these critics the beneficial outcome can be only marginal. It is swamped by the more dominant negative results which, it is judged, the insertion of aid achieves or promotes.

Whatever the varying strength of these types of criticisms, they share a common framework which is to widen the issue of aid effectiveness beyond technical macroeconomic and quantifiable relationships associated with 'growth theory' to a consideration of quantifiable relationships that attempt to capture patterns of poverty and distribution and, relatedly, social and political aspects of the development process. The central question is thus not 'does aid promote economic growth in aid-recipient countries?' but 'who gains and who loses in the process of economic growth that is promoted?' In drawing the conclusion that aid tends to (or does) harm the poor, the critics focus their analysis on the following parameters: the internal structures of recipient economies, the manner in which external forces act upon and react with different strata and sub-strata within recipient economies, and the role of the state and political forces both within recipient countries and as these interact with external governmental political forces.

That these factors (or some of them) are important in analysing the impact of aid on recipients and that their relevance extends beyond the radical leftist critics of aid has been, at least implicitly, recognised by aid donors themselves. Three concerns among aid donors can be highlighted in this respect. The prominence given to addressing basic needs and to the direct alleviation of poverty in the 1970s (discussed in Chapter 9) was an implicit acknowledgement of the failure of models of development which linked development exclusively to economic growth to address all the issues deemed to be of relevance to the aid debate. In this respect, the following statement by Robert McNamara, former chairman of the World

Bank in an address to the Board of Governors in September 1972 marks a watershed in conventional thinking:

> Increases in national income – essential as they are – will not benefit the poor unless they reach the poor. They have not reached the poor to any significant degree in most developing countries in the past, and this in spite of historically unprecedented average rates of growth throughout the sixties.

While the swing back in the 1980s to a concern for growth has lessened the visibility of redistribution questions among certain donors, the prominence now given to policy dialogue and the role of donor governments as a crucial determinant of aid effectiveness is an implicit acknowledgement that orthodox modernisation theories of development which ignore the role of recipient governments in the aid process are inadequate. And thirdly, growing recognition of the fact that prospects for Third World development are intricately bound up with the performance of the industrialised world and directly affected by world trade and growth levels, the degree of protectionism, and the pattern and prospects for international financial flows, indicates acceptance of the view that external factors are a crucial element in assessing Third World development prospects. It would thus seem that, contrary to the view which would maintain that the areas of analysis highlighted by the leftist critics of aid are at bottom irrelevant to the debate about aid effectiveness, the issues raised by them are now widely accepted as important. Indeed, one can probably go even further and say that the crucial discussion and analysis of the whole process of development and aid's role in this process owes much to the force of the leftist criticisms over the past two decades.

There is, however, a crucial difference between, on the one hand, placing the issues of the role of the state, internal and external structures, and their dynamic interaction on the agenda for consideration (and acknowledging their influence and importance) and, on the other hand, concluding that the effects of these influences preclude or substantially prevent aid's ever being able to assist in poverty alleviation in recipient countries.

When the aid debate broadens beyond an exclusive concern for growth to consider aid's role in the process of development, the pro-aid camp makes a number of virtuous assumptions. These include: that the recipient state is able and willing to use its power and influence to promote a pattern of development beneficial to the poor under its jurisdiction, that internal and external forces either interact to assist in this process or, at minimum, are incapable of providing insuperable impediments, and that in general aid is a force or influence capable of assisting dynamic development.

Critics from the radical left, however, maintain that the recipient state either is not able or will not choose to use its power and influence to promote a pattern of development beneficial to the poor under its jurisdiction. They argue, too, that internal and external forces interact to reinforce malevolent structural rigidity, thereby impeding the effect of benign social and economic forces that could lead to national development and substantial and effective poverty alleviation. Within this perspective, aid can be viewed as part of the problem – because it helps to reinforce negative dynamic forces frustrating development – or, for some leftist critics, as largely irrelevant because the critical factor in promoting development is seen as power relations rather than insufficient resources. In either case, aid is placed in a theoretical context which rejects the assertion that it can and probably does do good.

The fact that both sides in the debate are ready to acknowledge that, in terms of aggregate development performance, the contribution that aid can make will never tend to be large means that broadening the debate to a discussion of aid's role in the overall development process rapidly leads to the more substantial debate about overall development strategy and policy. Different conclusions about aid effectiveness are derived directly from different theoretical perspectives concerning the state, the origins and causes of underdevelopment, the perceived beneficial or harmful effects of capitalist development upon developing countries, and the distribution of benefits resulting from such development.

It is clearly beyond the scope of the present study to provide an in-depth analysis of all these wider issues. The discussion in this chapter is more limited in scope. It will attempt to do three things. First, to outline briefly the main criticisms of aid made by leftist critics. Secondly, to discuss and evaluate the different theories and perspectives of development from which these criticisms are derived. And, finally, to draw some conclusions about the leftist criticisms and their ability to challenge effectively the conventional view that aid can be a positive influence in recipient countries.

The criticisms outlined

Leftist critics of foreign aid can be grouped into two distinct, although related, categories: the institutional pessimists and the structural theorists.[1] The institutional pessimists focus their attention on recipient governments and, for a variety of reasons, conclude that the interplay of power and economic interests prevents them from utilising the aid provided in a manner conducive to poverty alleviation in their countries.

The structural theorists agree with the institutional pessimists that state structures and recipient governments are a major impediment to aid effectiveness but their analysis is both wider, usually international in scope, and historical. For them, aid is part of a structural relationship between rich and poor countries which has evolved over time to underdevelop the Third World. Rich country objectives are primarily and overwhelmingly to use poor countries to further their own economic interests. Rich countries are able to achieve these objectives by allying themselves with the dominant economic groups in recipient countries; these groups strengthen their own economic power by furthering the links already established between themselves and the rich countries. This they can do because the dominant economic groups control political power in the Third World. The existing international politico-economic structure provides economic benefit to the industrialised countries, which ultimately control and guide it, and to the elites in the Third World who gain economically and politically from its evolution. Obversely, it provides little material benefit to the mass of poor people in the Third World who are effectively excluded from achieving or obtaining political power in their countries and for whom poverty and exploitation remain the socio-economic result of this overall process.

As aid is part of this wider and dominant relationship between the developed and developing world it is incapable of addressing and alleviating the poverty of the developing world in a systematic and effective way. Rather it is seen as part of the problem. Within this perspective, if aid is shown to be assisting the poor in particular parts of aid-recipient countries at particular times, this outcome is viewed as extremely partial and is usually assessed as providing specific relief to ameliorate the excesses of the system, and perhaps to counter incipient political unrest which, in its absence, would effectively challenge the power of the elites.

It should be noted that the conclusion of the structural theorists that the development process fails to help the poor is not a conclusion exclusive to those who incorporate it into a systematic world view of underdevelopment. There are, as we shall see, other critics – and even friends – of aid who assert that rapid economic growth does not help the poor. For some, the answer to this problem is to place greater emphasis on redistribution to accompany growth strategies; for others a fundamental and radical restructuring of wealth and assets is required. It is this latter group which provides a radical challenge to the conventional pro-aid perspective.

Influential among the institutional pessimists are Seers and Myrdal. Their criticisms of aid are based on two negative assessments of recipient governments and recipient states. They assert, first, that much aid is frittered away through corruption and, secondly and more substantially, that the aim of Third World rulers, as we saw in Chapter 5, 'is not to relieve poverty, rather the contrary, to make sure that the incomes of the masses are kept low and social services retarded' (1982). This conclusion has been derived from a number of early writings of Myrdal, whose concern about the less than altruistic nature of Third World governments and administrations led him to coin the phrase and analyse the weaknesses of 'the soft state'.[2] In addition, Seers and Myrdal challenge the distributional consequence of expanding present patterns of growth, arguing that where economic growth has been rapid it has rarely been of much benefit to the poor (1982).

Lappé and her colleagues agree with the Seers and Myrdal pessimistic conclusions about the state and extend this to a discussion of power relations within recipient countries. They assert that recipient governments 'represent narrow, elite economic interests' (1980:11), that the poor lack political power, and that the crucial issue for development is 'for the poor to achieve the power they need to direct a development process in their interests' (12). Official aid, they conclude, cannot help because it 'reinforces the power relationships that already exist' (11). As for the additional resources provided as aid, they argue 'that additional resources are usually not needed to eliminate hunger' (11). What is needed is 'a correct diagnosis of the root causes of hunger – a diagnosis that puts control over resources in the central position' (13).

In a more rigorously argued critique Mende, too, pinpoints the deficiencies of the state in developing countries and the fundamental requirement of mobilising mass support as the key to meaningful development. Aid, he views as a diversion from the main task at hand. He writes thus (1973:92):

> The new ruling groups represent only small urban elites and lack the means of communicating with the masses. They cannot mobilize their people. Yet to do so is an indispensable prerequisite of the mobilization of internal resources. Unable to do this, they are deprived of the major instrument of development and so become proportionately more dependent upon the other far less importance components: exports and aid.

It is, however, in the writings of authors like Jalée (1968), Hayter (1971 and 1981), Wood (1980), Carty and Smith (1981) and Hayter and Watson (1985) that one finds the most complete account of the structural theorists' critique of foreign aid. Writing within a Leninist 'framework, Jalée places the aid relationship in the context of imperialist exploitation.[3] According to his analysis, imperialism has shaped the pattern of production in the Third World for the satisfaction of its own needs and without regard for the needs of the inhabitants (1968:39), so that Third World poverty is not so much an original state but rather the result of imperialist plunder (19). For Jalée, aid is part of the process of imperialist exploitation. Distinguishing between bilateral and multilateral aid, he considers the former to be of greater importance. It brings, he argues, 'political servitude and economic subjection. It is given, received and applied in such a way as to strengthen business circles in the country giving it and the local oligarchies in the country receiving it' (83). Less directly, he adds, multilateral aid is designed to support the broad policy and interests of the imperialist camp in a general way (69).

Writing from a similar perspective, Hayter places aid within the wider structural relationships of the world capitalist system, arguing that it 'can be explained only in terms of an attempt to preserve the capitalist system in the Third World' (1971:9). Aid is a form of exploitation and its contribution to the well-being of the peoples of the Third World is negative. It can be seen 'as a means of maintaining, especially after the loss of colonies, a common interest between the elites of underdeveloped countries and the metropolitan countries, or as a kind of bribe to help make it worth their while to continue to co-operate with the drain of capital from their countries' (1971:83). It is also clear, she continues, that, however good or bad individual projects may be, they can never do much without changes in central government policies (92). Similar views are expressed in her most recent book written with Watson. Here the authors explain that much aid fails to alleviate poverty because its overall purpose is the preservation of a system that damages the interests of the poor in the Third World (1985:1). Capitalism and capitalist development provide no solution to Third World poverty, they argue, and aid cannot help, even if it is targeted to the poor, because it is channelled through Third World governments, the majority of which are authoritarian, often military, regimes, of a brutally repressive nature (239 and 250). Governments, they continue (252):

> have many ways of frustrating the supposed purpose of aid (directed to the poorest), either deliberately or merely from lack of concern to ensure that it reaches its 'target' and is not lost in corruption etc. along the way. Such governments derive their power from the support of rural land-owning classes and urban elites; they have no interest in disrupting rural systems of power and patronage or in any diminution of the exploitation of the rural and urban poor. Most aid officials will testify to such difficulties . . . The policy is unworkable.

For Wood, aid also needs to be analysed within the parameters of a global perspective, especially if one wishes to understand the role of the state and the impact of aid upon it in underdeveloped countries (1980:5). Because foreign aid offers the possibility of releasing the recipient state from the need to extract the economic surplus it requires totally from domestic sources, one might expect it to increase the state's relative autonomy and thereby facilitate statist patterns of development. But this does not happen. For one thing, the aid agencies constitute a powerful system of social control 'limiting one type of development and promoting another' (2). What is fostered is the 'structural dependence of the state on processes of private accumulation' which 'encourages a form of integration into the capitalist world economy that prepares a way for penetration by international capital' (6). Furthermore, foreign aid and private capital inflows are not, as might be assumed, two distinct and separate sources of additional finance; rather they are complementary and reinforcing. While this in part is the result of donor policy, it is also, according to Wood, a reflection of state policy within recipient countries. Thus, the state 'acts as conduit for the formation of a powerful class that uses its state power to develop an independent economic base in society' (31). And, finally, 'reliance on foreign aid contributes to the creation and consolidation of capitalist states in the underdeveloped societies' (33).

The more popularly oriented book by Carty and Smith summarises well the perspective of the structural theorists and their conclusion that aid is 'part of the problem, not the solution to poverty and underdevelopment' (1981:6). They write (11):

> Underdevelopment . . . didn't just 'happen' – nor is it a problem solely generated within the Third World. External forces have substantially created it. In every situation of underdevelopment, there are *underdevelopers* – structures, powers and governments which ride the backs of the southern nations and choke off their development possibilities. The peoples of the Third World are not unfortunates suffering from a deficit of what the advanced capitalist countries can offer them, nor are they poor because the North has neglected them or left them out of the development process. . . . The Third World is trapped in the poverty cycle, not because western countries have failed to commit their capital overseas, but because they are continually draining massive amounts of capital from the South. . . .
>
> Within this analytic framework, development is not so much an economic process as a political one. What the Third World's poor most critically lack is not aid or northern inputs, or even reformist measures labelled a NIEO but *power*. Foreign aid policies that ignore or justify the current power balance between and within nations are integral problems of the underdevelopment problem, not imperfect solutions. Lobbying for this and that aid reform in an attempt to create a more nearly perfect assistance program can divert attention from the central issues. It's like fussing over a flat tire on an automobile with a dead battery.

We return, finally, to those radical writers who challenge the orthodox view that promoting growth without giving attention to wealth and income distribution will ever lead to the alleviation of poverty in Third World countries. The implication of this perspective is that aid which attempts to accelerate growth, or even aid that is targeted towards marginal changes in redistribution through basic needs-type strategies, will ultimately fail to solve the widespread and structural features of poverty that characterise recipient countries.[4] One example, from among many, that adopts such a critical perspective is the lucid contribution by Griffin and Khan. They start with some stark statements (1978:295):

> Development of the type experienced by the majority of Third World countries in the last quarter century has meant, for very large numbers of people, increased impoverishment. Certainly there is no evidence that growth as such has succeeded in reducing the incidence of poverty.

The answer, they conclude, to the question why poverty has increased is not a lack of resources nor a lack of economic growth, but 'has more to do with the structure of the economy' (299). One structural feature is the degree of inequality, and income inequalities lead to the concentration of the surplus in a very few hands. Another is the inequitable distribution of wealth and assets, of which land is a critical component in most developing countries. These factors, together with a fragmented allocative system, 'constitute a socio-economic context in which powerful dynamic forces tend to perpetuate and even accentuate low standards of living of a significant proportion of the rural population' (300). The implication of their analysis is that efforts to alleviate poverty need to confront these structural problems. They pinpoint the interaction of different classes in society and the role of the state as necessary factors to be considered in such an analysis, concluding that a structural understanding of poverty will reveal why 'both micro- and macro-economic tinkering are almost certain to fail. The remedy lies in structural change, in changing the distribution of productive wealth (and consequently the distribution of economic power) and in increasing the participation of the poor in decision-making (and consequently enabling them to exercise political power)' (303).

Radical development theories

It is not so much the assertions of the leftist critics that official development assistance has a negative impact on the poor in recipient countries that concern us here. Of primary interest is the theoretical perspective underlying their assertions, for it is this perspective which provides them with the framework for their generalised and frequently absolutist conclusions about the harmful effects of foreign aid.

Pinpointing this perspective is not an easy task, however. In general, the critics have failed to elaborate in sufficient detail the precise theory of development they are utilising to derive their negative conclusions, and radical theories of development do not unanimously lead to the conclusion that aid is harmful. If aid, for example, is part of the problem rather than a contribution to its solution (Hayter, Lappé et al., Carty and Smith), the problem needs to be specified very precisely. But it is not. Or if the state is unable to act so as to promote a pattern of development that benefits the poor (Lappé et al., Seers, Wood, Hayter), then what is the theory of state intervention which leads to these pessimistic conclusions about its mode of operation? This question is not rigorously examined. Or, again, if the capitalist system is to blame (Hayter), how does this system function in a dynamic framework to prevent the poor from ever, or scarcely ever, receiving benefits from it?

Even a superficial reading of radical development theory reveals that the use of concepts such as underdevelopment, exploitation, and imperialism is wholly inadequate for deriving unequivocal conclusions that aid's effects will be negative, that capitalist development either cannot take place in the Third World or that, if it can, the result will always be detrimental to the poor. There is far from a consensus among radical leftist scholars that because Third World countries are dependent upon and dominated by capitalist forces originating in the industrialised countries of the North, aid's effects will therefore be negative. There are Marxists, for example, with a history going right back to the writings of Marx, who believe that the only route to progress is through capitalist development. There are also writers within the dependency school of thought, who, while acknowledging that forces of the centre are dominant in peripheral economies, can also argue that dependent development is not the only consequence of the capitalist development initiated at the centre. And there are also Marxist writers who maintain that states in Third World societies not only have a certain autonomy but that they adapt and in doing so can reflect a shift in class interests over time. Thus it is important to recognise that not all radical development theory leads to the conclusion that aid's impact upon the Third World necessarily has to be negative.

Dependency theory

The strand of radical development theory most closely bound up with the negative conclusions of the leftist critics is one particular sub-category of dependency theory associated with the writings, for example, of Baran, Frank, Wallerstein, Quijano, Nun and Marini. Its views on the possibilities of independent development in the periphery are that these are non-existent short of engineering a radical severing of links with the capitalist centre, and this is itself dependent upon socialist revolution. It is within this perspective that the writings of Jalée are located.

From a theoretical viewpoint, this particular perspective has been rigorously attacked: by those in general sympathetic to the dependency school, by the non-dependency Marxist literature of the more orthodox camps, and, not without significance, by its former adherents. Some attacks from within the radical framework have been extremely harsh. For example, Booth has recently written thus (1985:762):

> It is now reasonably clear, I would argue, that the dependency position is vitiated by a variable combination of circular reasoning, fallacious inferences from empirical observation and a weak base in deductive theory.

The Baran/Frank/Jalée perspective on Third World development provides a generalised rejection of the possibility of the full development of the capitalist system ever taking place there. What occurs, rather, is the 'development of under-development'. For these writers poverty is not an original state but the consequence of the penetration of market forces into the peripheral Third World from the capitalist centre, which creates and deepens the process of underdevelopment. Self-reliant development is inhibited because the economic surplus which is produced is either siphoned off by foreign capital or its representatives in the peripheral economy or else spent on luxury consumption. A key negative element in the whole process is the state. State power in the periphery is in the hands of a small elite which itself benefits from the dependent capitalist relations that have been established. This elite is in close relationship or alliance with the advanced nations; as it gains power and economic benefit from the furthering of this external alliance, the evolution of the capitalist system in the periphery both reinforces, and is reinforced by, the process of underdevelopment, with external forces providing the overwhelming determining force that sets up and furthers the pattern of under-development. The bulk of the population of Third World societies is marginalised by the development of underdevelopment, so that accelerating the process provides no hope that the poverty of the mass of the people will be alleviated.

It is within this overall dynamic perspective that aid's negative role and effect are evaluated. Various factors are involved. First, aid is viewed as an element in the dominant relationship of the centre (the donors) to the periphery (the recipients). Secondly, and relatedly, the type of development that aid funds stimulate is necessarily the dependent development that is already taking place; thus aid accelerates a growth process whose major characteristic for the recipient country is under-development. It is in this respect that aid is viewed as part of the problem rather than a counter-force geared to providing a solution. Thirdly, because official aid is channelled to or through recipient governments and these governments are a central mechanism for perpetuating the process of underdevelopment, aid further reinforces the process of underdevelopment by providing additional resources for domination. And finally, because it is the power of the elites which controls the operations of the state, state power is a critical factor in perpetuating and reinforcing the process of dependent development. Thus to the extent that attention is focused on providing additional *resources* (the aid debate) rather than on the basic requirement of altering *power relations*, discussion about aid is fundamentally irrelevant to addressing the major causes of continuing poverty and underdevelopment.

That this wholly pessimistic assessment of Third World development prospects represents only one view within the radical perspective is brought out clearly when it is contrasted with that provided by Warren within the Marxist paradigm. For Warren, far from dependency being the central feature of the relationship between industrialised and Third World countries, it is in fact a myth. Economic contact between advanced industrial society and the Third World, he maintains, can not only promote development but does do so. Using industrialisation as the yardstick for economic development, Warren argues that the prospects for successful capitalist development are quite favourable in many underdeveloped countries. Indeed, he goes further to suggest that direct colonialism, far from having retarded or distorted the indigenous capitalist development that might otherwise have occurred, acted as a powerful engine of progressive change. There is a rise in indigenous capitalism which is continually loosening the ties of subordination binding the Third World and the imperialist world and furthering the evolution of autonomous capitalism in peripheral countries. Thus he can state that 'the overall net effect of the policy of "imperialist" countries and the general relations of these countries with underdeveloped countries actually favours the industrialisation and general economic development of the latter' (1980:9–10). As for the state, Warren is broadly optimistic about its role in promoting development. While he acknowledges that 'major policy blunders' have occurred which have resulted in a 'squandering of many of the benefits of Third World postwar economic development', he goes on to suggest that the selection of a different set of policies 'would have permitted the promotion of a more efficient and humane capitalist development than occurred in practice'. However, even these mistakes have 'failed to halt the gathering momentum of capitalist advance' (235–6). In contrast, then, to the dependency perspective, capitalism, in the words of another Marxist scholar, Kay, 'created underdevelopment not because it exploited the underdeveloped world but because it didn't exploit it enough' (1975:x).

It is easy to see how this particular radical view, which extols the virtues of capitalist development (as the route to the generation of proletarian revolution), would assess the impact of aid in very different terms from those of the pessimist critics. From the Warrenite perspective, aid would be seen as a positive force because it promotes capitalist development; it would be seen as virtuous because it provides additional resources that can be used to accelerate the process of industrialisation, and because it provides greater flexibility to recipient states to promote development and extend capitalist relations to all parts of their economies.

What both the pessimistic dependency theorists and the optimistic Warrenite view of the world have in common is, of course, the attempt to outline a general theory of dynamic development applicable to all Third World countries. It is precisely here that both views have been vigorously criticised. Just as Warren criticised the dependency view by providing evidence which revealed that rapid industrialisation has taken place in a number of Asian countries, so he too has been criticised for ignoring, for instance, the record of many poor countries in sub-Saharan Africa. Neither theoretical perspective has satisfied scholars as providing an adequate explanation of the manner of dynamic Third World development, although the extremes that each represents and the fact that both purport to be general theories indicate the wide-ranging theoretical options that are apparently on the agenda for debate and analysis. Of course, the fact that these extremes have been put forward as alternative theoretical perspectives neither indicates that both are wrong nor that a middle path between them is necessarily correct. It is clearly crucial to try to analyse precisely what the process of dynamic development characteristic of Third World countries is so as to be able to assess the constraints impeding that development and the forces assisting the process. For it is only then that it will be possible to evaluate the effects that aid is likely to have both now and in the future. While the implication of the Warrenite view is that the pessimism of the dependency perspective is entirely misplaced, it is necessary to analyse this perspective more closely.

It is important to recognise that *within* the dependency perspective itself the overtly negative conclusions linked with Frank, Baran, Wallerstein and Jalée – with their associated adverse conclusions about the role of foreign aid – are far from universally accepted. Warren's writings have evidently been influential here in alerting writers to what to many now appears self-evident, namely that the development of underdevelopment is not an iron law with no exceptions. In his authoritative analysis of the evolution of dependency theory, Palma points out that some writers within the school argue that it is misleading to regard dependency as a formal theory and that no *general* implications for development can be abstracted from its analyses, while others regard it as a formal theory and maintain that it *can* be operationalised into a practical development strategy for dependent countries (1981:20). What the evolution of analysis within the dependency framework has attempted to do, in brief, is to prise apart the deterministic and pessimistic conclusions about the interaction of political, economic and social forces in the light of more rigorous historical analysis and highlight those forces which have had (and therefore can have) influence in altering the parameters analysed.

In the view of the theorists of the Economic Commission for Latin America it is quite possible to break out of the dependent relationship characteristic of the periphery, largely through the process of import-substitution and, at least in some degree, autonomous industrialisation. To Cardoso, it is the political determinism of Frank that is the focal point of his criticism. Frank asserts, for example, that 'the economic basis of a developmental national bourgeois class . . . has been entirely eliminated or prevented from forming at all, thus precluding further or future development under capitalism' (1978:10). But for Cardoso this is an historically naive and mistaken view. He rejects the notion that the local bourgeoisies no longer exist as an active social force and that the only political alternatives lie between the extremes of socialism or fascism. Writing with Faletto, Cardoso rejects the view that the lot of the poor in Third World countries is hopeless and determined entirely by others (1979:10–11):

> We conceive the relationship between external and internal forces as forming a complex whole whose structural links are not based on mere external forms of exploitation and coercion, but are rooted in coincidences of interests between local dominant classes and international ones and, on the other side, are challenged by local dominated groups and classes. In some circumstances, the networks of coincident or reconciliated interests might expand to include segments of the middle class, if not of alienated parts of the working classes. In other circumstances, segments of dominated classes might seek internal alliance with middle classes, working classes, and even peasants, aiming to protect themselves from foreign penetration that contradicts its interests.

It is the determinism, the lack of rigorous analysis, the highly abstract nature of the theory, and the failure to provide a satisfactory explanation of the actual process of development in Third World countries that are the main elements of dependency theories (most of them!) which have been criticised most vigorously by both more orthodox and neo-Marxist writers. Perhaps the most telling criticism is that dependency theory, in all its various forms, quite simply does not fit the facts. There is a wide cross-section of countries mainly in Asia, dominated by the Newly Industrialising Countries (NICs) (but Japan must also be included as a challenge to the general inapplicability of dependency theory), which show clearly that underdevelopment is not by any means the only possible result of capitalist penetration in Third World countries. There is no doubt that the growing strength of the NICs in the mid to late 1970s inflicted a severe blow to the influence that dependency theory had enjoyed in development theory circles in the late 1960s and early 1970s. It is also important to recognise that within the original home of dependency theory, Latin America, the experience of a number of key countries also challenged the excessively negative assessment of development in that sub-continent, as Randall and Theobald, for example, explain in relation to Argentina and Brazil (1985:122ff).

A second major problem with dependency theory is its unsatisfactory treatment of the related issues of political power, the role and function of the state, and public policy, in spite of the efforts of writers like Cardoso to provide more realism and relevance to the extremely monolithic views of Frank, Jalée and Wallerstein. There are various issues here. Laclau, from a Marxist perspective, has argued that the dependency theorists have failed to recognise (or acknowledge) that the penetration of capitalist forces into the periphery has by no means led to the total destruction of pre-capitalist relations (see Randall and Theobald, 1985:132–4). Moreover their crude interpretation of capitalism glosses over what could well turn out to be critical factors in understanding the nature and evolution of the political process and the role of the state, by lumping quite complex factors together under the generic notion of class struggle. The continued existence of pre-capitalist relationships highlights the fact that alliances between groups are likely to be complex and to change over time. Of importance, too, is the fact that analysis of the state by Marxist and mainstream writers indicates that the Third World state can have in theory, and almost certainly does have in practice an autonomous role which is distinct and separate from the predictable and deterministic role representative of external forces as suggested by dependency theory. Country studies covering Asia and Africa as well as Latin America have repeatedly supported this critique of dependency's superficial analysis of political and state forces, also bringing questions of ethnicity, for example, into the analysis of the development process which is now recognised as a highly complex phenomenon. The rich variety of experience forcefully challenges the dependency view that the state in Third World countries is a rigidly mechanistic sub-element of worldwide economically determined forces, with no power substantially to alter its subservient position and with no internal forces to provide countervailing tendencies against the prevailing power structure.

Finally, dependency theory has been under its most vicious attack from Marxists for being tautological and logically flawed. As an example of this type of criticism, Booth writes as follows (1985:762–3):

Satisfactory development is identified as 'self-sustaining' or 'autonomous' and (hence) industrial growth; this is the meaning attached to 'classically capitalist' development. But this amounts to saying that it is non-satellite . . . development. Hence the empirical demonstration that in historical fact satisfactory development occurs only to the extent that metropolis-satellite or dependency links are broken or weakened is nothing of the kind, but an exercise in tautology.

It appears therefore that mainstream development thinking and Marxist theoreticians alike are correct in rejecting this particular perspective as an unsatisfactory explanation of the process of development. Thus, inasmuch as radical leftist criticisms of aid are rooted in the dependency framework of analysis and particularly (though not exclusively) in its more pessimistic manifestations, they provide an inadequate basis for concluding that aid necessarily harms rather than helps. Nevertheless this conclusion by no means closes the issue. To reject dependency as a theoretical perspective does not mean that the issues highlighted by dependency theorists are unimportant. They have, to their credit, alerted theoreticians and concerned scholars to the need to take serious account of real and influential forces which were wholly absent from the narrow perspectives of modernisation theories and their growth-specific variants. Within Marxist theory, the debate has inspired a new enthusiasm to grapple with key areas of analysis brought to prominence by the dependency writers. Within liberal theory it has highlighted the naiveté and inadequacy of many of the models that ignored the influence of political forces.

For the aid debate four structurally related questions central to an assessment of aid's impact still need to be discussed, even when the dependency perspective as an explanatory theory is rejected. First, what is the impact of capitalist development within Third World countries? This question opens up others: what has happened to growth, and what has happened to poverty and to income distribution? Secondly, what is the nature and role of the state in Third World countries, and does it hold out the hope or possibility of utilising its power to promote rather than frustrate a pattern of development beneficial to the poor? Thirdly, what is the role of additional resources in accelerating the process of development and lifting the poor out of their poverty vis-à-vis political and power relationships viewed by some as the key factor in development? And fourthly, what are the prospects for alternative paths to progress, and in particular what hope is there for the revolutionary alternative and what benefits is it likely to bring? If capitalist development is necessarily inequitable and if it fails to alleviate poverty, if the state is unable or unwilling to change this outcome, if additional resources are not necessary to improve the lot of the poor, and finally if revolution provides a viable alternative, then foreign aid in its present form would clearly be indefensible and the leftist critics would be vindicated. We shall now examine these issues in more depth.

The role and nature of the state

An assessment of the role and nature of the state remains a fundamental element in evaluating the impact of aid, for it is now widely recognised as a crucial determinant of the possibilities for development. As Higgott points out 'in a strange kind of way . . . we have a situation nowadays in which both Marxists and non-Marxists have a similar view of the behaviour of the state – albeit operating from a different normative base and utilising different terminology. Both scholars recognise the fundamental role of the state in political and economic activity' (1983:78). We now need to consider the following question: are the radical structural theorists and institutional pessimists correct in their assertion that the nature of the state in aid-recipient countries prevents it from exerting a role beneficial to the alleviation of poverty? Liberal theorists would of course reject this pessimistic viewpoint, although possibly admitting that in particular circumstances negative forces could be critical when a recipient state is wholly corrupt and oppressive. What is of more interest to us at the theoretical level is the Marxist view of the state and the question of whether this particular perspective leads to the negative conclusions of the institutional pessimists.

There are two elements from within the ongoing debates in the Marxist literature which cast doubt on the wholly negative conclusions about the state suggested by the critics of aid. First, there is as yet no single theory of the state found in Marxist writings within the perspective of either the industrialised or the developing world. Thus at the theoretical level, firm conclusions have not yet been reached and the range of possibilities for state action remains far from closed and pre-ordained.

Secondly, there is growing recognition amongst Marxist writers that a deterministic view of the state, its role and its function is woefully inadequate as a basis for analysing the process of change at the political level. There is an increasing recognition of state autonomy – autonomy both from external forces and, of particular importance, from the interests of the classes and representatives of powerful economic interests within particular countries. While these analytical developments by no means lead to the view of modernisation theory that the state is a neutral umpire above and beyond the play of economic forces present in the country, they do signal a great advance in thinking over the past ten or fifteen years. For instance, whereas in the mid-1970s the radical left attacked the political feasibility of Third World governments embarking on a policy of redistribution with growth because, it was argued, such a policy would contradict the class interests of those who controlled the state, such a sweeping dismissal of this type of strategy because of its political naiveté would be far harder to find today.

Traditionally, the character of Marxist thinking about the state was defined in two assertions. First, the form and function of the state reflect and are largely determined by the economic base of society. Secondly, the state is seen as an instrument used in its own interests by the economically dominant class. It is this second aspect that has been adapted by modern writers under the influence of, most importantly, Gramsci, Miliband and Poulantzas, who have all placed increasing emphasis on the relative autonomy of the state. Miliband, for example, has stated that he does not subscribe to the view of the state simply as a passive instrument of class rule (1969:66–74), while Poulantzas (1973:284–8) sets out to show that, in order to defend its ultimate survival, the state could never be the instrument of the short-term interests of the bourgeoisie or of even one fraction of it. In a society dominated by the capitalist mode of production, he argues, the state can and indeed must maintain a considerable freedom from the dominant classes. Two elements are highlighted. First, it needs to be recognised that the dominant classes have competing interests so that commercial, financial, industrial and also regionally-based fractions compete to advance their sectional interests. In these circumstances, the state must exercise some autonomy in deciding how to aggregate the interests of these competing interests with policies favouring some class interests at the expense of others. But secondly, and of perhaps more importance for the present discussion, Poulantzas goes on to point out that the state, in order to survive, also has to respond to pressures emanating from one or more of the dominated classes and in so doing will be disposed to act in some measure at variance with the interests of the dominant classes. He goes even further by arguing that these accommodations may be contrary to the short-term and even the long-term economic interests of different fractions of the dominant classes (see Sandbrook, 1982:78–9).

It is important, for our purposes, to recognise that these new insights into Marxist theory refer to the state in the industrialised world – a world in which Marxists would be the first to acknowledge that the capitalist system and class relations are far more completely formed than in Third World societies. A fortiori, therefore, the unpredictable nature of the state and the complexity of its changing make-up will be far more evident in Third World societies. Here not only are classes less than fully formed but class relationships tend to be more fluid, overlaid as they are by different alliances between and within groups – as many urbanites still have rural links and as ethnic, religious and regional influences add yet further dimensions to a simple class analysis. In addition, as Hyden points out, control of the state is almost certainly different from control of society, with, again, critical implications for policy intervention possibilities (1980:31ff). These factors have led leading Marxist analysts of the state in the Third World – Roxborough, Cliffe, Saul, Cohen, Shanin and Leys, for example – to be increasingly cautious both as regards defining class allegiance as more than provisional and as regards predicting the pattern that state evolution will take. There is now, for example, little sympathy for the view that the political elite, either in Latin America or Africa, is necessarily an agent of the internationalist capitalist class.

Of course, increased recognition of the 'openness' of the state to potential change and of its uncertain structural role does not lead Marxist scholars to disregard or set aside the notion that capitalist development throws up certain forms of group association of the powerful and powerless which are influenced crucially by prevailing economic forces, or that external linkages (so prominent in dependency theory as to eclipse other forces) are not an important element in the dynamic process. It is rather that the fluidity of class formation and the relative autonomy of the state and its bureaucratic baggage will by no means predetermine future power relations and economic gainers and losers. Two important implications arising from this perspective need to be highlighted for our purposes. First, returning to the debates of the 1970s about the possibilities of states embarking upon redistributive policies, these arguments no longer appear to be as naive as they initially seemed (to radical scholars) to be. And secondly, there would appear to be far less certainty that capturing the commanding heights of state power through revolution is either a widespread and durable possibility or that it will necessarily lead to policies directly beneficial to all poor groups in a country in a recognisable and sustained manner. The practical thrust of these conclusions will be discussed and confirmed in Part III, Chapter 16, below.

The 'redistribution with growth' literature sets out reasons why a government that one would initially suspect of being opposed to measures directed at redistributing income and assets to poor and marginalised groups might well embark upon such a strategy. For example, Bell (1974) pinpoints two reasons: enlightened self-interest, for fear that the absence of such policies would increase the likelihood of revolution, or because constituent groups of the elite could have conflicts among themselves, so that providing benefits to poor groups could lead also to ensuring the long-term power of dominant elite groups. However, Poulantzas' perspective could add to this range of possibilities, for example, through the state introducing measures in opposition to even the long-term interests of dominant classes who still remain part of the *powerful* as opposed to the *powerless* system. Each of these strategies can, in short, be incorporated into a Marxist perspective of state strategy and policy in Third World countries, and each rejects the narrow deterministic conclusions of the radical institutional pessimists.

At the other extreme, the view that taking over the state necessarily leads to the automatic achievement of non-contradictory gains for those assuming state power appears equally naive and superficial. It is, for instance, no easy task for a state, even if it *wishes* to do so, to opt out of the world capitalist system; the forces of the market will still tend to be present in such circumstances, if not critically important. As Murray, in an influential study, correctly asserts: 'Even when the underdeveloped area is organized on socialist rather than capitalist principles, historical experience has shown how difficult it is to insulate the growing economy from the international law of value' (1972:236). In relation to the alliances operating within the nation state, Bienefeld and Godfrey point out (with regret) that (1982:23):

Unfortunately when a state comes to free itself from the domination of private capital interests as exercised through control of the ideological or the political sphere and backed up by control of the material means of production, there is no guarantee that such a state will represent the interest of the population as a whole. There is unfortunately no self-evident set of practices which serve some homogeneous interest of 'workers and peasants', quite apart from the issues of a separate bureaucratic interest which may or may not come to dominate in such a situation.

. . . the idea that gaining political control of the state is to open the door to unambiguous policies emerging from some permanent consensus emanating from the total political involvement of the masses in a sort of perpetual cultural revolution is an unrealistic picture produced by the hyperactive imagination of people who have not had a great deal of responsibility for co-ordinating complex processes of production, requiring a vital concrete and measurable output at a time when it is needed for further reproduction.

There is thus no guarantee that a change at the political centre will itself provide the sufficient conditions for political change to be replicated at the regional, town or village level. Contradictions and local power alliances are likely to be far more durable than revolutionary theorists would have us believe. Hence there is no iron law that leads one to be believe that all political obstacles to development occurring in a capitalist-type framework will vanish once central state power in Third World countries is under the 'control' of the conflicting alliance of various peasant and worker groups. In fact, the evidence would tend to suggest that they may even be heightened (see Randall and Theobald, 1985:137ff. and Part III, below).

There is little doubt that, as Randall and Theobald explain, much of what passed for analysis of political change in the revolutionary optimism of the late 1960s regarding revolution as a normal phenomenon was naive in the extreme. This naiveté severely underestimates the capacity of societies to maintain and adjust their systems (183).

The extreme pessimism and determinism of the dependency perspective are thus found to be wholly inadequate. Hence, the conclusion that therefore aid provided to recipient states necessarily accentuates poverty by reinforcing antagonistic power relations has also to be rejected. Similarly the conclusion that the taking over of state power by the poor and marginalised necessarily provides the answer to poverty is to be rejected as naive and historically superficial. These conclusions are rejected on the basis of a wide consensus of theoretical work from both liberal and Marxist viewpoints which provide a far more robust perspective. At minimum, they suggest that the complexity and fluidity of state and state-related alliances in Third World societies point to the realistic possibility of autonomous state action that could be beneficial to the poor. But even more they suggest that states in the Third World could well act to further the interests of the poor, even when politically they do not represent those interests directly. In a less authoritarian and more democratic context, state action favouring the poor through redistributive measures would be even more significant. However, as Streeten points out, there has been a woeful lack of research analysing these issues sufficiently (1983:18):

political constraints should be neither ignored nor accepted as ultimate facts. They too call for analysis. . . . Relatively little research has been done by political scientists into the question of how to build constituencies for reform, how to shape reformist coalitions or alliances between groups whose interests can be harnessed to the cause of reform.

One needs, however, to be equally wary of replacing the naive negative determinism of the dependency school with an equally naive optimistic determinism that 'all will turn out all right in the end'. What the theoretical literature on the role of the state suggests is that there is *no* general and predictable pattern of state activity that can lead to firm and uncontestable conclusions. What is required is a case-by-case analysis to determine within particular circumstances how far the state in particular countries is autonomous, how far it wishes to support aid programmes targeted to poverty alleviation, how far the economic structure inhibits redistributive growth, and how far that structure can change and in what directions. That said, however, it needs to be stated that the (ongoing) theoretical debates currently taking place give, in the mid-1980s, far fewer grounds for pessimism than the conclusions reached by the radical leftist critics of aid have suggested.

Indeed, although Seers in the late 1970s launched, as we have seen, an attack on the naive conventional view (developed in part by himself) that aid would be beneficial to the poor in Third World countries by highlighting the problems of recipient states, he himself provides a critique of the extreme deterministic viewpoint with which he more recently became associated. He argues that Third World states experience not single external pressures but a variety of pressures, some competing with each other, thus challenging those who use an oversimplified world model and label all countries as either 'imperialist', 'neo-colonial' or 'socialist'. Indeed, he concludes that 'the room for manoeuvre is much greater than it was a couple of decades ago when the ''Three Worlds'' model reflected reality more closely and most of the ''Third World'' could only turn to one or two developed countries for political and economic support'. He also places increasing emphasis in his later writings on the influence of personal leadership in effecting policies either for or against the wider interests of marginalised groups in poor countries.[5]

The record of Third World development

Other radical leftist criticisms also need to be considered. There is no point in pumping aid into Third World economies, it is argued, when the process being furthered is resulting in low or negligible economic growth or when the growth that is achieved does not lead to the alleviation of mass poverty because the poor are by-passed in the growth process. In such circumstances, providing aid is no help because the resulting pattern of development fails to address and meet the needs of the poor. These arguments lead to the following central questions: have Third World economies experienced economic growth, and if so has that growth led to a reduction of poverty? If the answer to these questions is clearly 'no', then the leftist critics of aid would provide a crucial challenge to the assumptions upon which official development assistance is provided.

We consider first the question of economic growth. Different analysts have produced different conclusions not only by using data from different countries at different time periods but also by using similar data bases. However, taken in historical perspective, the available evidence points strongly to the conclusion that in the 30-year period from 1950 to 1980 Third World economies not only grew at comparatively high rates but at higher rates than in previous time periods. Taken together, all the substantial analyses that have been conducted bear out this broad conclusion, even though there have been geographical differences and for particular countries (the minority) over particular time periods negative growth rates have been recorded. Of importance, too, is the fact that historically high rates of growth have occurred across the range of different types of economies: low-income, middle-income importing and middle-income exporting countries. In addition, major aggregate indicators of national welfare in Third World economies have also recorded significant improvements; in all regions, life expectancy and literacy have improved, while child mortality rates have declined. These conclusions are drawn not only from the time series and cross-country statistics provided by international agencies such as the World Bank but from leading scholars like Kuznets, Chenery, Morawetz, Meier, Reynolds, Sen and Stewart.

Table 11.1, taken from the work of Kuznets and Morawetz, shows clearly that, compared with previous time periods for the industrialised nations, the period 1950–75 was one of historically high growth rates per head for the developing world. Table 11.2 (from World Bank data for the period 1965–80) reveals in more detail that, with the exception of sub-Saharan Africa in the latter period, the aggregate growth rate per head for different types of Third World economies was also positive and high compared with the industrialised nations.

Table 11.1: *Long-term Growth Rates of Per Capita Income, Selected Countries, Regions and Periods (% p.a.)*

	1870–1913	1913–60	1950–75
1. All Developed Countries	...	...	3.2
of which:			
a) France	1.4	1.3	3.8
b) Germany	1.7	1.6	4.5
c) Japan	2.2	2.5	7.6
d) United Kingdom	1.3	1.5	2.2
e) United States	2.2	1.7	2.0
2. All Developing Countries	...	...	3.4
of which:			
a) Lower-income countries	...	...	1.1
b) Middle-income countries	...	...	3.7
c) Africa	...	...	2.4
d) China	...	...	4.2
e) East Asia	...	...	3.9
f) Latin America	...	...	2.6
g) Middle East	...	...	5.2
h) South Asia	...	...	1.7

Sources: 1870–1960: Kuznets, 1966, Table 6.6;
       1950–1975: Morawetz, 1977, Tables 1 and 4.

Table 11.2: *Growth of Per Capita Income, 1965–80 (% p.a.)*

	1965–73	1973–80
1. Low-income developing countries	3.0	3.1
a) Asia		
i) China	3.2	3.5
ii) India	4.9	4.5
b) Africa	1.3	0.0
2. Middle-income oil-importing developing countries	4.6	3.1
a) East Asia and Pacific	5.6	5.7
b) Middle East and N. Africa	3.5	4.3
c) Sub-Saharan Africa	2.0	0.5
d) Latin America and Caribbean	4.5	2.9
3. Middle-income oil exporters	4.6	3.1
4. ALL DEVELOPING COUNTRIES	4.1	3.3
5. High-income oil exporters	4.1	6.2
6. Industrial market economies	3.7	2.1

Source: World Bank, *World Development Report 1985*, Table A2.

Recent studies by Sen and Reynolds on cross-country growth rate comparisons confirm these general trends, while also helping to explain the poor growth performance of those economies that have failed to record average high growth rates per head. Sen highlights low levels of investment as a crucial factor in low growth achievers, while Reynolds includes the following additional elements: low export growth, low levels of agricultural production, population density, and what he terms the 'political element' (Sen, 1983b:748–50, Reynolds, 1985:387–418). These factors, as well as the slowdown in world trade, balance-of-payments constraints and deflationary policies implemented in industrialised countries, help to explain why growth has slowed considerably in the first half of the 1980s and why, with the incidence of drought in large sub-regions, Africa's growth performance after 1973 has been particularly disappointing.

One of the major conclusions from the discussion in Chapter 10 was that the charge made by the critics that aid inserted into recipient economies has a direct detrimental effect on aggregate growth is unsustainable: the data do not provide evidence to support their view, and the theoretical justification for it is decidedly weak unless a series of questionable assumptions are held always to apply. We are now in a position to go further. The historical record reveals that in aggregate terms Third World economies have in the post-war period been generally characterised by positive rates of economic growth per head. The criticism that aid cannot help recipient economies at the aggregate level because it assists a process that of its nature retards economic growth has therefore to be rejected as a general proposition in the absence of substantive cross-country evidence showing that growth, development and poverty-alleviation could have been better achieved without aid.

This conclusion, however, does not mean that where economic growth is *not* being achieved, aid will provide the missing ingredient to reverse the negative aggregate trend. If particular circumstances, for example, war, widespread unrest, all-pervading corruption or gross economic mismanagement, are the causes of economic decline, then it is exceedingly unlikely that aid – however large the amounts provided – will reverse this trend. Hence, rejecting the assertion that aid contributes to overall economic stagnation or negative growth does not have to lead to the additional conclusion that aid on its own will reverse a process of economic decline. It probably will not.

Of far greater importance, however, is the criticism directed at the effects of prevailing patterns of development, and the part played by aid in furthering this development process, upon the alleviation of poverty in Third World countries. Even when growth is achieved in recipient countries, a fundamental leftist criticism is that without radical changes the achievement of growth fails to benefit the poor. Thus, because aid helps to promote 'development' that does not alleviate poverty it fails to resolve the basic problems that it is intended to address. As Griffin and Khan put it, the socio-economic structure of recipient states creates the conditions in which powerful dynamic forces tend to perpetuate and even accentuate low standards of living for a significant proportion of the population (1978:300). These assertions raise the crucial questions of the evidence available to support such conclusions: has the development process into which aid is inserted increased or decreased the incidence and extent of poverty in recipient countries?

The distinction being made by these critics of aid is not between the desire to promote economic growth on its own and the desire to ensure that the benefits of growth are distributed or redistributed to the poor. Rather, it is the distinction between growth either with or without distributional measures and an entirely different growth path based on radical and above all structural change in recipient economies which is said to be a pre-condition for equitable growth and poverty alleviation ever taking place. Thus the radical criticism is a rejection not only of growth-expanding initiatives but also of redistribution-with-growth approaches to development and their basic-needs-related cousins in which aid funds play a role. It is a rejection, for example, of the perspective offered by the World Bank and most leading Western donor countries that a mix of growth-directed and poverty-specific initiatives will help to solve the problems of Third World poverty, as expressed, for example, by World Bank Chairman Clausen's valedictory address to the 1985 Board of Governors meeting in South Korea in October 1985 when he stated:

> Our task in the years ahead is not merely to resume growth, not merely to assure that this growth is on a sound, sustainable basis – important though that is . . .
> We must assure that growth is accompanied by programs to alleviate poverty, that a resumption of growth in investment in new productive facilities and infrastructure is accompanied by expanded investments in education and social services . . . Sustainable growth requires true development of human capital, the alleviation of poverty and the maintenance of the environment.

These types of approaches are rejected by the radical leftist critics because the measures taken to alleviate poverty assume that the current growth path and its structural determinants are to remain substantially in place, albeit trimmed and improved by implementing measures to improve resource efficiency. For the critics, the record suggests that attempting to alleviate poverty within this framework is doomed to failure. Are they correct?

Before considering the available evidence, it is necessary (although to the general reader doubtless annoying) to have to report that the data base for measuring poverty, and particularly for analysing changes in the incidence of poverty, is far from reliable, particularly when attempting to compare data between different countries over time. Indeed, it is distressing that, as recently as 1980, Chenery had to admit that acceptable time-series data were available only for a dozen or so developing countries (1980:27). And in the World Bank's 1985 *World Development Report*, income distribution data are given for only 18 out of 72 listed low-income and lower middle-income developing countries, the latest figures being already 10 years old (228). Not that one can be entirely confident about the accuracy even of these data. Albert Berry, a long-time analyst of income trends in developing countries, observed recently that 'it appears unlikely that we know . . . the direction of change in economic inequality in any less developed country' (1985:337).

Most studies of poverty and growth comparisons between countries have been of the cross-section variety over a single or short time period. Making deductions from these data about generalised patterns over time assumes that countries will tend to follow much the same pattern in their development experiences as are found in the cross-section, an assumption fraught with difficulties (see Meier, 1984:33). Of equal importance is the awareness that poverty can be identified in different ways: by social or economic class, by residence, by asset or income distribution, by access to specified basic needs, by relative or absolute norms, or finally, by money or real income shares (see Streeten, 1978:241–3). Clearly different measures will reflect different types of poverty or in some cases will be based on the particular themes to which theoreticians wish to draw attention. Finally, it needs to be remembered that inequality and absolute poverty are different concepts. If the reason for providing aid is to help in the alleviation of absolute poverty, this objective could well be fulfilled even when the distribution of income and assets is widening, while, obversely, poverty could well be affecting more people, both relatively and absolutely, when income differentials are narrowing.

Expressing concern about a superficial understanding of poverty and the different ways of measuring it, however, need not minimise an appreciation of the extent of poverty in the Third World and its almost all-pervasiveness in many countries. Based on minimum standards of nutrition, health, clothing and housing etc., it is estimated that some 800 million people are living today in absolute poverty, the vast majority in Third World and aid-recipient countries. Assuming that the economic trends of the past 20 years are repeated in the next 20 years (in the mid-1980s this, by common agreement, is a very optimistic assumption), it is judged that by the year 2000 the absolute number in absolute poverty will be no lower than in 1960. These figures on their own would tend to suggest, and forcefully, that the prospects for development are exceptionally bleak and that more of the same – more of the type of development so far generated and aid funds to promote such development – would be hopelessly inadequate to address the problems of poverty.

However, when viewed in relative terms, the figures look different. In 1960, some 50 per cent of the world's population were judged to be living in absolute poverty; this was reduced to about 30 per cent in 1980 and there are prospects for a reduction to 20 per cent by the year 2000 (Meier, 1984:43). With world population increase at over 2 per cent a year, this indicates that tens of millions will have escaped from absolute poverty over the 40-year period – a far less depressing picture. Using these latter figures, more of the same – particularly if promoted more quickly – provides grounds for more optimism, especially when radical alternatives on a global basis have no test of history to support them.

The basis for much of the pessimism supporting the view of the radical critics is derived from the work of Simon Kuznets, and particularly his inverted U-shaped curve hypothesis. Based on a mixture of data analysis and some speculation, Kuznets argued in part that, at low levels of development, economic growth involves and indeed requires a widening of income inequality within nations so that measures to accelerate growth necessarily lead to the poor becoming relatively worse-off (1955:1–28). To this are added the fact that income distribution in Third World countries is highly inequitable and the widely acknowledged tendency for those with economic power – high incomes and a disproportionate access to national wealth and assets – to control political power and thereby to hold on to their economic gains. In such circumstances the possibility of reversing these inegalitarian tendencies looks bleak indeed, although Kuznets did provide a rider stating that at higher income levels the tendency to greater inequalities would be reversed. But for most Third World countries the prospects for this occurring within a generation appear exceptionally grim.

To the theory has been added the evidence. Kuznets based his theory on data available up to the mid-1950s; in 1973, Paukert at the ILO examined the figures for the next 20 years, which, he said, confirmed the Kuznets hypothesis (1973:121). Country studies of Argentina, Brazil, the Philippines, Malaysia, Mexico and Turkey have shown that rapid or moderate growth in the 1960s and 1970s led to growing inequalities even if not always an absolute increase in impoverishment, while for Bangladesh and the poorer countries of Africa low growth has been accompanied by increased absolute impoverishment (Streeten, 1978:242). To this evidence can be added the 10 empirical studies of seven Asian countries discussed by Griffin and Khan. They suggested that in Bangladesh, India, Indonesia, Malaysia, Pakistan, the Philippines and Sri Lanka, comprising 70 per cent of the rural population of the non-socialist world and covering a time period of between 10 and 25 years, there has been both a worsening of income distribution and declining real incomes of the rural poor, even in periods of rapid economic growth. It is, they argue, the structure of the economy rather than rates of economic growth which is responsible for the observed increased poverty (1978:299).

It is this type of evidence which has provided the radical aid critics with their ammunition for challenging the assumptions behind the conventional view in favour of providing aid to relieve poverty. They contend that as both the theory and the evidence indicate that expanding the present capitalist development path fails to solve Third World poverty, providing aid to assist in this process is no solution.

There are, however, serious grounds for rejecting these conclusions as inevitable general truths at both the theoretical level and on the basis of other evidence. First, the Kuznets inverted U-shaped hypothesis has been challenged increasingly in more recent years. A substantial review of the literature by Cline indicates that recent available evidence over time for individual countries throws strong doubt on the inevitability of initially increasing inequality during development (1975:394). Also studies by Papanek (1978) and by Anand and Kanbur (1981), using the same data-base as those who found support for the inverted U-shaped curve hypothesis, drew the opposite conclusions. More recently, Skolka's hypothetical model finds no general support for the Kuznets view, highlighting both the complexities of dynamic change and the very different results achieved if agriculture or industry are given priority in the strategies carried out (1983). Work by the World Bank and the Institute of Development Studies at Sussex concludes that the wide diversity of experience of development paths in different countries leads to two important conclusions. First, that there is little empirical evidence for deducing that higher rates of economic growth inevitably generate greater inequalities and, secondly, that increases in the concentration of income are not inevitable even in capitalist-type economies advancing from low levels of per capita income (Ahluwalia 1975:10). Israel, Yugoslavia, Taiwan, Costa Rica, Sri Lanka and Tanzania are all cited as examples of countries where growth has been accompanied by a reduction in poverty (Chenery et al., 1974:xv). There are few, if any, scholars today who would challenge the conclusion that two leading capitalist NICs, South Korea and Taiwan, have over a decade and more achieved high growth, narrowing inequalities, and substantial poverty reduction.

Studies by Morawetz, Chenery and Syrquin, and Stewart all conclude that the available evidence is mixed and that, as such, it is not possible to make generalisations about growth, income distribution and poverty reduction performance across all countries. Morawetz (1977), for example, lists the following countries as those in which over the period 1950–75 the share of income accruing to the poorest has either increased or remained constant: Iran, Israel, South Korea, Singapore, Taiwan, Sri Lanka, Costa Rica, El Salvador and possibly Colombia. However, he lists eight countries where the share to the poorest has declined. Interestingly, Sri Lanka is cited by different authors as a country in which income distribution has both widened and narrowed; India, Pakistan and Indonesia are other countries in which conflicting conclusions about the pattern of growth and equality have arisen (Streeten, 1978:242).

A detailed breakdown of recent trends in poverty alleviation has recently been published by the World Conference on Agrarian Reform and Rural Development (WCARRD) of the FAO in Rome. Its findings in summary form are as follows (FAO, 1984:x):

> The analysis shows that over the last decade some progress has been made towards alleviation of poverty. Out of 96 countries for which data were analysed, 67 experienced growth in per capita calorie supply in relation to their minimum requirements. As a result, the proportion of these countries facing high or medium risks of food inadequacy has been reduced from about 80 per cent in 1970–72 to about 65 per cent in 1978–80. On average, the child death rate has been reduced by about 4.3 per cent and the infant mortality rate by 2.5 per cent per annum. . . .
>
> However, the incidence of absolute rural poverty in recent years (1975–80) is still very high. Out of 68 countries for which information is available, 31 are in the high poverty and 18 are in the low poverty groups. A closer investigation also reveals that the progress in poverty alleviation as measured by different indicators has been poor in high poverty countries. Improvement in calorie requirements met over the period 1970–80 was two per cent on average in the high poverty countries compared to 6.1 and 8.3 per cent for medium and low poverty countries respectively. Out of 29 countries which had an absolute decline in per capita calorie supply in relation to requirements over the period 1972–80, fourteen are in the *African Region*. Similarly, countries with high levels of infant mortality (over 150 per thousand) were able to reduce infant mortality rates by only 0.9 per cent per annum, while countries at low levels of infant mortality (below 100) could reduce it by 4.2 per cent. Latin America has achieved a reduction in the child death rate which is three times as much as in *Africa* and in the infant mortality rate twice as much.
>
> Absolute rural poverty still remains a matter of serious concern. In 1980, out of nearly two billion people living in 68 developing countries for which the estimates of the incidence of rural poverty are available, 1.34 billion are in rural areas and nearly a half of them still live below the estimated poverty line. Nearly two thirds of the poor are in the *Far East* and three fourths are concentrated in eight countries.

Not only has performance differed between countries over time but marked differences have occurred between countries following a broadly capitalist path of development. Moreover, capitalist economies have grown both faster and slower than socialist-type economies and have increased welfare gains to poorer groups faster and slower than the gains achieved in more centrally-planned economies. As Lipton argues: 'the data suggest no plausible indicator of an LDC's degree of socialism or capitalism, of external dependence or autarchy as causally linked to either the efficiency or equity of its overall performance' (1977:74). These variations point to two important conclusions for the present discussion. First, the historical record indicates the fundamental failure of a deterministic explanation for characterising changes in growth, income distribution and poverty alleviation. And secondly, and relatedly, the mixed experience highlights the crucial role that policy initiatives can play in altering patterns of growth, income distribution and poverty. Thus the role of the state remains central to the discussion of development strategy.

There is further common ground to be found in the conclusions to most studies on growth and poverty, that is relevant to leftist criticisms of aid. One is that resource availability, past performance and current patterns of asset and income distribution have all played a crucial role in determining the future possibilities for growth and poverty alleviation. Another is that poverty alleviation and improvements in living standards are crucially determined by changes in *per capita* income. Whether growth leads to a narrowing of income differentials or not, the evidence points strongly to the conclusion that absolute levels of living are only raised in the context of economic growth (Stewart, 1979:24, Hopkins and Van der Hoeven, 1983:108 and Weisskopf, 1983: 453).

This conclusion is argued for succinctly in the 1984 FAO Report thus (p. xi):

> Economic growth, particularly increases in *per capita* agricultural production, appears to be a necessary condition for alleviation of absolute rural poverty. Most of the countries which experienced a decline in food adequacy and marginal improvements in child death and infant mortality rates, had either negative growth or only marginal increases in *per capita* GDP during the period 1970–81.

To many people this is self-evident: Third World countries are classified as such because they have lower levels of income per head than industrialised countries, and Third World countries contain the overwhelming majority of people living below the poverty line. What this means is that economic growth and an increase in resources appear to be fundamentally important conditions for alleviating poverty. It does not necessarily mean that poverty will be eliminated by raising growth levels (as the previous discussion has indicated), but it does suggest that economic growth cannot be held up as the cause of increased or perpetuating poverty. The point is being laboured because a number of critics discussed in this chapter, notably Lappé *et al.*, contend that access to power is a *sufficient* condition for poverty to be eliminated in poor countries. While it may be *necessary* in certain specific countries or sub-regions to obtain an increase political power so as to correct a highly inequitable distribution of assets, such as land or human skills, on their own these gains will not solve the problems of poverty.

And this brings us back to the study by Griffin and Khan. Two of their main conclusions are that the initial distribution of wealth and income has a decisive influence over the pattern of economic growth and hence over the rate of amelioration or deterioration in the standard of living of the lowest income groups, and that given these initial conditions it is difficult to change the distribution of income by manipulating standard policy instruments (1978:301). These conclusions are similar to Morawetz's hypotheses that the initial distribution of assets and incomes may be a crucial determinant of trends in inequality and that once growth is taking place and incomes are being earned it seems difficult to redistribute incomes by means of taxes, public employment, etc. (1977:41). What the thrust of these points suggests is, in general, the following: in a poor country, the greater the inequalities in asset and income distribution and the greater the need for increased access to particular assets to raise income levels (particularly access to land for an agriculturally dependent and poor population), the less likely it will be for growth to solve widespread poverty in the absence of *substantial* changes in income and asset distribution. It is this type of circumstance which has led even writers like Chenery and his World Bank colleagues to state quite explicitly that in certain cases 'we consider an effective land reform to be a necessary condition for the type of strategy propounded in this volume' (Chenery *et al.*, 1974:119).

The crucial question that these issues raise is whether in these particular types of situations there is a positive role that aid funds can play in seeking to achieve the objectives of poverty alleviation. In many respects, the answer lies in the field of politics rather in economics, as even Chenery *et al.* readily admit (119). We are thus back to the critical role of the state in effecting substantial structural change. It does appear that even in *these* particular circumstances there is far more scope than was previously assumed for policies to be implemented which do address crucial structural constraints inhibiting poverty-alleviating growth, even if state power is firmly in the hands of groups that exclude the poor majority in the poorest countries. This conclusion is considered and developed in more detail in Part III below, which reviews country and project-specific evidence in some depth.

But more can be added. If aid is to be provided to assist in the alleviation of poverty, if additional resources are needed to raise the levels of living of the poor, and if the political power equation can be altered by changing the relative economic strength of competing political groupings, then aid funds can be a significant force in altering the politico-economic power balance even in countries where the poor are formally unrepresented in the state power structure. Aid may well help: by providing or expanding credit or marketing facilities to rural farmers or education and technical skills to these groups and to the landless poor, and by increasing the power of those within the political system supporting such measures. Aid that permits governments to allocate resources to poor groups without loss to the prime beneficiaries of an inegalitarian politico-economic system could also be a positive force for change. It could even be argued that aid that increases aggregate wealth provides greater possibilities for material gains to be provided to the poor by a state apparatus that does not reflect their interests, precisely because the provision of such gains at higher levels of 'development' involves fewer losses to the economic and political elites. In other words, in a dynamic context it is not always a zero-sum game that is being played. Clearly only a case-by-case analysis will reveal the room for manoeuvre in particular circumstances.

Importantly, too, one needs to consider the alternatives. Withdrawing aid funds because the likelihood is minimal – in these particular circumstances – of recipient governments carrying out policies that either directly or indirectly provide gains to the poor (whether the aid funds themselves directly benefit the poor could well be a secondary issue), removes an important instrument in government-to-government dialogue and policy leverage. Such action condemns the poor to their perpetual poverty, short of hoping that withdrawal will accelerate the process of radical change occurring internally. And this, if history teaches us any lessons, is far less likely to arise from within groups living on the margins of existence, though its occurrence should not *a priori* be excluded as unfolding events in South Africa tend to suggest. These important points are discussed further in an analysis of aid to Haiti in Chapter 17 of this book.

In this respect, it needs to be stated that the substitution of aid funds from non-official channels may be unlikely to provide an effective alternative. This is in part because, if the problem is diagnosed as essentially and immediately political rather than economic, then successful non-official aid, by improving living standards which lead to an increase in the political power of the poor, is as likely to meet the same resistance from an unrepresentative and intransigent Third World regime as would official aid targeted to the same objectives. But, as the quantities of funds voluntary agencies are able to provide typically fall far short of those that can be channelled officially, these agencies are often better able to achieve their objectives. Few if any would challenge the view that voluntary aid has undoubtedly been successful in assisting poor and marginalised groups. What is more often at the heart of the controversy is not, *contra* the radical critics, whether any aid can ever do any good in particular countries, but whether 'bad' aid – that is aid which neither immediately nor in the long term benefits the poor – can be replaced with aid that does do so.

That said, however, it is not the intention here to go to the other extreme and make a general statement to the effect that there is never a case when official aid should be ruled out because the possibility of its effectively benefitting the poor is so slight as to be, for all practical purposes, nil. It is quite possible in theory to outline circumstances in which the economic structure and the character of the regime are such that the poor are in practice highly unlikely to gain from official aid. (In these instances the moral case for action in a different form from official aid would then almost certainly be paramount.) However, in practice it would appear that these circumstances would probably not include most of those selected by Griffin and Khan. Perhaps Nicaragua in the final years of the Somoza regime would be one such country, although even then there would be some who could argue, with some credibility, that providing Somoza with funds to be channelled immediately into private US bank accounts accelerated his exit. On the other hand, there would appear to be good grounds for providing assistance to relatively stable countries that are by and large excluded from many Western donors' portfolios at the present time: Cuba, North Korea and China. All too frequently, it is the political perceptions of the donors rather than the politico-economic realities and the poverty of the recipient countries which determine the selection and pattern of aid flows.

The argument of the critics that *all* aid should be withheld because the development process that it lubricates is of its nature detrimental to the poor is thus rejected as a proposition with general applicability, and in practice is likely to apply to only a handful of Third World countries. The fact that growth has not led to poverty reduction in particular instances or that aid has had negligible results in redressing such trends, by no means has to lead to the conclusion that therefore growth can never lead to poverty reduction nor that aid cannot have a different effect if inserted in a different manner or in a different form. Clearly a case-by-case evaluation is required and this is the subject of Part III of this study.

Concluding observations

The main conclusions to be drawn from the foregoing discussion are that radical leftist criticisms of aid which maintain that the structural and political constraints are so great as to make foreign aid incapable of assisting recipient economies, and especially of helping to alleviate poverty, have to be rejected. At the theoretical level, they are exceptionally weak, being considerably influenced by largely discredited perspectives within the dependency approach to development and narrow deterministic views of the role of the state in the dynamics of Third World change. An assessment of the (limited) cross-country evidence indicates that poverty certainly has been reduced when economic growth has been achieved within a capitalist-type framework, and that a radical socialist revolution is no guarantee that poverty will be eliminated.

But it would be wrong to conclude that these leftist criticisms and, more broadly, leftist analysis of the development process have little to offer the aid debate. Not only have they highlighted the critical influence that political factors, external economic forces, and patterns of income and wealth distribution can and do play in dynamic development, but their work also challenges the naive view that development professionals have sufficient understanding of the development process to be able to pinpoint accurately and on a basis that can be generalised the 'correct' path to follow. For the aid debate this means that not only is there no automatic link between providing aid and a positive measurable outcome resulting, but that in countries which need more aid - based upon a poverty-reducing requirement - the insertion of aid is likely to be less easy to target and its effects less easy to quantify. In poor countries that have a greater potential for growth and

are implementing policies aimed at poverty reduction with a governmental structure oriented to such an objective, aid funds can more easily be inserted to accelerate this process. Here, there is far less controversy over involvement by donors,
and the evaluation of projects and programmes can provide useful insights into
perfecting the efficiency and effectiveness of aid. Yet for poor countries whose
growth prospects are poor, whose income and asset distribution is highly inequitable, and whose political system is resistant to implementing poverty-reducing
policies, it is far less easy for donors to ensure that aid is used to assist the fundamental transformation required for poverty-reduction to be effective. It is perhaps
ironic, but at the same time depressingly true, to have to admit that the influence
and impact of aid are likely to be less in situations where it is needed most and
where its ability to entrench structures that require change rather than transform
them is far too easy. Leftist aid critics are correct to highlight these issues and to
place them firmly on the agenda, but they are almost certainly wrong, except in
very extreme and probably very few particular instances, in their insistence that aid
in general should be withdrawn or withheld. The question of the optimal response
of donors in the non-extreme situations becomes critical.

It may be that leftist critics and the aid lobbies pressing donor governments to
target aid funds more directly to poverty-reducing projects are in too much of a
hurry. Where millions of people are living on the edge of starvation, this is of
course understandable. However, a clear distinction needs to be made between
emergency aid targeted to specific and recognisable crises and development assistance whose objectives, while still directed at poverty alleviation, are necessarily
more long-term in perspective. And it is the difficult cases – where structures need
to be changed in a growth-oriented strategy, but where they are most resistant to
change – that provide many real problems for concerned donors and their aid
lobbies.

One set of problems is political. If a reorientation of the politico-economic
structures of a recipient economy is an important factor for poverty-reduction to
be effective, what room for manoeuvre is there for donors to insert aid funds that
have the effect, directly or indirectly, of influencing the prevailing balance of
group-interests in favour of the poor and marginalised? Both leftist critics of aid
and even the redistribution-with-growth literature have alerted us to the fact that
this question is of critical importance, but the literature remains woefully silent on
providing answers. Donors tend to ignore the question by attempting, vainly, to
maintain that aid issues can be separated from politics, or by attempting to avoid
the issue by not providing aid to certain countries where the political question
becomes exceptionally transparent. In the former case, the question of the room
for manoeuvre remains unanswered; in the latter, the donor has washed its hands
of the plight of the poor. Clearly both responses are inadequate as a means of
addressing seriously the problems of Third World poverty in the grey areas where
poor countries are characterised by inhibiting structural and political rigidities.

Another set of related problems concerns the time-horizon. There is little doubt
that donors and aid lobbyists share the conviction that Third World poverty
constitutes a problem requiring urgent attention: for some because of a moral
imperative, for others because extensive poverty is seen as a threat to world stability. There is little doubt, too, that this concern has been in large part responsible
for the popularity of basic-needs types of strategies of development and the
emphasis given to channelling aid more directly and explicitly to the poorest. In
some respects, the quick-fix response of the public – elicited by pictures of the
famine in Africa – of throwing money at the aid agencies to enable them to throw

food at the starving is replicated by the quick-fix attitude of the aid-to-the poorest lobby. While attempting to channel aid directly to the poorest is in many respects praiseworthy, it is by no means certain, even when political and structural conditions in recipient countries are favourable, that this is exclusively the best path to follow. Assisting the poor, and especially more of the poor in a more lasting way, might well be achieved better by indirect means which provide them with no or few immediate tangible gains. The fact of poverty, and the identification of poverty groups, neither guarantees that direct aid is a better way of eradicating poverty nor that it is the most efficient way, given especially the different skills, expertise, and appropriate products available among different donors. There are certainly grounds for believing that, had aid to Africa over the past 15 years been directed more to rehabilitating infrastructural and particularly transport facilities, then the crisis affecting so many countries might well have been less acute (See UN, 1986:18).

In the case of countries characterised by structural and political rigidities and highly inequitable asset and income distribution patterns, the objective of utilising aid resources to reduce poverty is clearly far harder to achieve. Here time-horizon questions are intricately related to the political room for manoeuvre. Accepting the theoretical arguments discussed above that political rigidities and non-poverty-oriented regimes are by no means permanent features of the Third World political landscape, it would appear that there is often scope for providing assistance that is, on the one hand, of long-term benefit to the poor, while, on the other, not supporting or reinforcing those rigidities that are a major part of the problem. Again, while this should be a critical area for research, it has tended to be by-passed by analysts working in the aid field. This occurs at least in part because the difficulty of channelling aid directly to the poorest in these countries leads aid lobbyists to downgrade them in the public eye, thus lessening the need for politicians to venture into these grey areas and examine the possibilities of initiating effective change. Meanwhile, the poor in these countries remain unaided, poor and marginalised.

Our conclusions, therefore, on the radical leftist attacks on aid turn out to be far less critical than would at first appear. While the arguments they put forward have to be rejected as general propositions with wide applicability, their work has enriched the aid debate considerably. They have isolated key weaknesses in conventional aid theory, highlighting the critical need to incorporate wider historical, structural, political and external factors into any comprehensive assessment of aid's impact and its potentially harmful effects. But, in addition, their analysis has pointed to important areas of the aid debate that have still not been sufficiently considered by either aid practitioners or donor governments. As with the aid, savings and growth debate, this can only assist in providing a greater understanding of how external and internal factors can change or be changed to enhance future aid effectiveness.

Notes

1. There are a wide variety of theories and sub-groupings of theories of development associated with leftist scholars. Some of these are associated – either by the scholars themselves or the critics – with the term 'structuralism'. The term 'structuralism' in the text is used here to embrace all groupings

that include structural elements in their theoretical writings, and should not be interpreted narrowly as a consideration of only those theories that more narrowly are referred to as structuralist.

2. Myrdal develops these ideas most fully in his three-volumed work, *Asian Drama: An Inquiry into the Poverty of Nations* (1968). A more popular and accessible analysis of the soft state is provided in *The Challenge of World Poverty* (1970), especially Chapters 7 and 8, where he explains that (208): 'The term "soft state" is understood to comprise all the various types of social indiscipline which manifest themselves by: deficiencies in legislation and in particular law observance and enforcement, a widespread disobedience by public officials on various levels to rules and directives handed down to them, and often their collusion with powerful persons and groups of persons whose conduct they should regulate. Within the concept of the soft state belongs also corruption. . . . These several patterns of behaviour are interrelated in the sense that they permit or even provoke each other in circular causation having cumulative effects.'

3. It is not our intention here to provide a rigorous treatment of imperialism. Suffice it to note that not even all writers on imperialism within the Leninist perspective argue that imperialism cannot lead to positive benefits for the victims of imperialist forces. For a good historical treatment of the different views see Palma (1981), Higgott (1983) and Randall and Theobald (1985).

4. The literature on basic-needs strategies of development embraces a wide variety of different approaches, some more closely associated with more orthodox growth-oriented development and some including radical structural change on their agendas for action. Some authors, for example Hopkins and Van Der Hoeven (1983), reject the notion that there is a general basic-needs strategy that is distinct and identifiable as a general theory.

5. This is developed in 'The Political Room for Manoeuvre' in an unpublished manuscript prepared for graduate students in development studies, Institute for Development Studies at the University of Sussex, 1975 (mimeo).

12 Criticisms from the Right

Foreign Aid and Market Forces

Conventional aid theory, as outlined in Chapter 9, asserts that the insertion of external resources into the recipient economy can help to accelerate the development process through relieving specific bottlenecks caused by limited domestic resources and limited access to external resources channelled through non-aid mechanisms. The theory is at the same time both market-based and market-pessimistic. Aid intervention is perceived as desirable because of the inadequacy of the market in poor countries to deliver high levels of economic growth and development, but aid is also inserted in the hope and expectation that there will eventually no longer be any necessity to provide it, because markets will then be sufficiently developed to throw up signals and lead to responses that no longer require sustained non-market external intervention.[1] Within this general perspective, the basic needs-type approaches of the 1970s can be placed. Here emphasis was placed on market failures, and it was concluded that direct action targeted at the alleviation of poverty was a necessary component of aid intervention resulting from market failure. However, within this framework market-oriented growth was still seen as the final objective to be attained, even though aid intervention was now viewed as a more long-lasting necessity than had previously been assumed.

It is within this context that the influential rightist criticisms of foreign aid, especially as advocated in the late 1970s and the 1980s, need to be placed. Rooted in neo-classical economic theory, the rightist perspective asserts that intervention through aid frustrates or, in its most radical form, impedes the development process. At its centre is an extreme optimism about the efficacy of the market, and the overriding benefits of a non-distorted price system and private enterprise to achieve sustained and accelerated development on their own. Like criticisms of aid from the radical left, this attack is broadly-based and at its root is not dependent upon an evaluation of what aid achieves in practice, for, as with the leftist criticisms, aid is perceived as part of the problem impeding the achievement of faster growth and development.

At their most extreme, rightist critics give no place to aid, for of its nature, as a form of intervention channelled to recipient governments, it is said to frustrate the free operation of the market, to distort the price system, and to impede private-sector development. Less extreme *laisser faire* theorists would favour a type of aid that is directed at private-sector expansion in a framework characterised by less direct government intervention in the economy, usually in the context of declining overall aid flows. Even in its less extreme manifestation, this general perspective is clearly at odds with the aid intervention associated with basic-needs-type approaches to development, for this intervention is seen to be market and price distorting. However, the extreme pro-market approach also challenges the more traditional theory of aid intervention. While it agrees that bottlenecks and domestic resource shortages are impeding more rapid development in poor countries, it rejects any government-based interventionist strategy to relieve these shortages even in the short term. For the *laisser faire* theorists, the efficient operation of the market provides the only sure basis for sustained development and so it should always be promoted: if external resources are needed for development, then it is market signals which will both pinpoint this need and also provide the necessary price signals for these resources to flow to where they are required. In short, scarcity of capital or other resources that poor countries are experiencing is a symptom of market failure or price distortion, to be remedied not by interventionism but by policies that address these failures and distortions.

It should be stressed that much of the aid debate at the policy level in the 1980s has not been concerned with arguing for extreme positions – whether aid intervention or sole reliance on market forces be viewed as mutually exclusive alternatives. Rather, it has been concerned to move the middle ground either more in the direction of an interventionist or a non-interventionist strategy in a world where intervention and market forces are both part of the given reality. None the less, the debates that have been taking place in the middle ground have been critically influenced by the merits that the more extreme *laisser-faire* perspective is perceived to hold out for sustained and accelerated development in poor countries today. The fact that greater emphasis has been placed on non-interventionist strategies and that market forces are accorded a greater weight in policy dialogue than heretofore has had a significant influence upon aid intervention policies and perceptions about the role that aid should play in the development process. Thus an evaluation of the rightist criticisms of aid is important, not only to examine the merits of the extreme rightist perspective but equally to help inform the debate about the emphasis to be placed upon intervention and market forces at the margin.

In the next section of this chapter the views of major rightist critics are outlined; we then examine the theoretical basis for the rightist perspective, and thereafter look at the theory in relation to the real world, particularly in the context of conditions currently prevailing in the economies of poor countries.

The criticisms outlined

The general flavour of the rightist perspective is well illustrated in a two-volume report published in 1984 and prepared by President Reagan's Task Force on International Private Enterprise.[2] The Task Force explains that foreign assistance resources should be used to foster economic and social development but stresses that past strategies have been flawed by placing emphasis on social rather than economic development. What is needed, it is argued, is essentially the promotion of economic development, for with it come the resources needed to pay for social programmes which can, in turn, help accelerate development. Promoting economic development means promoting 'the role of private enterprise, free markets and competition' (Vol. I, 1984:30).

The Task Force maintains that this is the essence of the Reagan Administration's private-sector initiative, based on the fundamental belief that greater reliance on private enterprise, individual initiative and free competitive markets is essential for sustained equitable growth in the Third World (Vol. II, 1984:87). Specifically spelt out is the role that recipient governments should adopt to promote development in their countries (Vol. II:70):

Pursuing a private enterprise strategy does not imply that there is no role for government. A country's government must decide initially to allow market forces to find full commercial expression, assist in creating an environment conducive to risk-taking and innovation and provide the necessary infrastructure. It does suggest that government must define its policies carefully and avoid impeding private sector growth.

Amongst economists, the *laisser-faire* viewpoint and its applicability to the aid debate has been developed by writers such as Friedman, Bauer, Yamey and Krauss.[3] Their ideas have been described in some detail in Part I of this study; we shall consider here only the main outline of their particular perspective. All four authors share the view that, because economic development is best promoted by extending and expanding the penetration of market forces, then aid as presently distributed and channelled should be reduced or, better still, eliminated. Bauer, for example, has written 'I think that official aid should be terminated as soon as possible' (1979:239) because, he maintains, aid has tended to obstruct rather than promote development (1984:43). In similar vein, Friedman has written that 'Foreign aid is likely to retard improvement in the well-being of the masses' (1958:78). Krauss, more stridently, has stated that the absence of aid is 'an essential condition for economic development' (1983:90).

Bauer, Yamey and Friedman place particular emphasis on the role of individual initiative and market forces as key essential factors for promoting sustained development; Krauss highlights in particular the distorting effects of government intervention in recipient economies. For Bauer, the essential component of development is 'the extension of the range of choice of people as consumers and producers', which is most likely to be achieved in a freely operating market system 'in which firms and individuals largely determine what is produced and consumed, where they will work, how much they will save and how they will invest their savings' (1984a:22 and 25). Again, with his colleague Professor Yamey, Bauer has written (1981, quoted in Meier, 1984:294):

> Economic achievement has depended, as it still does depend, on people's own faculties, motivations, and ways of life, on their institutions and on their rulers. In short, economic achievement depends on the conduct of people, including governments. External donations have not been necessary for the development of any country, anywhere.

They go on to argue that if poor countries need capital from abroad and can use it productively, then they are able to borrow it, even to finance the enhancement of a country's physical infrastructure. Friedman makes a similar general point, arguing 'what is required [for economic development] is an atmosphere of freedom, of maximum opportunity for individuals to experiment, and of incentive for them to do so in an environment in which there are objective tests of success and failure – in short a vigorous free capitalistic market' (1958:71).

For Krauss, one of the fundamental obstacles to economic development, understood as dynamic and competitive market expansion, is 'big government' precisely because it impedes effective market signals and distorts the price system. If, he argues, 'there is a secret formula for economic growth, it is that no economy can prosper with the monkey of big government on its back' (1983:187). Now because foreign aid involves a transfer of income between governments, according to Krauss it necessarily increases the role and influence of governments in the economic sphere, thereby accentuating the essential impediment to economic progress. Foreign aid 'is part of a strategy of activist and interventionist government . . . for the recipient country, foreign aid allows big government to pursue policies that damage the competitive sectors of the economy and thus its economic base'

(188). This is also a point stressed by Bauer, who more concretely explains that 'aid has made it possible for governments to pursue such policies as subsidised import substitution, forced collectivisation, price policies that inhibit agricultural production . . . inflationary financial policies and the maintenance of over-valued exchange rates' (1984:49). Poor people, maintains Krauss, can escape poverty if the right policies are put in place which permit capitalist accumulation and international exchange (1983:54).

For all these rightist critics, the proof of the soundness of their ideas lies in the evidence they believe exists to support their perspective. Friedman's view is that, to date, a free market without central planning has been 'not only the most effective route to economic development but the only effective route to a rising standard of life for the masses of the people' (1958:72). For Bauer, the example of cocoa growers in Ghana and rubber producers in Malaysia provides evidence to show the effect of individual initiative on development, and the fact that so many so-called Third World countries with centralist governments receiving aid have failed to achieve dynamic growth is put forward to prove his point that 'foreign aid can do little or nothing for development or relief of poverty' (1984:51) Krauss maintains that the economic success of countries like Taiwan and South Korea began precisely when aid flows were halted and they adopted policies based on market signals and international competitive pricing (1983:160). The prosperity of the Gang of Four, he argues, is attributable to their ability 'not to handicap themselves by crippling the dynamic and competitive sectors of their economies with big government' (187).

Though each of these authors is clearly against foreign aid, it is Bauer who has been most influential in the English-speaking world in shifting the middle ground in the 1980s towards the free market perspective. This is because he has recognised that official aid flows to recipient countries are likely to persist and, accepting this reality, has put forward proposals for altering the nature of the aid relationship. Not that his views have all been incorporated into the new policy initiatives of governments influenced by *laisser-faire* ideas. For example, he has proposed that commodity aid agreements should end, that soft loans should be replaced by outright grants, and, in relation to overall economic policy, that industrialised countries should reduce their often severe barriers to imports from poor countries (1984:61–2). Few of these policies have been adopted by donor governments, indeed commodity aid agreements have been extended further in the 1980s and trade protectionism appears to be on the increase. None the less, his most fundamental proposal – that aid should go to governments that have attempted to promote economic progress through establishing a more effective administrative structure and pursuing liberal economic policies – has certainly been influential in aid policy circles both bilateral and multilateral. Moreover, his views that 'The Prime Minister should resist attempts to expand and entrench foreign aid' (*The Times*, 11 April 1983), and that the relief of immediate need should become far more the responsibility of voluntary agencies than official donor governments and their aid departments, have also been a major component of the rightist rhetoric of the 1980s.[4]

That the Bauer view has been important in the policy field is apparent not only from the strong parallels between his proposals and those of President Reagan's Task Force and the fact that he was raised to the peerage by Mrs Thatcher, but also by specific references to his views made by senior policy-makers. For example, as we saw in the Introduction to Part I of this book, the US Under-Secretary for Economic Affairs, Allen Wallis, in a speech in 1983 to the Heritage Foundation, made direct reference to the 'powerful case' made by Bauer and Yamey against official development assistance and the important job they had done in 'demolishing' many of the arguments in its favour.[5]

The theory of the market[6]

Lying behind the rightist criticism of aid interventionism, in both its mild and its radical form, is a central belief in the beneficial characteristics of the market, which is rooted in the theory of perfect competition and central theorems of welfare economics and equilibrium analysis. Economic policies highlighting the operation of free markets are based either explicitly or implicitly on what is termed general equilibrium theory, the most complete model of the free-market economy. General equilibrium analysis is concerned with the interaction of a large number of economic agents, individuals, and firms, connected together by various inter-linked markets in a co-ordinating mechanism through the price system.

The equilibrium price in one market is the one which will clear the market, that is, where all demand is satisfied and all goods are sold and where all consumers and producers are satisfied with the quantity of goods exchanged. Furthermore, if, for some reason, demand for particular products increases, the price for this product will increase, resulting in producers supplying more; the price mechanism will thus have smoothly transformed an increased desire for a product into increased output. At this stage equilibrium in that particular market will have been restored through a supply response brought about by a price change initiated by a change in demand.

So much for the situation prevailing in a single market. The total economy is made up of a whole array of different markets – for different products, different factors of production, and different service industries. General equilibrium is the economic state in which all different markets are simultaneously in equilibrium. This occurs if all these various markets, connected together by the price mechanism, are permitted to operate freely; individual choices of consumers and producers will determine the structure of the whole economy, what and how much it produces and consumes.[7] And there is more. The effects of these multitudinous individual choices not only benefit every individual in the economy, they also result in an outcome that is beneficial in a far wider framework. Welfare economists have been able to prove to most people's satisfaction, using complex mathematical techniques, that a fully free-market economy produces out of all possible economic outcomes the best for the welfare of its people. This best-possible outcome is known as 'Pareto-optimal', occurring in a competitive economy in general equilibrium. Any attempt to interfere in the operation of the free market which will shift it away from its general equilibrium position will induce a result that is in welfare terms non-optimal: some people will necessarily be made worse-off. Moreover, work by the Franco-Swiss economist, Léon Walras, in the last century was able to prove, again using sophisticated mathematical techniques, that a state of general equilibrium is stable and in theory can exist and persist.

These different theoretical insights provide the foundation for the rightist criticism of aid intervention; their influence cannot be emphasised too strongly. They show clearly, with logic and mathematical precision, not only that free markets based upon free and perfect competition and the absence of interventionism in the economy create the conditions for maximum economic efficiency, but that the interaction of different perfect markets in the whole economy results in both the best use of all resources and circumstances in which optimal welfare gains can be achieved.

Two major and interrelated questions need to be raised, however. First, how relevant to the real world is the theory and, secondly, given the fact that the real world is far from that constructed for the theoretical model to work as predicted, what are the implications for the debate about interventionism? We shall examine each of these issues in turn.

For the Walrasian general equilibrium model to function as predicted a number of assumptions are necessary. The main ones include the following: there is full and free competition in all markets; there is no historical, only instantaneous, time: the model is essentially static; there is perfect and instantaneous information available; there are no externalities in the economy: all costs and benefits are included in private transactions and there are no 'public' goods, such as defence, public administration etc., that either exist or which distort prices reflecting solely full and free competition; all products in different markets are completely homogeneous; and there are no economies of scale. For Pareto-optimality to be achieved additional assumptions are required. In particular, it is necessary to assume that the distribution of wealth and income, the state of technology, and people's preferences for goods and services remain unaltered and unchanged. Severely restrictive conditions are needed to achieve free-market equilibrium in just one market, and as the economy becomes more complex and interactive these conditions have to be extended to all the different markets that make up the whole economy.

It does not require a degree in economics to realise that these restrictive assumptions are far removed from the world of the real economy, and especially the real world of poor countries. Some crucial differences can be listed. Most fundamentally, the world does not consist of markets characterised by full and free competition where prices are flexible, responding instantaneously to changes in consumers' demand and initiating an immediate increase in supply. Markets certainly exist but, especially in the Third World, they are often made up of a few firms which tend to dominate in the production sphere, and there is a far from perfect informational link between consumers and producers. Distance and the lack of communication provide major barriers to informational flows, thereby creating partial or distorted rather than complete and perfectly inter-linked markets. Most poorer developing countries are characterised by dualistic rather than homogeneous markets: traditional structures exist with different types of organisational structures from those in the modern sectors of the economy, frequently with different labour and capital markets, different price structures for resources, and different access to technology. Advances in communication technology in the industrialised world, still far from complete, illustrate starkly that Walras' assumption of perfect and instantaneous information is an assumption that simply does not hold.

Another characteristic of modern economies, again seen more extremely in the Third World, is that products in different markets are far from homogeneous, and product differentiation tends to be the norm rather than the exception. Thus yet another assumption is challenged. Similarly, technological change and benefits of economies of scale are particularly important for aid-recipient countries trying to establish new industries and new production processes, either where none have existed before or to replace traditional or less efficient methods of production. This, together with changing consumer tastes brought about by structural changes and internal migration in Third World economies, illustrates another major difference between the perfectly competitive model and the real world.

Many of these particular differences between the assumptions necessary for the model to operate and the reality of Third World economies could be considered as characteristic of low levels of economic development, and there is certainly hope that in time some of the more extreme differences between the freely-competitive model and Third World economies might be lessened. As countries develop so markets are likely to become more complete and interrelated, information flows to improve, product differentiation to decrease, and the effects of economies of scale likely to be less discontinuous. Although even here it is highly doubtful that all the conditions necessary for full and free competition in all markets will ever be achieved (see Hahn, 1982).

There are, however, other assumptions that could never be expected to hold, whatever progress is likely in the future. For instance, the model is based on free markets in a single economy, whereas the world consists of individual economies bounded by the reality of nation states. These states are not only of different size and composition, but they cut across markets creating structural rigidities and barriers that seriously and permanently challenge the applicability of the free-market model. Admittedly for those economies without exchange-control restrictions and with free-floating exchange rates (few, if any of the Third World economies) financial and capital markets are more international, and companies do move across national boundaries making decisions on an international basis. However, this is the exception, and even in relationships between economies there is little likelihood of a free flow of resources, particularly labour, or even the likelihood of a system of free international trade. Moreover, public goods are a significant and influential part of real economies and there is little chance of their disappearing; even the minimal state will continue to exist, integrated into the economy by employing people, raising revenue and spending money. Then, too, there is the problem of relating the notion of the invisible hand to the workings of real economies. As Hahn writes (1984:117):

> one cannot invoke the classical theory of the invisible hand in dealing with economies in which agents have market power. If such an economy attains some coherent state to be called equilibrium, all market information will not be summarized by prices. The signals to which the agents respond will be much richer and the kinds of things they would like to know much more varied. One can, however, assert that the outcome will, in general, not be Pareto efficient.

In poor economies these structural characteristics are even more pronounced and market-distorting than in industrialised economies, although even here the differences between the abstract model and the real world remain profound.

Another permanent distortion arises in the real world, because of the crucial influence that information plays in economic development. While the freely competitive model assumes that information is a freely exchangeable good and perfect foresight attainable, this is never likely to hold because information about new techniques of production and new products is acquired at a cost. The establishment of patent laws and copyright procedures is a recognition of this fact, and recent developments in the world of informatics indicate that this crucial area of 'distortion' is going to become more marked in the years to come.[8]

There is, then, no doubt that the model from which the beneficial conclusions are derived bears little or no relation to the world of developing economies; moreover, it is never likely to do so. That much is clear. This leads to the crucially important question of the relevance of the model for policy-making in the real world. In a world radically divorced from the constructs of the theoretical model, what policies should be implemented to accelerate economic growth and achieve maximum welfare gains?

For the rightist critics of aid intervention, the answer lies quite simply in implementing policies which address as many of the distortions in the real world as possible so as to move the real world closer to the world of the free-market model. This strategy is advocated because of a crucial and fundamental belief, namely that, in attempting to move from the real world to one closer to that of perfect competition and general stable equilibrium, there is a better chance that the outcome predicted in the theoretical model will be achieved than if alternative policies are adopted. In short, because it can be proved that the competitive model will lead to maximum resource efficiency and definable welfare gains, it is assumed that policies promoting the extension and penetration of market forces, removing price distortions and subsidies, favouring private enterprise, and decreasing state intervention in the economy will be more beneficial than any other set of policy prescriptions, particularly those that are market and price distorting or which favour either the maintenance or increase of direct interventionism. If this assumption is found to be universally correct, then the rightist critics of aid intervention will be substantially vindicated. At the theoretical level, however, there is much left to answer.

The first thing to say about this pro-free-market assumption is that, although it is widely held, there is no formal theory available to prove its general validity. Indeed, doubt about its validity is highlighted by work that has been conducted to analyse what is likely to happen to the model when the assumptions upon which it is based do not hold. The effects are profound.

This is illustrated clearly in examining the welfare implications of the model. Pareto-optimality, in particular, falls victim to the realities of the real world. The theory of the second-best, generalised by Lipsey and Lancaster (1956–7) and, as with Pareto-optimality, demonstrated mathematically, shows that the marginal conditions of the Paretian-optimum are not valid criteria of an increase in welfare in a context where they are not *all and simultaneously* satisfied. If even one condition cannot be fulfilled anywhere in the economy, then a first-best solution cannot be achieved. Moreover, the belief that it is necessarily better to try to fulfil some of the conditions rather than none or even one is found to be false. There is no corresponding set of rules for the achievement of a second-best solution or even a better position where the first-best is not attainable. As Winch (1971:111) explains, the importance of this principle is difficult to overestimate. He continues:

It is not true, for example, that public utilities or nationalised industries should price at marginal cost when other industries do not. Repeal of an apparently distorting marginal tax might reduce welfare if other marginal taxes remain in force. Repeal of tariffs on certain commodities, or on all commodities from certain countries by formation of a customs union, is not supported by the case for free trade unless free trade is universal, and the case for free trade is not substantiated on Paretian grounds unless all countries simultaneously achieve Paretian optimum positions internally.

Another worry about the supposed beneficial effects of increasing market power in the absence of full and free competition relates to individual action. The free-market model is based fundamentally on the assumption that individuals and firms act out of self-interest. In the model, the potential excesses of individual action are kept in check by the actions of others which prevent the emergence of gains from monopolistic or oligopolistic power. However, in the real world of market distortions and far from perfect competition, this same self-interest operates with, at minimum, the potential for maintaining or expanding market distortions (through, for example, withholding information or gaining access to privileged information) so that those exerting their market influence can gain at the expense of others. There would seem, in other words, to be a built-in tendency to frustrate the beneficial results suggested by the model, indicating that in the imperfect world in which we live the consequences of relying more on market forces are unlikely to be entirely benign. There is every reason to believe that these adverse consequences will be greater in poorer less developed economies than in more sophisticated ones. There is thus no guarantee or theoretical justification for supposing that giving freer rein to market forces when market distortions are prevalent will either lead to a more efficient use of resources or to more widespread welfare gains. It could be that in this very imperfect world controls and intervention will be required. It is an unresolved dilemma for *laisser-faire* theorists that there is a case for natural monopolies to be at least overseen by the state if they are to be run by private concerns – as has occurred in Britain in the conditions of sale of British Telecom to the private sector. At minimum, this suggests that information is required *outside* the market mechanism and that some sort of intervention or countervailing force is needed to monitor and control excesses, even in situations where structural change – a fundamental component of development – is ignored.

Laisser-faire theory places great stress on prices and upon the need to remove price distortions caused in particular by state intervention and subsidies. The central questions this poses are at what level prices should be set and what power prices should exert. To argue that removing price distortions in a non-free-market economy will lead to the best allocation of resources calls into question both whether all distortions can be removed and, even if they can, whether the prices thrown up by the present non-competitive markets are indeed the best possible set of prices available. But even if prices are altered (for example, by removing price subsidies) to reflect better the current interaction of supply and demand, there is still a need to ask if getting prices 'right' will be sufficient to achieve rapid development. One problem concerns information. The fact that millions of dollars are spent in industrialised countries on advertising, market research and demand forecasting indicates that prices on their own are insufficient for decision-making. In poorer countries, these information gaps are even more pronounced. In many instances, prices are simply not known. But even if they are, there is no guarantee that either suppliers or consumers will be able to respond to them in an efficient manner. The beneficial effect of rising prices to call forth higher levels of supply is itself determined by access to the resources needed to raise production levels and access to the markets to sell what is produced. In poor countries this generalised access simply does not exist for large numbers of the population, limited as they also are by geographical and financial constraints. Consumers, too, frequently have no money to purchase goods on the market and no means of travelling to purchase goods, if they are available in specific, often urban, parts of the country.

Moreover, to have faith in the ability of prices to lead to a more efficient allocation of resources, it is necessary to assume that short-run price elasticities are high and that price shifts lead to a rapid shift to a new equilibrium position. To the extent that groups in Third World countries are living either outside the market place or only marginally linked to it, this assumption becomes highly questionable. Furthermore, much economic decision-making in more sophisticated economies depends critically upon the ability to anticipate correctly future price changes; those at the centre are better able to do this and thus to benefit more than those in peripheral areas. In this case overdependence on the price mechanism can have the effect of distributing benefits unevenly, with implications for long-term growth for different groups.

Theoretical work by Clower and Leijonufvud raises additional questions about the merits of dependence upon the price system to achieve the desired objectives of *laisser-faire* theory when the economy is in a state of disequilibrium. At disequilibrium prices, some potential sellers will be unable to sell all their products (markets will not be cleared); their incomes will therefore be lower than the optimal level. It follows then that the economy will face a demand problem which, through the multiplier effect, will lead to both unemployment and less than full output. In poor countries characterised already by high levels of unemployment, these problems are magnified: there are people who would like to work but cannot, and who would like to purchase goods but cannot because of their lack of purchasing power derived from their unemployment. The price system fails to provide the information required to connect potential demand with the ability of the economy to produce. What is more, this particular problem will not be solved by inducing wage cuts, and it is beyond the power of any single firm to correct this type of distortion. As Leijonufvud (1981) explains: 'the market signals presupposed in general equilibrium analysis are not transmitted' (quoted in Smith, 1984:181).

The general conclusions from this part of the discussion are well summarised by Smith (1984:182):

> So question one on the agenda is whether economic theory gives us any grounds for belief in free markets and free market economic policies as a basis for solving our problems. The answer seem to be 'no'. Keynesian theory, and the work of some general equilibrium theorists, suggests that market economies are *not* the self-stabilising, welfare-maximising machines which neoclassical economics would have us place our faith in.

If there is uncertainty about the applicability of the insights of the free-market model to market economies, then *a fortiori* there should be even more concern about its applicability to poor countries where market forces are even less fully developed. This point is developed by Nugent and Yotopoulos, who question the appropriateness of 'excessive reliance on the market mechanism at the early stages of development' (1979:541). While these authors could in no way be categorised as anti-marketeers, they believe that in the least developed economies the logic of the market is to increase 'biformity or backwash forces' rather than spread effects. This is in part because firms that are already established not only have a market-dominant position but are better placed to take advantage of new opportunities arising, thereby building further on their success in the process of technological change and capital accumulation. Factor movements from the traditional to the more market-oriented sectors simply do not occur in the manner suggested by free-market theorists. The consequence is that development in market-oriented developing countries can by no means be assumed to be dominated by automatic, equilibrating and development-spreading effects as the free-market model and policies derived from it would seem to imply (550). If, as Nugent and Yotopoulos suggest, disequilibrating forces are an important factor in the long-run evolution of market-oriented poor countries, then it is clearly necessary to provide counter-vailing forces to correct these endogenous distortions. They maintain that interventionist policies should be adopted 'in order to offset the systematic biases attributable to the operation of the market in the early stages of development' (550).[9]

One particular element of the free-market case that is emphasised by foreign aid critics like Bauer and Friedman is the role of individual choice and motivation in the process of development. In a recent critique, Sen has argued that the view that the 'invisible hand of the market will turn the quest for private profit into generalised visible social gains is not very convincing'. 'This is because the formulation of the incentive problem in terms of carrots and sticks, in which the individual is driven by lust for gain (the carrot) and the fear of losses and impoverishment (the stick) to give their best to society, is fundamentally misleading.' He continues (1984:2–3):

> While some economic relations operate through the market, involving prices and profits, many of the more important ones do not. When, for example, we move away from individual farming to modern industrial enterprises, the relationship between one worker and another is not a price-based involvement, and indeed even between the worker and the management, the relationship incorporates a variety of complex nonprice relations including trust, obligation and a socially conditioned sense of duty. Indeed, only in rather limited areas of economic interaction can it be said that interrelations between persons can be sensibly based on the pure pursuit of selfishness. Social norms emerge and reflect – to various extents – social and economic necessities, or *perceived* necessities.

Or, as Dasgupta and Ray put it – countering Bauer's view that people in Third World countries, including the poor, value individual choice – while the poor certainly do value free choice, what is fundamentally at issue is the inability of prevailing markets to offer them choices that will have an impact and lead to material improvements in their economic well-being (1985:36). As Salazar-Xirinachs goes on to explain (1985:43–4), not only are markets in the real world myopic because of insufficient foresight and information and insufficient learning, but economic agents especially in less developed countries

> have imperfect perceptions in the more fundamental sense that their perceptions of interest and obligation do not coincide with the perfect or pure individual gains . . . of the neoclassical theoreticans' economic agent. These imperfect perceptions can affect economic performance in two ways. They could be obstacles to development or they could smooth the behaviour of markets and constitute important factors in their own right in explaining successful economic performance. As long as economic theory adheres rigidly to a narrow view of what is viewed as a carrot and what is seen as a stick by individual agents, it will remain blind to consider those determinants of economic performance and development which go beyond the 'system of incentives' narrowly defined.

A final aspect of this debate needs to be highlighted. The free-market model is in essence a full-employment model: it assumes that all resources are fully utilised and that marginal changes can quickly bring the economy back to stable equilibrium.[10] Contrast this with the economies of Third World countries, where a prime characteristic is that resources lie idle or are severely underutilised. Development therefore requires not simply growth and more efficient use of resources that are already touched by the market, but structural change in addition. It is a lumpy, not a smooth and homogeneous process, and has as a key objective the raising of the incomes of the poor. Furthermore, social and political factors *do* have an influence on growth and development and these are affected by non-market factors. The free-market model simply does not address the question of market extension into non-market areas, and is based on the assumption that the distribution of income remains unchanged. It is surely for this reason that so much attention has been focused on basic needs and redistributive issues – in part because of the recognition that addressing needs and raising incomes of the poorest can have a beneficial effect on long-term growth as well as on immediate consumption levels. A related issue is one of timing. Developing countries not only desire to grow but, given the extent of their poverty, they have the additional objective of needing to accelerate their rates of growth. Harry Johnson, no particular friend of intervention, was ready to agree that even if markets are operating perfectly they will not produce as high a growth rate as society desires and that to achieve more rapid growth 'state action is desirable to raise the rate of growth' (1962, quoted in Meier, 1984:714).

Aid and market theory

The previous discussion has said little specific about aid. It has, however, provided the background necessary for evaluating at the theoretical level the views of the rightist critics. The weaknesses of their position should now be apparent. Their theoretical attack on aid intervention is not based directly on insights drawn from economic theory, but rather on the assertion that the conclusions of abstract free-market theory are applicable to aid-recipient economies and therefore that market-based solutions are preferable. The implication is that the market rather than intervention offers a surer way of achieving sustained development and thus where aid is inserted it should always be in a manner supportive of the market.

Thus the main criticisms of the rightist perspective lie not in the theory of the free market but in applying – and frequently applying wholesale – the conclusions derived from the abstract model to the real world of aid-recipient economies. This application of the model is illegitimate as a basis for generalised policy conclusions for two reasons. First, the assumptions on which the free-market theory is based are substantially divorced from the realities of aid-recipient economies, but, secondly, there are theoretical grounds for suggesting that, when these assumptions are relaxed and replaced by crucial elements reflecting actual conditions in these economies, outcomes in direct conflict with the beneficial conclusions of the critics could well result.

To use the free-market equilibrium theory as the basis for advocating exclusive market-based policy prescriptions in contrast to interventionist or even mixed economy solutions is fraught with difficulties. For as Professor Hahn puts it (1973:322).

> I have always regarded competitive General Equilibrium analysis as akin to the mock-up an aircraft engineer might build. My amazement in recent years has accordingly been very great to find many economists are passing the mock-up off as an airworthy plane and that politicians, bankers and commentators are scrambling to get seats. This is at a time when theorists all over the world have become aware that anything based on this mock-up is unlikely to fly, since it neglects some crucial aspects of the world, the recognition of which will force some drastic redesigning; in particular it provides no account of the actual working of the Invisible Hand.

What does this mean for the aid debate? Simply that there is no adequate theoretical basis for maintaining as a general truth either that no aid or that less aid or that aid targeted at the private sector or at expanding market forces will necessarily lead to beneficial results for the economic growth and development of poor countries. There is, in other words, no theoretical justification for arguing, as the rightist critics do, that a switch to greater market discipline, a more significant role for the private sector, and a deregulated price system will necessarily be more advantageous for Third World development.

It is important to stress, however, that this rejection of the rightist theoretical criticism of aid implies neither a rejection of the role of markets in development nor a green light for all interventionism. Conventional aid theory is market-oriented but not market-exclusive: it sees a specific and important role for aid interventionism, because it recognises defects and failures in market systems in poor countries and because it believes, given a favourable response in aid-recipient economies, that external resources can assist in raising income levels and accelerating the growth process. To reject the rightist critique of aid is by no means a rejection of this perspective. Similarly, to argue that there is no sound theoretical justification for implementing market-exclusive policies by no means vindicates a perspective advocating the abandonment of the market and total state control and planning. There are few if any theoreticans who would advocate such an extreme approach and no economy that has completely abandoned evaluation of and response to market forces.

In one sense these conclusions are exceptionally mild: they simply point to the need to regain the middle ground. They are also inconclusive for policy-making, because they imply the need to move on from theoretical debate to an evaluation of conditions in the real world. For, as Stern correctly pointed out over ten years ago, 'whether or not planning and government intervention will produce improvements when the market is defective is a matter of judgement and analysis in any situation' (1974:201). Whether aid is required to accelerate the development process and how much is required, whether aid should be accompanied by market expansion and greater reliance on the price system, and whether there should be more or less state intervention or intervention of a different type, simply cannot be decided without evaluating the conditions and economic circumstances of different poor countries.

If these conclusions are so banal, why was it necessary to devote so much space to a discussion of these issues? The answer lies in the fact that the rightist critics have been increasingly influential in recent years in asserting their views, and that these views have had an effect on attitudes to aid resulting in changes in aid policy. Moreover, the manner in which the media have failed to draw attention to the rigorous conditions under which the conclusions of free-market theory would lead to the results predicted has contributed to increased and wide support for the rightist viewpoint.

A final point needs to be stressed. The preceding discussion has been concerned overwhelmingly with theoretical questions. Its conclusions are that there is no sufficient *theoretical* basis for arguing that a switch to either an exclusive or more market-oriented development strategy and away from aid intervention will *necessarily* lead to greater economic gains for Third World countries. This does not preclude the possibility that in practice greater emphasis on market signals could benefit the development process – and decisively – or that the manner in which aid is inserted into an economy or utilised by a recipient could on balance be detrimental, or even that a decrease in aid could in specific circumstances set off changes in policy that would achieve greater benefits than maintaining current aid flows. Indeed, conditions in which the last two outcomes could result have already been discussed in Chapters 10 and 11 above.

In the next section we shall begin to examine the type of evidence put forward by the rightist critics to support their arguments in practice. However, consistent with the procedure adopted in previous chapters, discussion of more detailed and particularly country-specific evidence will be left to Chapter 17 in Part III, below.

Aid and market forces in practice

The central question to be addressed in this section is whether the evidence provided by the rightist critics is sufficient to support their extreme optimism about market-based policy prescriptions to be applied to aid-recipient countries. At issue here is not whether markets are important – for conventional aid theory has always accepted this – but rather whether the evidence shows that exclusive reliance on market-based policies has in practice proved more beneficial for Third World development than a mixed economy approach, or, less trenchantly, whether a significant swing in favour of market-based policies has likewise resulted in a substantial boost in development. If there is evidence to indicate these outcomes, then the case for aid intervention would be considerably weakened. The discussion will be fairly narrowly focused to avoid going over ground already covered in previous chapters.

The most frequently cited evidence to support the views of the rightist critics is of those developing countries that have achieved especially high growth rates, especially in the 1970s. South Korea and Taiwan are cited specifically, for example by Krauss, while Japan, too, is named as a country that has moved in a comparatively short time from being a poor underdeveloped nation to being one of the foremost industrialised economies in the modern world. There is common agreement that these economies have experienced rapid economic growth and that they have significant and dynamic private sectors, and most recent studies indicate that growth has been accompanied by a reduction in poverty. However, detailed analyses of the newly industrialising countries (NICs) show quite clearly that the successes that have undoubtedly been achieved can by no means be attributed to exclusive reliance on the market and to minimal state interventionism.[11] Bienefeld, for example, lists five policy measures adopted in the NICs that have played an integral part in their economic performance: protection of infant industries using both tariffs and subsidies, direct state intervention to establish and support major production projects, overseas state borrowing to help shield the private sector from risk, state involvement in the labour market to minimise wage and labour costs, and, finally, direct state encouragement of the growth of indigenous technological capacity.[12] Referring to South Korea especially, Sen (1983a:13) argues that no country outside the socialist-bloc ever came near to such a measure of control over the economy's investible resources.

The Japanese case also challenges the view that the free-market path provides the surest way to economic prosperity. Japanese economic policy-making has been characterised by three features: decisive interventionism in international trade matters concerning both product choice and import controls; the broad adoption of expansionary demand-management ideas associated with Keynesian macroeconomic interventionism; and an intricately interrelated policy of combining a high degree of state intervention with the deliberate promotion of competition (Smith, 1984:218). As a former Japanese vice-minister for International Trade and Industry, Mr Ojina, describing the strategy adopted by Japan explained (quoted in Smith, 1984:220):

It was decided to establish in Japan industries which required intensive employment of capital and technology, industries that in consideration of comparative costs of production should be the most inappropriate for Japan, industries such as steel, oil refining, petrochemicals, automobiles, aircraft, industrial machinery of all sorts, and electronics including electronic computers. From a short-run, static viewpoint, encouragement of such industries would seem to conflict with economic rationalism. But from a long-range viewpoint, these are precisely the industries where . . . demand is high, technological progress is rapid, and labour productivity rises fast.

Thus, far from these countries providing incontrovertible evidence of the merits of a blind free-market approach, they would tend to provide support for the mixed-economy policies, albeit policies that do place importance on markets and incentive structures. Indeed, in reviewing the performance of poor countries in recent years, Sen comments thus: 'In fact it is remarkable that if we look at the sizeable developing countries, the fast growing and otherwise high-performing countries have all had governments that have been directly and actively involved in the planning of economic and social performance' (1983b:13). It would thus appear extremely foolish to adopt a radically different approach with, as we have seen, very restrictive theoretical support and hope that more rapid development could thereby be achieved. There is also doubt whether the example of the NICs, with their more market-oriented approach to development, can be replicated in other developing countries, given the adverse circumstances of the late 1980s. Indeed, at a time when the industrialised world is adopting or extending significant interventionist influences, for example in the international trade sphere by increasing protectionist measures and through more central bank intervention in foreign-exchange markets, we need to ask why the poor countries with their far more limited power to influence the international economy should be thought to be in a position to gain significantly by relying more on market forces that are neither free nor necessarily acting in their interests.

There are additional grounds for doubt. Latin American experience, reviewed recently by Fishlow, suggests that investment opportunities have simply not been taken up by private concerns even where they existed and when private firms were in a privileged, protected position in the market (1985:126). Additionally, and more commonly, there is no evidence to indicate that the private sector, whether indigenous or foreign, has moved into, or been willing to consider, investing in large infrastructural projects (with the more recent exception of telecommunications) or to take on state welfare activities, for example in basic education and health programmes targeted especially at the rural poor, or to fund projects, for example in the field of agricultural research, geared to increasing the participation of small poor farmers in the modern sectors of the economy. Nor has it shown interest in investing in projects to improve the environment; indeed the most common complaint is that private firms have contributed to environmental problems. Soil erosion, desertification and general ecological degradation are important characteristics of poor countries that provide major impediments to sustained development and in particular to raising levels of agricultural production. These problems are not going to be tackled or systematically addressed by relying exclusively on private initiative, and in practice it is only state intervention (inadequate though it frequently has been) which has attempted to solve these sorts of problems. Beyond these issues, in many poor countries the state intervenes in the economy quite simply because there is no private sector in existence: in these circumstances, to advocate a reduction in state activity is likely to lead to the abandonment or erosion of the products or services provided.[13]

Perhaps of central importance for the 1980s is the evidence that private financial institutions, most particularly the commercial banks, have become increasingly unwilling to provide additional funds to a wide range of poor developing countries either to finance balance-of-payments deficits or to provide foreign exchange to import basic necessities. In short, the argument of the rightist critics that if poor countries require additional resources from abroad, then they can borrow is simply not supported by the facts especially in the case of the poorest and least developed economies which are not creditworthy enough for commercial financial institutions to risk providing finance for development. Whatever the cause of the reluctance to lend – and the cause is usually related to an assessment of poor pay-back prospects, itself a sign of underdevelopment – the fact is that poor countries require additional funding for which there is no readily available private source. It was the failure of commercial banks to increase their new lending commitments to Third World countries in 1983–5 which led US Treasury Secretary Baker to put forward interventionist proposals for additional funding in an attempt to encourage the banks to lend.[14]

There is also evidence to show that policies to remove price distortions can be far from costless. For example, work by Sen (1981b) indicates that many famines take place not because of any change in food availability but because millions of people are not able to use market signals to gain access to the food. He cites the case of Sri Lanka where the removal of rice subsidies led to an increase in child mortality.[15]

Again we must stress that these instances are not being cited to argue the case either for maintaining price distortions or for ignoring market signals. There is also plenty of evidence to indicate that, in the last two decades and more, many mistakes have been made through costly interventionism. Economic planning has had a particularly dismal performance record, especially in post-independent Africa; parastatal economic enterprises have frequently been high-cost and poorly run; over-valued exchange rates have led to severe balance-of-payment difficulties, and state intervention has on occasion heightened distortions and lowered resource utilisation, often through favouring sectional interests.[16] Similarly, price structures have been characterised by biases and distortions which have discouraged production and favoured subsidised consumers often in urban areas, leading both to welfare losses for the rural poor and lower growth rates in economies as a whole.[17] Clearly the blind acceptance of interventionism or the blatant disregard of market forces or price signals are almost certainly contributory causes of low growth rates, as the consequences of the abandonment of extreme non-market policies in China would confirm. But there is an important difference in strategy between, on the one hand, the extremes of abandoning all controls or of imposing blanket controls blindly and, on the other, controlling an economy and using market and price signals in a flexible manner that acknowledges the fundamental problems of either extreme. In short, the fact that in particular circumstances the state has been a poor deliverer or participator in development is by no means a sufficient reason for excluding it entirely or for reducing its role when the outcome is likely to be unpredictable and uncertain.

A final area of the debate about interventionism versus the market needs to be discussed, which brings us back more explicitly to the aid debate. Rightist critics frequently oppose aid because it is said to frustrate market-based solutions and private-sector expansion. While this outcome could result, it is by no means the only possibility and in practice aid has been vigorously criticised by leftist critics as being an important bearer of market forces (see Wood, 1980). The truth is that aid can be and frequently is used to stimulate the market and to encourage private-sector development, even though official aid is channelled through state structures. Its beneficial effect on private-sector activity can be direct or indirect.

Commodity aid – funds provided for the purchase of goods supplied by and usually manufactured in the donor country – is increasingly channelled to private-sector firms in recipient countries who can purchase products that, because of balance-of-payments constraints, are frequently otherwise unobtainable. All programme lending, too, assists the private sector by easing the foreign-exchange constraint on production and expansion. But more significantly, of the few studies that have been carried out, a US Treasury study found that only between 6 and 8 per cent of multilateral development bank lending went to final uses that were in the public sector but would have been in the private sector if the US definition of public/private sector boundaries had applied. In some cases, this occurred because there was no private-sector alternative available. Figures from the Asian and African development banks reveal a similar destination breakdown.[18]

The indirect and positive effects on the private sector of aid destined for use by the recipient government are many and various. Aid which reinforces the strength and extent of the minimal functions of government, either by increasing the efficiency of the law and order agencies or by raising the general level of administrative competence, will benefit the private sector. Aid which goes to raising the level of education or extends the physical or economic infrastructure can also assist the private sector.[19] Even aid which goes to expanding the state's direct involvement in the productive economy will provide gains for those private-sector firms supplying materials to these enterprises or goods and services needed by state employees.

Similarly, consumption-targeted aid, and more generally aid aimed at meeting basic needs, will, if successful, lead to an increase in demand for consumer goods that is frequently and increasingly supplied by the private sector. Against the argument that this aid would be better spent if channelled directly to the private sector and to policies aimed at more rapid direct economic growth, is the point that there is often a very real trade-off between economic efficiency and political stability. As discussed in the previous chapter, given widespread inequalities in wealth and income, one consequence of an over-reliance on the market is likely to be increased growth accompanied by growing distributional inequalities. To the extent that this outcome is likely to lead to political instability, the longer-run benefit to the private sector could well be achieved by targeting aid to raise the living standards of the poor directly in order to ensure greater political stability, even perhaps at the short-term cost of lower growth. Furthermore, there is no guarantee that because distortions exist in an aid-recipient economy and these are judged to be damaging to its full economic potential, then the removal or reduction of aid will necessarily lead to their being corrected. As market and price distorting elements tend to be worse in developing countries, the removal or increase of aid is unlikely on its own to be a critical influence in perpetuating or eliminating them. Even the poorest economies are likely to be too complex for single and simple policies to provide durable solutions.

Conclusions

The general conclusion of this discussion should now be clear. At a cross-country level, the grounds for concluding that in practice free-market policies and greater reliance on the private sector provide a better hope for sustained and more rapid development than mixed economy approaches appear weak. The successes achieved have not resulted from sole reliance on market forces and private sector initiatives, while there are serious grounds for questioning whether the private sector is able or willing to respond in the positive manner suggested by the critics.

Thus there are not sufficient grounds for arguing either that aid should be reduced or that it should be channelled exclusively into projects consistent with a free-market approach. The perspective of the rightist critics therefore remains a theoretical oddity, largely divorced from the practical questions facing poor countries and especially the need to raise productive investment with inadequate domestic resources. Indeed, the fact that the financial needs of poor countries are increasing and that, especially in Africa, non-aid finance is inadequate to meet these needs gives substantial grounds for suggesting that aid money should be increased.

As with the leftist critics, however, there are some positive insights emerging from the debate about the free-market approach. To the extent that aid-recipient countries have failed to evaluate sufficiently the benefits that market-based solutions, the private sector, and the removal of price distortions could make to their development prospects, then the costs and benefits of relying on these policy measures more than in the past need to be evaluated. This is not to suggest that resulting policies will necessarily lead to a better use of resources and a more rapid and equitable pace of development, even if markets can be extended and made to work more efficiently. Nor that reducing aid will be beneficial for recipient countries; it almost certainly will not. However, the rightist perspective does highlight the need to question the merits of naive interventionism and to weigh carefully the costs and benefits of market solutions and the perpetuation of price distortions in recipient economies.

The problems of development remain complex and thus they are unlikely to be solved by resort to oversimplified solutions derived from abstract theory. What they require is a case-by-case assessment that includes analysis of the role that markets, prices and the private sector do and could play in accelerating the development process, as well as analysis of the structural, political and external factors that influence the economic variables. To the extent that the aid debate and shifts in aid policy in the 1980s have been based not on such an analysis but upon a generalised a *priori* belief that the free-market approach to aid and development should be increasingly tried and adopted, then there are few if any intellectual grounds for supporting such a belief.

Notes

1. The word 'sustained' bears emphasis, for Keynesian theory gives an important role to state intervention to stimulate demand at certain times in the business cycle and to address problems of longer-term unemployment.
2. Vol. I, *The President's Task Force on International Private Enterprise: Report to the President* and Vol. II *The Private Enterprise Guidebook: The President's Task Force on International Private Enterprise*, Washington DC, December 1984.
3. See bibliography for major publications of these authors on the foreign aid/free market debate.
4. In Britain in the autumn of 1985 the government announced a small increase in the aid budget, reversing a downward trend in real aid funds that began with the coming to power of the first Thatcher Administration in 1979. However, much of this increase was to be linked to British commercial interests and export credit expansion. When the Ethiopian famine began to receive significant media coverage in October 1984 the government minister with responsibility for Africa, Mr Malcolm Rifkind, responded initially in Parliament by stating that relief for the famine victims should most appropriately be addressed by concerned individuals contributing to voluntary agencies. Both the increase in the aid vote and the decision to provide state aid to countries in Africa affected by the famine (though in the latter instance not by allocating additional aid funds) were due in large measure to public pressure strongly at variance with these Bauer-based proposals.

5. A. Wallis, *Economics and Politics: The Quandary of Foreign Aid*, US Department of State, Bureau of Public Affairs, Washington DC, March 1983, Current Policy No. 461.
6. Assistance in writing this and subsequent sections of this chapter comes from discussion with Keith Smith and from his book *The British Economic Crisis*, Penguin, Harmondsworth, 1984.
7. As Smith observes, in abstract theory, Soviet-type centrally planned economies could also achieve this outcome (1984:124).
8. See, for example, the whole issue of *Development*, the journal of the Society for International Development, Rome, Vol. 1, 1985 devoted to a discussion of informatics.
9. See also Helm (1986) for a discussion of these points in the industrialised economies.
10. For a discussion of this point see F.E Banks, 'Economic Development, Foreign Aid and Vintage Growth', *Journal of Development Studies*, Vol. II, October 1974, pp. 106ff.
11. See, for example, Bienefeld and Godfrey (1983) and IDS *Bulletin*, Vol. 12, No. 1, December 1980.
12. See M. Bienefeld, 'Dependency and the Newly Industrialising Countries' in D. Seers, *Dependency Theory A Critical Assessment*, Francis Pinter, London, 1981, pp. 79–96.
13. For a discussion of these issues and for particular examples, see Overseas Development Institute, *Privatisation. The Developing Country Experience*, Briefing Paper, 1986.
14. The different Baker initiatives and general financing problems in developing countries are discussed in Overseas Development Institute, *The US and International Financial Reforms*, Briefing Paper, May 1986.
15. These and other welfare effects of such policies are currently under investigation in a major research project under the direction of T. Addison and L. Demery at the Overseas Development Institute, London.
16. See various publications of T. Killick including, for example, 'The Role of the Public Sector in the Industrialisation of African Developing Countries', UNIDO, Vienna, 1981 (mimeo).
17 M. Lipton discusses these issues in depth in his book *Why Poor People Stay Poor*, Temple Smith, London, 1977.
18. These results are discussed in R. Cassen, 'North and South Economic Links and Their Implications', Address to Annual Meeting of the British Association for the Advancement of Science, Brighton, August 1983, p. 16.
19. This, however, is not always true. In particular, aid-funded prestige projects (unnecessary airlines, motorways etc.) can hurt the private sector if taxes have to be increased in order to finance loan repayments and recurrent cost expenditure. I am grateful to Paul Spray for this point.

13 The Theory and the Critics

Three initial conclusions can be drawn from the discussion in this Part of the book. First, that aid is neither sufficient nor necessary for development to occur; even conventional pro-aid theory only asserts that it can help in accelerating the process. Second, that the case for aid at the theoretical level is far from clear-cut: there is no general basis for asserting that foreign aid will always and necessarily help to promote economic development in aid-recipient countries. To make such an assertion is far too ambitious. Conventional aid theory itself bases its claim that aid is a positive force in development on certain specific assumptions, for example, about efficiency in resource use and a supportive political environment; it assumes that recipient governments are growth-maximisers, that aid monies are always used productively and, at least implicitly, that the external economic environment is benevolent. These assumptions can often remain in doubt and no satisfactory cross-country statistical tests have been carried out to show conclusively that aid does contribute to development. That it is positively correlated to development when its use and purpose are to assist in adjustment policies would be even harder to prove. These two conclusions would, doubtless, be accepted by the critics of aid.

The third initial conclusion is that the views and conclusions of the different critics also find no general support. No general validity has been found for the claims that aid frustrates the development process, that it is irrelevant to poverty alleviation, that structural and political constraints necessarily prevent it from making a positive impact, and that development could better be achieved either by reducing or eliminating aid or channelling it exclusively to the private sector and to initiatives directed at expanding free-market penetration in recipient economies.

The implication of these three initial conclusions is simply that it is not possible at the theoretical level to give a direct and unambiguous answer to the question 'does foreign aid help to promote economic development?'. Its impact will depend, *inter alia*, upon the form in which it is provided, the manner in which it is used, the political and administrative structures and the income and asset distribution mechanisms existing in the recipient economy, and the quantity of aid provided. If these were the only conclusions to be drawn from the preceding discussion it could be argued that they provide more comfort to the critics than to the supporters of aid, for if one cannot prove conclusively that aid can help, or that providing it is preferable to not providing it, there would appear to be little substance to support the notion that its role should be perceived as critically important. Why, it can be asked, should donors spend a total of more than US$35 billion a year on aid when no convincing theoretical proof can be provided that it will do any good and when a plausible case can be constructed to show that it may do harm?

It is because comments such as these can readily flow from the discussion above that stress was placed on the word 'initial'; these are only the initial conclusions to be drawn from the preceding chapters. Far more can and needs to be said. First, some general points need to be raised. In any social or behavioural science, one can never expect absolute certainty of an outcome; there is thus nothing odd about the fact that one cannot be certain that aid will have the intended beneficial effects. What is important in social science theory is to be able to judge two things: first, the likelihood of a particular result occurring, and secondly the conditions likely either to cause a positive outcome or to result in a negative outcome. If any outcome is 99 per cent likely to occur and the result is desirable, then, especially if the costs are small and the outcome particularly beneficial, there would seem to be powerful reasons for encouraging it to be produced. If an outcome is 10 per cent likely to occur, also with desirable results, low costs, and a beneficial outcome, and if, in addition, it is possible to indicate with 90 per cent certainty the conditions when this beneficial outcome will occur, then, again, there would seem to be powerful reasons for both paying the price for the 10 per cent of cases where the benefits will result and for attempting to alter the conditions that are inhibiting the beneficial outcome from occurring (providing, of course, the costs of this action are themselves weighed against both the initial costs and the importance of the eventual outcome to be achieved). Raising the question of the conditions required for a specific outcome to result is of particular relevance when various and different inputs interact to produce that outcome, for it indicates at once the complexity of the relationships involved and, especially in the social sciences, the impossibility of predicting outcomes with a degree of certainty akin to that expected in the natural sciences.

What the discussion of these general points has sought to show is that the absence of theoretical proof indicating that foreign aid will help to promote economic development is a quite normal and reasonable conclusion to draw. It would therefore be quite illegitimate to deduce from this conclusion that the case against providing aid is thereby strengthened. But the preceding discussion and the third initial conclusion have also indicated that no adequate theoretical proof has been provided by aid's critics for arguing either that all aid is harmful or that alternatives to aid intervention will necessarily be more beneficial than aid. This is important because, as we have seen, there are critics who assert or would like to convey these extreme views. To the contrary, however, this part of the book has sought to show that blanket theoretical criticisms of aid are unfounded and can be rejected, both because the assumptions upon which they are based can be seriously questioned and because the available evidence fails to prove the universalistic conclusions they seek to draw. This, of course, is by no means the end of the discussion. It now becomes critical to assess the likelihood of aid being effective, to identify those conditions which are likely to promote or inhibit aid effectiveness, and to ascertain the possibility of altering any conditions that are major obstacles to its achievement. How has the preceding discussion helped to address these issues?

We can begin by considering the rightist criticisms. Here extreme faith is placed on a more efficient price system, an extended market system, and an increased role for private enterprise to deliver higher rates of economic growth than those achieved as a result of traditional aid intervention. The conclusion in Chapter 12 was that there is little or no theoretical basis for believing that the abstract insights of *laisser-faire* theory would provide a surer way of achieving sustained development. Traditional aid theory must therefore be considerably strengthened. Debate about methods of achieving development then returns to the middle ground and revolves around consideration of the best mix of interventionist and market-oriented solutions. It is precisely because conventional aid theory is a theory of the middle ground that it can take up the insights of a more market-oriented approach and test them against other approaches so as to determine their relative effectiveness in particular circumstances.

The conclusions drawn from the leftist critics and the critics of aid located in the aid/saving/growth debate have rather more complex implications. While their absolutist claims are likewise rejected, their work has raised crucial questions about the likelihood of aid being effective. Conventional aid theory puts forward the proposition that under certain conditions (assumptions) aid can play a positive role in accelerating the development process. Because these conditions were thought to be relatively easy to fulfil, a general sense of optimism was initially created that aid *would* help to promote development; the likelihood of its not achieving its stated objectives was perceived to be small. What the critics have done is challenge this optimism in two ways. First, to question the ease with which these various conditions will be fulfilled and, secondly, to highlight additional key factors, either ignored or played down by conventional theory, that could have a significant influence on the impact of aid in recipient economies. However, a problem remains. Although the critics have highlighted (correctly) the need to examine a variety of conditions necessary for aid to have a positive impact, they have provided little guide to understanding in what manner particular constraints should be perceived as binding and unalterable. In many cases this has simply been assumed. The discussion in Chapter 11 suggested that the constraints pinpointed were almost certainly not as rigid as the critics maintained, and in part this conclusion was derived from recent developments in the thinking of the leftist citics themselves.

If these conclusions are correct, they would suggest that the most significant contribution made by the critics of aid has ironically been to help refine and improve upon conventional aid theory and to assist our understanding of when aid will help to promote development. At its simplest level, aid intervention is built upon the elementary proposition that more means more. At their simplest, criticisms of aid point to circumstances when more can lead to less. If an underweight person increases his food intake he will gain weight, but he will not do so if his stomach is incapable of absorbing more food or if he takes so much more exercise that the extra energy intake is more than used up. Aid theory is based on the view that additional external funds can assist a poor recipient country in a variety of ways by helping to increase efficiency in resource use, by raising savings and investment levels, by promoting human resource development, by making foreign exchange available, or, perhaps, by raising consumption levels directly. It asserts in particular that aid can be especially helpful in relieving bottlenecks and specific constraints in poor countries, the results of which could well prove dramatic. Given the extreme poverty pervading most Third World countries, the need for such assistance is clearly urgent.

The major contribution of the critics has been to identify those circumstances that are likely either directly or indirectly to prevent or hinder this assumed positive outcome from resulting. And in doing this they increase understanding of how to raise the effectiveness of aid and to ensure more precisely that it will contribute to development, especially in situations where the need for assistance is great but, as a result, the ability to trace through its effect is often most difficult. A subsidiary gain is to make more transparent the transfer of aid that is channelled for the achievement of political and other non-development objectives.

That aid theory is not able on its own to lead to the conclusion that aid will necessarily help promote development and that the theoretical advances to date have been extremely limited is apparent from the tentativeness with which the 'fundamental' case for aid has been put forward in a recent DAC annual report (DAC, 1985:11–12):

> The basic proposition of international co-operation for development has been that pre-industrial and relatively stagnant economies *could* be launched on the course of dynamic economic and social transformation, ultimately sustainable without prolonged dependence on concessional aid; further, that this process *could* be set in motion, broadened and accelerated by the efficient use of internal and external resources in *combinations appropriate* to the particular case in an environment of policies and leadership *conducive to* sustained development (italics added).

Conventional aid theory at the macro-level falls far short of being able to predict the precise effects of aid – a weakness that is shared by economic theory more generally. As Hahn and Matthews have argued, there have been substantial differences in rates of economic growth between countries over different time periods but it would be difficult to claim that any theoretical model 'goes far towards explaining these differences or predicting what will happen to them in the future' (1964:889). Aid's effect will depend upon a range of factors, quite possibly in different circumstances and over different time periods. What the evolving debate described here between the critics and aid theorists has done is to provide greater insight into these different variables, their importance and influence. For example, the impact of aid depends crucially upon how governments choose to use it and the critics have certainly helped to advance our understanding of the constraints and positive circumstances determining the complex link between government action and aid impact. We now turn, in Part III, to a consideration of the micro-studies of that impact in order to ascertain the extent to which these throw more light on the central issue debated here: whether aid in practice helps or hinders Third World development and whether alternatives to aid provide a surer way of alleviating poverty.

PART III
Assessing the Evidence

14 Introduction

This part of the book considers explicitly the lessons from experience, in part by examining the performance of aid in practice and in part by discussing the likely effects on developing countries of a non-aid or different aid strategy – the latter outcomes being of particular importance to both radical leftist and rightist critics of the aid relationship. The basic question to be examined is this: does an assessment of what aid has done, or not done, support or challenge the views of the critics? We shall examine both the macro-effects of aid intervention in particular countries – the aspect of the relationship of most concern to aid theory – and also the effects of particular forms of aid, and specific projects and programmes in recipient countries.

It should be stated, at the outset, that this examination of the evidence by no means attempts to provide a comprehensive analysis of the detailed effects of all forms of official aid that are currently or have historically been channelled to developing countries. To do so would be a massive undertaking, and would have to include separate treatment of, for instance: aid to different productive sectors of the economy, technical assistance in all its various forms, infrastructural aid, aid channelled to social sectors like health and education, aid and the environment, aid, energy and renewable resources, aid for research and development, commodity import programmes, aid to the private sector, bilateral vis-à-vis multilateral aid, different types of programme aid including balance-of-payments support, commodity support programmes, and aid related to macroeconomic adjustment policies and, most generally, to policy reform in developing countries.

The approach adopted here is far less ambitious and, initially at least, of a different sort. It is, in the first instance, to step back from the rapidly growing evidence of the effects of the various categories of aid – which have been analysed and summarised in the recently published book by Cassen *et al.* (1986) *Does Aid Work?* – and to consider in more detail the prior methodological questions which need to be raised about the data and the use to which they can legitimately be put. This is the subject of the next chapter.

This chapter is considered fundamental to the overall assessment of the impact of aid because it helps to place the different examples selected by critics and supporters – chosen to 'prove' the correctness of their different perspectives – within an overall framework. Critics, especially, are very ready to cite examples of aid failure to illustrate that their assessment is the right one. Advocates of aid, and especially bilateral and multilateral official agencies, for their part maintain that on balance aid 'works', even though they do admit – especially when pressed – that some aid has for different reasons been a failure. What has been, and still often is, missing, is a rigorous analysis of the ways the types of evidence are utilised in the aid debate to support different arguments. All too often those citing particular examples fail to explain how typical or representative those examples are.

Following on from this methodological chapter, a few key areas of aid intervention are selected for particular examination, with Chapter 16 considering some evidence of aid at the micro, and largely project, level and Chapter 17 addressing some specific aspects of the macro-effects of aid on particular countries. The emphasis in Chapter 16 is on the crucial question of judging whether aid at the micro-level does achieve the objective of reaching down to and assisting the poor to improve their living standards; food aid and agricultural and rural development projects are discussed within this context. Chapter 17 falls into two distinct sections. The first provides a rapid overview of the different country-specific studies that have been carried out to ascertain aid's general impact on their development. The second addresses the important criticism of foreign aid which maintains that aid is inappropriately inserted if the recipient government and its administration are corrupt, inefficient and not committed in their policies to the development of the people. These issues are discussed in the context of the Caribbean state of Haiti. While this selection of topics for more detailed analysis is in some senses arbitrary – other authors would doubtless choose a different set of issues to examine in depth – it does, it is hoped, address the main areas of controversy in the current aid debate.

One conclusion emerging from this part of the book is that, although there is plenty of evidence to indicate aid's inadequacies especially in the alleviation of poverty, both in the past and in the contemporary world, this by no means lends support for the generalised conclusions that are frequently made: that aid therefore cannot help in the alleviation of poverty or that poverty alleviation and growth can best be achieved without aid. Part of aid's failure lies in the very nature of underdevelopment itself, so that expectations lifted out of the context of its insertion need to be tempered by both an appreciation of the complexities of the real world into which it is inserted and realistic alternatives. Another conclusion is that critics and advocates alike have far too little understanding of the complex nature of development and too little data upon which to base the respective conclusions they readily draw. To date, aid evaluation has been a very blunt and inadequate tool with which to construct firm and incontestable conclusions: in many cases there is simply insufficient evidence available, in others the evidence is too ambiguous. Assessing aid through an exclusive and single prism of economics, politics or science and technology, as commonly occurs, simply fails to capture all the variables that in the real world *do* have an effect upon outcome.

If these conclusions are correct, then they indicate that the available evidence of aid in practice is at present inadequate not only to prove the critics right but also to prove the supporters right. If, however, as was argued in the discussion in Part I of this book, the moral case *for* aid is based largely on its beneficial effects, what do these far from unambiguous conclusions about aid in practice mean with regard to the moral case for providing it? This question will be discussed in the final part of the book, Retaking The Middle Ground.

15 How to Assess the Evidence

The quantity of evidence available

Compared with the open-endedness of the discussions on the ethics of foreign aid and macro-theory, it would appear that we are on firmer ground in assessing the evidence of aid in practice and will thus be able to come, in this part of the book, to more definite conclusions about the merits of donor governments and multilateral agencies providing aid to recipient countries. Certainly there are grounds for believing this: not only do the critics of aid provide long and detailed examples of aid's effects but donor agencies themselves are increasingly concerned to record the effect their aid has had, and some agencies, like the World Bank, have been evaluating their projects in recipient countries for some two decades. There is a wealth of documentation available recording the performance of aid; according to the DAC in Paris, some 9,000 evaluations of official aid have been carried out by major donors in the last 10 to 15 years.[1]

Important though this body of documentation undoubtedly is for judging overall aid performance, one needs to know just how representative is the available information. And here our first concern needs to be raised. According to DAC statistics, some $420 billion of net aid has been channelled to less developed countries since 1970.[2] On the assumption that an average aid programme or project is valued at $6 million, this would mean only some 12 per cent of all aid since 1970 has been evaluated, and as many aid projects are far smaller than $6 million, the proportion evaluated would be far lower.[3] Although one can only guess at the exact percentage formally evaluated, there would be few, if any, observers or practitioners of aid who would argue that more than 10 per cent of aid has been subject to such analysis since the late 1960s, and even less before then.

This raises the question of how far the evidence available is representative of all the aid disbursed. While there is no quantitative assessment of this, what we do know about the evolution of aid evaluation reveals that there has been a mushrooming of evaluation studies in recent years, indicating that most of the available evaluation material is of quite recent origin. For example, out of 154 evaluations of UK bilateral aid recorded by the Overseas Development Administration as of January 1986, 105 (68 per cent) had been completed in 1980 or more recently.[4] More generally, in 1985 the DAC judged that, compared with the approximately 9,000 studies they were aware of, some 1,100 were currently being carried out each year. We also know that proportionately more large aid projects and programmes have been evaluated (for the reason that there is greater concern about accountability for large sums of money), so that large numbers of the smaller but more numerous ones will have escaped the evaluation net. Also some donors who do carry out evaluations keep these confidential or restricted, thus providing an added bias to the available literature. The World Bank's audit reports, although including aid-specific funded projects (International Development Association), do not contain details on particular projects, and the UK's ODA has failed to release evaluations of programme aid and of the Aid and Trade Provision (ATP). In addition, there are very few reports of aid evaluations of either OPEC or Comecon aid in the aid literature.[5] All this suggests that the evaluations that have been carried out and are widely available are not a representative sample of all aid, and hence an assessment of these studies will not necessarily represent an unbiased sample of official aid.

Recognition of this problem and a not untypical response to it are provided in the non-partisan study by Bachrach (1980) for the OECD. In an attempt to reduce bias in project selectivity, he made an effort to include 'good' and 'bad' examples of aid on the premise that 'both types can be very instructive'; however, he was careful to comment that 'whether a different set of evaluation summaries would yield conclusions similar to those contained in this paper is an open question' (1980:51). More generally, discussing the results of World Bank aid, Weiner comments that 'clearly this evidence cannot be extrapolated to other development assistance. It is a matter for regret that there is no comparable evidence overall' (1984:65).

We need, however, to pursue a little further the fact that official aid agencies have recently carried out far more evaluation studies of aid effectiveness than previously. All bilateral agencies that are DAC members and all UN multilateral agencies carry out aid evaluations and have increased their number and coverage over the past six years. However, while the World Bank and its affiliates evaluate all projects and programmes, these are usually not available for academic scrutiny. Most bilateral agencies, including the ODA, do not evaluate their aid on any systematic basis either by type or size of project or by recipient country. A recent DAC study reviewing evaluation methods and procedures of member countries states that most donors evaluate 'roughly at least 10 to 20 per cent of their projects annually', adding that these evaluations tend to be planned on a narrow project-by-project basis ignoring broad and systematic issues, and that they are influenced by field staff or donors having specific questions they want answered (1985:7). Thus it is questionable whether analyses of bilateral agency reports are representative of current practice or that details of IDA and other multilateral projects that do emerge in the literature (sometimes by illicit means) are a reflection of the general impact of all IDA projects.

This latter point highlights a matter of great relevance to criticisms of particular forms of aid. Published reports or evaluations of aid are not likely to reflect the effects of *current* aid practice, unless – as has not been the case – aid practice continues unchanged over time. Published evaluations most commonly refer to aid projects or programmes initiated many years previously; thus they are likely to reflect the donor's state of the art knowledge at that time. In the light of experience it is quite possible that mistakes highlighted in evaluations *published* today would not occur, at least with such frequency, in similar projects or programmes *initiated* today.

The implication of this time lag needs to be examined more closely. It was some 14 years ago, in September 1973 following Mr McNamara's Nairobi speech to the Board of Governors, that the World Bank and leading bilateral DAC member donors began consciously to re-orient aid policies specifically towards the poor. Now this may seem a long time ago. However, it was only in the World Bank's 1984 annual review of project performance audit results, published in 1985, that the bulk of projects examined were for loan or credit agreements made after 1974.

In the 1984 review, only 46 per cent of the projects analysed began in 1975 or later. In the 1982 review, published in 1983, 57 per cent of the projects considered were started in 1973 or earlier. Furthermore, the date of project commencement itself occurs on average some three years after initial identification, selection, preparation and design of a project. Given this lead-time, less than 30 per cent of all projects considered in the most recent 1985 World Bank project review could be said to have been influenced by the switch in Bank thinking acknowledged to have taken place following McNamara's speech. In general, the Bank estimated (1982:31) that a period of some 10.3 years elapsed from initial identification to the completion of *ex-post* project evaluations for its IDA projects.

Similar time lags would appear to apply to bilateral donor projects. For example, of all the ODA evaluations made public in the financial year 1984/5 and excluding those projects that have not yet been completed, 57 per cent were studies of aid projects that began in 1972 or 1973, some three years before the publication of the White Paper *The Changing Emphasis in British Aid Politics: More Help for the Poorest*. What this time lag means is that, to the extent that criticisms of aid, for example those concluding that aid is a failure because it does not reach the poorest, are based on the evidence currently available, there are good grounds for indicating that this judgement could well be premature. Indeed, more recent work by DAC members suggests that, especially for 'people-centred' projects where delays in project implementation are more frequent, a period of 10 to 15 years from project start-up to the stage where evaluation is likely to indicate firm results could now be considered normal.

So much for the evaluation material on official aid projects and programmes and our concern about the lack of evidence available in order to be able to derive unbiased and representatively-based conclusions about aid's impact. Are we on firmer ground if we consider the studies conducted to judge the impact of aid upon particular aid-recipient countries over time?[6] Certainly if either a large number or smaller but representative number of country studies have been carried out pinpointing the impact of aid on overall development, then, even in the absence of detailed project- or programme-specific studies, there would appear to be a useful body of material from which at least initial judgements could be made.[7]

Alas, on this score, too, the information gap is vast. Only a handful of detailed country-specific studies attempting to analyse the impact of all aid from all major sources have been carried out. The most detailed are those produced for the Task Force on Concessional Flows of the joint World Bank–IMF Development Committee (now widely referred to as the Cassen study). Most have not been published separately.[8] In all, seven country studies were carried out as part of this study, for Bangladesh, Colombia, India, Kenya, Malawi, Mali and South Korea. In addition to these country studies, some were included in another major study published in 1983 and carried out by Krueger and Ruttan for USAID. This study included case studies of India, South Korea, Turkey, Ghana and Ivory Coast. In addition, a number of studies of aid to the Indian subcontinent, in particular, have been carried out by various authors, such as for Bangladesh, Sobhan (1982) and Faaland (1981), and for India, Rao and Narain (1962). Apart from these studies, DAC officials are aware of no other country-specific studies of all aid from major sources.

There have, however, been a number of studies of aid provided by particular donors to particular recipients. Where the donor in question is the largest donor, providing half or more of the aid received, then these studies could be considered to be important contributions to the country-specific literature. Included here would be Jacoby's 1966 study of US aid to Taiwan, Jones' 1977 study of British aid to Lesotho, Botswana and Swaziland, and Morton's 1975 study of aid to Malawi.[9] In addition, a series of studies has tried to draw conclusions about the overall impact of aid on the recipient. Here one would include Holtham and Hazlewood's study of aid in Kenya (1976), some recent studies of Canadian aid to Haiti, Bangladesh, Tanzania and Senegal, recently conducted by the North-South Institute in Toronto, and the Swedish National Audit Bureau Studies of their own particular policies and aid programmes.[10]

While the Cassen case studies stand out for their detailed analysis, if all the specific ones listed above are included they only account for 17 developing countries,[11] or some 12 per cent of the over 140 countries in the developing world that are recipients of aid. What is more, among those authors drawn to comment on the potential lessons to be learned for other aid-recipient countries, none has argued that their selected countries are typical of others; most have cautioned against making worldwide generalisations. As the 1985 report of the Chairman of the DAC reviewing 25 years of official aid experience puts it: 'The most conscientious effort to avoid subjectivity in assessing the multifaceted and evolving story of developmental assistance cannot ensure scientific objectivity. The issues are essentially judgemental' (DAC, 1985:16).

None the less, widespread positive and negative generalisations about aid impact and performance *are* continuously made. For example, the Cassen study is quoted in the 1985 DAC Review as concluding that, although aid's performance varies by country and by sector and there is a substantial fraction of aid which does not work. 'Most aid . . . succeeds in its developmental objectives . . . contributing positively to the recipient countries' economic performance . . . not substituting for activities which would have occurred anyway'. And even as cautious a scholar as Hyden can be drawn to comment that 'for every official success, there are at least ten failures. Billions of dollars have been spent on projects and programmes that never achieved their intended objectives' (1986:246). As for the views of aid's vigorous critics discussed in this book – Bauer, Krauss, Griffin, Seers, Lappé *et al.* and Hayter etc. – to the extent that their views are based upon the evidence of aid in practice, it needs to be stated that the quantity of evidence available is almost certainly far from sufficient to support their conclusions. In short, both critics and supporters of aid appear to have been far too eager to draw general conclusions about aid's performance than the evidence available would justify.

It could, however, be argued that if the evidence that *is* available points repeatedly, reliably and consistently to either beneficial or detrimental effects of aid on recipient countries, then the lack of comprehensive quantitative data becomes less important. We now address this question.

The quality of the available evidence

Overview
The process by which aid's performance is judged is most commonly referred to as *evaluation*. While there are a number of different definitions of aid evaluation, a recent one agreed by the DAC provides a helpful starting point. Here evaluation is defined as:[12]

> An examination as systematic and objective as possible of an on-going or completed project or programme, its design, implementation and results, with the aim of determining its efficiency, effectiveness, impact, sustainability and the relevance of the objectives. . . .

where impact is defined as

> a term indicating whether the project has had an effect on its surroundings in terms of
> technical, economic, socio-cultural, institutional and environmental factors.

To judge the effect of aid from the evidence available would appear at first sight to
be a comparatively simple exercise: examine the evaluations of performance and
from the results of these conclude that aid has performed either better or worse
than would have occurred without its intervention. Tot up the individual scores
and come to an overall judgement. If the results show success in achieving objectives and also that better results occur than without aid, then the evidence vindicates aid intervention; if the results show failure to achieve objectives and also that
the objectives could have been reached better without aid, then the critics' case will
have been confirmed.[13]

The initial trouble, of course, is that some evaluations indicate success while
others indicate failure. A few fairly simple and straightforward examples reveal
these different outcomes quite dramatically. First, the failures.

In 1962 the European Development Fund (EDF) of the European Community
agreed to build the Sibiti-Niari valley road in the Congo, stretching for 75 kilometres at a cost of 3.7m. écus. By 1983, it had financed the project four times over
and paid for road construction and supervision twice. The total cost had increased
over nine times to 34.3m. écus yet only 20 kilometres had been built and three-
quarters of the constructed part had already been ruined. The whole project has
absorbed up to 80 per cent of the Congo's indicative aid funding from the EDF and
has had the effect of reducing to almost nothing the aid that the country was
entitled to expect for other projects covered by the second Lomé Convention.[14]
Two other failures of EDF aid, this time in the Central African Republic, are given
in the 1985 European Court of Auditors report. In one case, the EDF has funded a
cotton-growing project for 20 years at a cost of 17.3m. écus, yet the project has
nothing to show for the time and money expended. In the most recent period,
1970–82, the number of cotton planters had fallen, the area planted to cotton had
decreased and total production had contracted. In the second case, the EDF-
funded Ecole Nationale Supérieure opened in 1982. The kitchen-refectory block
has never been used except occasionally as a conference centre, for the building has
no ventilation, mechanical or natural; the bars protecting the windows in the
administration block were constructed so that the windows could not be opened
and the only access to the cinema projector room is by way of a step ladder which
needs both hands to climb so that no equipment can be put in the room.[15] Of
course, it is not only EEC projects that have failed, and it is to the credit of the
EEC that such explicit examples of aid failure are published. For example, the
World Bank reported in 1985 that one of its agricultural projects in West Africa
was considered 'a major economic and social failure'. Not only did it achieve a
negative rate of return but the co-operative system which was to provide the institutional framework for input supplies and marketing had completely disintegrated
and, in addition, the project generated strong opposition among the supposed
beneficiaries.[16]

It is far easier to reveal aid failure than aid success, at least to the sceptic,
because blatant inability to achieve *any* objective can render a project a failure,
while *all* objectives need to be achieved to satisfy the critics. Three initial criteria
for aid success would appear to have to include the following: the attainment of
objectives, cost effectiveness, and whether there were any losers or negative effects
resulting from the project. Some examples of aid success that broadly meet these

criteria, and which have not been challenged specifically by the critics would include the Mauritius electricity generation project, an irrigation project in Malaysia, and a food and nutrition centre in Tanzania.[17]

Britain provided two pairs of medium-sized generators to Mauritius in 1974 and 1975 to contribute to the expansion of the island's electricity system, at a cost of £1.3m. These generators enabled Mauritius to complete its rural electrification programme by 1979 so that not only were virtually all dwellings in reach of power supply but by 1982 over 90 per cent of all dwellings were connected, with some 84,000 of the 155,000 domestic consumers falling into the lowest category of electricity users.[18] The World Bank's irrigation project in Malaysia not only achieved a double cropping of rice covering 96,000 hectares for the farmers on the project and a 100 per cent increase in farmer incomes, but the increase in the wages of the landless farm workers exceeded the incomes of the farmers directly benefitting. In addition, for every $1 worth of paddy rice produced there was another 75 cents in downstream benefits in construction work, transport and services.[19] In 1974, the Swedish aid agency, SIDA, provided financial support for the establishment and subsequent running of the Tanzanian Food and Nutrition Centre. Sweden's financial and technical support declined after 1979. The Centre was almost exclusively Tanzanian-run by 1985. It successfully carried out nutritional research, training and publicity programmes; its results are utilized by different line ministries and its success has been acknowledged both nationally and internationally.

To point out particular and relatively clear-cut examples of aid success or failure is only the first, and easiest, task in attempting to evaluate performance. There is also the requirement, as discussed above, to attempt to ascertain whether better or worse results would have been achieved with or without the aid. Two project-specific examples illustrate success and failure in this regard. The first, a failure, concerns British aid to supply diesel generators to Nepal at a cost of £2.54m. agreed in September 1978. The intention was to reduce the effects of power cuts pending the completion of further hydro-electric capacity and at that time to move the diesel generators to other areas of the country. The success of the project depended upon its completion by December 1979 in time to meet the critical winter demand for electricity in 1979/80. The generators were commissioned over a year late, in March 1981, and the bulk storage fuel tanks and raw cooling water tank were not available for another six to nine months. Various difficulties, including lack of diesel fuel, meant that the generators were never operated for more than one or two hours a day. The new hydro-electric scheme came on stream in May 1982. Since August 1982, the generators have neither been used nor moved: skid-mounters were never provided. Seven out of the 11 local personnel trained to operate the project have left. And finally the original project submission noted that domestic consumers would be better-off with kerosene rather than diesel-generated electricity for energy purposes, and that the private sector most probably invested after all in their own standby electric plants.[20]

In contrast to this is a World Bank project in Jakarta, Indonesia, that involved a massive slum-upgrading programme, consisting of 1,000 hectares a year benefitting some 450,000 people annually. According to the appraisal report, Jakarta has been the first major Third World city that 'has been able to mount a long-term program at a level sufficient to catch up with need within a reasonable period of time'.[21] What is important for this part of the discussion is that, as a result of the project's performance, the fundamental concept of slum-upgrading became widely accepted in Indonesia and had a major impact in re-orienting the whole national housing effort of the government in the desired direction. In short, aid not only had wider beneficial effects but without the aid it is highly unlikely that these benefits would have taken place.

Someone coming fresh to the aid debate might now go on to ask about the results of attempts to assess the success or failure rate of all aid that has been evaluated – the 9,000 plus evaluations that have been carried out – or of a representative sample of them. But this sort of analysis has never been attempted for all the different aid agencies, even though much aid has been subject to some form of audit for the purposes of public accountability. The best that has been done is that selections of particular types of aid or all aid from a few donors have been processed and assessed and conclusions drawn. The comments of the critics on these limited assessments indicate why no-one has seen fit to attempt to carry out a comprehensive assessment of all the material: the conclusions made have been vigorously challenged, the challenges ranging from 'inadequate' to 'worthless'.

To expand upon this point, let us return again to the examples of aid success and failure discussed above. Interesting though these undoubtedly are, if there is one thing that the critics and supporters of aid *are* agreed upon it is that the uncontroversial effects of aid's performance – those for which there is little or no debate about the outcome achieved – are the rare exception rather than the general rule. And, as explained above, controversy appears to be far greater when agreeing success rather than failure. When aid agencies and supporters of aid state that 'on balance aid is successful', or that there is sufficient evidence that projects on average do produce satisfactory results in a very large proportion of cases, or 'when eight major agencies have examined the experience of a large number of their recent projects and conclude with similar conclusions that between two-thirds and three-quarters broadly achieve their objectives', the critics and even many broad supporters of official aid simply do not believe them.

Excluding those attacks argued solely from *a priori* starting-points (discussed in Part II above), differing views about aid's performance tend to revolve around four main factors: whether the objectives were achieved; what the overall impact of the aid was; whether the costs involved justified the expenditure; and, finally, what the overall development result was compared with different (probably non-aid) alternatives. The dispute about performance turns upon how these different factors are to be assessed and weighted in coming to an overall judgement of success or failure. For the critics the assessment is, on balance, negative; for the supporters it tends on balance to be positive.[22]

Does this mean that the supporters and critics have both gone round the world evaluating different aid projects and programmes separately, sometimes coming to their respective conclusions for different types of aid and sometimes for the same intervention? Surprisingly not. Most criticisms have not been based on evaluations made by the critics, rather they have most often been based on the same evaluations made or commissioned by the donor agencies themselves, although at times supplemented by visits, journalistic reports and the obtaining of additional unpublished records from the respective agencies. For example, the most recent book by Hayter and Watson (1985), highly critical of World Bank projects, especially in Latin America, is based almost entirely on the World Bank's project performance Audit Reports (PPAR), other project documents, and interviews with World Bank staff.

It is far from uncommon for very different conclusions about aid to come from similar source documents. One example of this comes from British aid to Colombia. Two senior ODA officials have referred to an ODA sheep project in that country as relatively successful, citing the fact that it had 'built up considerable knowledge of sheep and cattle diseases in the area'.[23] However, according to the evaluation summary published by ODA, a very different picture is provided. The project involved introducing Scottish blackface sheep into the Colombian mountain areas and the setting up of a demonstration farm with the imported breed. The main findings were that: the demonstration farm was not cost-effective; the choice of the Scottish breed was a serious mistake since it was suitable neither for wool nor meat; the females could not breed properly and the lambing quality was poor; and, finally, the Colombians were not really interested in sheep farming.[24] How then could the project be termed a success? The answer lies in the fact that a sheep health component was later added to the project, the resources of which were used to solve problems of local dairy herds – with apparent 'success'.

Given the fact that most assessments of performance are derived from donor or donor-sponsored studies and evaluations and that these do not appear to provide unequivocal answers on effectiveness, we need to delve a little deeper into the quality of this principal source of information.

Aid evaluation: the state of the art

As an attempt to judge the performance of aid in practice, the general objective of evaluation appears to be clear: to derive a universal system of evaluation that reduces subjective judgement to a minimum while analysing all relevant aspects of the aid/development relationship in order that reliable and uncontroversial conclusions can be drawn. As will quickly become apparent, we are, at present, very far from achieving this ideal. This itself is one cause of the present controversy over aid performance and a reason why one needs to be sceptical of unqualified generalisations about performance, whether from the camps of the critics or the supporters of aid.

Surprisingly, not least because of the controversies that have raged since its earliest days, evaluating aid is of comparatively recent orgin. It is only in the last eight to ten years that most donors have established separate evaluation units with permanent staff. In spite of this advance, there is still no agreement either among the agencies or among academics about how best to evaluate aid. As a result, different approaches are used by different agencies and changes in approach even within agencies are far from rare. Attempts to work towards a common framework for analysis are only now beginning to be discussed within the DAC, and still have a long way to go. Outside the DAC, aid evaluation techniques do not appear to have been much debated or systematically used and even within the DAC grouping, it is uncommon for agencies to distribute evaluation material among themselves or to circulate these to a wider audience, partly because of the costs and the volume of paper involved. A further problem, highlighted above, is that the selection of aid projects or programmes for evaluation tends to be haphazard. In a review of much recent evaluation material, Bachrach comments thus (1980:56):

> on what basis are projects selected for evaluation? By what criteria are evaluators chosen and work judged? On what grounds are evaluations made public or kept confidential? . . . the lack of information on the crucial decisions of evaluation leaves the (perhaps unfair) impression that the process is *ad hoc* rather than planned. That is, without knowing who the evaluation is for and what it is for, evaluation appears neither as a planned response to specific programme characteristics nor as a systematic action to alter certain programme characteristics.

The current lack of a common framework for analysis arises because there is much ambiguity about three crucial and interlinked building blocks for evaluation: what to evaluate, how to evaluate, and when to evaluate. We shall consider each of these in turn.

What to evaluate

Initially it might be thought that the first issue – knowing what to evaluate – is uncontentious; however, there are major problems even here. Not infrequently, donors are unclear about the objectives for which particular types of aid are given, as a recent DAC report (1986b) on evaluation methods and procedures among member countries confirms. Lack of clarity can and does arise for four different reasons; first, the objectives can be so general that the effects of the aid cannot be pinpointed; secondly, they can change during the course of the project or pro- gramme; thirdly, sometimes a set of contradictory objectives can be set; or, fourthly, they might in certain circumstances not be known.

General as opposed to specific objectives are most common with non-project aid including technical assistance and programme aid which account for some 30 per cent of all DAC bilateral aid. In these instances, evaluating the success or failure of particular types of aid intervention is fraught with difficulty because the aid component usually constitutes only one, and often a minor, element of a broader policy package. Is technical co-operation a failure or a success if those instructed in a particular skill pass their examination of competence but fail to use that skill? How does one judge the results of programme aid if the external economic influences before and after the start of the programme are markedly different? The subjective judgement of different evaluators plays a critical role in coming to conclusions about such aid intervention.

For project aid, even if the objectives are clear at the outset, it can happen that these are changed during the course of a project's life. The likelihood of this happening is illustrated by the World Bank's 1985 review of ten years of project performance: the Bank states (1985:9) that only 42 per cent of its projects were implemented as agreed, and 56 per cent were changed significantly during the implementation process. The question then arises whether success is to be judged by the degree to which original objectives were achieved, changed objectives were achieved, or objectives were not changed when they should have been. Quite quickly an apparently simple exercise can become extremely complex. The third complication arises because projects can and sometimes do have contradictory objectives. This can arise from the donor perspective where, for example, aid linked to structural adjustment programmes frequently has contradictory policy and welfare implications, or it can arise from different views of donors and recipients about the achievement of objectives. This latter problem can be illustrated by a decision to use aid monies to build village halls for rural communi- ties in South Korea. Although the halls were built, no village meeting ever took place in them. However, the villagers deemed the project a great success both because the buildings were viewed as symbols of modernisation and because they were fully used – but as storage and living quarters.[25] The donor judged the aid a failure, the recipients judged it a success. The fourth difficulty arises if objectives are not known when the decision is made to provide aid. New emphases on participation of the potential recipients of aid, stimulated for example by agencies such as the ILO, stress the necessity of not having pre-conceived objectives. Thus the ILO writes (1985:20–21):

> As meaningful participation involves the rural poor in setting their own objectives, no outsider can know in advance what training is needed to attain those objectives. . . .

Specialists from outside cannot arrive with pre-conceived ideas about the training they think is needed.

It is not only donors and recipients who can have different views about the objectives of aid; the issue is of central importance to a number of critics. Aid is not only criticised because the objectives specified have not been achieved but also because some critics judge aid performance against other objectives which they (the critics) deem as either major or dominant ones that should be considered. For instance, one major criticism of aid is that it fails to reach or benefit the poor. This general question is of such importance to the aid debate that it will be discussed more fully in the next chapter. What concerns us more immediately here is how far the effect of aid on the poor is the subject of initial assessment and subsequent evaluation. The answer is that far less aid is evaluated in this respect than the non-specialist might think. Of the evaluation material that does exist, much does not consider this impact explicitly or at all. The bulk of the evaluations of aid provided for infrastructural, energy, industrial, programme and technical assistance objectives rarely consider the effect of this type of aid on the poor – and this accounts for over 60 per cent of all official aid. It is only in the case of rural development projects and some urban projects – and then only recently – that questions have been asked in this regard and by no means all donors even today require evaluators to examine these effects. For example, the UK's Overseas Development Administration only lists the general question 'who were the intended beneficiaries, how were they to benefit?' in its most recent checklist of objectives in its publication *Guidelines for the Preparation of Evaluation Studies*, and even then notes that 'not all questions are relevant to all projects (eg some projects may not have specific targeted beneficiaries)' (1985:12). Thus while the critics could well be correct that aid, or some of it, does not directly benefit the poor, there is far less evaluation material available which addresses this question explicitly than one might imagine from the vigour and consistency with which this particular criticism has been voiced.

There are other objectives besides poverty alleviation which have received greater prominence in the aid literature in recent years. These include ecological and environmental issues and the appropriateness of technology transferred to aid recipients. As with poverty alleviation, there are two questions that need to be separated out. First, are these different factors taken into consideration in deciding what to evaluate and, secondly and distinctly, are these objectives achieved? While much aid can certainly be criticised, perhaps even condemned, if it fails to relieve poverty and if it creates environmental ruin, one needs to take care in condemning it for these results if they were not considered in the decision to provide the aid and hence in devising ways of ensuring that these objectives were achieved. Failure to achieve certain objectives that are not set at the outset does not necessarily have to imply that aid will never achieve these objectives once they are considered explicitly. For instance, it would have been illegitimate to criticise US aid to Taiwan in the 1950s for its failure to consider the direct effects of that aid on the poor when it was believed at the time that the trickle-down theory of growth was correct. While donors can certainly be criticised for failing to assess the effect of aid on all factors crucial to the achievement of development, this criticism is in the first place directed at the complex question of what constitutes sustainable development. It is only when these factors are understood and incorporated into the evaluation process that aid evaluation will be able to throw light on the question of its effectiveness. At present, because a number of factors such as the effect of aid on the poor and on the environment have not been incorporated widely into the aid evaluation process, a judgement about aid's part in achieving these objectives cannot always be made.

Of course, raising issues that need to be considered in the evaluation process still leaves open the question of the weight to attach to each of them. This brings us to the question of *how* to evaluate aid performance.

How to evaluate

In many cases there are close links between the questions of what to evaluate and how to evaluate. For example, quite soon after Independence in Zimbabwe USAID began to provide micro-computers and technical assistance to the Ministry of Education in Harare. How far does one go in assessing the performance of such aid: the time taken to install the machines, the costs of the machines vis-à-vis alternative use of funds, the functioning of the machines, their use by US technical staff, the training of nationals to use the machines, the increased efficiency of the ministry, the impact of the ministry in increasing the efficiency of the educational system, the effect of education in the development of the country, or, finally, to take the criticism just discussed, the effects of these machines on the poor, the environment or alternative technical solutions? This example highlights two questions upon which there is still no general agreement among donors. First, precisely what are the factors that need to be included in an evaluation and, secondly, how exactly does one measure effectiveness or impact? These questions are equally pressing for programme as well as project aid.

As the Zimbabwean example indicates, measurement is clearly a problem to the extent that the outcome is not quantifiable. However, even if it is quantifiable it will almost certainly be the case that in practice some of the primary data required for evaluation will simply be unavailable, thus necessitating the use of secondary data, the accuracy of which is itself often unknown. The quantification problems in aid evaluation are often severe and only rarely, if at all, minor. They tend, too, to be often ignored in assessing aid effectiveness when a major part of the relevant evidence does not appear in a form that can easily be measured, or alternatively when only a part of the project life-cycle is covered by organised data collection (see Wheatley *et al.,* 1985:18).

When evaluation depends on qualitative assessment, the problems quickly escalate. At its simplest, as Faaland points out, 'The objective that aid should benefit the poorest groups in least developed countries is important but it is too general to form the point of departure for an evaluation' (1983:6). Two questions need to be addressed: first, who is to judge the effect and, secondly, how is the judgement to be determined? A central issue is the extent to which judgements made are verifiable by others.

By and large donors have attempted to ease (not solve) these difficulties first by choosing as evaluators people expert in particular disciplines and/or secondly by attempting to quantify the qualitative data. But some have also gone further. Not satisfied with making judgements about whether the range of objectives have been achieved for particular projects (frequently there is more than one objective and sometimes, for example in the case of rural development projects, there are many), some donors have attempted to provide a single figure for projects that 'captures' the overall effectiveness of a particular project. In doing this a judgement is made not only about how far the different project objectives have been achieved but also about the importance of some objectives vis-à-vis others. Agencies like the World Bank have used rate of return analysis, usually using a benchmark figure of 10 per cent as the cut-off point: if a project has a rate of return above the 10 per cent level it is deemed a success, and the higher the rate the more successful the project. Some donors have been attracted by some sort of scoring method for judging effectiveness: different objectives are scored (for example, on a scale of one to ten) and then weighted to give an overall score for the project. This latter method is judged by many bilateral donors more appropriate than rate of return analysis both because it is more amenable to the incorporation of a wider range of criteria and also because it is easier to use and apply. However, it needs to be stressed that many donors favour neither approach, preferring instead to let evaluators choose their own specific methods of evaluating success or failure, although usually within broad parameters. For example, ODA's guidelines state (1985:13):

> As far as practicable, evaluators should seek to compare the project's results with what was intended in terms (among other things) of: total costs, completion dates, output levels, rates of return (social and financial) and (if applicable) effect on target groups. The evaluation should, where appropriate, include a social cost/benefit analysis comparable, as far as possible, with that carried out at the appraisal stage.

There are major problems with each of the different methods used to assess aid performance and these centre particularly around data inadequacy and subjective judgement. One particular danger is that approaches which emphasise mathematical and financial rigour can be incorrectly assumed to escape the judgement problems that other approaches use. However, while these methods certainly try to reduce subjectivity by emphasising consistency and rationality and so are an advance on unstructured individual assessment – and they would certainly benefit by having different people with different outlooks involved in assessment, as suggested for example by Wheatley et al. (1985:57) – they do ultimately depend critically upon subjective judgement. As Stewart points out, judgement comes in all the time in social cost-benefit analysis: 'It is the nature of any exercise which is designed to put figures on and add up the resulting costs and benefits that the results should appear to represent scientific and objective conclusions, although in reality they are largely based on hunch, guesstimate and judgement' (1978:158). More critical still is Misra who maintains that 'there is no project which cannot be justified. Much depends upon who wants the project, who is going to finance it and who has been hired to approve it' (1981:51).

Rate of return analysis does not escape these problems either. Not only are much of the data that are used in project appraisal of dubious accuracy, especially when considering social criteria, discount rates and measurement of benefits, but individual judgement can have a profound effect on the results that are achieved. For example, Chambers cites the case of an agricultural project evaluated by three teams which separately gave rates of return of 19 per cent, 13 per cent and minus 2 per cent for the same project (1978:212). More generally, these issues are highlighted in a review of some 25 World Bank projects by Jones (1985). She points out that 'about one third of the audit or project completion reports reviewed noted that an economic rate of return could not be re-estimated with any degree of accuracy . . .' (1985:55) and that (60):

> many of the projects with the most sophisticated data collection systems have not generated the information needed to estimate project impact with some degree of confidence. Furthermore, even where project impact data have been generated through sample surveys, the audit reports do not provide enough information to determine the statistical significance of the reported differences in production achieved by project and non-project farmers. Very few audit reports even provide information on the size of

sample, much less the survey methodology. . . . While this information may be available from a careful mining of project files, its omission from audit/completion reports may leave the reader with a mistaken impression of the validity of project impact data.

She continues by stating that only about half the projects she examined appeared to have enough data to calculate the rate of return 'with some validity' because of weaknesses in baseline studies, failure to account accurately for exogenous variables, and dubious or incorrect assumptions made about the shadow price of labour (63–4).

There is also a need to question precisely what is being calculated when a rate of return figure is produced. It is important to know not only about relative inflation and interest rates between countries in order to judge performance across countries and over time, but also about the general success of other non-aid projects in different countries. As Berg comments, if a project achieved a rate of return of 2 per cent in Ghana today that might well be a miracle of development, but if a return of 15 per cent was achieved in Singapore the project manager might need replacing (quoted in Cracknell, 1984a:128). There is, too, the question of cause and effect. One needs to know, but is seldom told, how far the scores achieved are the result of the project process and how far the achievements (successes or failures) are due to external factors. As Cracknell correctly points out (24): 'sometimes a project has a good internal rate of return but only because producer prices have risen much more than expected or could reasonably have been foreseen, ie it has turned out to be a good project but only because of good luck!' World Bank evaluations are also exceptionally weak in pinpointing beneficiaries of projects. As Ayres, no enemy of the Bank, comments, 'neither Bank documents nor interviews with Bank project staff revealed a great deal about this aspect of project implementation' (1983:134). These problems and the subjective nature of rate of return analysis are implicitly acknowledged by the Bank, which recently stated that the results of its own evaluations of its projects raise the question of the context in which those results should be seen (1985:viii):

> It is our belief that no external context would be truly valid and that the Bank's performance has to be judged in its own terms, with reference to the objectives set for the operations that it supports, and that the level of achievement over time is essentially self-comparing. The Bank's own high professional competence, and the generally privileged position it enjoys in borrowing countries and in their investment planning and policy-making, would rule out any other context in which to evaluate its performance and the operations it has supported.

For World Bank rural development projects in Latin America, the author of a recent staff working paper is even more explicit about the inability of current evaluation material to provide an objective assessment of project success or failure. He writes (Lacroix, 1985:22-3):

> There are surprisingly few publications relating objectively the experiences of integrated rural development. And even those publications that are available repeatedly mention that cost figures, production data and quantitative information are not available. This leads to the conclusion not only that monitoring and evaluation are not reported, but that there is also a lack of systematic documentation, collection of data etc . . .
> Evaluation is more of a public relations effort than an information gathering exercise. As a result, little is known about the objective successes and failures of projects and little agreement can be reached in this respect with regard to specific projects. What some call successes, others will call failures, both opinions based on subjective and intuitive interpretations of actual or imagined events. Human development efforts such as rural

development are particularly prone to such confusions about what constitutes success or failure since many intangible benefits and costs can be counted and interpreted quite differently, following personal, subjective viewpoints.

And this itself raises the question: how far *can* one trust the judgement of the evaluators? Most evaluation units, the World Bank included, are staffed predominantly with economists, although aid projects involving technical details are commonly evaluated by engineers competent in that particular field. This introduces evaluator bias. For instance, because of the compartmentalisation of skill competence, engineers and economists tend not to evaluate or even notice factors analysed by other disciplines and which could prove critical to assessing project results. For example, even a desk study of four British aid projects by a sociologist revealed major gaps in analysis and in understanding what went wrong and why.[26] And as the 1985 DAC review argues, 'the composition of the evaluation team has a large influence on which factors are examined and particularly whether social issues are addressed' (1985:6).

More generally, a major gap exists in present knowledge because of the failure to incorporate political questions into evaluation methods and procedures. This statement may seem strongly at variance with experience because, from the viewpoint of many leftist criticisms of aid, politics and political questions are frequently highlighted as the major factor contributing to aid failure, while among donors there has in recent years been increasing recognition of the importance of the political environment, leading to a consensus view that a sympathetic political context is a major element in achieving aid's objectives. While this donor view is certainly correct (see Cohen *et al.*, 1985:1216), it has led to little or no progress in incorporating political variables systematically into evaluation methods. As for the perspective of the leftist critics, beyond *a priori* assertions and statements about power structures etc., there has been little attempt to examine the specific contribution and weight of political factors in judging aid's achievements or lack of them.

Tendler and Chambers have been among the first writers to draw attention to the political gap in evaluations. Tendler writes: 'political economic variables and their influence on development projects have received little attention (from within the agencies) partly because project successes and failures have seemed to be satisfactorily explained by more obvious factors closer to the project'. Yet against this explanation 'support of projects by strong interest groups has been central to the successful execution of all projects whether redistributive or not', (1982b:ii). For his part, Chambers pinpoints the gap in appraisal techniques thus (1983:163):

Political feasibility is not (regrettably) part of standard programme or project appraisal. There are well established procedures for assessing technical, financial and economic feasibility, deficient though their use often is but none in any formal sense for assessing the power and interest of groups, how they converge or conflict and how they will support or impede the achievement of a project's objectives.

Important though it is to highlight this gap, a weakness of leftist criticisms of aid is to place too much emphasis on political factors. In what has become a classic text, Tendler's book *Inside Foreign Aid* goes meticulously through the different political criticisms of aid and analyses other, most frequently institutional, organisational and bureaucratic, explanations that could just as easily be used to pinpoint causes for aid failure. Although the book raises many key issues for the aid debate (to be taken up here in subsequent chapters) its importance for the present discussion lies in its highlighting the complex nature of the aid relationship and hence of the difficulties in evaluating how aid's performance should be judged. She explains that 'the difficulty of tracing today's development assistance problems back to . . . organisational factors explains to a certain extent why critics have singled out other more visible causes' for aid failure (1975:3).

Of course, highlighting institutional and bureaucratic factors for inclusion in aid evaluation is only a first step. The next is to draw up a set of criteria for judging their importance, their influence and, of course, their scope for instituting change. But, as with the political factor, very few advances have yet been made in this regard. While DAC donors, for example, recognise the importance of a sound policy framework for achieving aid's objectives, they also admit that there is still considerable uncertainty about how policy dialogue should be conducted to obtain the most beneficial results. As the Cassen study explains, 'if there is a general weakness in the aid process . . . it is that understanding of institutional, political and social constraints to aid effectiveness lags very far behind economic and technical competence in virtually all agencies' (1986:10/37). And, of course, these weaknesses apply equally to the criticisms of aid, for, as Tendler pithily points out, 'knowledge that is still to be learnt cannot, by definition, be more abundant in one part of the world than another' (1975:11).

The problems of evaluator judgement apply particularly in evaluation using scoring techniques.[27] This is well illustrated in an exercise carried out by Jennings to assess UK aid by scoring 40 out of 100 project evaluations completed. He clearly believes in the methodology used, for he concludes that 'the highly successful scores achieved on average for the ODA projects scored confound much of the conventional wisdom which sees aid as a culprit in the disastrous performance of many developing countries' (1984:23). His scoring methods were suitably weighted for project value, with sub-scores for the following sub-criteria: achievement of project objectives; efficient achievement of project objectives and wider project impact.

Many questions need to be raised about the scoring methods used here and more widely in aid assessment. First, why should one necessarily believe the judgement of the assessor? That variations between assessors arise is brought out clearly in the Jennings paper, as the principal researcher asked four other people (all in general friends of aid) to put their own scores on a selection of the 40 projects. The results showed no unanimous agreement on *any* criteria for *any* project. Variations were in some instances very wide indeed; for example, one assessor believed that for one project a score of 10 out of 10 (100 per cent) should be given for 'immediate objectives achieved', while another believed a score of 5 was appropriate. For another project, one assessor gave a score of 4 for the criterion 'wider project impact favourable', while two others gave a score of 8. Even in their more rigorous approach to scoring techniques, Wheatley *et al.* readily admit that every individual colleague would no doubt have arrived at a somewhat different solution, although they do recommend that two assessors should work independently and then discuss their (differing) results (1985:55–6).

A second issue raised by the ODA scoring exercise is the basis upon which an overall success rating should be deemed to be the arithmetic average of the assessment of three prior performance criteria. Who is to judge that the achievement of immediate objectives, their efficient achievement (how calculated?) and the wider project impact (how assessed?) should be given equal weighting? And, to raise a previous question, how precisely does one quantify qualitative data? Moreover, why should other criteria, such as the effect on income distribution or alternative uses of aid funds or sustainability, not be considered important in evaluating aid success? These questions are simply not addressed in this or indeed most other aid scoring evaluation exercises. In their more detailed approach, Wheatley and his colleagues use a similar approach and end by adding up the scores arrived at in the evaluation of different criteria, arguing, with little conviction, that this 'reflects the explicit finding that no sound basis has been identified for adjusting the relative scores of sub-items in order to give them more or less weight in relation to each other as aspects of project success' (1985:67).

Finally, why should one necessarily regard the findings of aid evaluation studies upon which scoring methods are based as a reliable source for assessing aid performance? The Jennings study considered a UK aid project to provide 3,850 UK tractors to India between 1971 and 1974. This project was evaluated by Dr G. Dalton and, on the basis of this evaluation, Jennings, the assessor, gave overall scores of 9 with a sub-score of 10 for the achievement of immediate objectives, 6 for efficiency in achieving objectives and 8 for achieving wider impact. The (Dalton) evaluation report itself concluded, *inter alia*, that the provision of tractors did not reduce on-farm employment and by increasing land usage led to increased farm profitability.[28] However, Lipton rejects if not the conclusions then any generalisations that could be drawn from the study. He argues that it was based on a short two-month survey relying largely on evidence provided by the tractor industry. Dalton, according to Lipton, seemed completely unaware that 'careful studies establish beyond doubt that tractorisation in South Asia has in most cases greatly reduced workplaces, hasn't significantly raised output when other variables are held constant and has damaged poor people', and that there is also massive evidence to show that tractorisation *does* reduce employment per acre (1984:13–14). Lipton adds the following (12–13):

> No blame attaches to the author, who imaginatively sought to achieve his aims, eg to make some assessment of the social costs and benefits (using shadow prices) of these machines, including their effects on employment and food production (p.vii). What is unfortunate is the choice of such a low level of funding that the investigator was compelled to rely upon (a) the casual empiricism of rapid trips to accessible places, and (b) interlocutors inevitably biased towards presenting a favourable picture of the impact of tractors.

It was these factors, Lipton continues, which could lead to the conclusion providing 'an astoundingly complete justification of a policy that sent 3,850 tractors of five different makes as aid to a country with massive rural unemployment and poverty, yet hardly any spare land that was economically arable' (13). Clearly to base assessments of aid performance on evaluation reports makes the assumption that these are accurate and reliable. The UK tractor aid example reveals the dangers in making this assumption. This suggests that an assessment is certainly needed of the reliability and accuracy of aid evaluation reports which to date constitute the prime source of data for assessing aid performance. No such assessment, however, has been carried out.

When to evaluate
Although the literature on the weaknesses of techniques used in evaluation is large, enough has probably been said here to indicate the profound methodological problems that still exist. We shall therefore now turn to the question of when aid should be evaluated. Superficially it might appear that if the intention is to judge the overall success or failure of a project, then the best time to evaluate is immediately the project has been completed. If this *is* a good time, then a number of bilateral donors would fall at the first fence if Mosley is correct in his 1983 study

that some 34 per cent of evaluations of UK aid have been carried out while the project was still in progress (1983:594).

There are however, two reasons for wishing to lengthen the time between project completion and evaluation.[29] One is because of the increasing recognition that sustainability is a problem: a project cannot really be deemed a success if it is not capable of maintaining its objectives once the donor input has been withdrawn. The other reason for delay is because of increased concern (among donors and critics) to evaluate the impact of the project on the wider society into which it has been inserted. While it is clearly self-evident that it will take some time for the wider impact to be felt, there is no golden rule pinpointing precisely when an impact study should be carried out; it will vary from project to project and region by region (see UN Administrative Committee on Co-ordination, 1984:45).

Important though the reasons might be for delaying the time when evaluations are undertaken, most evaluations carried out by bilateral donors still tend to be undertaken close to completion. Hence while the wider issues (discussed in the last paragraph) are now recognised as relevant and important to the evaluation process – and this is itself an advance that has only occurred in the last five or six years – this recognition has not yet been incorporated widely into the evaluation procedures. As Cracknell, the former head of the Evaluation Department of Britain's ODA, has readily acknowledged. 'Because impact evaluations are still relatively few in number and cannot be considered by any means as representative, they can seldom be used as conclusive evidence when one is trying to answer very broad questions such as "Is aid in general effective?", ie "Does aid work?" ' (1984a:22). By the end of 1983, USAID had completed only 50 impact evaluations spread largely between rural roads, agricultural research, water supply, local education and rural electrification projects (Hoksbergen, 1986:287–8). One manifestation of this area of weakness has been the reluctance of donors to assist project sustainability through expanding and increasing funding for recurrent cost expenditure; another has been a reluctance to examine and take up again projects that have 'failed' in preference to using aid funds to finance new projects or programmes.[30]

The importance of timing in aid evaluation is illustrated by the World Bank's 1985 annual review of project performance. The Bank recently went back to 25 agricultural projects some five to 15 years after project completion and re-assessed performance. All had been deemed successful at the audit stage. The results, based on the Bank's own criteria and methodology, showed that subsequently 12 had achieved 'adequate sustainability', but for the majority the projects had failed, with rates of return for all well below 10 per cent, negative for two projects and on average 2.7 per cent. Failure was attributed to a range of factors including: institutional organisation, failure of technology, lack of services surrounding the project, and lack of finance for recurrent costs to sustain initial success. On the other hand, five of the 25 projects had achieved benefits that exceeded those anticipated at the project completion date (1985:32–44). Clearly, then, timing is of considerable importance in judging aid effectiveness and general impact, although, as we have seen, there is no satisfactory way of knowing, *in abstracto*, precisely when evaluation should take place.

There is, finally, an added complication. If too much emphasis is placed on overall project impact, then there is a danger that important implementation problems are ignored, down-played or simply forgotten. Consultation with field staff could well draw donors' attention to key obstacles of aid performance, which would be lost if evaluations were postponed. Thus although impact studies have rightly been given recent prominence, they should not be seen as a complete substitute for earlier assessments of aid's effects.

Other questions

Besides these detailed problems, other broader issues need to be raised. One is that evaluation is conducted principally as a management tool to guide donor agencies to improve aid effectiveness – both for projects that are in the process of implementation and for future projects.[31] This is acknowledged as the core reason for carrying out analyses of aid performance; as the recent DAC report argues, 'The overriding purpose of evaluations of development assistance is to serve the interests of donor and recipient nations in improving their policies and procedures in delivering and receiving aid' (1985:5). This implies that the growing quantity of evidence available from evaluations is not being gathered to answer the broader question of whether aid does or does not contribute to overall development in recipient countries. It is likely to be even less helpful in addressing specifically the question asked by some (especially rightist) critics of whether development would be promoted better without aid. This point is explicitly acknowledged by a former senior official of the UK's ODA (Browning in Cracknell, 1984a:9–10):

> But what can evaluation work achieve? Experience suggests that we cannot expect too much from it on larger issues. Discussion among donor countries in the Organisation for Economic Cooperation and Development (OECD) suggests that, at least as at present conceived, the results will not answer fundamental broad questions such as 'Does aid result in development?' or even 'Would more aid lead to faster economic growth in developing countries as a group or individually?'

The point is probably made too strongly, however, for if it can be assumed that the whole is in some measure the sum of the parts, then a consistent pattern of successful or unsuccessful aid performance would go a good way towards judging whether aid does or does not result in development. Indeed, to the extent that aid evaluations do attempt to monitor aid performance against a 'control' – assessing development performance with the aid input against a similar context where aid has not been provided – as does occur in at least some evaluation exercises, then even the latter point raised by Browning above is met. Moreover, as impact studies explicitly attempt to evaluate the wider effect of projects, including the 'broader socio-economic and political implications' (Cracknell, 1984a:21), these wider issues are by no means disregarded in current aid evaluation practices. None the less, it is important constantly to bear in mind that the principal purpose of aid evaluation is *not* to attempt to answer the more general questions of aid effectiveness, even though the critics *do* use evaluations precisely for this purpose; they have after all little other detailed and rigorously analysed data upon which to base their criticisms.

Another methodological weakness in judging the performance of aid by analysing separate evaluations of particular aid interventions is that these tend to be framed on the assumption that the world external to the project or programme remains unaffected and uninfluenced by it. This is by no means always (or ever) true. The effect of external influences could be either beneficial or detrimental to the intended impact of aid. An adverse effect now increasingly recognised by donors is that a proliferation of separately promoted projects which often require a maze of different documentation can be a drain on the administrative capacity of the recipient country, although in some of the poorest countries even a single project could have the same result. Various outcomes are possible: individual projects could suffer from institutional inefficiencies inhibiting implementation;

some projects that attract the scarce administrative resources in the recipient country could, as a result, perform comparably better than others; or, again, if aid projects in general attract recipient-country administrators to the detriment of non-aided work, aided projects could stand out as significant successes vis-à-vis a deteriorating wider national performance. In all cases, however, the wider effects of aid insertion will be missed by single-project evaluations. And, of course, there are a wide range of other potential external influences besides administrative ones that would also be likely to affect performance. These are discussed below.

It is also quite possible for circumstances to arise in which either two or more particular projects are evaluated as successful but the combined effect of both results in a less than efficient outcome or, alternatively, where particular projects are evaluated as failures but the eventual outcome is successful. An example of the first could be the separate decision of two donors to build power stations to increase electrical capacity in a country, with the result that overall capacity vastly in excess of projected requirements is installed; even so, the individual evaluation reports could each conclude that the objectives were achieved on time, at minimal individual cost and, as a result of increased capacity, the poor now have access to cheap electrical energy. On the other hand, two projects, one to introduce cotton production in a remote area and another to set up a ginning factory, could both be deemed failures on completion because the cotton produced could not be marketed and the factory received no cotton to gin. However, once an all-weather road with bridges was built to provide a permanent link between the two, the expected benefits could be reaped. The general point is that because evaluations tend overwhelmingly to be project– and time–specific, external factors which can have a bearing on success or failure tend to be ignored. It is in part because the evaluation of aid performance is initiated by individual donors that narrow project-specific bias tends to be so prevalent in the available evaluation material.

A final and common practical weakness of much aid evaluation material is the failure to assess the possibility of repeating the successes (or failures) accruing to either pilot projects or geographically-specific interventions. If lessons of project performance are not to remain project-specific but are to have wider appplicability, then it is necessary to ask whether and in what circumstances successes or failures will be repeated. This issue is of crucial importance to both the critics and defenders of aid because examples of differing aid performance form the basis of many of the generalisations made about aid or different forms of aid. In many cases donors merely assume that a 'successful' project can be replicated while critics tend to assume that specific failures imply that these failures will be repeated. The literature reveals few if any attempts to test these assumptions with any degree of rigour. For example, a recent study on the twin issues of replication and scaling-up[32] by Yaser found little or no attempt to consider these issues in evaluation analysis. Of seven major DAC donors consulted, several had nothing to offer on the subject, although indicating 'interest' in the question. Two donors stated they were considering the question, one was 'alluding' to the problem, while a fourth (CIDA) had included specific relevant questions on 'continuation and duplication' (in the appraisal stage) in its project evaluation handbook (Yaser in Miller, 1980:115).

Does lack of success imply failure?

Thus far, the discussion in this chapter has focused on the quantity and quality of the micro-data available to enable firm conclusions to be drawn about the impact of aid, the implication being that if evidence of sufficient quantity and/or quality *were* available the case either for or against aid intervention could then be made. There are, however, serious doubts about the truth of this assumption: would reliable quantitative and qualitative data on aid's impact, even if they were available, clinch the argument?

There are various and different implications that can be drawn from evidence that convincingly indicates aid failure. While consistent evidence showing that aid has not worked points to aid failure (in relation to a set of objectives or in comparison with alternative policies), it does not necessarily follow that either aid does not work now (given the considerable time lag in producing the evidence from project commencement) or that it cannot work in the future. Indeed, given the fact that major official donors use aid evaluation as a management tool for improving aid effectiveness, there is, even for aid's advocates, a built-in assumption that aid intervention can never – or only rarely – achieve its objectives entirely and that improvements can always be made. This suggests that aid is provided in the full knowledge that it will not be completely successful. But beyond this qualification the question still remains whether changes can be made to ensure that, if aid has persistently been a failure, its performance can be improved to tip the scales in its favour. The crucial question, then, is whether the lessons of past failure are capable both of being learned and of leading to changes in design or implementation which result in greater success and a better performance than for alternative (non-aid) policies. It is only if aid can be shown not to have worked, and not to be capable of working in the future, and that an alternative strategy would work, that the perspective of the critics of aid will have been vindicated. The difficulty for the critics is that this question is unlikely to be capable of being answered solely by reference to the evaluation material available which analyses past or even present performance. The case against aid based on performance criteria can be validly sustained only on the assumption that constraints are permanent and incapable of change; this is open to challenge by both historical experience and, as discussed in Part II above, by theoretical considerations.

There is, too, the question of homogeneity. Official aid today consists of a wide range of different forms of intervention linked together by the common thread of concessionality. It includes technical assistance, food and commodity transfers, budget support, rural and urban projects, infrastructural and institutional assistance, sectoral specific assistance targeted, for example, to agriculture, education, health and industry, and bilateral and multilateral channels for intervention. If aid fails to work in one particular form it does not thereby necessarily follow that it has to fail if applied in a different form. Similarly even if it can be shown that aid is never likely to succeed in one form or if provided to specific recipients, either because the lessons of failure will not be learned or structural constraints are all-pervasive, it does not necessarily mean that these blockages will apply to other types of aid or to all other countries. In instances of aid evaluation revealing a mixture of success and failure, the implication of failure is not that all aid should be cut off but that by and large aid should be channelled into areas where it is most likely to achieve success.[33]

Beyond these types of question there are other elements in the aid relationship which suggest that failure should not always and inevitably be taken as the benchmark for a rejection of aid. Not only would one expect, even without much detailed evidence, that different types of aid will achieve different results in different countries but one would also expect a greater degree of failure in poorer aid-recipient countries where, on needs-based criteria, the obligation to provide it would be greater. Poorer countries tend to be characterised by greater uncertainties, weaker institutions, fewer socio-economic linkages and greater vulnerability of their economies to external influences. In these circumstances expectations of what aid can achieve must be lower than in countries which have a more supportive environment, and thus a greater degree of failure will be anticipated and indeed expected even at the time when the aid is initially given.

In poorer countries and societies, especially, our understanding of the development process and its contributing factors will be limited. Hence the outcome of aid intervention is not likely to be fully predictable; and it is likely to be far different from the outcome that one would expect from hot-house laboratory conditions. To judge aid's results on the basis of these ideal criteria is to judge them wrongly and prejudicially. Indeed, to the extent that donor agencies attempt to increase aid effectiveness by controlling the recipient-country environment, they will stand accused of challenging the recipient's sovereignty and of imperialistic behaviour. It is simply misplaced to expect that there ought to be a 100 per cent success rate for aid intervention. On the one hand, not even commercial banks expect their lending to have such a high performance rating even in the industrialised world; in lending to Third World borrowers the margin for error is even wider. Why then should one expect aid funds – frequently provided because commercial institutions judge the projects too risky – to achieve higher or even an equal rate of success? On the other hand, as Tendler points out, when large amounts of money are involved in aid transfers it is unreasonable to expect norms applied to public funds in donor countries to be the sole criteria for judging performance (1975:42):

> Whenever large amounts of money are being spent there will be an unavoidable minimum of misspending, inefficiency and graft. The number of possible mistakes in a program like AID's therefore will be much greater than in the State Department simply because the latter doesn't have to build projects and rely on outsiders for essential inputs. State under criticism could close ranks, AID on the other hand (is) exposed on all sides.

The criteria therefore by which aid is to be judged should be more in relation to whether some benefits have been achieved, given the existing constraints, and whether these benefits have been achieved more effectively and efficiently than would have been possible without aid, rather than whether all the objectives set have been achieved with maximum success.

There is, of course, a crucial difference between arguing that some failure is part of the nature of the aid relationship and should be acknowledged as such, and arguing that failures should be carefully analysed and, if possible, corrected. The point is not to condone waste and to justify misuse of funds, rather it is to highlight the risky and uncertain environment in which any policy intervention, including aid, is carried out. Furthermore, in certain circumstances as Yaser points out (in Miller, 1980:111), donors sometimes embark on aid projects with the full knowledge that they will probably fail, in order to learn more about the determinants of a particular phenomenon or the means to address the problem in order to apply that knowledge to other countries or to assess wider impact possibilities in the future. In these cases 'aid failure' is all but built into the justification for intervention and in no way leads to the blanket policy implication of withdrawal.

This brings us to another important factor in assessing aid, namely the bias towards failure in the evaluation material available. Donor agencies not only evaluate aid in order to improve aid management; their evaluations also tend to be highly critical texts. Evaluators are predominantly social scientists whose academic training not only emphasises criticism but rewards it. As Chambers points out, 'Social scientists in part are taught to argue and find fault'. Moreover, they tend to be better able to obtain funding for research on projects that are new or innovative because the lessons here are unknown, in the same way as official evaluation departments are more interested in doing evaluation of new initiatives. 'Because these are new, they are precisely those where most is going wrong and the studies occur before the main early lessons have been learnt and corrections made' (Chambers, 1983: 30-31). The implication is clear; the evidence of aid performance available through evaluation material tends both to highlight the problems rather than give a balanced judgement of successes and failures and to give greater prominence to those interventions that are more likely to face difficulties in implementation and completion. Conversely, there is little interest generated in analysing projects that are known to be successful, and hence these tend not to be the subject of detailed studies and evaluation. In a recent review, Muscat describes well the inherent biases in evaluation material available on technical assistance programmes (1986:70):

> aid project evaluations are negatively biased. The evaluators tend to be regarded by operating personnel as outsiders, looking for faults that need correction, the identification of which appears to confirm the value of evaluation more than does the identification of things done correctly. More importantly, the evaluation literature does not include many studies in the engineering and scientific fields, such as telecommunications, meteorological services, civil aviation, remote sensing, geological services, where TC is commonly recognised as being relatively successful. These fields tend to be focused more institutionally, they require far fewer recipients for successful technology transfer, and have less need for cultural adaptation. In addition, non-biological technologies are relatively easy to transfer between countries which are ecologically different, while biologically-based fields (like agriculture, animal husbandry, health) require extensive local adaptation.

The general conclusion from this discussion is that to judge the overall performance of aid on the basis of the evidence of aid evaluation material could well be premature. Lack of evidence of success by no means has to lead to the conclusion that all aid will always fail, nor should one assume that a judgement of failure cannot be revised or reversed by the passage of subsequent events. The questions that are seldom asked, probably because firm conclusions are far more difficult to arrive at, are these:[34] with limited resources at their disposal and in the difficult circumstances in which they have to work, what is it reasonable to expect aid agencies to achieve, and could these goals be achieved better without aid or through different donor policies and intervention? The available evidence is unlikely to provide clear-cut answers to either of these questions.

Wider influences

The aid evaluation and aid impact debate is focused specifically on the question whether particular types of aid intervention do or do not contribute to development and (even if all too infrequently) whether alternative policies would be preferable. It is based on the assumption that aid is provided and received to achieve development objectives; other objectives and influences are by and large ignored. Thus discussion takes place in a sanitised world of the perfect donor and perfect recipient where wider political, foreign policy, strategic, commercial, and economic influences are not considered. The problem is that these influences can not only be important, they can sometimes be crucial to aid performance in the real world. The purpose of this section is to highlight a range of pressures and constraints which can and do have critical effects on aid and its impact on development. To the extent that they are unexpected, uncertain and unpredictable – as many are – these influences lessen even further the ability of aid's critics or supporters to make firm generalisations about its performance.

It is no secret that donors, and especially bilateral donors, provide development aid within a context consistent with broad international and foreign-policy perspectives. The US, European, OPEC and Eastern European donors have historically, and at minimum, refrained from giving aid to their enemies and more generally have provided more aid to their Third World allies and/or to territories with which they have strong historical links. Similarly, both bilateral and multilateral agencies have tended to provide aid to recipients that adhere to broad policy directives approved of by them.

The problem that needs to be highlighted here is not so much that aid always has an important political dimension but that political considerations are a dominant force which can and does result in substantial variations in aid flows to countries and regions and from bilateral to multilateral agencies. These variations can have a marked effect on aid performance right down to the micro-level, because changes in total flows can disrupt projects by halting funds or by leading to key staff withdrawals, by re-ordering aid priorities, or by playing havoc with intra-project co-ordination. For the USA in particular, political considerations have always been influential but quantitative volatility has been more particularly marked in the 1980s.[35] Yet it is not only the US which incorporates political considerations into aid flow decisions. For example, in a recent and comprehensive review of Western European donors, Stokke comments: 'When aid programmes are implemented, however, it seems as if most donor governments tend to look after their own political and economic interests first, even at the cost of reducing the real value of the aid to the recipients' (1984:13).

Dramatic examples of changes in US aid to particular recipients are illustrated by the cases of Zimbabwe, Sudan and Ghana. US aid commitments to Zimbabwe began at $24m. at Independence in 1980, rose to $84m. in 1982, fell to $59m. in 1984 and were set to fall well below $20m. in early 1986 prior to a decision in September 1986 to cancel all future aid programmes. These differences were caused in large part by political considerations evaluated in Washington, including Zimbabwe's refusal to vote in the Security Council to condemn the shooting down of the South Korean airliner and more recently its criticism of US foreign policy. US aid to Sudan stood at $64m. in 1981, rising to $121m. in 1984; in 1986 total US military and economic aid to Sudan stood at $158m. prior to total suspension in late February with only $50m. of food aid being disbursed, following Sudan's developing relations with Libya. US aid to Ghana totalled $22m. in 1981, $11m. in 1982, $7m. in 1983, $18m. in 1984 and $12m. in 1985 when all aid was suspended, related to the uncovering of the destabilisation efforts of the CIA.[36]

Variations in US funding have also seriously and significantly affected the funding and aid planning efforts of multilateral agencies. Reductions in contributions to the seventh IDA replenishment affected World Bank aid projects, while withdrawal from UNESCO had an even more serious effect on the latter's ongoing programmes. More generally, US funding for international organisations, including all UN agencies, was 16 per cent lower at current prices in 1986 than in 1980 and is set to fall another 17 per cent in 1987.[37] Given the lead time in planning and executing projects, discussed in an earlier section of this chapter, these variations in funding are likely to have serious effects upon aid performance.

The general effects of aid flow volatility can also have ripple effects on third countries which can seriously disrupt aid planning and project effectiveness. For example, total UK aid to sub-Saharan Africa (including technical assistance) was almost static between 1980 and 1984 – £244m. in 1980 and £247m. in 1984. Yet this regional stability included a £20m. cut in aid to Zimbabwe, from 1980 to 1984, a 500 per cent variation in annual flows to Uganda and a 75 per cent drop in aid to Ghana.[38]

A second major factor influencing aid performance results from donors using aid to further their own economic interests. While donors give aid with the intention of helping recipient countries, they also make no excuse for intending also to promote their own economic interests. This poses the crucial question of whether there is in practice any conflict between these two objectives, and if so what the consquences are. The most common way that donor self-interest is achieved is through aid tying – stipulating that the aid provided is used to purchase goods or services originating in the donor country. Three sorts of distortions to aid performance can arise from this practice: first, when the goods and services offered by the aid donor are not of priority to the recipient; secondly, if the goods and services provided by the donor are needed by the recipient, but are more costly than those from alternative sources; and thirdly, if the types of goods and services are inappropriate to the needs of the recipient at its particular stage of development.

Compared with aid provided as freely convertible currency, each distortion entails some costs to the recipient. Thus the ideal of completely untied aid would result in these distorting consequences being reduced.[39] Against this, however, it could equally be argued that this is not the distinction that matters, for if aid is provided tied to donor purchases or else not provided at all, then the choice for the recipient lies in accepting the less than perfect tied aid or the even less preferable option of no aid at all. In practice, neither extreme is of much policy interest. The evidence indicates that considerable distortions do arise from aid tying and, at the margin at least and probably well beyond it, donors do have an option to increase or decrease the amount of aid that they provide in a tied form. Of greatest importance is that donors have consistently maintained that the *primary* objective of providing development assistance is to promote recipient-country development; donor self-interest is acknowledged only as a secondary or, at worst, a mutually achievable benefit. No donor has yet explicitly stated that it gives development assistance primarily to further its own economic interests, with recipient development as a secondary and desirable but not sufficient aim. To do this would fly in the face of DAC agreements stretching back to the early 1960s. In the UK, for instance, the law under which the Overseas Development Administration spends public money requires that it be spent primarily on development.

That aid tying does lead to the different sorts of distortions listed above is confirmed by a wide array of evidence.[40] DAC figures reveal that, excluding EEC aid, some 31 per cent of all aid from DAC donors is tied, and more significantly only 31.5 per cent of DAC bilateral aid is not subject to formal procurement restrictions.[41] Certain sub-categories of aid are subject to far higher degrees of tying. For example, UK technical assistance is 'practically all tied to the UK', (ODA, 1985:xii) while most DAC donors insist that commodity aid programmes are used almost exclusively to purchase goods from the donor country (well over 90 per cent of commodity aid provided). In addition, it is rare for donors not to insist that most if not all foreign purchases of goods are obtained from the donor, if available. A recent study of Canadian aid to Tanzania found that over 82 per cent of its aid was tied to the procurement of Canadian goods and services, although DAC figures state that only 51.7 per cent of Canadian bilateral aid is tied (see Young, 1983:89).

Recent new initiatives to increase donor self-interest have come from arrangements that encourage the use of aid monies increasingly for trade promotion activities. In Britain the Aid and Trade Provision (ATP) instituted in 1977 uses aid money to lower British companies' commercial export costs so as to obtain orders, often in the hope of outbidding firms from companies in other donor countries using similar aid-backed trade facilities.[42] More generally, the use of mixed credits, which reduce the effective interest rate on project loans to developing countries by combining normal export credits with aid or very soft loans, has expanded in recent years to be worth an estimated SDR 5.8 billion in 1984 and over SDR 6 billion in 1985.[43] Recent agreement to limit the extent of mixed credits, by prohibiting aid financing for higher-income developing countries and raising the aid element for the poorest countries, is recognition of the fact that aid monies have increasingly been used to promote donor economic interests at the cost of development objectives in recipient countries.[44]

Tying can also extend beyond these more transparent practices. For example, in the USA Tendler lists a series of executive restrictions and amendments to the foreign assistance legislation: 50 per cent of AID-financed commodities to be carried in US-flag carriers; procurement to be limited to US sources; assistance to be terminated not only when expropriation without adequate compensation occurs but also when there is unpaid uncontested debt to a private US citizen in a recipient country; no assistance to be given for productive enterprises competitive with US industry unless the recipient country agrees to limit exports to the US to 20 per cent of assisted enterprise output; and, finally, if PL-480 wheat is imported, recipient-country exports of corn and rice are prohibited (1975:38).

Evidence that aid tying adversely affects recipient countries comes from a variety of sources. While Bhagwati acknowledges the weaknesses of aggregate data, he estimates that the extra cost to recipients of having to accept tied aid lies between 20 and 25 per cent (1970:17). These figures are confirmed by more recent work. For example, the US Task Force study on India found prices 20-30 per cent higher as a result of tying, Riddell (1983:32) estimated a figure of between 10 and over 20 per cent for US aid to Zimbabwe, and Holtham and Hazlewood found that for Kenya 15 per cent of all UK aid was 20 per cent overpriced (1976:58). More dramatic instances can also be cited. For example, in the 1970s Bangladesh railways arranged for the procurement of passenger carriages from South Korea and Pakistan under a Japanese credit scheme. At the same time carriages were imported from Denmark under a Danish aid initiative. The first procurement was arranged by international tender, the second on limited tender only in Denmark. The cost of the Danish carriages was three times the international price. Subsequently the tendering and procurement procedure was repeated with the tied aid originating this time in Britain: the UK carriages were 50 per cent more costly than South Korean and Indian-sourced carriages obtained through untied Saudi Fund aid (Huque, 1985:28).

Price, however, is only one factor. When aid tying is considered along with the pressures that widely exist to commit funds quickly, then further distortions arise.[45] One is a bias towards projects with a high foreign-exchange content; another is pressure to accept larger projects (see Bridger, 1984:4). A third bias is a frequent reluctance on the part of donors to have a high or rising local cost component in projects, the implications of which can be very significant. As Tendler puts it: 'availability of project financing for only foreign exchange costs causes the priorities of recipient countries to almost re-arrange themselves around foreign exchange intensive projects and encourages maximisation of the foreign exchange component of any desired project' (1975:74). Duncan and Mosley point to yet another distortion caused by aid tying: the proliferation of types of equipment leading to the familiar problems of staff training and procurement and maintenance of spare parts as well as the use of equipment of unproven worth under local conditions (1985:25). This problem tends to increase when a large number of donors are active in particular recipient countries. For example, as the DAC review put it, in the early 1980s, Kenya was trying to cope with 600 projects from 60 donors. Similarly the UNDP has estimated that there were 188 projects from 50 donors in Malawi, 321 projects from 61 donors in Lesotho and 614 projects from 69 donors in Zambia' (DAC, 1985:195-6).[46] While a proliferation of donors puts considerable strain on recipients in the attempt to co-ordinate these different projects with each other and with domestically initiated development projects, aid performance also suffers from lack of donor co-ordination. As the 1985 DAC report admits, this issue has hardly been faced by donors (195):

> close co-ordination both among aid institutions and between them and the recipient countries, has long been prescribed as an indispensable condition for enhancing the development effectiveness of each participant in the development process. Rarely, until recently, has such country-centred co-ordination been fully or consistently attempted.

The proliferation of different types of equipment highlights the technological bias of aid tying. There are a wide range of examples of tied aid leading to products judged inappropriate to recipient countries. Duncan and Mosley cite the example of 9 per cent of aid to Kenya having gone to water projects leading to 18 different types of water-pump currently being used in the country; many do not work and 89 per cent of the population still does not have protected water supplies (1985:118-25). The EEC Court of Auditors draws attention to the installation in Mauritius in an isolated spot without adequate technical facilities of a thermo-dynamic solar pump of a very experimental kind costing a staggering 413,290 écus. It worked for only a few hours in 1980 and would have required 40,000 écus in annual charges to maintain and repair. If it had worked it would have irrigated 20 hectares of land. Its cost was roughly that of 50 ordinary motor-driven pumps which would have irrigated some 500 hectares of land.[47] Of course, as discussed above, there are as yet no reliable data to suggest how typical these examples are. In contrast, an ODA evaluation report speaks positively about the use of windmills imported into Kenya in terms of the appropriateness of the technology used, which was the specific perspective of the evaluation study.[48] None the less, of the evaluation reports that are available (and which I have seen) a significant number do cite examples; often unsolicited, of technological problems with goods imported under tied aid arrangements. Typical of these is the case of UK forklift trucks supplied to Sudan. These, according to the evaluation done, not only had tyres of the wrong size, so causing serious maintenance problems, but the design was inappropriate for the hot conditions under which they were to be used.[49] Sometimes the commercial pressures to use aid funds for uses inappropriate for recipient countries is extremely transparent. For example, an evaluation for ODA of the commercial implications of its aid quotes another evaluation report thus:

> In 1979 St. Vincent and Montserrat were each recommended to acquire a Britten-Norman Trilander aircraft and aid funds were made available. A serious case for these two small islands to own and operate a particular type not represented in the fleets of local operators – one aircraft airlines – was not attempted. The consultancy report . . . reads more like a sales brochure. The aircraft was provided out of aid funds and both

islands have now put them out of service and want to dispose of them. . . . The proposal to provide BA 146 to the Sudan has been resisted. These activities are the reverse of project identification . . . offers of surplus goods without evidence of need or developmental objective should surely be resisted by the ODA.

There are also instances of aid being refused because the goods required by recipients are not obtained from the donor in question. A clear-cut instance of this comes from Bangladesh. In 1981, Sweden agreed to finance a power station with untied aid, the main component being the purchase and installation of power-generating turbines. The bid went to international tender and the tender committee selected a lower Japanese bid rather than one by a Swedish firm. After a number of Swedish protests, Bangladesh decided to accept the Japanese bid, at which point the aid offer was withdrawn (Huque, 1985:33-4). The frequency with which these particular types of aid distortion occur is not known, a major reason being that these sorts of problems are simply not addressed in the normal process of aid information gathering.

A final wider influence on aid performance can and does arise when changes occur in economic circumstances due either to non-aid-specific policies of donors, singly or as a group, or to other economic factors. A few of the many examples will be cited to illustrate the range of such influences. At a general level, consider the rise and fall of OPEC aid. It rose to a peak of $9.7 billion in 1980, accounting in that year for 24 per cent of total aid disbursements. Since 1984 the world oil price has fallen, hovering around $10–$15 a barrel by April 1986 compared with an average of $28 in 1980 and between $26 and $30 a barrel in 1985. There is little doubt that this recent price drop will make even more significant inroads into the level of OPEC aid. There is little doubt, too, that this progressive fall in OPEC funds will affect particular country programmes because over 80 per cent of OPEC aid is channelled bilaterally to over 40 Third World countries.[50]

Also at the general level, the downturn in world economic activity since the late 1980s, lower commodity prices, and increasing balance-of-payments constraints all lessen economic options in aid-recipient countries and adversely affect their economic performance. It is these broader constraints which increase the likelihood of recipient-country policies inhibiting the goals set for particular aid projects. Not that they are all of recent origin. For example, over 20 years ago Hirschman recounted the tale of the Owen Falls hydro-electric scheme in Uganda. The plant was built to enable the creation of an industrial centre in Uganda to counteract the industrial dominance of Nairobi in adjacent Kenya. However, economic constraints within Uganda led to the Ugandan Electricity Board having to build a transmission line direct to Kenya and sell the electricity generated to industrial users in Nairobi (1967:106-7). More recently, the EEC reported on a water supply project installed in Mali. Drinking fountains were built which would have provided clean water to the majority of the population. However, because the local authorities do not have the finance to pay for the water the fountains have been cut off and most people still have to purchase water from private vendors at inflated prices.[51]

A perhaps extreme example of a far from uncommon phenomenon – non-aid-specific economic policy initiatives indirectly affecting aid performance – comes from Thailand. Since the early 1950s, the US has provided Thailand with significant amounts of foreign economic aid, a large proportion of which has been channelled to rural development projects.[52] The US has been joined in its efforts by other major donors, like the World Bank through IDA, and more recently by

Japan and West Germany.[53] A major thrust of the agricultural aid effort has been focused on increasing rice yields, by extending the land cultivated, improving traditional production techniques, and expanding the use of high-yielding varieties. This aid effort combined with domestic initiatives has been highly successful; Thailand's rice production has expanded dramatically, as have exports which are the single most important foreign-exchange earner. For example, between 1978 and 1984, the volume of rice exports trebled to 4.6 million tonnes, their value rising from $511m. in 1978 to $955m. in 1984.[54] In December 1985, however, the US Farm Act was signed into law by President Reagan. The effect of this legislation will be to provide a subsidy to US rice farmers which halves the price of US rice exports thus making US rice cheaper than the Thai product. According to the Thai Board of Trade, Thailand stands, as a direct result of this measure, to lose 40 per cent of its export markets to the US, with over one million tonnes lost in Middle East and African markets alone, estimated, in 1986, to deprive the country of over $200m. of foreign-exchange earnings.[55]

To sum up, it can be seen that there is an array of wider influences that can and do have a marked effect on aid performance, with the macro-factors often reaching down quickly to the level of particular project performance. Pinpointing these influences, however, by no means has to lead to the conclusion that they prevent aid from achieving the development objectives for which it is predominantly given or that they are likely to do so in the future. Indeed, some wider influences, such as the original increase in oil prices, were positive, while others, like the lack of donor co-ordination, have hardly yet been addressed (so that the issue of whether lack of co-ordination is a significant constraint, and if so will remain one, is still unclear).

Concluding remarks

The discussion has indicated some serious inadequacies in the available data on the performance of aid. The bulk of the micro-evidence systematically produced comes from evaluation material, almost exclusively carried out by donor agencies or commissioned by them. Not only is the quantity of such material severely limited and with built-in negative biases, but its quality is far from satisfactory. Aid evaluation methods are still very crude and many of the observations made in evaluation reports are unreliable for drawing wider conclusions about aid's effectiveness because of their narrow focus, data unreliability and subjective judgement that cannot readily be verified. Moreover, even if the evidence were available to support the critics' contention that aid projects have repeatedly failed to achieve their objectives, it by no means follows either that failure will be repeated in the future or that development performance without aid would be any better. The data are simply inadequate to draw such conclusions.

It should not be inferred, however, that the available evidence is without value and that no generalisations whatsoever can be made about aid performance. The fact that evaluation of aid performance is now being treated seriously by official donors, that over a thousand evaluations by DAC and multilateral donor agencies are now being conducted annually (if not yet widely distributed), that attempts are being made to reduce or at least pinpoint data weaknesses and to expose subjectivity in evaluation, and that analysing the effects of aid on beneficiaries and non-beneficiaries is increasingly accepted as an intrinsic part of the evaluation process, are all major advances that must be acknowledged. As a result, in the next five to ten years it would appear that the available micro-evidence will provide some useful general indicators of aid performance. It should also increase knowledge about the range of constraints impeding performance, the strength of these and the room for manoeuvre.

Of course, the complexity of the development process and the wide range of variables influencing change in society mean that it will never be possible to monitor aid performance with scientific objectivity and laboratory-type accuracy; to attempt to judge against these norms would be both naive and unrealistic. What is realistic is to increase the level and breadth of expertise examining aid performance so that aid success and failure are analysed with greater precision and with more verifiable indicators in order to narrow the present gap between superficial guesses or narrowly-based assessments and the desirable (but unachievable) objective of achieving near-scientific accuracy. Recent work, for example by Wheatley *et al.* (1985), is a significant step in this direction, although it has not yet been tested and tried in practice.

Weaknesses in the data on aid performance at the general level do not imply that there is also no evidence available to draw conclusions about particular types of aid inserted in specific settings. While the evidence on structural adjustment lending and the effects of a wide range of non-project aid, including technical assistance, is readily acknowledged as poor (in the case of aid provided with structural adjustment loans, evaluations are only now beginning to be carried out and these remain largely confidential), there is a widespread and increasing literature on certain types of project aid including rural development, food aid and certain types of infrastructural projects. This literature includes a broader consensus about causes of failure, lessons learnt and the identification of different positive and negative forces assisting or hindering aid impact and effectiveness, although it also reveals conflicting effects which challenge generalisations even for specific types of intervention. The evidence of the effects of particular types of aid at the micro-level will be the subject of the next chapter.

Notes

1. Author's discussion with the DAC Secretariat, Paris, February 1986. Interestingly in a review of evaluation studies prepared for the OECD, Bachrach comments that although the amount of evaluation material available is overwhelming 'very few *ex post* evaluations could be found' (1980:51).
2. Calculated from DAC, 1985 Tables 11 and 25 and DAC, 1983 Table A2.
3. Out of 80 projects evaluated by the Overseas Development Administration, excluding food aid and disaster relief, the total cost to ODA amounted to £347 million, averaging £4.3 million per project. These varied from less than £100,000 to £47 million for particular projects. World Bank projects tend to be far larger than bilateral and other multilateral agency projects. Of 1,014 World Bank projects evaluated between 1974 and 1983, the average cost was approximately $67 million, of which World Bank lending averaged $21.8 million per project. However, these projects were not all classified as aid projects. IDA-specific projects from 1961 to 1982 averaged $9.9 million of disbursed funds per project. See World Bank, 1982:101 and 1985a:5.
4. ODA, 'Index to EVSUMS as at January 1986,' 1986 mimeo.
5. For example, two recent books on OPEC aid by Hunter (1984) and Achilli and Khaldi (1984) provide no analysis of the evaluation of any aspect of OPEC aid.
6. I have already discussed the profound weaknesses in methodology and data reliability for cross-country studies in Chapter 10.
7. The quality of such reports and their ability to address the crucial questions of aid's impact are issues secondary to whether any studies have been carried out or not. The content of the studies that have been carried out is discussed in Chapter 17, below.
8. A detailed synopsis of the work of the Task Force has been published as R.H. Cassen, *Does Aid Work?*, 1986.

9. The ODI book on aid to Kenya by Holtham and Hazlewood (1976) points out that British aid to Kenya only exceeded 50 per cent of all aid in 1964 and 1965.

10. These include Haiti (1984) by E.P. English, Tanzania (1983) by R. Young, Bangladesh (1983) by R. Ehrhardt and The Swedish National Audit Bureau reports, 1974, *SIDA* in *Tanzania* and 1976, *SIDA* in *India*. See bibliography for full references of these and other country case studies.

11. Of course, there is a vast literature on various aspects of development in most if not all aid-recipient countries, some of which includes comments upon or sections devoted to aid questions. However, this literature falls well short of providing in-depth analysis of the effects of aid inflows from all major sources on specific recipient countries.

12. DAC, *Evaluation Methods and Procedures: A Compendium of Donor Practice and Experience. Annex, 'Glossary of Terms Used in Evaluations'*, OECD, Paris, 1985, pp. 7 and 18. Under 'Types of Evaluations', the following are listed: Identification, Appraisal *ex-ante*, mid-term, *ex-post*, Self-evaluation, Incorporated, Built-in Internal, External, Project, Sector, Programme, Process Evaluation/Evaluation of Procedures. Similar sorts of definitions are provided for the UN agencies. See, for example, *The United Nations ACC Task Force on Rural Development Panel on Monitoring and Evaluation* (1984) pp 11-17. There are, however, other concepts and approaches that are also being utilised, for example 'performance evaluation'; see Skeates and Whitlam, 1983.

Some critics might argue that even these definitions are too narrow because they pre-judge the question of whether aid insertion is needed at all. However, if the term 'relevance of the objectives' (undefined by DAC) is taken to include these particular perspectives, it is believed that these definitions provide an adequate starting-point for judging aid performance which encompasses these types of concerns. Clearly evaluation can be extended beyond projects or programmes to whole countries. In this section attention is focused primarily on project and programme evaluation of different aid donors. The methodological problems of cross-country evaluations have been discussed in Chapter 10. Specific problems of country evaluations are discussed in Chapter 17.

13. Both of these differing conclusions do, of course, also depend upon the assumption that results from specific instances of aid intervention are not unique and hence that at least some generalisation beyond the particular can be made. This crucial assumption to the arguments is made both by aid's advocates and its critics and is discussed in the section on 'When to evaluate' below. Interestingly this was a point raised in the 1985 DAC Chairman's report which comments thus: 'if a particular society develops, or fails to develop, the explanation will always need to take many different factors into account, few of which lie within the command of aid agencies. The traditional tool used by economists to resolve this problem, such as multiple regression analysis, fails to carry conviction. Economists, with their pretensions to scientific method, have still found no way of handling the proposition that everything is a special case' (1985:256). If one held rigidly to the view that everything is unique, then a general discussion of aid effectiveness would cease at once. That this book is being written at all is an admission that the extreme assumption of uniqueness is rejected.

14. *Official Journal of the European Communities, Information and Notices*, Vol. 26, C357, 31 December 1983, pp. 135-6.

15. *Official Journal of the European Communities, Information and Notices*, Vol. 27, C348, 31 December 1984, pp. 129-31.

16. World Bank, *Tenth Annual Review of Project Performance Audit Results 1984*, Washington, 1985, pp. 34-5.

17. The food and nutrition centre is of particular significance because of the positive evaluation it received from an author highly critical of aid – Radetski, 1986:38-9.

18. P.W. Beard and B.P. Thompson, *Mauritius Electricity Generation Project*, EV 301, ODA, London, 1983 and *EVSUM 301*, ODA, London 1983.

19. DAC, 'Evaluation Methods and Procedures: A Compendium of Donor Practice and Experience', OECD, Paris, 1985 (mimeo) pp. 31-2. The complete project is evaluated in Bell *et al.* (1982).

20. J.N. Stevens and P.W. Beard, *An Evaluation of Diesel Generators in Nepal*, ODA, London, EV 326, 1984.

21. Ayres, 1983: 158. Ayres does discuss criticism of this particular project in relation to displacement of people and increase in rents and land values; however, even the critical consultant who drew attention to these problems is quoted as admitting significant data unreliability (Ayres, 1983:196).

22. The word 'tends' is important. As will become clear below, it is quite possible to support aid even if its past and present performance is assessed as negative, provided one is convinced that its performance can be improved or if one believes alternative approaches are likely to be even less beneficial.

23. G.D. Gwyer and J.C.H. Morris in Cracknell, 1984:54.

24. ODA, *Colombia Sheep Industry: 1983*, ODA, London EV 276, 1983.

25. Tendler, 1982b:137.
26. P. Devitt, *The Role of Sociological Factors in Four ODM Projects*, ODA, London, EV 101, November 1978.
27. Wheatley et al. (1985) provide perhaps the best description of the scoring technique, its scope and its inherent difficulties.
28. G. Dalton, *British Aid Tractors in India*, ODA, London, EV 36, 1976.
29. Some agencies, notably the World Bank, do project completion studies and then, on a selected basis, carry out impact studies some time later. However, this is the exception rather than the rule: most bilateral agencies have neither the staff nor the finance to adopt such a wide-ranging approach to aid evaluations.
30. There are exceptions. Both Sweden and Canada have been increasingly receptive to examining both these questions in recent years and acting upon the results.
31. See Cracknell, 1984a:23 for the UK view.
32. 'Scaling-up' refers to expanding a project from a pilot stage covering a small area to a wider area; 'replication' refers to *duplicating* or *repeating* a particular project in another area.
33. This conclusion is qualified by the term 'by and large' because there could be circumstances when, say, a 10 per cent success rate is preferable to the zero 'success rate' associated with aid withdrawal.
34. These questions are raised in part in DAC, 1985:253.
35. See Office of Technology Assessment, US Congress, 1984:59-61.
36. Aid figures taken from OECD (1986), Section B. See also *African Economic Digest*, 5 April 1986, *The Guardian*, 4 April 1986 and *Financial Times*, 4 September 1986 for references to US aid suspensions. US commodity aid to Zimbabwe, the most significant item, has been set at only $10 million in 1986 compared with $66 million in 1983. See Economist Intelligence Unit, *Quarterly Economic Review of Zimbabwe and Malawi*, No. 1, 1986, p. 18.
37. Overseas Development Council, *Policy Focus, The Budget and US Foreign Aid: More Tough Choices?* ODC, Washington, 1986.
38. ODA, *British Aid Statistics 1980-1984*, ODA, London 1985, Table 18.
39. It might be argued that free foreign exchange would result in these distortions being completely eliminated. However, this would only arise if the recipient had perfect knowledge of its development requirements and of all possible purchases it could make to fill resource gaps. In practice, this is unlikely to be the case, hence my use of the term 'reduce' rather than 'eliminate'.
40. See DAC, 1985:243-7 and reports of meetings of donors as reported, for example, in *Financial Times*, 4 and 7 April 1986.
41. DAC (1985) Table XI, 'Tying Status of ODA by Individual DAC Members 1982-83', p. 244.
42. The arrangement, its inconsistencies and its adverse effects on recipient countries is discussed in Toye and Clark, 1986.
43. *Financial Times*, 4 April 1986.
44. *Financial Times*, 7 April 1986. This was recently acknowledged by a former Permanent Secretary of the UK's ODA. He wrote thus: '. . . there is the Aid and Trade Provision or the ATP, the British mechanism for providing aid in the form of mixed credits, where aid is linked with ordinary export finance. The borderline between aid to developing countries and aid to British industry is sometimes hard to find. The philosophy underlying the arrangement is that the two can be reconciled, and so they can; but our experience of this programme is that business pressures grow and the emphasis tends to shift towards the interests of exporters' (Ryrie, 1986:8).
45. This pressure arises because aid budgets have commonly been determined by donors on an annual basis, although there has been some movement in recent years among some donors, including the Scandinavians, to extend this to a three-yearly period. Pressures become particularly acute if aid funds allocated by donors increase significantly from one year to another because projects and programmes then have to be established within a limited time-frame.
46. However, one does need to be careful in playing this sort of 'numbers game' for in a recent article Hewitt and Kydd (1986) suggests that in Malawi the problems of donor and project proliferation are not so acute.
47. *Official Journal of the European Communities, Court of Auditors, Annual Report For Year 1983*, Vol. 26, C357, 31 December 1983, p. 123.
48. Economists Advisory Group, *Evaluation of Selected Appropriate Technology Projects*, ODA, London EV 325, February 1984.
49. B.E. Cracknell, *Evaluation of ODA's Co-financing Aid with IBRD for Cargo-handling Equipment in Port Sudan*, ODA, London, EV 344, October 1984.
50. This point was raised in April 1986 by the President of the African Development Bank who stated that the oil price fall would be 'accompanied by a sharp decline in concessional aid from oil exporting countries', *Financial Times*, 8 April 1986. OPEC statistics from DAC (1985) pp. 91-3 and 316-17.

51. *Official Journal of the European Communities, Information and Notices*, Vol. 28, C326, 16 December 1985, p.127.
52. Between 1962 and 1975, US economic assistance totalled $450 million, of which over 30 per cent and on occasions over 45 per cent went to rural development. From 1950 onwards US aid went to rice-growing projects (See World Bank, 1959:66).
53. IDA commitments to Thailand totalled $125 million from 1961 to 1982 of which $37.5 million went to agriculture. For accounts of IDA aid to Thai agriculture and German aid to increasing rice yields in rural development projects see Fremery (1983) and Hoare (1984).
54. Figures from IMF, *International Financial Statistics*, January 1986, p. 456–9.
55. See *Financial Times*, 13 February 1986.
56. NGOs and their supporters also base their particular case for private aid intervention on an assessment of private aid in practice; hence the method of arriving at conclusions about private aid or private versus official aid is broadly similar.

16 Aid at the Micro-Level

Aid, the poor and the poorest

In this first section, we consider what is for many people the bedrock question about foreign aid: is it, or is it capable of, reaching and assisting the poor in aid-recipient countries? This is a central issue not only for many leftist critics who argue that official aid usually cannot do so, but also for those whose moral basis for supporting official aid programmes is founded upon needs-based criteria. It is also a central question for many donor agencies, highlighted, for example, in the US by the 'New Directions' mandate (see Morss and Morss, 1982: 28-46) or in the UK by the 1975 White Paper *The Changing Emphasis on British Aid Policies: More Help for the Poorest*. For major multilateral agencies the question is also crucial. For instance, Alan Berg, a senior World Bank adviser, has pointed to a major conclusion of World Bank studies, that 'the nutrition problem cannot be expected to be solved in an acceptable period through the normal course of development, even with a substantial expansion of food production. Special measures for the malnourished are needed' (1985:32). More strident still is the FAO (1984:68):[1]

> A conclusion of decisive significance for policy is that for many developing countries, reduction in rural poverty to acceptable levels through the route of growth alone will take either an unacceptably long period or will require a level of income unattainable in the foreseeable future.

The implication is clear: if aid is to assist in the alleviation of poverty it needs to tackle the problem head-on; it is no longer adequate to argue that the poor will be helped by concentrating exclusively on growth-oriented policies. The 1985 DAC Chairman's report highlights for the Western donor community as a whole the importance of the issue (1985:259-60):

> Large parts of concerned public opinion want foreign assistance to be used primarily for helping the poorest people in developing countries. And foreign aid is criticized often and perhaps increasingly for having failed to reduce the incidence of poverty. . . . Helping poor people in poor countries remains the most widely shared, essential and noble rationale of foreign assistance. Aid effectiveness must in the end be assessed against this standard.

Can the poor be reached?

While this broad poverty-directed objective is clear, at the micro-level fundamental objections are raised about aid's ability to help solve the poverty problem. These revolve around the circumstances of poverty, the nature of the aid provided, and the political and broadly structural environment in which the poor live vis-à-vis the wider society.

One objection is simply that the poorest cannot be reached directly or only at such a high cost that the efficiency of providing them with aid is put into question. Alternatively, it is argued that the poorest are incapable of being incorporated into the wider development effort of recipient countries; the best that can be achieved therefore is to provide them with charitable hand-outs and to cease pretending that they can be assisted by projects that could be considered developmental. Another objection is that, even if the poorest can be reached, any aid projects for them will fail because the benefits accruing will be hijacked by local or regional elites for themselves, thereby ensuring that elite dominance is maintained or even increased, with the position of the poorest remaining the same or worsening. A final set of objections concerns participation of the poorest in aid projects and programmes. Such participation is assumed to be the key factor in development at the local level. But at the same time it is argued either that foreign aid, because it is externally initiated and controlled, precludes the participation of the poorest at all stages and so *a priori* is deficient, or, alternatively, that genuine participation will not be possible because the poor, for various reasons – lethargy, fear, indifference – simply will not wish to involve themselves in these alien projects. Either way, the aim of helping them by providing aid will be doomed to failure.

There can be no doubt not only that these issues are important ones but also that they need to be answered. However, the available evidence indicates that they have tended either to be avoided or else not yet answered by the donor community in such a way as to convince the doubters, never mind the more strident critics, that all is well with aid projects to the poorest. Indeed, it appears that the aid debate has reached a stage analogous to that reached in the late 1960s and early 1970s at the macro-level in relation to the trickle-down theory. Up to the late 1960s, donors were apparently content to believe that the promotion of overall growth was a sufficient condition for ensuring that the poor were assisted. By the mid-1970s, however, they were clearly unconvinced and thus proceeded to talk explicitly of aid to the poorest and to re-orient aid projects with these objectives to the fore. Now, in the latter part of the 1980s, donors are recognising the complexities involved at the practical level in attempting to provide gains to the poorest through aid intervention, although to date – and even this is by no means universal among the donor community – there is little more than a recognition that serious problems can and frequently do exist. The stage appears to have been reached where the critics have made some telling points but the donors have yet to assess seriously and systematically the validity of the objections raised and to adapt policies when the criticisms have been found to be valid.

We shall argue in the next few pages that for the 'aid to the poorest' strategy to be made more effective the points raised above need to be examined and analysed far more carefully than they have been. We shall conclude, however, that, even though our knowledge in this area remains extremely limited, what we do know suggests that there is a role that donors can continue to play in effectively providing aid to the poorest, even if project success in the future is likely to be far more limited than donor rhetoric would lead the public to believe and even if to date it has, overall, been extremely limited.

That assisting the poor is bound to be a difficult undertaking is evident from a consideration of the characteristics of poverty. The poor in Third World countries, as Chambers points out, are likely to be often sick or malnourished, with few assets and large families, and to be inarticulate, uneducated, unorganised, isolated and non-mobile. They are less likely to use government services than the non-poor and to be relatively powerless or dependent upon local patrons for a range of their basic requirements. Further, they are likely to be relatively invisible, higher proportions of them being women, children and older people (1978: 209 and 1983:109-10). Because the poor live near to the limits of basic survival, they will tend also to be suspicious of change for the reason that pursuing bad risks can so quickly and easily bring disaster, and because long periods of alienation and isolation will have made them distrustful of outside intervention.

But the wide diversity of these different characteristics also suggests that the poor in Third World countries do not constitute an isolated and unreachable underclass, good only for welfare hand-outs. Lloyd (1979) argues convincingly that the urban poor, especially, contain within their group features of upward mobility that frequently remain unseen in static or short-term analysis of them and their environment. More generally, Lipton compares the poverty underclass of the industrialised world – those with mental or physical disability and those suffering because of demographic circumstances – with that existing in the Third World. His review of the available evidence indicates, *contra* the critics, that the *great majority* of the ultra-poor in developing countries are not an unreachable underclass (1983:3):

> Their extreme poverty is associated with lack of promising human and physical assets; with weak labour-market positions; with large families, high dependency ratios and with very high infant mortality and with serious risks of nutritional damage. Only tiny proportions of the Third World's ultra-poor could survive as drug addicts, alcoholics, mental defectives or even single-member families. These ultra-poor are mostly a resource, not a burdensome underclass.

Analysing the phenomenon of poverty and isolating its characteristics, however, does not necessarily reveal the causes of Third World poverty. One view is that poverty is multi-causal. Chambers, for example, argues that it is difficult to judge to what extent one particular cause may or may not be primary or dominant or may indeed vary in importance over time or by season, country, region, community, village, household or individual (1983:43). Sometimes single characteristics of poverty are addressed by providing aid in the form of particular goods and services that the poor lack. This could be termed mono-type aid intervention – the provision of food or health services to address problems of sickness and malnourishment; schools to increase educational levels; credit and other agricultural inputs to increase the assets of poor farmers; and site and service plots to address housing needs. Sometimes a broad approach (multi-targeted aid intervention) is adopted by providing a package of inputs required by the poor, most typically in the rural areas by promoting integrated rural development projects discussed later in this chapter.

Some evidence
Such mono-type aid interventions have met with mixed results. Some have been successful in reaching the poor and in helping to alleviate specific problems; others have failed either to reach the poor or to solve the problems.[2] Examples of success are given by Ayres (1983:177) who records the ability to provide site and service plots to the lowest decile of urban income distribution levels in four countries – Brazil, Botswana, Thailand and Tanzania; by the International Fund for Agricultural Development (1985) which records success in reaching the poorest farmers with credit facilities in a number of countries; by Muscat (1986:75) who cites benefits to the poorest from specific health measures to eradicate smallpox, to address vitamin deficiency and prevent infant deaths from diarrhoea in Bangladesh and elsewhere; by evidence from India which reveals that high-yielding crop varieties have assisted a variety of poor groups, increasing crop yields (Pinstrup-Anderson and Hazell in Gittinger et al., 1985: 89-92); by Clay and Singer (1984:23) who cite the case of food aid to Kerala in India which has had

a positive impact on lower-income households and vulnerable groups; and by Tendler (1982b:101) who records the case of projects in Colombia where information provided to Indian communities enabled them to work with government agencies and obtain basic services that, theoretically, were 'readily' available. Clearly, other instances of similar successes could be cited.

Of perhaps more interest are examples of mono-type interventions which have had positive ripple effects on other characteristics of poverty. Rahman and McDonnell point to food aid in Bangladesh which not only raised the nutritional status of the poor but also, through parallel pricing policies, led to an increase in domestic food production (1984:60). Lipton argues, and provides evidence to show in India and elsewhere, that efforts to reduce sickness among the ultra-poor have had an indirect and positive effect on their income levels because they can spend more time working. He states (1983:22):

> a carefully designed attack on the causes of illness and disability (especially if combined with appropriate timing and placing of education to cut its opportunity costs) will increase the productivity not only of whole communities, not only of the poor relative to the non-poor but in particular, via the impact on participation ratios, of the poorest relative to the poor.

For her part, Tendler cites cases of the poor not only raising production levels through project aid but of this resulting in both a reduction in landlord dependence and an increase in wages to those still dependent upon wage labour. She observes that 'A marked substitution of own-plot work for hired-out labour has taken place in some of the [World] Bank's projects in northeast Brazil, resulting in a decrease in supply of labour to landowners and an increase in the daily wage rate in the project area' (1982b:22). And in a wide-ranging review, Burki and ul Haq provide other examples including, for instance, the case of Sri Lanka where it has been shown that better education improved health status in spite of the inadequate availability of clean water (1981:169).

Interesting though these examples are – to support the multi-causal explanation of poverty and to provide some evidence of official aid benefitting the poor and poorest groups in aid-recipient countries – their importance is challenged by those who contend that some specific causes of poverty are dominant and decisive for poverty alleviation. In particular, some critics argue that political power and institutional factors provide the major underlying constraint to eliminating poverty and that if these factors are not addressed in aid projects and programmes poverty will continue. They would probably argue that the examples cited above and others indicating the ability of aid to reach the poorest and to relieve certain characteristics of poverty are ways of easing suffering rather than solutions to the basic problem, and in any case are isolated rather than typical examples. Certainly not a few scholars who favour aid also maintain that their survey of the evidence suggests that aid has been particularly bad at reaching and helping the poor (see Chaudhuri, 1986:14–21 and, in general, Cassen, 1986).

While, as discussed in the previous chapter, there is no reliable evidence available to judge the extent to which particular examples are typical or not, there is increasing recognition that broad political influences are indeed a critical factor in achieving aid effectiveness at the micro-level, and also that the role of elites and powerful group forces are of increased importance in projects designed to reach and assist the poor. For instance, it is the donors and not their critics who have recently stated (DAC, 1985:34):

> We have seen repeatedly the crucial role of political leadership in the best examples of

both national development and development assistance. In a developing country, serious political commitment to development is essential to inculcate in traditional communities the belief that material progress is attainable, to mobilise popular energies, to evoke good performance from public agencies, to obtain and sustain adequate public funding.

Room to manoeuvre

The crucial question remains the degree to which political constraints at both the local and the national level are dominant in the attempts made to reach and assist the poorest. On the one hand, many critics argue that these constraints are central and, because they tend not to be addressed by official agencies, 'aid to the poorest' policies are often a sham. On the other hand, donor agencies, while gradually recognising their importance, still tend, as the critics correctly point out, to avoid addressing them overtly, even though their practical decisions can and sometimes do reveal attempts to overcome them. What the evidence, partial though it is, suggests is that the critics are wrong to insist that political and power factors constitute a binding constraint on official aid agencies attempting to reach the poor and help them even in apparently hostile environments. There is more room for manoeuvre than is often believed.

This is illustrated, in particular, by the work of Chambers and Tendler. They explicitly acknowledge the importance of political and power relations at the local level but convincingly point to different types of intervention which can either circumvent or lessen the influence of elites whom the critics would argue 'act as a net to trap the goods that are aimed at the poor, intercepting what comes down' (Chambers 1978:131–2). Projects targeted to the poor, they argue, can be split into three categories: those where gains for the poor occur only at the expense of local elites, most especially when scarce distributable goods are involved; those where elites can only benefit if the poor also gain; and those where the poor will gain but the elites are not interested in these gains. If aid to the poorest is targeted to the latter two categories there is little force in the argument that local elites will hijack it and that the intervention will be ineffective. The elites will certainly not oppose projects designed to eradicate human or animal disease in areas where the poor and local elites and their animals rub shoulders with each other, nor will they be much interested in disrupting projects designed to raise production of low-status food crops for own consumption which they do not themselves grow.

Chambers provides a useful table (see Table 16.1) to illustrate the respective gains and/or losses to the elites and the rural poor from particular types of intervention (1983:162).

As for the situations of direct conflict, all is not lost here either, and it is possible to devise projects that reduce the level or degree of conflict, thereby providing real gains for the poor. For example, evidence suggests that one constraint can arise from elites taking control of agencies delivering goods and services to the poor and utilising them for themselves. In certain cases the problem can be overcome by creating separate agencies for the elites and for the poorer groups. For example, Tendler cites the Water Board in Bangladesh and the drought prevention agency in north-east Brazil as instances of 'building agencies' being created which supported projects targeted to the poor and whose strength split local elite groups and increased the implementation of projects for the poor (1982b:41).

Alternatively, especially in acute situations, it may be necessary to provide explicit benefits to the elites in order to divert attention away from the gains for the poor, admitting this to be an explicit cost of reaching the poor. Local conflict can

Table 16.1:   Benefits distributed between the rural elite and the poorer rural people

Rural Elite	Poorer Rural People	Examples
Gain	Lose	Allowing or enabling elite to appropriate common property resources (land, groundwater, fish, forests, pasture, reeds, silt, stone, etc.); denying these to others.
Gain	Gain	New services accessible to all (health, water, education, shops with basic goods, etc.).
		Most public works which create new infrastructure.
		New irrigation or other technology which increases employment and raises wage rates.
		Canal irrigation reform from which all farmers gain.
No change	Gain	Extending the coverage of spread-and-take up programmes to be accessible to more of the poor.
		Credit enterprises for the poor.
		Subsidised rations for the poor (as in Sri Lanka)
		Appropriate technology (seed varieties, tools, cropping systems, etc.) for resource-poor farmers.
Lose	Gain	Land reform with inadequate compensation.
		Implementation of minimum wage legislation.

also be reduced in some instances if the alleviation of poverty in a particular region strengthens the total power of that region vis-à-vis others: local elites convinced of this would be more ready to assist the poor in their own locality. In other instances, providing the rural poor with certain central government services and increasing access to these while at the same time increasing the power of grass-root groups could also reduce the dependence of the poor on local elites for these services, so saving costs to the elites and providing greater self-reliance for the poor. Geography is also an important element. Gains for the poor are more likely to occur if they are relatively isolated from elites. While certain rural areas will thereby be favoured over others, there would also appear to be plenty of scope for providing aid to the urban poor who tend to be concentrated in specific areas and frequently far removed from the more affluent parts of cities (Tendler 1982b:iii).

It is only after careful analysis of the losses and gains to be expected from particular forms of aid intervention that conclusions can be drawn as to whether aid will or will not assist the poor. As Chambers stresses, in the rural context: 'The tendency is to regard land, water, forest, fish and grazing as resources to be appropriated so that one household's gain is another household's loss.' Yet he goes on to discuss instances where this assumption does not prevail; for example, by scheduling canal water irrigation facilities with care, the poor can certainly gain (1983:188). Tendler cites examples of agricultural assistance reaching the poor in a hostile environment through concentration on different crop varieties, and the provision of credit to non-landowner farmers and technical assistance in a form that elite farmers are not interested in using. She also highlights assistance which promotes the non-agricultural income-raising activities of the poorest households, for example in small trading, crafts, fishing, women-controlled activities, peddling, etc (1982b:53). Garcia-Zamor draws attention to the successful establishment of food and nutrition centres in areas where one would have expected the local elites to have hijacked the projects. He attributes the success to the wide array of conflicting elites, each with different group interests, the prestige perceived by elites in having such centres established, and the creation of jobs at the local level (1985:67-89).

Thus it would seem that, even in a political environment that is hostile to a type of aid intervention aiming to assist those in extreme poverty, there is scope for providing aid in particular forms that do lead to gains for the poorest. It is quite possible that failure to examine the implications of these different types of constraint and potentially beneficial outcomes is, at least in part, a cause of aid's poor record in helping to alleviate poverty. But even if it is acknowledged that there is some flexibility at the local level, the question still needs to be asked: would official agencies be allowed to intervene at this level in countries with non-democratic and elitist political regimes? Here again, there would appear to be grounds for arguing that scope for action is not as circumscribed as the critics would maintain. The Philippines, under the rule of Ferdinand Marcos, provides an example of far greater room for manoeuvre than, for instance, Lappé and her colleagues would admit. They cite the Philippines as a country, among others, with a reputation for neglect of the needs of the poor and, because of this, an instance where aid will not benefit the poor (1980:19-24). Yet, in 1985, an ILO report cited the Sarilakas project in the Philippines which had, since the early 1980s, been positively assisting the rural poor through the increased beneficiary participation of thousands of households and resulting in raised income levels (1985:37-40). More generally, in a review of Latin American experience, Huizer had recently argued that there is considerable evidence of help from sympathetic outsiders being a positive factor for the success of peasant participatory movements (in Lisk, 1985:198). Also in a recent publication, the International Fund for Agricultural Development provides evidence of credit aid rescuing the poor in yet another country condemned as a hopeless case by Lappé et al. – Pakistan (see IFAD, 1985). And in his book on the World Bank, Ayres cites a number of examples of poverty-oriented projects established in regimes far from committed to such a poverty focus: an agricultural project to benefit 3,600 poor rural families in Bolivia, a site and service and rural non-formal education project in El Salvador, and a rural development project for 7,000 low-income families in Paraguay (1983:211-12).

In a paper on national nutrition studies and country experience, Pines records examples of successful intervention in the most adverse political circumstances, arguing that for effectiveness identifying key decision-makers and responding to their interests requires as much attention as seeking the most efficient technical approach for addressing nutrition problems. He adds: 'By thinking more systematically about who makes decisions, whom they listen to and what information is likely to influence both, the nutrition community becomes more effective in using its modest power' (1982:278). In this regard, too, Tendler adds that 'governments that are not willing or able to commit themselves to redistributive policies or to empowerment of the poor . . . may accept projects with these implications if they are presented as technical solutions to technical problems' (1982b:38).

What these examples suggest is that it is too quick and slick to view and condemn project aid intervention solely through the prism, and assessment, of the adverse nature of the national or local political regime. There is clearly far more to aid performance than having a national government or local leadership committed or not to helping the poor, even though there is no doubt that a favourable political climate is conducive to the goals of aid being more easily achieved. Importantly, too, the reverse situation needs highlighting: acceptance of poverty-focused strategies by particular recipient governments by no means ensures the success of these projects. For example, in India there is a national commitment to reduce poverty but national policies are frequently obstructed by local power elites capturing the potential gains for themselves. Even in Tanzania, with a strong government commitment to poverty reduction and greater egalitarianism, recent evidence indicates that the beneficiaries of water development projects over a 13-year period have been the relatively better-off farmers and not the poorest (Radetski, 1986:29). These sorts of examples have led Hyden to comment (1983:182):

> Even when governments are committed in ideology to these values [helping the poor] their chances of putting them into practice are limited as long as the state remains an alien body to the bulk of rural producers. This poses a serious challenge to the view, prevailing in broad circles in the international aid community, that the most progressive aid policy is one that provides aid unconditionally to a government committed to redistributive policies. Conditions in Africa do not permit such a simple equation.

The essential point to strike home is that recognition that political factors are important – although this is a relatively new point to be acknowledged by donors – should not pull one into believing that they are always or necessarily primary or dominant. In a recent article, Cohen *et al.* have argued that the bureaucratic dimension can be just as important as the political, and it was in analysing the room to manoeuvre in the context of the complexities of recipient-country bureaucracies that Pines (above) was suggesting ways of improving policy effectiveness. It is because 'bureaucracies do not operate as administrative mechanisms solely [engaged] in executing the policy decisions of national leaders' and because they do play 'a significant and active role in framing the policy agenda, supporting particular options and undercutting others, assembling support for and affecting the course of policy program and project implementation' (Cohen *et al.* 1985:1218) that political constraints, at the national and local level, do not constitute the exclusive barrier to implementing poverty-targeted aid projects which the critics have so vigorously claimed. Political, administrative, bureaucratic and general power relationships are all important factors weaving a complex web of forces from the national down to the local level, sometimes clearly supporting and occasionally clearly impeding the objectives of poverty-focused aid intervention. (For the latter effect, see the case-study of Haiti discussed in the next chapter.) But more often than not the overall effect of these forces will tend to be uncertain and unpredictable. What this conclusion implies is that channelling aid to the poorest will never be an easy undertaking. Indeed, as two characteristics of the poor are their suspicion of outsiders or outside intervention and their unwillingness to take risks, even if intervention has proved successful in some regions or countries, there is still no guarantee that aid will be acceptable and adopted in others.

An examination of all the different constraints likely to affect project implementation in the rural areas leads Chambers to argue that the most effective poverty-oriented projects are likely to have the following characteristics: they are small and administratively-intensive; and they are likely to be difficult to monitor and inspect, slow to implement, and in general unsuitable for complex techniques of project appraisal (1978:210). A similar list of characteristics is provided by Faaland, although he adds that such projects will also tend to take some time to complete and to be not easily replicable elsewhere (1983:9). In addition, experienced practitioners and donor agencies now commonly cite the need for some form of participation by intended beneficiaries as an essential ingredient for success (see ILO, 1983:3 and Lisk, 1985:vii). Not that participation, any more than any other ingredient, should be viewed as holding the single key to success. Tendler, for example, describes in detail an aid-funded credit institution in Nicaragua that flourished and expanded in part because of its top-down and non-participatory mode of operation (1986:8–9). A major conclusion of this discussion, therefore, is that if aid's critics and even aid's friends are correct that projects specifically targeted to the poorest have been largely unsuccessful, then the cause of failure is likely to have been the nature of the intervention attempted and not always or exclusively the impossibility of ever achieving success.

We do not need to be over-precise, however, to point out that, given the conditions and constraints affecting all attempts at intervention to help the poor directly, it is simply not practical to expect that all the aid that official donors provide can be channelled directly to the poorest in this specifically targeted fashion. Hence to judge aid effectiveness on this criterion alone would be misplaced. Yet this conclusion by no means has to lead to the view that all aid not specifically targeted to the poor must be dismissed as 'bad' by either those donors whose basis for giving it is that it should help the poor or by aid's more general critics. It is quite possible, and there are numerous examples, for different forms of aid to assist the poor less directly. Indeed, the authors of *Real Aid*, whose basic critical perspective is to judge aid by its effects on the poor, include the following types of aid under this heading: fertilizer and cement plants, hand-tool factories, saw mills, certain engineering projects, rural roads and railways, power stations for rural electrification, and the development of human resources for health care, education and other services relevant to the poor (IGBA, 1982:18).

But there is no good reason to stop there. The urban poor would be assisted by the provision of clean water facilities and by certain urban electrification schemes, while both the urban and the rural poor would stand to gain from programme aid that eases balance-of-payments shortages and leads, for example, to an increase in the supply of basic vaccination kits, wheat flour for bread, cooking oil, clothing or blankets. As Green comments for Africa: '. . . import strangulation is a fact weighing heavily on poor people in at least half the region' (1986:26). One could go even further. A highly capital-intensive British aid project in Sudan successfully improved the efficiency of port-handling equipment in Port Sudan. There would seem to be little doubt that this particular project assisted the importation of emergency food aid in the 1985–6 famine, thereby saving the lives of a number of poor people in the country and in Eritrea in neighbouring Ethiopia, even though these benefits were neither considered at the stage of project identification nor in the completed evaluation report (Cracknell, 1984b). Similarly, Ayres provides examples of nation-wide projects that have indirectly and significantly assisted the poor, such as credit projects in Mexico and agricultural research and extension projects in Brazil (1982:95). Nor need aid be directed exclusively to the poor for the poor to benefit. It is possible for direct effects to be less beneficial to the poor but for second-round effects to provide a more direct and tangible gain. Ayres, for instance, also quotes World Bank staff as arguing that in Brazil the presence of rural development projects did not initially provide gains for small farmers but helped to make small-farmer-oriented agricultural development strategies politically feasible (1983:144).

Clearly the point can be pressed too far. There is a crucial difference between, on the one hand, initiating aid projects in the hope of their providing benefits to the poor, or even arguing that virtually any project can be legitimised because in some vague way some benefits can be traced to the poor and, on the other hand, specifically orienting all projects in a framework that places the needs of the poor as the prime consideration for project acceptance or rejection and focuses on this

particular objective through to the completion stage. The evidence of aid in practice, of course, provides a mixed bag of success and failure in this regard. To the
extent that commercial and political pressures dominate or even influence donor
decision-making – and, as discussed in the previous chapter, they undoubtedly do
– then the aid-to-the-poorest orientation of more general intervention will be
diluted or lost. There are also numerous examples of donors bowing to recipient
pressure to build inappropriate white elephants or cathedrals in the desert, as
Edgar Pisani, when overseeing the EEC's development directorate, made a point
of continually exposing. But there are also examples that reveal a reverse trend.
For instance, Britain refused to provide aid to the Kenyatta hospital in Nairobi,
favouring instead more rural-oriented health intervention strategies (Holtham and
Hazlewood, 1976:249). In practice, general aid projects consist of a medley of
motives, specific objectives and effects. Where the critics are on firm ground is in
highlighting those projects which are neither motivated nor designed with the
intention of assisting the poor at all.

We can, however, come to two firm conclusions *contra* the critics. First, that
aid does not necessarily have to reach the poor directly and at once for them to gain
from aid intervention. However, it should be added that, unless the impact on the
poor of all aid projects and programmes is in continual focus, their needs are
almost certain to lose out to those of more powerful interest groups. Moreover, it
would appear that, unless donors are trying continuously to reach the poor directly
through specific, although admittedly limited, project interventions, their adherence to poverty-focused aid at the more general level is likely to become increasingly rhetorical. Secondly, that if, as was suggested above, the poorest can be
reached directly in the difficult terrain of poverty-focused projects, then *a fortiori*
they can also be assisted in the more general aid interventions where the constraints
will be less acute. While in both cases it cannot be emphasised too strongly that the
gains to the poor will never accrue automatically, it can be demonstrated that at
the project level aid can reach them and help them both directly and indirectly, and
that it does so even in circumstances that are apparently hostile. Nevertheless, even
though the evidence is still decidedly incomplete, it does suggest that successfully
executing projects directly targeted to the poorest is far less easy than the donors
have been ready to acknowledge openly.

The poor and the poorest

A final issue concerns a distinction that critics often make between the general
level of poverty and the very poorest groups in Third World aid-recipient countries. The criticism is frequently made that, while some aid does indeed help some
poor groups, it commonly fails to assist the poorest groups in society; much leftist
criticism of World Bank projects, typified for example in the work of Hayter,
highlights this as a central focus of complaint about official aid. What response
can be given to this particular attack? In part, this question has been answered in
the previous discussion which explicitly examined the lot of the ultra-poor and
concluded that, although the difficulties should never be underestimated, not only
can they be reached but some aid projects have certainly assisted them. Indeed,
care was taken to distinguish above between the poor and local elites in part
because of the fact that the *elites*, although so named, could well be classified as
poor themselves, but less poor than other less visible groups, especially in rural
settings. The reason for highlighting this distinction was because of the evidence
suggesting that the lack of positive and significant trickle-down effects at the local
and regional level can be a major problem in aid-recipient countries.[2]

There are dangers, however, in pursuing this particular line of argument to extremes. If one were to be concerned solely with the bottom-most rung of society, then one could be manoeuvred into a position of directing attention exclusively to the misfits, the handicapped and those who, whatever opportunities they are given, will always be a burden on society. These people would certainly be categorised as the poorest in Third World countries.[3] While it is in no way the intention to argue here that any human being should be considered unworthy of assistance – and given the poverty of Third World countries, their ability to provide welfare facilities is clearly limited – if the dominant criterion for providing assistance were to be human inadequacy, then this group of the poor should be of first concern to donors. It is because this is not the group commonly referred to as the poorest-to-be-helped by those advocating *development* aid to the poorest that one needs to be wary of arguments which suggest that a consensus exists concerning precisely who falls into the category of 'the poorest' in aid discussions. The issue of who the poorest are and their relation to the 'less-poor' poor is a complex and still unresolved question. Some examples illustrate these complexities.

If aid is to be given on the basis of need, who is to play God and decide on greater and lesser needs when all groups are living at a totally inadequate level of existence and when measures of absolute poverty frequently contain elements of subjective judgement?[4] Should food supplements be denied to malnourished under-fives in an urban slum when their parents live above the breadline but do not provide their children with a balanced diet, if this means that there is not sufficient food for starving peasants in remote rural areas? And if the poorest in these rural areas cannot be reached, should one deny food supplements to these 'rich' urban children? As Amartya Sen might put it, if the poorest have entitlements then so too do the poor. Or again, if one is concerned with the poorest groups, should one sub-divide the income distribution into quintiles or deciles or a further disaggregated grouping to classify the neediest category of people? The divisions chosen will clearly play a crucial part in deciding who are the poorest deemed appropriate to help. And the arbitrariness of this decision needs to be considered along with the certainty that income levels are in any case not known with much accuracy for any poor groups in Third World countries.

If the objective of providing aid is to reduce levels of poverty, then there is a case for arguing that it is legitimate to assist all those living in extreme poverty. Elites in rural India may have more wealth than their poorer neighbours but, compared with many city dwellers and most industrialised world citizens, their living standard is appallingly low. Take the bottom rung away or provide aid to raise the living standards of this group, and the elites become the poorest and are now 'worthy' of support. Moreover, to the extent that aid in particular circumstances cannot reach extremely poor groups or only at a prohibitive cost, is it better to provide no aid at all or to provide it to the destitute – but not the poorest – who *can* be reached and for whom assistance can help to alleviate poverty? These issues are raised as questions precisely becasue no satisfactory answers have yet been given and because the apparent consensus, among aid donors concerned to provide 'aid-to-the-poorest' and those advocating such an approach, tends to conceal them.

There is, finally, the question of the short term and the long term. While there is now certainly evidence to suggest that the poor should be assisted through direct interventionist policies because the benefits of growth will not always or necessarily trickle down to them fast enough or, perhaps in some circumstances, at all, it cannot always and in addition be assumed that equalising growth, even with interventionist policies, will be either possible or desirable. This is not the place to pursue the issue of possible or optimal growth paths, but the following comment by Hyden, an author with all the credentials of a person concerned with the poor and their betterment, indicates the complexity of the issue as well as raising an important question for those advocating aid to the poorest (1983:534):

> . . . it must be accepted that the institutionalisation of class contradictions is a *sine qua non* condition for development. Such a process will facilitate the incorporation of the peasantry into a national economy controlled by a class of persons concerned, at least in the long run, with the necessary changes in behavioural and institutional patterns that sustain a 'civil public realm'. In the process they will no doubt make private gains and many peasants will suffer losses with respect to their present position in the economy of affection. Yet such a turn of events is a virtual necessity not only for the survival of African countries as macroeconomic entities but also for any effective pursuit of egalitarian societies.

Different types of aid

In this second section we take a closer look at the aid experience at the local level by examining the performance of different forms of aid intervention. Two broad areas are considered: food aid and aid to promote rural development. The purpose of the discussion is not to come to definitive conclusions about the merits of particular forms of aid over others but rather to select particularly controversial forms of aid intervention and to discuss the merits of providing these specific forms of aid in the context of criticisms that have been made against them.

Food aid

Food aid constitutes a significant and (in recent years) increasing sub-category of official aid. In the 1970s it represented some 10 per cent of all official aid, rising to 12 per cent by the mid-1980s largely as a result of the emergency in sub-Saharan Africa, and accounting for over $5 billion worth of official aid funds. Food aid in the form of cereals amounted to 8.8 million metric tons in 1982/3 and exceeded 9.5 million metric tons in 1985 (World Bank, 1985:184–5). Food aid is currently distributed to over 100 recipient nations by over 25 bilateral donors and by major multilateral organisations. The three largest distributors are the United States, the EEC and the World Food Programme (WFP) (set up in 1963 by the FAO). Between them, they distribute over 75 per cent of all food aid, with some 80 per cent of it originating in the United States (43 per cent) and EEC member countries (35 per cent).[5]

A central (though by no means the only) question for the wider aid debate is whether food aid assists or hinders developing recipient countries and in particular whether the poor and most vulnerable groups, especially those with a less than adequate food intake in the absence of aid, are assisted by food aid transfers. Before examining this question in more detail, a paradox that is frequently forgotten but none the less of more than passing interest needs to be highlighted: the nature of the problem out of which the requirement for food aid arises provides the very constraints that inhibit the success of food aid initiatives, and the greater the food requirement, the greater are the obstructions likely to be. What is more, the very existence of food aid and its acceptance by recipient countries are both a sign and an acknowledgement of failure; the failure to grow enough food, the failure to possess enough foreign exchange to purchase food on commercial terms, or the failure to obtain enough through commercial sources in abnormal times. Thus if the success of food aid intervention is ultimately to be judged by the absence of food aid, its continued existence is frequently a sign that past food aid has failed.[6] In the particular instance of emergency food aid, the link between the requirements for assistance and the difficulties in meeting these requirements is seen most starkly. Food needs arise in emergencies because normal methods and/or levels of production, storage, transportation and distribution have been disrupted, and often destroyed; yet it is the ability to provide, store, transport or distribute food quickly and eventually to grow food again which provides both the major challenge in the attempt to reach those without food and the ultimate criterion for judging the exercise a success or failure. The greater the needs, the greater the likelihood of emergency food aid not succeeding in achieving its objectives.

If this paradox complicates an assessment of emergency food aid, the complexities are increased by the fact that food aid extends well beyond emergencies. By no means all food aid is donated gratis; large amounts are sold, albeit on varying terms of concessionality, so that judgements about its effectiveness in these cases would have to embrace alternative uses of the money so allocated. Emergency aid only constitutes some 20 per cent of all food aid, 30 per cent is provided as project aid, with programme aid accounting for fully half of all food aid – the former provided in the context of wider projects, the latter in the form of subsidised imports or, although less widespread, money tied to direct food purchases by recipients.

Complexities, however, have not dampened the vigour with which food aid is criticised. Of initial interest are those critics who have concluded that its failures are so transparent and pervasive that it should cease to be provided by donors – with perhaps an exception made for some types of food aid in certain type of emergencies. Lappé et al. condemn food aid because, they argue, it does not reach the poor who need it and because a common form of project food aid – the provision of food for work – does not help the hungry or build self-reliance. They argue that food aid for emergencies can only alleviate suffering in response to a short-term emergency, adding that the record of emergency aid leads to serious questions about its widespread use; indeed, at one point they state that chronic food aid should be terminated (1980:93–136). In similar vein, Jackson (1982) provides a radical critique of food aid, the thrust of which is to conclude that on balance food aid does more harm than good; his particular criticism is of project food aid which he states is cost-ineffective and provides, in the vast majority of cases, no benefit for the poor (see also Stevens, 1983:56–7).

The evidence
The major difficulty in accepting this highly negative viewpoint lies not so much in the veracity of the evidence put forward as in deducing that it is representative of all or most food aid and that, if it is, the negative outcome will continue to occur even if changes are made in the form and/or insertion of food aid into recipient countries. On neither count can the critics' conclusions be sustained: the evidence is inadequate both to reach such deductions and to convince one that the constraints that do exist are permanent, immutable and widely applicable. Certainly, as even the critics are careful to point out, there are examples of successful food aid intervention not only in emergencies but also when it is provided in the form of project and programme assistance. Beyond this, however, if there is one thing that the systematic literature reviews reveal, it is that the evaluation of food aid is woefully incomplete, and major questions relating to its impact have simply not been analysed sufficiently. Maxwell, for example, rehearses many of the methodological weaknesses of aid evaluation, discussed in Chapter 15 above, in the

context of food aid studies. His considered judgement is that 'food aid has been inadequately studied in many respects, notably in terms of its impact on recipient countries . . . The validity of this general observation is not contradicted by the existence of competent individual case studies' (1983:32).

Moving from the general to the specific, in their thorough and comprehensive scouring of the evidence, including an analysis of all the major reviews of food aid conducted in the past ten years, Clay and Singer have found examples of particular forms of food aid having a negative impact, some having a positive impact and others having no clearly determinable impact one way or the other. They state that 'for every positive effect identified as an illustrative case cited in the literature it is possible to provide a contrasting negative case and vice versa' (1984:4). Their overall view is that at present (their most recent review was written in late 1985) the evidence is too partial and incomplete for general statements about food aid's impact to be possible. They add, and importantly, that significant changes in distribution, composition and targeting of food aid have taken and are continuing to take place so that criticisms of past food aid performance are now no reliable guide to present practice.

These conclusions, of course, not only challenge the general critics of food aid; they also question the faith that donors place in the benefits to be derived from food aid intervention and the assertions frequently made by donors justifying their various food aid practices and policies. The present state of knowledge of both food aid intervention and of donor and recipient policies is simply inadequate to draw the general conclusion that food aid is beneficial to those receiving it. That said, it must also be added that there is even less evidence available to show that less developed countries in general need of external food sources or with hungry sub-groups would be better-off by refusing food aid either in emergencies or in longer periods of food deficit.

While it is certainly important, and relatively simple, to disarm food aid's most radical critics, to foreclose discussion at this level of generality is to sidestep the central policy debates. Food aid exists and, given the maintenance of food surpluses in the industrialised West and political and economic pressures to dispose of them, it is going to continue to be distributed, spurred on, of course, by other pressures – of need – from the recipient and deficit country end, including the 'permanent' feature of disasters. The key issues, then, are not whether food aid should or should not exist – for it will – but rather the manner in which it will and should be distributed. Clay and Singer draw the conclusion that 'donor and recipient governments have some margin for manoeuvre to make more effective use of food aid resources' (1984:3), as, implicitly at least, do the radical critics when they acknowledge that some food aid can be effective. What is important is to analyse precisely where that room for manoeuvre lies, how present food aid forms and processes could be changed to improve effectiveness and to pinpoint those constraints that are likely to prevent food aid from achieving its goals. To inform this debate studies· of food aid experience, including particularly those studies that isolate constraints impeding greater effectiveness and expose weaknesses in the food aid system that could be eliminated or reduced, are crucial.

Not surprisingly, political and administrative factors and the self-interested motivations of donors play an important role in determining food aid effectiveness, as the critics have always pointed out and the donors are now, in the mid-1980s, ready to acknowledge. It is no secret that one of the original objectives of US food aid policy was to dispose of surpluses and one of its four purposes today is 'the achievement of foreign policy objectives' (Ezechiel, 1986:3.1). Studies also show that EEC policies are influenced by the 'push' factor of wishing to dispose of surpluses (see Jackson, 1983 for references). Britain, too, is ready to acknowledge these pressures. For example, the head of the UK's EEC aid programme has stated (Freeman, 1985:47):

> the motives for providing food aid are mixed: there are those who see it primarily as a means of reducing foods which are in surplus in Europe . . . most of the foods which are stockpiled are unsuitable for the victims of famine or (in the case of butter oil) have much cheaper substitutes which can supply equivalent levels of nutrition.

More recently the former UK Minister for Overseas Development criticised EEC food aid, arguing that 'the institutional links between food aid and the Common Agricultural Policy must be severed. Europe should provide recipients with food they need, not food we want to dispose of. We should be prepared to buy it when appropriate in other developing countries'.[7]

Various problems flow from these pressures: the desire to dispose of surpluses can affect the quantity of food aid available, the type of food provided, the countries to which it is given, and the speed with which it is distributed. The evidence shows that US food aid fell substantially in the 1970s when Third World needs rose, the fall arising as a direct result of lower surpluses exacerbated by increased commercial sales to the Soviet Union (Ezechiel, 1986:3.13). It also reveals instances of inappropriate products being distributed, such as much dairy produce by the EEC, severely criticised by reports from within the EEC itself (Jackson, 1983:53). Recipient country examples of inappropriate products being provided because of donor pledges include food aid to Pakistan for Afghan refugees and to North Yemen (Clay and Singer, 1985:62). It is important to recognise that these practices continue to occur in different parts of the world even after past mistakes have been exposed. In addition, the evidence indicates the tardiness with which some donors, like the EEC, respond to emergencies (Stevens, 1985), frequently because of complex bureaucratic procedures. Delays of a year or more are not uncommon; in 1986, Mali was still awaiting food aid promised in 1984 and Chad food aid promised in early 1985.

Administrative and political problems apply equally to the recipients. It does not require a degree in political science to demonstrate that when corruption is present at the national or local level, or when governments are not committed to distributing food aid to the needy, or when administrative structures are not functioning, the likelihood of food aid failing to reach its intended destination or being diverted en route is going to increase. Recent examples of this come from Guatemala, Zaire and Ghana and more generally in the Sahel where border smuggling has been a common and widespread problem (Stevens, 1979:17–18 and 142; Hopkins, 1983:198 and Clay and Singer, 1983:82).

But these negative factors by no means provide the complete picture. One of the most significant changes in donor food aid practices over the past fifteen years has been the rise in multilateral agencies, like the WFP, which has lessened the adverse political influence of bilateral donors (Clay, 1983:3ff). Even within the US itself, the objectives of surplus disposal and meeting foreign-policy objectives are balanced by the requirement under PL480 that priority consideration be given 'in helping to meet urgent food needs abroad, to making available the maximum feasible volume of food commodities required by those countries most seriously affected by food shortages' (quoted in Ezechiel, 1986:3.18). And to those who argue that this is mere eyewash, the co-ordinated and effective response of USAID to the 1985 famine in Africa provides recent evidence of the dominance of this principle. On the question of surpluses, the example of Canada indicates the way in which this potential and seriously debilitating factor can recede from policy influence (Ezechiel, 1986:4.3). There is also plenty of evidence of food aid achieving its objectives in countries with a wide array of political and administrative problems. Indeed, one of the most significant developments in the past five or six years has been the way in which many donors and recipients alike have co-operated to improve food aid delivery systems. Achievements have been noted, *inter alia*, in Tanzania, Jamaica, Tunisia, Cameroon, Senegal and Sri Lanka.

Moving to more specific issues, criticisms are voiced against food aid because of the adverse effects said to arise *even if* the broader influences are favourable. A familiar one is that food aid does not reach down to the poorest and food-deficient groups for which it is intended. An important influence in this debate has been Amartya Sen; in a study of famine in 1947 and in the 1970s, he shows that localised food scarcity is frequently caused not by an absolute shortage of food but rather by the fact that those in need do not have the power and ability to be able to draw the necessary food resources to themselves. As he (1981:156) goes on to explain, poor people's

> exchange entitlement may worsen for reasons other than a general decline in food supply. For example, given the same total food supply, food prices may rise because other groups are becoming richer and buying more food, causing a worsening of exchange entitlements. Or some economic change may affect their employment possibilities, also leading to worse exchange entitlements. Similarly, their wages fall behind prices. Or the price of necessary resources for the production they engage in can go up relatively. These diverse influences on exchange entitlements are as relevant as the overall volume of food supply in relation to population.

That distributional and entitlement questions are important is highlighted by the fact, elaborated in a 1986 World Bank study, that overall the world has adequate supplies of food to feed those who inhabit the globe. The study also stresses, quoting Sen, that a critically important way of reducing hunger is by raising income levels (1986:27).

Sen's analysis suggests a number of specific issues which need to be raised in relation to food aid. The first is whether an increase in food supply through food aid is a necessary condition for providing food to those who need it. There can be little doubt that in some areas of the world absolute food shortages exist. Regionally, sub-Saharan Africa is a particular instance of such a shortage both because, from an initial situation of inadequate food resources, food production per capita has progressively declined and because serious and growing foreign-exchange constraints severely limit countries' ability to purchase food commercially. FAO data for 1986, for instance, show total grain import needs for 26 countries in sub-Saharan Africa at 8.6 million tonnes and the inability of these countries to acquire 4.75 million tonnes of this through commercial channels or aid commitments already made. In the case of many countries in Africa, as Sen himself agrees, there is a need for food aid because of a national shortage of food, as indeed there is in any poor country with a national food deficit – Bangladesh for example. Of course, to put the case for food aid on the basis of national shortage is not necessarily to argue that cereals available in bilateral donor countries are the most suitable source of that aid: other sources could be nearer and could be provided more cheaply and quickly. As the FAO (1986:ii–5) points out, in early 1986 seven African countries had exportable surpluses of coarse grain sufficient to meet the import needs of 16 deficit countries in Africa. In response to multilateral pressure, some donors have purchased regional surpluses in what are termed triangular transactions,[8] thereby increasing food aid effectiveness.

National food deficits, however, raise only one – and probably the least contentious – set of issues highlighted by the critics. There are, in addition, the short-term effects of food aid intervention and the long-term consequences. On the first, critics question whether the food aid provided leads to increases in consumption and better nutritional status for the vulnerable groups. There are various strands to this criticism: the food aid provided does not reach those for whom it is intended; it is not eaten by them, perhaps because it is the wrong sort of food, perhaps because it is given away, perhaps because it is eaten by other family members; it is eaten but the overall food intake does not rise because the food aid replaces food that would otherwise have been eaten. These sorts of criticism could apply equally to emergency or project food aid. Clearly not even the harshest critics expect perfection, their criticism is based on the belief that these adverse consequences are the normal outcome: the food provided at the national level does not trickle down to those who need it.[9]

On the second issue, it is argued that even if the immediate results of food aid are beneficial the longer-term consequences will be adverse, reducing either absolutely or relatively the ability of the target group to command their food resource requirements. A variety of different criticisms are raised here: food aid depresses food prices and so adversely affects poor producers; food aid creates dependence on non-traditional foodstuffs and leads to increased import demand for these products; food aid provides recipient countries with increased resources, thus decreasing pressures to undertake necessary macroeconomic adjustments such as lowering exchange rates, and introducing other policy measures that would lead to earlier national self-sufficiency; *au contraire*, it is argued that the failure to provide multi-annual commitments of food aid prevents food-deficit countries from having the flexibility required to implement policies aimed at needed structural change.

Certainly the evidence shows instances where all these types of effects have occurred. Food aid to Guatemala during and following the earthquake undoubtedly did lead to production disincentives for other poor producers (Clay and Singer, 1983:82). Outside emergencies, food aid has tended adversely to affect poor producers in Jamaica, Egypt and Peru (Rahman and McDonnell, 1984:60–61). As for the advantages of supplementary feeding programmes in addressing the problems of malnutrition and undernourishment, Stevens' review of the evidence leads him to conclude that 'the flamboyant claims of donors and others that food-aided supplementary feeding is a major weapon for combating malnutrition cannot be justified by the available evidence' (1979:163). He cites a programme in northern Ghana where the more affluent mothers take the food rather than the poor, and a feeding scheme for schoolchildren in Burkina Faso whose effectiveness in reaching the poor is hampered by the fact that in some areas only 10 per cent of the children are in school (1983:137–44). As for the effects upon those who do receive food aid, a five-country evaluation reports mothers stating that 'they were able to spend less on foods for their family since being enrolled in the CARE feeding program' (quoted in Stevens, 1983:144).

What the available evidence on 'failed' food aid does indicate, and strongly, is that these types of adverse result tend to arise if and when specific action has not been taken to offset them. Thus food aid success would appear to be far from automatic, but rather related directly to addresssing the different constraints that often arise when food aid intervention is attempted. This conclusion would seem to be borne out by many of the examples of success. For example, in Bangladesh an evaluation of the Food for Work Programme indicates that 70 per cent of those involved are producers with holdings of less than one acre and significant income gains have been achieved precisely because of attempts to target aid to these vulnerable groups and to pinpoint potential income gains beforehand (Van Arkadie and de Wilde, 1984:98–100). The Bangladesh case also puts into perspective the claims of critics that political factors are the key issue in judging effectiveness. There is no doubt that corruption has existed in Bangladesh, affecting food aid especially. Yet, as Clay observes, greater attention has been paid by the government to food issues over the past ten years and there was no widespread famine in 1984 after crop failures comparable to those experienced in 1974 (1985:203–6). As Ehrhardt observes (1983:129):

> the cessation of food and commodity aid would likely have had a minimal impact or no impact at all on the policies of the government and would have only made conditions worse for the most vulnerable groups in Bangladesh.

Similarly the success of programmes in Brazil, Colombia, India, Tunisia and Sri Lanka came about because the support that food aid gave to subsidised consumer prices was combined with policies to raise domestic producer prices substantially in order to offset the potential negative impact of food aid on poor producers (Clay and Singer, 1985:92–3 and Stevens, 1979:168ff). Similar positive results appear to emerge from a wide array of recent World Food Programme projects which have not had a negative impact on local production (Ezechiel, 1986:2.21). As for supplementary feeding schemes, although literature surveys, like that conducted by Beaton and Ghassemi covering over 200 schemes, point to limited effectiveness, it is significant that the successes achieved have typically resulted when programmes have formed part of a combination of nutritional and health inputs precisely targeted and sutained through careful design, with detailed attention paid to the management of these complex interventions (Clay and Singer, 1985:96–100). Another factor highlighted in the success stories is the attitude of different groups to different food types. In South-East Asia wheat is considered an inferior product to rice, in Southern Africa yellow maize is considered inferior to the white variety. In both instances the provision of lower status foodstuffs undoubtedly improves the chances of the aid reaching the intended beneficiaries.

Mention should be made here of recent initiatives to provide not food but cash to the poor when there are sufficient food supplies available locally. In 1985, UNICEF established a targeted cash transfer project for over 7,000 families in Ethiopia, related in part to local employment schemes. Not only has this scheme lowered the costs of implementation, it has also helped to stimulate local agricultural production and, in this instance, has led to a decline in child malnutrition in the project areas (World Bank, 1986:39). However, caution needs to be used in generalising from this example. Work by Reutlinger and Katona-Apte (1985), for instance, reveals cases where food rather than cash has had a more favourable impact on health and nutritional status.

Conclusions

But even if successes can be achieved in food aid programmes it would be unrealistic to expect dramatic results. There are few if any examples today of food aid making a major and sustained positive impact. On the other hand, there are probably fewer instances of its resulting in massive failures than there were 10 or

15 years ago. Not that this should lead to complacency. As noted above, there is still far too little evidence available of food aid performance for generalised conclusions to be drawn, even though there continues to be evidence of donors providing food aid that is inappropriate, misdirected or provided in a context that is conducive to negative ripple effects resulting. In such instances the case for exposing these deficiencies is unquestionable and for altering the type of intervention is strong. Of perhaps more concern, however, is the extremely low level of understanding of the importance of different impediments inhibiting success at the international, national and local levels and the possibilities of removing or lessening their impact. Until more work is done in this area it will be impossible either to generalise about the impact of food aid on the poor in developing countries or to pinpoint with sufficient accuracy those constraints which will prevent or impede it from achieving its stated objectives.

Where the critics have provided a service is in exposing the ignorance of donors and recipients and challenging the claims that food aid is necessarily beneficial. Where they have erred is in concluding that these adverse effects can never be overcome.

Agricultural and rural development projects

Aid-funded agricultural and rural development projects (RDPs) are of considerable interest to the broader aid debate both because they constitute a major feature of official programmes and because the available evidence reveals such a low degree of success.[10] What is of particular interest here is not only the attacks made on RDPs by the virulent critics of aid but also the fact that over the past four or five years the failures of rural and agricultural development projects pinpointed in the evaluation reports have been increasingly acknowledged by the donors themselves. Where the more radical critics and the donors and their evaluators part company is not so much in the analysis of aid's particular and often dismal performance but in the different deductions and recommendations made as a consequence of this analysis.

The 1985 DAC Chairman's report acknowledges the importance of agriculturally-oriented aid thus: 'Today all DAC Members, without exception consider that food and agriculture must have priority in their aid programmes' (1985:213). This commitment is revealed in the aid funds allocated to agricultural development by bilateral and multilateral agencies, up from $6.9 billion a year in 1975–6 to $11.6 billion in 1982–3 (at 1982 prices and exchange rates), rising to 17 per cent of all DAC bilateral commitments and 24 per cent of all multilateral commitments by 1983.[11] World Bank agricultural projects implemented and substantially completed in the period 1979–83 cost $10.9 billion, with World Bank loans and IDA credits amounting to $4.1 billion (World Bank, 1983:44).

Two major and broadly based weaknesses characterise many donor-promoted RDPs; the failure to reach down to the poorest groups in rural areas and the frequent inability to achieve their specified objectives, particularly those directed at raising living standards. Reviews by a number of authors either sympathetic to or employed by the World Bank explicitly raise the poverty question. Its importance is emphasised by Lacroix who, in a Bank publication, maintains that it was the focus on poverty that led to the very concept of integrated rural development projects (IRDPs) (1985:1). However, the importance of this poverty focus contrasts with difficulties in reaching the poor. For example, Ayres (1983:103) states that for the vast majority of RDPs undertaken by the Bank the targeted beneficiaries excluded the landless, tenant farmers, sharecroppers and squatters. He cites the case of the massive Rio Grande do Norte project in Brazil, where the directly reachable target population constituted less than 20 per cent of the total project area population, adding that this is far from untypical of other Bank projects. The point is confirmed by Tendler in a Bank staff Working Paper (1982b:22). More recently, in a review of Bank projects in African countries, Jones asks whether the post-1973 emphasis on poverty and equity has received explicit treatment in agricultural reports. She answers thus (1985:94):

> Income distribution objectives don't appear to have been the over-riding objective, as many sector reports give priority to investments in high potential areas and recognise that the needs of 'progressive' farmers and estates should be catered to as well. . . . While all of the reports are careful to point out that smallholders are the primary beneficiaries of most of the proposed investment programs, equity concerns appear to take second place to a concern for rapid growth within the smallholder section.

Perhaps most revealing, however, is the discussion of poverty in the World Bank's ten-year review of project experience. The audit review draws attention to the fact that agricultural projects are classified as 'poverty-oriented' and 'non-poverty-oriented', the term poverty-oriented referring not to projects where the overwhelming majority of the intended direct beneficiaries are members of specified target groups but only where these groups constitute 'at least half' of all the beneficiaries. While the review falls short of explicitly revealing either the proportion of total projects so classified as poverty-oriented or the relative share of total funding earmarked for poverty and non-poverty projects, some indication of a non-poverty bias is reflected in the fact that re-estimated economic rates of return were available for 56 per cent of non-poverty-oriented projects, with the remaining 44 per cent being projects termed by the Bank 'poverty-oriented' (1985:49). More recently, Beckman indicates that, in the 1980s, the Bank's commitment to poverty-focused RDPs has become considerably diluted (1986).

The tendency to direct RDPs at the not-so-poor groups in rural areas is not confined to the World Bank. For example, a recent all-party parliamentary report on UK aid to African agriculture made much the same point, arguing that the most significant feature of British aid to African countries 'is the continuing low allocation to subsistence farming. This means that little UK aid is directly supporting the majority of African farmers in drier regions who grow primarily food staples for domestic consumption. There is little support also to the large number of herders holding small numbers of livestock as a source of insurance against crop failure' (APPGOOD, 1985:32).

The record of failure

Setting aside the poverty-orientation of RDPs, the second weakness of these projects is their failure to achieve the objectives set. The World Bank's ten-year review highlights major problems in crop/area and livestock development projects. For the former, the overall success rate (on Bank criteria which themselves, as we have seen, are open to serious question) is 62 per cent, but far worse in Africa, with over half the projects in East Africa deemed a failure. For livestock projects, severely criticised by Hayter and Watson (1985), the Bank is even more forthcoming about its failures. It states that 'the five year perspective of this review confirms earlier conclusions that livestock has continued to perform less than well, fully 52 per cent of projects being "unsatisfactory". ' In Africa only one livestock project in 12 'turned out a good performance'. This failure record elicits the frank comment that there is a need 'for a complete re-thinking of the approach to livestock in Sub-Saharan Africa' (1985;46).

Bilateral aid efforts to promote rural development have evoked similar comments. For example, a recent review by an AID official concluded that at least a third of all AID agricultural projects have had no lasting impact and that 'very few have operated after the end of donor support at more than 75 per cent of installed capacity' (Billings, 1985, quoted in Johnston and Hoben, 1986:1.3). And in their recent book on rural development projects, Morss and Gow observed that 'almost all projects encountered serious problems during implementation' (1985:iv). The all-party parliamentary report quoted above points to major difficulties of IRDPs in Gabon and Tanzania, and an unpublished study of UK aid to Nepal also highlights major failures, pointing out that this experience is repeated in similar projects initiated by other donors in Nepal (Howell, 1984:7). More generally, a former ODA official, Gordon Bridger, has expressed 'mounting concern' about IRDPs (1984:1), while a recent semi-official book on ODA evaluations admitted general weaknesses, although hastening to add that the projects were 'not necessarily failures' (Cracknell, 1984a:47).

EEC reports also highlight the high failure rate of their multilateral projects. For example, the 1984 Court of Auditors report examined 12 agricultural projects in Mali, Mauritius and Senegal and concluded that not one was profitable, that none could survive without continued assistance, and that half could only be made viable if radical change was effected.[12]

It should be stressed at this point that, given the lack of comprehensive and rigorously processed data, these broad and adverse conclusions about official RDPs must remain somewhat tentative. However, because attention has been drawn repeatedly to these weaknesses by donor organisations and their supporters and friends rather than being solely repeated by the radical critics, it would seem more likely that they are typical and characteristic features of most of these types of projects. There would thus appear to be good reason for suspecting the accuracy of comments such as those of Lacroix stating that RDPs do work (even if not exactly as intended and particularly in the early years of implementation), especially as he is ready to acknowledge the absence of any systematic evaluation and monitoring of RDPs (1983:16-22).[13]

It is not, however, being argued that the picture is one of total failure for there have undoubtedly been instances of success. From the British aid programme, the Orissa rural development programme in India (which is a fertilizer education project concentrating on extension and credit in specific areas) is at least proving partially successful inasmuch as the smallest farmers are increasing yields on small unirrigated plots. The project is regarded by the ODA as one of its best focused and most effective schemes.[14] And from Africa, a recent IFAD publication describes major successes in nine of its rural projects in as many countries including: swamp reclamation and land reform leading to a sixfold increase in rice production for 2,000 poor women cultivators in The Gambia; water and soil conservation measures raising crop yields by 64 per cent for 5,000 farmers in Somalia's backward regions; 300,000 families receiving seeds and tools in Ethiopia, preventing famine for the recipients; and self-managed village associations improving health and water systems in Mali and raising incomes from $40 to $365 a year (IFAD 1986).[15] Important though these examples certainly are – not least to the tens of thousands of poor people who have gained from official aid interventions – it would appear that these are the more infrequent exceptions rather than the, regrettably, more common outcome of RDPs.

If it is accepted that the facts point to a high record of failure, what are the implications for official aid intervention aimed at assisting the poor to raise their income levels and improve their general economic well-being in the rural areas of the Third World? The radical critics use the evidence available to conclude that official aid for rural development should cease altogether or, for some critics, should only be inserted when the broad political climate is deemed favourable (see Hayter and Watson, 1985, Chapters 8 and 11). There are, however, grounds for challenging such conclusions as incorrect or, at minimum, premature.

Ignorance and Complexities
While the available evidence reveals widespread failure, it also indicates that the process of rural development is highly complex. This is widely acknowledged by donors; indeed the shift to IRDPs, with their multi-faceted components, was in part a recognition of the complexity of the rural development process.[16] However, this complexity is married to still considerable ignorance of how best to promote rural development – what should be attempted, in what order of priority, and with what type of interventionist mechanisms. As neither aid donors nor the critics have been keen to expose their ignorance on these matters, the debate about the role of aid in promoting rural development has tended to become both confused and confusing.

The core problem lies not so much in the failure of particular types of aid intervention but more fundamentally in the failure of all the different actors and observers – the official aid agencies, the recipient governments, the critics and the poor themselves – to pinpoint how precisely to promote rural development and to improve the economic well-being of the poor.

In their eagerness to achieve quick and tangible results from their interventions, donors have projected an image suggesting that they know the answers and that these answers lie comfortably and consistently within the context of the assistance they have to offer. At the same time and paradoxically, as Ruttan points out (1986:56-8), donors have constantly changed the details of their programme approaches (often in line with fads and fashions, and frequently proclaiming that single and specific constraints provide the fundamental barrier to development), while also failing to learn from past experience. For their part, the critics have built their case against rural development aid more on attacking the exaggerated claim of the donors than on carefully worked out, consistent and tested alternative strategies to achieve the same objectives, while also placing the blame for failure on a single or narrow set of constraints judged to be obstructing potential development – usually related to power relations and political pressures. Neither the exaggerated claims of the donors nor the partial responses of the critics focus sufficiently on the fundamental issue of how to promote rural development in the extremely hostile environment of most Third World countries.[17]

One of the dangers of proceeding along these lines is that the very objectives for providing aid – the needs of the poor – could become obscured, and in some cases appear to be becoming increasingly so. Wider recognition and acknowledgement that RDPs are achieving extremely limited results, especially, though not exclusively, in relation to the poor, is leading in some donor quarters to a retreat from this particular form of intervention. For example, as the recent UK parliamentary report observed (APPGOOD, 1985:49):

Over the past five years, we might have expected a gradual build-up of technical expertise and a gradual expansion of productive investments. Instead, we have a slow retreat from poorer marginal areas and a reluctance to consider similar 'integrated' projects. Indeed, there has not been any new IRD project since the late 1970s and no obvious attempt to find alternative ways of assisting poorer regions now so dramatically exposed by several seasons of shortfalls in rainfall.

More generally, the 1985 DAC Chairman's report observes that 'A greater share of aid resources would probably have gone to food and agriculture over the past decade if the difficulties of working in this sector were less daunting' (1985:216). Aid failure and the problems of achieving tangible and positive results appear to be lessening the will to continue trying or attempting alternative aid interventionist approaches, while the problems of rural development remain and no viable different strategy has been put forward.

Of course, there are a multiplicity of constraints impeding the successful outcome of RDPs and it is these factors which have been increasingly identified in the evaluations carried out. A variety of technical factors have been highlighted especially in relation to agriculture: inappropriate products, lack of on-farm testing, insufficient knowledge of existing farm systems, lack of localised research, too hurried attempts to shift from pilot scheme to large project, and failure to monitor project evolution and to adapt to changed circumstances. Bureaucratic and managerial factors have also been emphasised to explain the failures of the different elements of the larger and more ambitious RDPs. These include (DAC, 1985:216):

> the lack of institutions able to serve as effective links between central government and the farmers; the scarcity of competent technical and management staff at local and national level; imperfect understanding of the critical role played by women in agricultural development; and above all the lack of effective village-level organisations for enlisting the participation of producers, especially small farmers in technical, financial and marketing actions associated with aid programmes.

Some evaluations attribute failure to the absence of a distinct and separate institution to promote the project, others to having such an institution but with little power and able to be manipulated by different existing central and local government agencies (see, for example, Howell, 1984:28). Others again see a key weakness in inadequate local administrative capability upon which success is judged to depend (Ruttan, 1984:399). Some see failure as caused by the very complexity of the whole enterprise which simply has too many constraints to grapple with. Then, too, there are the explicit political factors that are highlighted, together with instances of corruption and graft inhibiting the completion of projects or the channelling of resources to those for whom they are intended.[18]

Moving beyond these more direct factors, other evaluations attribute failure to the inadequate training provided for local people involved in the different project enterprises or the insufficient attention paid to the need to provide recurrent cost funding for a phased period after the project has been established. Then, too, there are the problems caused by the donors. These include 'preference for large capital projects, reluctance to provide aid to cover local and current expenditures, the rigidity of aid procedures, lack of staff competent in both the technical and socio-political aspects of rural development, as well as with know-how in the field of stimulating the role of women in agricultural development, and lack of coordination among donors' (DAC Review 1983:216). More generally, Morss and Gow (1985:1) add that many constraints lie beyond the control of project managers altogether.

While each of these various constraints is doubtless important in different projects, with a number probably widely applicable, and addressing them will be likely to improve performance, many evaluation studies provide a vivid sense of the wide array of different constraints that will face *all* RDPs, even if they are trimmed of their more ambitious characteristics and become more limited in scope. This should warn one against the constant danger, indulged in particularly by donors and aid advisers, of believing that success lies simply in removing a single constraint. Contemporary fashions in this regard include those who believe that the lack of market forces or inadequate price incentives provide the key constraint to rural development failure and aid's role in achieving greater success.[19] In some quarters the single 'solution' now appears to lie in administrative inadequacies. For example, in the African context, Daniel *et al.* comment thus (1983:131):

> Probably the most widely cited reason for the failure of rural development projects and programmes in Sub-Saharan Africa is poor administration – a combination of a lack of administrative skills in the first place and maladministration once the project is in place.

But these 'single solution' answers can equally be faulted on other grounds. To the extent that the path to improved rural well-being remains unknown or unclear, there can be little confidence in believing those who maintain that removing particular constraints holds the key to success. What is noticeable today, especially although not exclusively in relation to Africa, is that serious and experienced professionals are now more ready to admit their ignorance. As Eicher observes, 'Donor agencies are frequently as misguided about the role of agriculture in development as their hosts', adding that 'Research by economists on livestock is about 25 years behind research on crop production. There are many assertions and beliefs and a sparse supply of facts' (1986:6–7,18). The point is developed by yet another analyst also with wide experience of African rural development problems (Johnston in Johnston and Hoben, 1986: IV,10):

> Given the complexity of the issues of agricultural development and the lack of knowledge concerning the distinctive and extremely heterogeneous characteristics of African agriculture, it is important to recognize that ignorance and uncertainty with respect to the design and implementation of agricultural strategies are unavoidable and serious handicaps. In fact one of the most serious sources of failure and frustration in Africa has been misplaced confidence that 'we' had the answers.

Conclusions

The three features most characteristic of efforts to accelerate rural development and improve the lot of the poor would appear to be the high degree of complexity of the process, widespread ignorance and considerable uncertainty. Where aid has succeeded in achieving its rural objectives, it has been in this general context. That success, admittedly limited, has been achieved is an indication that the enterprise is not without hope. That failure appears to have been the dominant outcome is a sign more of the difficulty of the endeavour than the hopelessness of the task at hand. Donors, recipient governments and aid advisers have all contributed to specific failures and will certainly continue to do so. No one can doubt that improvements are needed: in project design, delivery and continuity, and in the timeframe in which donors expect positive results to be visible.

Thus, while one can readily agree that 'large quantities of money and good measures of professionalism are not the magic movers of progress that they have so universally been held to be' (Hyden, 1983:187), there is even less assurance that their absence will further the progress of rural development. In short, aid for RDPs to date and in general has failed to achieve significant and far-reaching results for the rural poor directly or indirectly engaged in agriculture, but that is no good reason for not continuing to strive to improve Third World agriculture through the medium of aid, given the evident lack of success of alternative non-aid strategies.

Notes

1. Debate about the extent to which the poor are assisted and benefit through the process of national economic growth, with or without direct redistributive measures, has already been discussed in Chapters 11–13, above.
2. Readers are referred in particular to Griffin and Khan (1978), Lipton (1977 and 1972) and Chambers (1983) for a discussion of this point.
3. They have been treated differently in different traditonal societies: in some they have been well cared for within the means of the communities where they live, in others they have been cast aside to fend for themselves in isolation.
4. For example, after reviewing the literature on absolute poverty Cubitt and Riddell came up with the following definition of the basic poverty line: 'the income required to satisfy the minimum necessary consumption needs of a family of given size and composition within a defined environment in a condition of basic physical health and social decency' (1974:5). Once it is acknowledged that 'social decency' is a criterion to judge even absolute poverty, then much objectivity will be lost.
5. Some 20 per cent of total food aid now passes through the WFP; the EEC provides some 35 per cent of all food aid of which two-thirds is under Community programmes and one third bilateral from member states. In 1984, the EEC provided 1.85 million tonnes of wheat or the equivalent in other cereals, and 122,500 tonnes of skimmed milk powder and 32,760 tonnes of butter oil as food aid.

   US food aid, commonly known as PL 480, consists of four categories, known as Titles. Title I provides for concessional sales of commodities to less developed countries; under Title II food commodities can be donated through US or foreign private voluntary organisations, multilateral agencies and bilateral arrangements with recipient governments for humanitarian purposes, including emergencies; Title III provides for Food-for-Development programmes and forgiveness of debt incurred under Title I; and Title IV covers mainly administrative and reporting arrangements. Title II covers the main US food aid channel and in the 1985 Farm Bill the minimum quantity channelled through Title II was raised to 1.9 million metric tons per year with a minimum for non-emergency programmes of 1.425 million metric tons. (See Ezechiel, 1986 and Freeman in ODA, 1984:46).
6. The point could possibly be made for all aid intervention, although it is seen most clearly in the case of food aid.
7. ODA News Release, 20 June 1986.
8. These are arrangements whereby donors act as intermediaries between surplus and deficit countries, sometimes to purchase food from the surplus country which goes to the deficit country and sometimes to engage in swap arrangements where a product from a donor country is provided to country A with a deficit in this product but a surplus in another, on condition that an agreed quantity of that surplus product is channelled to the deficit country. In the period 1984–6, for example, the USA, Japan and Australia undertook triangular transactions using Zimbabwe's surplus maize crop. However, in 1986, even though Zimbabwe had a maize surplus of many hundreds of thousands of tonnes, neighbouring food-deficit Mozambique was supplied with 20,000 tonnes of maize from the US under a food aid agreement. (*The Financial Gazette* (Harare), 25 April 1986, p.2).
9. It is possible to use a 'trickle-down' argument in favour of food aid even in circumstances when there is a national food surplus. It could go like this: in country A with a national food surplus there are people who lack basic food necessities; by providing more food in the form of aid it is likely that, with an even greater surplus, there will be decreasing pressure to divert the excess away from the neediest. Hence, in the absence of any effective donor ability to alter structural constraints in the short term, food aid should be provided to surplus countries as the best practical way of bringing food resources to those who need them. Donors rarely, if ever, use such arguments because to do so would be an admission both of a very cost-ineffective method of providing aid as

well as of an inability to influence recipient-country policy. However, the fact that donors do provide grain to recipients with national grain surpluses indicates that the point is not entirely academic. In practice, inevitably, matters can be very complex on the ground. FAO (1986) observed that in 1986 Sudan required immediate emergency assistance and yet it was also one of the seven countries named as having an exportable surplus of coarse grain. This anomaly is explained by the fact that eastern Sudan has a sorghum surplus which cannot be transported to western Sudan where a severe deficit is causing acute starvation.

10. The history of the evolution of rural development projects and aid is well summarised in Ruttan (1984 and 1986) and in Lacroix (1985). RDPs include those more specifically concerned with different aspects of agricultural development. Within the last fifteen or so years there has been a shift of emphasis in some regions in the scope of RDPs, widening their range of activities to include components such as the provision of credit, the supply of inputs and the provision of rural infrastructure as well, in some instances, as the introduction of programmes of social welfare and community development. Some of these wider and more ambitious projects have been termed integrated rural development projects.

11. *Inter alia*, aid included here embraces aid for services and rural infrastructure, integrated rural development projects and associated technical co-operation. Lacroix defines integrated rural development projects as 'those that try to bring a basket of goods and services, consisting of production, social and infrastructural components to poor rural areas' (1985:15).

12. *Official Journal of the European Communities, Information and Notices*, C.348, 31 December 1984, p.125.

13. Lacroix's conclusion that IRDPs are 'on balance successful' reads uneasily with his comment that 'little is known about the objective success and failures of projects and little agreement can be reached in this respect with regard to specific projects' (1985:23).

14. J. Elliott, 'Aid Reaches The Poverty Line', *Financial Times*, 22 March 1986. The Orissa scheme is not without its critics or its problems. It is expensive to operate; it excludes the landless; the small farmers are those with land of less than 2.5 acres and these only constitute 70 per cent of the project beneficiaries; also there are doubts about the maintenance of performance after ODA withdraws, with estimates suggesting 20 per cent of farmers are likely to go back to their old ways and only 40 per cent will continue to apply the correct quantities of fertilizer. The fact that, with these problems, the project is deemed highly successful highlights the difficulties encountered in RDP implementation.

15. As IRDPs contain a range of different elements frequently including credit schemes, research and extension programmes, road building, school construction, water, nutrition and general health projects, there is evidence of the respective successes and failures of these sub-sets of larger schemes. As the general discussion in previous sections has indicated, the success rate has tended to vary, although notable successes have been achieved, especially for those elements where the gains for the poor have not entailed a zero-sum game with the non-poor. Explicit mention should, perhaps, be made of the gains achieved from agricultural research especially of high-yielding crop varieties in parts of Asia. Recent research has tended to suggest (in some areas at least) that 'contrary to expectations, the Green Revolution did not displace small farmers. The evidence seems to be that where agro-climatic conditions were favourable, the small farmers, after a time lag, adopted the new technology as readily as large farmers. A decade ago . . . it was not recognised that the principal beneficiaries of the high yield revolution would be the low income consumers' (Yudelman, 1984 quoted in DAC, 1985:217). For a discussion of the performance of rural roads, see important studies by Tendler (1979) and Howe and Richards (1984).

16. Since the mid-1970s there has been some indication of a trend away from multi-faceted RDPs to what is termed a 'minimum package approach' whereby the overall strategy is broken down into stages with different aspects addressed sequentially rather than concurrently. While this phasing certainly reduces the administrative and logistical complexities of initiating and sustaining rural development, it by no means eliminates them or necessarily reduces other constraints.

17. The word 'hostile' in this context is not used to refer either exclusively or particularly to political hostility. The term refers to the complexity of constraints including, for example, inadequate physical resources, environmental factors, lack of access, poor human resource capability, lack of effective markets, and bureaucratic and administrative inadequacies which prevail in the rural areas of aid-recipient countries.

18. In this context mention could be made of an IRDP in Colombia that had substantial political support at all levels from national to local and also involved considerable support from among the local population. However, as Lacroix points out, 'unfortunately this support is a mixed blessing since the project and its institutions are coming under pressure from politicians trying to use them to advance other than project related interests. Also, the high visibility of the program has revived bureaucratic struggles for control. Currently, the Ministry of Agriculture is laying claim to the

co-ordination responsibility of the . . . food supply program to the poor urban consumers' (1985:31).

On the other hand, Howell's evaluation of the UK's IRDP in Nepal leads him to state that 'in the current context of administration in Nepal integrated rural development and particularly integrated rural development planning at the district level is not a practical proposition. The structure does not exist for it and there is no genuine interest in it.' The root cause of the problem he attributes to the central government and its lack of interest in development in the Koshi Hills area. However, he does not thereby conclude that the project should be abandoned and British aid to rural development withdrawn. He continues thus (1984:57–8): 'Despite the difficulty for KHARDEP in performing its IRDP role, there are arguments for its continuation. Firstly, for district and regional programmes a donor such as ODA would have much less control working with central ministries than working with a regional agency such as KHARDEP. Second, in implementation it is only an agency such as KHARDEP, within the MPLD, which can effectively work with district administration which is involved in a wide range of activities. Third, for local infrastructure projects there is no alternative but to persevere with a planning agency within MPLD able to influence the panchayat structure; and fourthly, the concept of district and regional planning, while currently weak in Nepal, can only be strengthened if support is given to an agency such as KHARDEP.

If, as I suggest below, there is a narrowing of project and more careful design of projects and involvement in implementation, KHARDEP becomes less important than the central ministries. In the circumstances, there is a better prospect for effective utilisation of UK aid, both capital and TC, if there is a more close involvement with central ministries. This is likely to provide greater support at the national level for particular programmes, and at the regional and district level it would allow ODA a closer involvement in the ways that its funds and expertise are deployed. Virtually all TCOs, and most advisers, would support a move to have closer links with the ministries involved in implementation at the expense of lessening links with KHARDEP or any successor to KHARDEP.'

19. The inadequacies of concentrating exclusively on prices is pinpointed in a recent article by Lipton in Rose (1985) which begins thus: ' "Getting the prices right", while desirable (if definable), cannot on its own do much for agricultural output in sub-Saharan Africa. Farmers switch to new crops when incentives so indicate; but with land becoming scarcer, and no dramatic new techniques near the margin of profitability, farmers – however rational – cannot greatly raise *total* output when prices rise. Price elasticities of total farm supply are notoriously low (Bond, 1983; Cleaver, 1984). We need somehow to apply, to sub-Saharan Africa, two lessons from South and East Asia: that, if agricultural output is to benefit greatly from "getting the prices right", a country has first to get the elasticities up, mainly through agricultural research (AR); and that *national* AR is needed to realise significant gains from adapting basic findings from elsewhere.'

However, Lipton does appear to fall into the same general trap of isolating single constraints impeding progress, for he continues by stating that 'It has long been clear that national AR elsewhere, is a winner', even if the rest of the article's thrust is to caution against these types of generalised and single explanations of success.

17 Aid at the National Level

The present chapter adds to the general overviews discussed in some detail in Part II above by considering the macro-evidence from the limited number of countries where in-depth studies have been carried out. While the partiality of the data currently available and their varied quality caution against being able to make reliable generalisations, they certainly do not add support to the views of the different radical critics either that aid frustrates development or that its absence could facilitate a faster, fairer or more favourable process of development.

This chapter has two distinct sections. The first provides a rapid survey of the available country-specific evidence largely through the prism of economics, considering particularly the effects of official aid vis-à-vis the rightist criticism that aid impedes market and price efficiency and by its very nature frustrates more rapid development. The second section places the political questions surrounding official aid intervention at the centre of the stage. Many overt criticisms and anxieties expressed about official aid both from the political left and from elements of the right reflect concern about the justification for providing aid to Third World governments and non-democratic regimes whose record reveals a lack of interest in promoting equitable development or, in certain instances, a complete disregard for the well-being of the majority or significant minority groups of the population. Taking the extreme case of the Caribbean island of Haiti, particularly in the period of the Duvalier regimes, this section highlights the complex issues raised in arguing whether official aid should or should not be provided to such governments.

The recipient country evidence

Three warnings need to preface the references that will be made here to specific country findings. The first, already highlighted, is the woeful lack of comprehensive and representative data. The second, referred to by those who have conducted country studies, is the tentative nature of their findings: most admit that the conclusions they draw are based on partial analysis, frequently dependent upon inadequate statistical and other quantitative information.[1] The third warning is that even the country studies that have been conducted are not strictly comparable because the methodologies used for analysing aid's impact differed widely from country to country and over different time periods. As even Western donors, who are eager to find evidence to provide justification for their interventions, agree (DAC, 1985:259):

> There is still no satisfactory methodology for assessing the impact of aid on the economy of an entire country, or even an entire sector. Such country studies as are available remain for the most part impressionistic. There is a whole set of questions here, on the

effectiveness of country programming, of general support for non-project aid, and of donors' collective efforts in the context of arrangements for co-ordination . . . In each of these areas there are major unanswered questions outstanding.

Moving to the evidence that the country studies do provide, some tentative conclusions can be drawn. Few, if any, studies of aid's long-term impact on a recipient country have ever provided statistical evidence that has been able to show unquestionably that it has had a positive effect at the macro-level.[2] However, all the analyses reviewed here either provide partial or at least circumstantial evidence that aid's insertion has been accompanied by improvements in certain key indicators – such as economic growth, investment levels and domestic saving – or else highlight dominant external factors which have led to an apparent negative aid effect. Yet they all point also to failings and inefficiencies in the aid relationship, lowering effectiveness and impact away from a theoretically more perfect outcome. *Contra* rightist assertions, there is, in addition, no evidence to lead one to conclude that development would have occurred faster without aid, while, importantly for these particular critics, there is evidence to show that the private sector has been assisted through aid intervention and has certainly not been fundamentally impeded because of the insertion of aid.

For a number of countries, analysts have commented that aid has been critical for the very establishment of the nation following political independence and the ending of the colonial era, often when independence was preceded by armed struggle. In Southern Africa, Jones points to both the critical lack of local technical capability and the absence of domestically-generated revenue to conclude that for Lesotho, Botswana and Swaziland 'at independence these countries were not in a position to function without outside support' (1977:61). For Malawi, Hewitt and Kydd provide a similar assessment pointing out that at independence the country's very survival depended upon aid (1986:1). Outside Africa, the Bangladesh study contends that in 1971 aid put the country on the map and kept it afloat in the difficult first years after independence (Van Arkadie and de Wilde, 1984:6). Similarly Steinberg's analysis of South Korea points to the essential role played by aid funds for the survival of the new country in the early 1950s (1984:25). Even in less extreme circumstances, aid has provided a breathing space. For example, no-one has disputed the benefits that reconstruction aid provided to Zimbabwe following independence in April 1980 which was utilised to rebuild clinics, schools and agricultural services damaged and destroyed during the pre-independence war. The important general conclusion to be drawn is that, while it could legitimately be argued that all this is water under the bridge, these positive effects of aid have never been questioned by the critics. In other words, this particular advantage of aid does appear to be undisputed.

India

But what has been the longer-term impact of aid? We can start to answer this question by considering the case of India, the country that has received more aid from more donors than any other developing country.[3] It is also a country that Bauer has been drawn to comment on in relation to foreign aid, arguing that 'much of the aid received by developing countries, notably India, has not served materially to improve the income-earning capacity of these countries', but has saddled them with large debts without a commensurate increase in the capacity to service them (1971:108). While Bauer provides no evidence to support this assertion, the two recent country case studies of aid to India by Sukhatme, and Lipton and Toye provide a wealth of documentation pointing to a very different conclusion, put in the latter study in the following terms: 'No one would deny that aid, although small, has played and continues to play an important part in India's development' (1984:0.2).

Increased income-earning capacity has occurred in India and poverty has been reduced. This has, in part, resulted from aid's contribution to raising food production and to expanding employment opportunities. Aid has also played a wider but more indirect role, through its contribution to agricultural research, leading especially to increased yields of food crops. Lipton and Toye highlight specific gains for the poor, arising from agricultural aid especially through increasing food availability. But they also stress broader systematic effects: building up a cadre of local research personnel, the establishment of agricultural institutes, and technical assistance to improve the country's agricultural administration. They also maintain that the Government of India would not have proceeded nearly as fast or as far or in the chosen direction of rural credit, water management reform, urban development programmes in Calcutta, or extension services without donor involvement (II.52). None of these specific benefits of aid have been challenged by the critics. More recently, other evidence indicates some quite dramatic falls in the proportion of the population living below the poverty line. For instance, the most recent development plan quotes data from the National Sample Survey Organisation records that in 1983-4, 37.4 per cent of the population were living below the poverty line compared with 48.3 per cent in the period 1977-8.[4]

In aggregate, aid's contribution to the national economy has been far lower than in many other developing countries, amounting over the past 25 years to some 3 to 4 per cent of GNP. It is, therefore, not surprising (given other influences) that econometric evidence of its effects on growth has been ambiguous. There has, however, been a steady rise in both domestic saving and investment in the period that aid has been provided to the Indian economy. GDP *per capita* has risen by 50-70 per cent in real terms since Independence and there have been marked improvements in poverty reduction in a number of states. Also, *contra* Bauer *et al.*, some aid has been channelled directly to the private sector. Indeed, a major contribution has been to help to establish a wide range of financial institutions providing long- and medium-term finance to private business that the commercial banks had been unwilling to fund. Aid has also played a role in establishing capital markets in the country (Sukhatme, 1983:44).

India has also been helped to obtain finance at well below market rates. Lipton and Toye have calculated, for example, that foreign borrowing without aid would be $2.5 on IBRD terms for every $1 obtained on IDA terms (1984:0.7). Much aid has also contributed to the expansion of the country's basic infrastructure of roads and power plants, even though, today, there are still serious inadequacies in these facilities.

It would be incorrect, however, to argue that the aid relationship has been entirely smooth or beneficial. In the mid-1960s, especially, prior to the Aid Consortium, there were great tensions and conflicts between the donors and the Indian Government. Moreover, there is little doubt that some of the aid provided for human resources development and health projects has been inappropriately allocated, especially in the late 1960s and early 1970s. Yet some of the failures of Indian development have been failures of national policy rather than specific failures of aid. For instance, the low levels of private investment recorded in the late 1960s cannot be blamed on the aid relationship, they were a direct result of broader policy directives and restrictive legislation. None the less, there does seem to be evidence to suggest that the extensive tying conditions attached to donor aid funds contributed to distortions in investment decisions and priorities (Sukhatme, 1983:20).

Thus it is neither being argued that aid has always been used wisely in India nor that after over 30 years of receiving it India has solved its development and poverty problems. However, there is enough evidence available to show that aid has assisted the country's development in major ways, in spite of many bureaucratic and logistical problems and also donor ignorance of precisely how to help which have clearly inhibited its effectiveness. Importantly, too, there is nothing to suggest that India would be in a better economic position today without aid.

Africa and other Asian countries

The available evidence in other aid-recipient countries also provides little support either for the rightist criticisms of aid or for those challenging the conclusions of traditional macro-theories of aid. Even if, in general, the macro-statistical evidence is more suggestive than conclusive for Botswana, Lesotho and Swaziland, Jones found a positive relationship between aid inflow and investment levels and between aid and what he calls productive consumption, allocated largely to agricultural extension, health and education services (1977:55). Young's study of Tanzania also points to the positive role of aid at the macro-level in raising investment levels (1983:33). In Malawi, aid has been associated with a high tax level and there is no evidence of a lowering of national effort to raise revenue domestically. In the 1965–79 period, aid inflow was paralleled by both a marked increase in the investment to GDP ratio (from 14 per cent in 1965 to 38 per cent in 1979) and in faster growth of private vis-à-vis public investment (Hewitt and Kydd, 1986:10,112).

The recent Kenyan case study at first sight appears to provide evidence adverse to aid's supporters. It concluded both that domestic taxation rates could be higher than those prevailing and that aid could have been more effectively utilised (Duncan and Mosley, 1984:11,132). While on their own these conclusions would tend to provide support for the critics, the study found no statistically significant relationship at all between aid inflow and economic growth. And, of major importance, the authors concluded that over the 20 years that aid had flowed into Kenya the prospects for development had tended to become more difficult. They state (1984:7):

> the chain of causation runs from the condition of the economy to aid flows as well as *vice versa* and the high levels of aid in 1966 and 1981–82 for example, are better understood as a *response* to the stresses which the Kenyan economy was suffering, from decolonisation and the second oil shock respectively, rather than as a *determinant* of its condition in those years.

In general, therefore, the African case-study evidence provides support for the pro-aid camp and few broad instances of aid's adverse effects.

In Bangladesh, too, aid inflow has been associated with a rise in capital investment, while a rising or steady aid/GNP ratio has been associated with an increase in the domestic savings ratio (Van Arkadie and de Wilde, 1984:38–41 and Hossain *et al.* 1984:46). The work of Hossain and his colleagues also reveals a positive relationship of both the direct and indirect tax-to-GDP ratios with aid inflow over the period 1970–71 to 1980–81, although they add that 'the movement towards self-sustained growth in Bangladesh has received little help from the aid inflow', largely because of the channelling of the bulk of aid into infrastructural projects (72–4).

What is more, Bangladesh has had few, if any, alternatives to foreign aid for external financing. The country is incapable of feeding itself and has had a continuous foreign debt problem since independence: in 1984 total debt amounted to $1,011m. and the trade deficit was over $700m.[5] As Van Arkadie and de Wilde argue, there is no effective means of funding the imports needed and Bangladesh is not a plausible candidate for non-concessionary private finance. They estimate future projections of $200m. a year to the year 2000 to service the country's external debt with little near-term hope of increasing exports dramatically or of a significant rise in commercial financial inflows (1984:4,44). The debt burden has certainly increased in recent years but the blame for this cannot be laid at the door of the aid relationship.

Taiwan and South Korea

The country studies of Taiwan and South Korea also highlight the positive impact of foreign aid. Jacoby's study of Taiwan covers the period 1951–65, so his findings are largely of historical interest. However, for this phase of Taiwan's development, his analysis reveals a strong positive impact of aid on economic growth. He judges that, at minimum, 30 per cent of the annual gain in GNP was attributable to economic aid, although he also states that the average rate of economic growth would have been 9 per cent a year rather than the 7 per cent achieved if Taiwan had not had to divert resources to military expenditures (1966:37,46). Most aid went to infrastructural projects and was utilised for public-sector investment projects raising, overall, the rate of capital formation from 12 to 17 per cent of GNP over the period. While generally in favour of private and market-initiated development, Jacoby nowhere argues that aid to Taiwan squeezed out the private sector. Indeed, he states that 'an economy like Taiwan needs a development strategy because market forces provide incomplete guidance to investment decisions and an efficient capital market is lacking' (53). He also reveals that, in spite of the public sector/infrastructural bias of the aid distributed, much aid did go directly to private industry.

He attributes his assessment of aid's positive impact to favourable complementary government policies, an agricultural structure, including substantial land reform, conducive to sustained expansion, and the fact that even by the early 1950s Taiwan was already partly developed, having iron and steel, paper and aluminium industries established as far back as the 1930s. With this favourable environment, aid could and did assist in the development process, leading also to the spread of economic benefits to large population groups. It also helped to ease specific bottlenecks as they arose, for example by expanding electrical energy capacity. However, Jacoby also highlights certain failures. These include less than fully efficient resource allocation because of corruption, incorrect advice from the US donor, too much aid given for hydro-electric rather than thermo-electric plants, too little aid channelled to agricultural research, and numerous errors of individual projects caused by lack of initial surveys, lack of independent project appraisal, and pressure to spend aid funds before the end of the US fiscal year. He also comments that the efficiency of aid funds was adversely affected because of US unwillingness to commit funds over the long term.

While Jacoby's study does not explicitly raise the question of whether Taiwan would have been better without aid, he does provide ample evidence with which to base his conclusion that 'The Taiwan experience demonstrates that, given the necessary conditions, foreign assistance can successfully assist a country to develop economically' (90). In view of the debates about the merits or otherwise of foreign aid intervention that have ensued since he wrote his study over 20 years ago, his sensitive comments about the role of foreign aid in development are worthy of repetition here (39,85a):

> Both *a priori* theory and historical observation strongly suggest that a fast pace of development cannot be maintained over an extended period of time unless there is a stable government, a minimum degree of monetary and financial discipline, a literate, adaptable economically orientated population, entrepreneurial and technical leadership and an adequate supply of capital. The science and art of foreign aid to semi-developed countries consists in identifying the on-coming bottlenecks to sustained and rapid growth and concentrating assistance upon ways of removing them, one by one, as they appear.
>
> Because foreign aid is normally a minor fraction of total development resources – about 1/3 in the case of Taiwan – and because the allocation of aid is crucial to the results obtained, economic policies are a much more weighty determinant of the pace and progress than the level of aid.

We turn, finally, to South Korea, a country whose development performance has been cited as providing perhaps the strongest country-specific case that aid impedes development and that the absence of aid in a context of *laisser-faire* policies is the surest way to advance and prosper.

These particular conclusions are based on the following evidence of South Korea's development and aid performance.[6] In the 1954–60 period, the country was dominated economically, politically and militarily by the United States, which provided over 90 per cent of all foreign aid, totalling very large amounts. Broad macro-statistics for this period reveal only minimal economic gains, especially in contrast with the post-1961 era. For example, average annual economic growth in the period 1954–60 was 4.2 per cent, with *per capita* income rising from $67 in 1953 to $82 in 1961. Few gains were achieved in rural and agricultural development, especially in rice production. Export levels in 1961 were no higher than in the early 1950s and there was very little improvement in infant mortality and other health indicators. Yet over this period the US channelled over $1,892m. in economic aid to South Korea, averaging $236m. a year. Aid accounted for some 8 per cent of GNP, half of all resources used for investment, providing one-third of all government revenue and paying for 75 per cent of all imports. Since the early 1960s, the economic record of South Korea has been remarkable. Annual economic growth rates averaged 8.3 per cent a year in the period 1961 to 1981, double the rates achieved in the 1950s. *Per capita* income trebled in the 1960s and increased at an even more rapid rate in the 1970s. Infant mortality rates halved, exports expanded by an average of 30 per cent a year and rice production expanded. On the aid front, US project aid ceased in 1959 and in the period 1962–70 general US aid funds averaged only $55m. a year.

It is the comparatively poor performance of the economy in the pre-1960s period, the turn-around in economic performance thereafter, and the associated dramatic reduction in US aid flows that occurred at this time which apparently provide aid's critics with the evidence for arguing that aid is an obstacle to development and that its removal is a major factor in encouraging Third World governments to pursue a growth-oriented strategy dependent upon market forces rather than on foreign hand-outs. It is, however, relatively easy to show that this particular interpretation of South Korea's economic fortunes is a gross over-simplification: the critics' case is far from proven.

While there is little question that the pre-1960s period was one of a low and disappointing economic performance accompanied by very high and sustained levels of aid inflow, the precise nature of the association between aid and economic performance was more complex than the 'aid equals low growth and no aid leads to high growth' scenario implies[7]. In the first place, aid inflows did play a crucial role in ensuring the survival of a country devastated by war. Food aid, for instance, was critically important because of the destruction of much of the country's agriculture during the war. More generally (Steinberg, 1984:25–6):

> The Republic of Korea could not have survived on its own at that time. It could neither feed its people nor provide them with basic needs – let alone amenities; it could not run the government without outside assistance, nor could it protect the state. The standard of living had dropped below World War II levels and was not to equal them again until 1957.

Beyond these immediate effects (never seriously challenged by the critics), aid did also play a positive role in laying some of the key foundations for subsequent development by helping to build up the physical and social infrastructure of the country, the positive benefits of which were not readily apparent in macro-economic indicators for the 1950s. Three areas were of particular importance: assistance with the all-embracing land reform programme; projects to expand and develop the country's infrastructure, especially for transport and power facilities in general and for rural infrastructural projects in particular; and finally, technical assistance both to assist the incipient expansion of the educational system and in the technical skills imparted to thousands of military personnel within the country and in the United States (see Krueger and Ruttan, 1983b:13–49).

Over and above these achievements, however, there is little doubt that, given the scale of the aid inflow in the pre-1960s period, the economic results were disappointing. Where the critics are correct is in pointing this out, where they are wrong is in using the specific example of South Korea prior to 1960 to suggest that the adverse results were part of a normal or inevitable consequence of aid intervention. Failures there certainly were, but their cause lies more in questionable development policies, not directly caused by aid, and in the political and economic conflicts between the US and the Syngman Rhee regime. As Mason *et al.* explain (1980:192–3):

> The Korean government of Syngman Rhee wanted to build a modern economy similar to, but independent of, the Japanese economy. Their desire was for new factories and heavy industry financed through foreign aid having little regard for the inflationary impact of the heavy investment programs or the longer-run issues of comparative advantage. The United States, on the other hand, was concerned about moving the South Korean economy towards self-sufficiency as rapidly as possible while holding down the aid requirements and minimizing instability and inflation in the process. Thus, there was clear disagreement over the issue of resource mobilization, with the Korean government wishing to rely mainly on external resources, or if necessary on inflation as a means of mobilizing domestic resources, and the American government urging greater Korean efforts at domestic resource mobilization through increased taxes and private savings.

Blame for economic failure can be attributed to both sides. US aid was biased towards imported consumer goods and not the basic capital materials needed to assist the building of a self-sufficient and dynamic economy. Also the PL480 programme did suppress producer prices, especially for rice, thereby inhibiting the process of agricultural expansion. On the other hand, corruption, mis-use of aid funds and political interference in economic issues occurred and were largely due to South Korean failings (Steinberg, 1984:31 and 37). The issue of where the most blame lay will probably never be satisfactorily resolved but the critics do have valid points that should not be brushed under the carpet. To underplay the conflicts and to argue that the aid provided in the pre-1960s period must have been effective because of the notable successes of subsequent years is to fall foul of equally misplaced generalisations. There were significant failures of aid in this period even if some aid, as indicated above, did assist future development prospects.

Perhaps, though, the greatest error the critics make is in misreading the post-1960s period of South Korea's development. The essential differences were not of aid and low growth followed by high growth and *no* aid but of aid and low growth followed by high growth *and* aid, with each of the periods marked by fundamentally different economic policies and attitudes to the aid which did flow in. The 1961 *coup* and events surrounding it should not be seen as causing a reversal of attitudes to aid in general; rather these events led to a fundamental shift in overall development strategy in which aid, although in different forms and from different sources, continued to play a role. This interpretation is borne out by the evidence of aid flows. While US aid quantities did fall dramatically, with general support assistance dropping by $86m. between 1960 and 1962 and falling progressively to $9m. by 1970, total US economic aid still averaged $139m. a year from 1962 to 1970, with PL480 aid totalling $85m. a year in this period compared with $44m. a year in the period 1954-61 (Steinberg, 1984:D.6). Furthermore, Japanese aid, non-existent in the 1954-61 period, amounted to a massive $1,898m. in the period 1965-81. The crucial difference between the pre- and post-*coup* eras related to key changes in economic policy. These included: a major currency reform, a sustained export drive, the nationalisation of commercial banks and increased state control of credit, a more systematic approach to rural development, rapid industrialisation, a major expansion in education, normalisation of relations with Japan, and diversification of sources of foreign finance.

It has been the far more favourable economic and political climate in this latter period that led to the aid provided being utilised much more efficiently than in the 1950s. Steinberg's review of the evidence leads him to conclude that it 'probably speeded the adoption of various reforms and the development of certain industries and institutions. More importantly, it probably also encouraged the Korean government to make certain investments (such as in various types of technical education) more comprehensively and quickly than they otherwise might have done' (1984:56-7). And as Krueger and Ruttan have argued, the continued and increased amounts of food aid provided 'allowed the Korean government to pursue a policy of urbanisation without the uncertainty of bad harvests as a constraint . . . As the PL480 program declined in importance the Park government instituted stronger programs of agricultural and rural development' (1983b:13-45).

While aid has certainly been a contributory factor to South Korea's economic expansion over the past 20 years, the critics are correct in downplaying its role. It certainly has not been pivotal; far more important in quantitative terms have been non-aid sources of foreign finance including, initially, use of World Bank and Asian Development Bank funds which totalled over $6.5 billion from 1962 to 1984, and, more importantly of late, commercial bank borrowing, as well as rising levels of private and particularly Japanese foreign investment.

But where the critics are also wrong is in arguing that South Korea's successes are the result most fundamentally of *laisser faire* economic policies. The country's economic and export achievements have certainly been built on a response to world prices, but a response that, like that of Japan, has been planned and engineered. The following essential characteristics of South Korea's economy, fundamental to its success, are far removed from the tenets of *laisser faire*: export

incentives and subsidies, government control of credit and large investment decisions, state control and influence of the large conglomerates which dominate
economic activity, rail and electricity subsidies, and the presence of an extensive
and active planning machinery.[8] Certainly South Korea has made use of the price
system and market signals in steering the direction and expansion of its economy,
but this has been in a manner far removed from *laisser faire* orthodoxy. It has also
been expansion assisted by aid funds, even though it is apparent that foreign aid
has not been vital in this latter period for development to proceed. For South
Korea, as for Taiwan, economic policies have been a 'a much more weighty
determinant of the pace and progress than the level of aid' (Jacoby, 1966:39).
And, finally, given the very high rates of economic growth that were achieved in
the 1970s with aid, there is little to suggest that even greater growth rates could
have been achieved in its absence.

Conclusions

This brief survey of the major country study evidence, then, does appear to
support the orthodox pro-aid view that aid can be and frequently is a positive force
in development, even if it could have done far more had institutional and political
circumstances in recipient countries been more favourable and had donor self-
interest been pursued less vigorously. Of course, besides the inherent limitations of
this country-specific evidence already mentioned, macro-critics of aid may be
quick to point out that all the studies cited here have been undertaken by friends of
aid and are therefore a poor basis for challenging opposing views because of
subjective bias. While it is true that the studies have indeed been carried out by
analysts broadly in favour of official aid intervention, they by no means give the
impression of a conspiracy to manipulate the data, and in a number of cases,
especially those studies prepared for the World Bank's aid effectiveness study,
many harsh words were expressed about aid's failings. But what is perhaps most
telling is that the most vigorous critics of aid have themselves failed to undertake
detailed country-study analyses to prove to anyone's satisfaction either that aid is
not effective or that its absence is the critical factor in accelerating the development process.

Poverty and political pariahs: the case of Haiti

The case for aid

If extremes of poverty are to be the criterion on which to base the case for providing aid to Third World countries, then Haiti is without any doubt a country to
which aid should be given. It is classified among the least developed countries of
the world and is the poorest country in the Caribbean, indeed in the whole of the
western hemisphere. Not only is it poor in comparison with most other countries
but the numbers of those living in absolute poverty are large, and the evidence
points to increasing poverty at least over the past twenty years and probably for a
far longer period.

A few facts and figures illustrate the extent of its poverty and deprivation. With
an estimated population of 5.3 million in 1984, GDP *per capita* stood at $341,
having fallen by over 10 per cent in the first four years of the 1980s following
increases of 3 per cent a year in the decade of the 1970s and stagnation in the 1960s
(see Burgaud, 1986:4 and 41). Yet even these low aggregate figures mask the extent
and depth of the poverty. According to English (1984:9), Haiti has the most
skewed income distribution in the world with one per cent of the population

controlling 40 per cent of national income. At the other end of the scale, World Bank estimates are that in 1981 three-quarters of the population lived in families with *per capita* income of less than $140 a year, while the UNDP judges that the 'really poor' population increased from 48 per cent of the total in 1976 to 68 per cent by the early 1980s, in spite of the most substantial increases in GDP recorded in the past 25 years (1982:1). While poverty is the norm for the 80 per cent of the population living in the rural areas and dependent upon primitive methods of subsistence agriculture, it is also widespread in the urban areas, especially in the capital, Port-au-Prince. For those in urban employment, the minimum daily wage in 1981 was $2.60 a day, with $0.56 of this spent on transportation; the urban unemployment rate in 1985 was judged to be 35 per cent (UNDP, 1982:1; Burgaud 1986:41). The majority of the urban population live in rat-infested slums: less than 30 per cent have potable water or access to any sort of sewage system and in the past ten years no new low-cost housing has been built by the government. A USAID study in the late 1970s judged that *per capita* farm income was well under $200 a year, usually under $100 and also certainly declining (Zuvekas, 1978:131). Haiti's rural population density is twice as high as that prevailing in India (Pietrodangelo, 1985:16). Soil erosion and ecological degradation are considered among the worst in the world: one third of agricultural land is no longer cultivable and the FAO recently judged that on present trends the country's forest resources will have been completely exhausted by the end of the century (Zuvekas, 1978:62 and 190). Haiti does not grow enough food to feed the population and food aid is provided to both urban and rural poor (Prince, 1985:46).

Poverty and underdevelopment are also illustrated by reference to health and social indicators. Malnutrition and gastroenteritis are responsible for over half of all deaths in Haiti and an estimated 75–80 per cent of all children suffer from malnutrition. Official statistics put the infant mortality rate at 150 per 1,000 but many observers believe the figure to be far higher. In a worldwide 1974 study of 129 countries, Haiti came 127th in calorie intake and 129th in protein consumption (ibid.:62). Less than 15 per cent of the population have access to safe water and malaria, tuberculosis, tetanus and typhoid are endemic and deadly (English, 1984:15; Pietrodangelo, 1985:16). Some 80 per cent of all children under the age of six have malaria (Prince, 1985:59). Functional literacy for the majority rural population is put at only 10 per cent, primary school enrolments were only 26 per cent of the respective age cohorts in the late 1970s and less than 4 per cent of those entering primary school finish the course (Zuvekas, 1978:155–157).

The case against

In spite of these horrific indicators of poverty there are many who believe that official aid should not be given to Haiti, or at least should not have been provided during the period of the Duvalier dictatorships of father and son that lasted from 1957 to February 1986. Three main reasons have led to this conclusion: that the government was corrupt in the extreme; that it was not in the least interested in the plight of the poor; and thirdly, that official foreign aid provided political legitimacy to the regime and because of this, and the provision of external finance, the life of the dictatorship was perpetuated. These problems constitute what the World Bank would term the 'policy environment'. There is considerable evidence to support each of these assertions. We shall look briefly at this evidence before considering the broader question of whether foreign aid should have been cut off.

That Haiti has been characterised by an undemocratic dictatorship of the most extreme form is scarcely in doubt. As Rotberg expresses it, 'Haitians experienced tyranny, rapacity, and an all encompassing disfiguring dictatorship which has surprised all of its third world counterparts in single-mindedness of purpose, tenacity and lack of redeeming social and economic features' (quoted in English, 1984:3). The abuse of human rights has been widespread and enduring, as the International Commission of Jurists and reports to the US Congress, amongst others, have highlighted (Plant, 1987). Besides the army, the Duvaliers created and used widely the *Tontons Macoutes*, a band of semi-trained thugs whose role was to suppress opposition and provide 'law and order' through barbaric methods of killing and torture. Under Francois Duvalier over 50,000 people were killed; under his son, President-for-Life Jean-Claude Duvalier, the killings diminished in number but the regime continued to make 'widespread use of arbitrary arrest, imprisonment without proper trial, ill-treatment and torture' (Prince, 1985:36). One indication of the reign of terror has been the rate of emigration: since 1970 an estimated 20,000 people a year have fled Haiti. One author has estimated that some 85 per cent of skilled and professional Haitians now reside outside the country (Prince, 1985:69). Not only did the Duvaliers appoint all magistrates and judges but for nine months of the year the President ruled the country by personal decree.

Dictatorship and tyranny have been the backdrop for the evolution of an economic system whose benefits have been channelled consistently to a very small and influential elite. In 1982, a Canadian parliamentary committee, after visiting Haiti, called it a 'kleptocracy' in which anything of value was liable to be appropriated by the ruling elite and their officials at every level of the system (quoted in Prince, 1985:8). The economy, as Thoumi explains, functions more through personal connections than anything else: the economy and economic progress are associated not with risk-taking nor are they dependent upon the market mechanism, but rather with a dominant power structure where personal contacts and graft are the fundamental determinants of economic gain. Laws are not applied fairly but rather according to official interpretation (1983:213–17). Lack of concern for the poor or of orientation to their needs is cited frequently in analyses of Haiti's economic development under the Duvaliers. In 1974, for example, a USAID report stated (LeBeau quoted in Zuvekas, 1978:284):

> The greatest single constraint to an effective attack on these problems [of further agricultural development] is the evident lack of concern for the rural population on the part of the urban elites and certain elements of the responsible ministries.

Four years later another USAID report stated (Zuvekas, 1978:279 and 284):[9]

> while there have been some improvements since then, it is our view that government support for agricultural development is still weak and continues to constitute a major constraint . . . it is important to single out as an important constraint the government's role in discouraging production through its direct and indirect support of monopsony power.

More generally, Lundahl, perhaps the most respected economic analyst of Haiti, has recently commented that 'hardly a single author writing on the economy of Haiti has failed to make the observation that the lack of government commitment to the agricultural sector constitutes one of the major constraints to development in Haiti' (1983:273).

It is, however, the degree and extent of corruption that was the most visible sign of the Haitian 'kleptocracy' under the Duvaliers. Of the many instances of overt corruption that have been discovered and documented (and, given the nature of the regimes, these constitute barely the tip of the iceberg) the following capture the flavour of the regimes' practices. Prior to his dismissal as Finance Minister in July 1982, Marc Bazin, a former World Bank official appointed after pressure from Western donors, judged that $15m. a month was being regularly diverted from Haiti for 'extra-budgetary expenses', including to the President's own Swiss bank accounts. Earlier, the US Department of Commerce judged government mis-appropriation in 1977/8 to be valued at $69m., equivalent to 63 per cent of all *recorded* government revenue. This latter emphasis is important, for significant sources of government revenue are not accounted for, including the lucrative taxes obtained by the *Régie du Tabac et des Allumettes* (RTA). The proportion of central government revenues channelled through the Ministry of Finance's budgetary process declined from 53 per cent in 1970–71 to 43 per cent by 1975–6.

More explicit examples of corruption come from monies provided from inter-national agencies. The IMF lost $6m. out of a $20m. standby credit. The Minister of Sports once allotted $2m. for a sports complex that cost $200,000 to build, providing some 29,000 government employees with double salaries and various kickbacks. CIDA cancelled a rural development programme in frustration after half the $17.7m. spent had gone on administration and because half the 700-odd employees on the project's payroll did not actually work for the project. After the project was cancelled the Canadian Auditor-General revealed that in the final year fraudulent payments detected amounted to $110,664, with an additional $127,513 suspected.[10]

The evidence that official aid to Haiti played a role in maintaining the Duvalier regimes in power is less direct but certainly points quite forcefully to that conclu-sion. First, foreign aid constituted a consistently high proportion of government revenue. In the late 1970s and early 1980s, it financed some two-thirds of govern-ment investment. In 1984, official grants and credits totalled $145m. nearly 50 per cent of the value of all imports, having averaged over $110m. a year (net receipts) in the late 1970s and 1980s (DAC, 1986:120); not only have foreign aid funds helped to maintain a steady foreign-exchange inflow, but without these funds the country would have had to take even more notice of IMF conditionality, which it violated consistently in the 1980–86 period (see Burgaud 1986:43–50). Foreign aid also helped the regime indirectly to maintain its oppressive socio-political struc-tures and anti-poverty-focused development practices. For instance, 65 per cent of state funds were spent on state security in the early 1970s, while foreign funds also helped to maintain an extremely low tax regime for the wealthy – according to World Bank data, one per cent of the population receives over 40 per cent of national income yet pays only 3.5 per cent of that income in taxes (Prince, 1986:51; English, 1984:3 and 31).

The dilemma

So much for the evidence of Haiti's extensive poverty, the corruption of the elite-centred dictatorships and the indications that aid funds have assisted in main-taining the regime. There is no doubt that these contrasting realities of the Duvaliers' Haiti provided official aid donors and those supporting aid with an acute dilemma: the depth of the poverty forming the basis for advocating inter-ventionist action by those with resources to help, and the depth of the regime's depravity forming the basis for advocating restraint and withdrawal. The question we wish to pursue here is whether the critics have been correct in advocating a 'no official aid' policy in Haiti over the past 28 years.

If the critics are to have a watertight case upon which to base their conclusion, then it would appear that they need evidence additional to that already provided in the preceding paragraphs. Three broad elements need to be considered: the effect of aid provided on the poor; the effect on Haiti's general politico-economic orientation, and on the poor in particular, of aid withdrawal; and, finally, the likely effects of action beyond the aid relationship by donor governments on the country's development prospects. If the critics can show that the poor have not benefitted from the aid provided, that withdrawal of aid would have had a positive outcome at least in the medium to long term, and that, besides aid withdrawal, political and/or military pressure and/or other action by donor countries would have led to beneficial change in Haiti, then their case would be as watertight as anyone could hope to make. It would also be far more convincing than the case for providing official aid.

While it is certainly true that the evidence available to address these issues is unsatisfactory – both because no systematic country study of aid to Haiti during the Duvalier regimes has yet been carried out and because analyses of 'what might have been' are open to a considerable amount of speculation, in Haiti as elsewhere – it is equally unsatisfactory to hide behind these data inadequacies and use them to argue that until the benefits of alternative policies can be proved the aid option is preferable. We need to examine these three different and crucial aspects of the donor–recipient relationship and on *this* basis attempt to form an overall judgement of the critics' viewpoint. As the discussion in the rest of this section indicates, my own view is that the evidence is inconclusive. Some points decidedly in favour of the aid withdrawal option but other evidence suggests that aid withdrawal and non-aid intervention would not have provided the outcome that both supporters and critics of aid wished to see.

Aid's impact on the poor

While some aid has certainly benefitted some of the poor – and food aid in particular has provided a necessary dietary supplement, especially to the urban poor – it also appears that the overall gains have been minimal, particularly in relation to the effort and money involved. Bilateral aid has been provided predominantly by the United States, and also by Canada, West Germany, France and even Taiwan and Israel. Multilateral aid has been provided by the World Bank, FAO, UNDP, UNICEF and the WHO, while, in addition, well over 700 voluntary aid organisations have been active in Haiti, many, but by no means all, having church links. The distinction between official and voluntary aid has not been as clear-cut as in many other aid-recipient countries, in part because the adverse political conditions led official donors to channel substantial amounts of aid through voluntary agencies or to carry out joint projects with them. Although a number of the large projects have had similar sorts of structural, organisational and impact problems to those experienced in other parts of the world, in Haiti it is particularly noticeable that the voluntary aid agencies have been as frustrated in achieving positive results for their projects as have the official agencies. Thus on this evidence it would seem that a switch from official to voluntary aid, following a supposed official withdrawal, would not have led to a significantly different degree of success in projects oriented to the poor.

The most detailed published account of aid to Haiti is English's 1984 study of Canadian aid flows, partly channelled to voluntary agencies, partly funding joint projects and partly used to support official projects. The overall effects are assessed as profoundly disappointing, with the largest integrated rural development programme cancelled in 1981. Yet some successes were achieved, for example in primary school construction and literacy programmes, in health projects (spring-capping), and agricultural credit and extension. Disappointing results have been especially prevalent in more complex efforts, including an irrigation project and a rural development centre that became over-extended.

On the positive side, English maintains that foreign aid inflow has helped to train and strengthen the hand of development-oriented civil servants vis-à-vis traditional and corrupt ones and that to the extent that aid has required counterpart funds from the government it has increased the government's financial commitment to development (1984:33). However, it needs to be added that in the overall context of Haiti's pre-1986 policies, these gains appear to have been extremely marginal.

The UNDP highlights a number of specific aid initiatives including water projects, land terracing, training institutes, coffee growing, canal and road building, and a new housing project in Port-au-Prince. However, the UNDP's Haiti publication (1982) fails to evaluate project impact and other authors have questioned the level of success of multilateral aid. For example, Zuvekas reports that a recently completed UN soil conservation project was characterised by crumbling terraces (1978:195), Fass (1982) describes in detail the UN water projects in Port-au-Prince which were intended to provide water to the poor but, at great expense, ended up benefiting high and middle income areas, and Prince (1985:72) highlights the concentration of aid in the Port-au-Prince area supporting the elite's economic ventures by bias towards the modern-sector infrastructure, and cites over 200 million francs of French aid used to upgrade the telephone system and runway at Duvalier airport. More generally, some aid agencies have certainly inhibited the potential impact of their programmes by choosing or being forced to work so closely with the corrupt and inadequate administration. For instance, the US strategy has been to 'place maximum possible responsibility on the Haitian government for the selection and design of projects' (Zuvekas, 1978:323), thereby reducing considerably the potential impact of its projects.

The failure of aid is, not surprisingly, acknowledged as at least in part attributable to the adverse political environment which affected official and voluntary aid alike. For example Prince, a supporter of voluntary aid, writes that many NGO projects 'are founded on the principles of encouraging community participation and self-reliance; but in the authoritarian political environment of Haiti, an approach of this kind is not without problems, as is shown by the inclusion of a number of development workers among those arrested in the November 1984 roundup of alleged "subversives" ' (1985:73). However, both Zuvekas and English attribute failures in large measure also to the almost complete absence of co-operative effort and grass-roots organisations, and the lack of incentives to form local groups in the rural areas. And there is certainly evidence of the limited gains made at the local level through co-operation being wiped out by direct action initiated by government servants (English, 1984:114). Whatever the particular reasons for the failures of different projects, there does appear to be widespread agreement both that aid overall has not done much for the poor and also that the prevailing conditions point to little hope that any significantly different outcome could be expected. Yet, and this is important for the aid withdrawal option, the point has also been made that aid has provided a role in helping the situation from deteriorating further. For example, a confidential report from a British NGO with long experience in Haiti states:

On the basis of experience during the 1970s, current levels of aid and methods of assistance are unlikely to do more than slow down somewhat the decline in living standards among the rural population . . . We were awfully good at expressions like 'liberating people from natural and human constraints that would permit them to be masters of their destiny'. It sounds particularly good in French. But these ideas have been dormant among the majority of the people since Independence (1804) and only recently has it been possible to voice such ideas among fairly intimate groups.

But the most telling summary of aid's failures comes from USAID. For instance, a 1982 report of the US General Accounting Office observed that 'the AID program to date has had limited impact on Haiti's dire poverty, and many projects have had less than satisfactory results' (quoted in Pietrodangelo, 1986:18). More detailed is the Zuvekas USAID report which evaluated the long-term efforts of this the most important and influential of all Haiti's aid donors. He concluded (1978:327):

> A significant improvement in the level of living of Haiti's rural poor must be viewed as a very long-term objective. For the medium-term, a reasonable objective would be simply to halt the deterioration in living standards which most rural residents seem to have been experiencing for at least two decades and perhaps much longer . . . It must be admitted that the obstacles to radical socio-economic change in Haiti are formidable; and without such radical changes, improvements in the lives of more rural Haitians will be slow in coming.

Haiti without aid

If aid has performed so poorly in alleviating poverty and changing the government's general orientation, would the country in general and the poor in particular have benefitted more without aid or through wider non-aid pressure or activity? From what has just been said, it does appear that aid has had a positive effect as a holding operation. Thus in the short term it seems that aid withdrawal would have had an adverse effect on poor groups touched by aid projects, especially those in the agricultural, health and food aid areas of intervention.[11] However, even if that point is acknowledged, can a case be made for arguing that aid withdrawal would have had an even greater impact on a greater number of the poor by leading to a change in development policies towards a more direct rural and poverty focus?

Certainly there *is* evidence that various pressures and changes in aid commitments by certain donors did have an effect on policy. At least three times during the Duvalier dictatorships the US either cut off or substantially reduced aid: from 1963 to 1973 (English, 1984:22–24), during the Carter years (at least in the years 1977–9), and more recently under President Reagan just prior to the flight of Jean-Claude Duvalier in February 1986.[12] English argues that after CIDA's withdrawal in 1981 from its massive IRDP, other donors reported better co-operation with the government over their own projects (1984:135), while Burgaud has pointed to positive results of pressure being applied to the government both by individual bilateral donors and by the IMF and the World Bank (1986). These have resulted, at different times, in the following effects: more rigorous accounting methods being applied: financial and wider political and human rights considerations being acknowledged by the government, especially in its 1982 development plan; specific and concrete actions to orient development towards agricultural, environmental and primary health care interventions; and, finally, the appointment of technocratic ministers and some senior officials on the recommendation of external agencies.

However, if these initiatives were intended fundamentally to alter the government's basic orientation, then they certainly failed, for the dictatorship survived for nearly thirty years in spite of the pressures exerted by the donors. Lundahl points to the ineffectiveness of these pressures on the economy by highlighting the case of 'as powerful an organisation as the World Bank [which] has for more than a decade insisted that the accounts of the *Régie du Tabac*, whose funds are used eg for paying the *tonton macoutes* and for other purely political purposes be opened to public inspection [but] without any trace of success' (1983:276). On the other hand, some observers believe that the reforms announced by the government in the Spring of 1985 and supported with considerable additional bilateral aid inflows from, especially, the US, Canada, France and West Germany, hastened the end of the Duvalier regime (Burgaud, 1986:42). If this interpretation is correct it does suggest that aid intensification rather than withdrawal was a factor contributing to political change. But can it not be argued that a total withdrawal of all bilateral and multilateral aid in a co-ordinated multi-donor effort would have led to more substantial political change far sooner and in a manner which would have brought greater gains for Haiti's poor and deprived majority?

While this is certainly implicit in the writings of some authors, for example Pierre-Charles (quoted in Lundahl, 1983:273-4), there are serious doubts about the effect that a total and sustained withdrawal of all official or even bilateral official aid would have had upon development prospects. These doubts are centred around the absence of a viable alternative form of government and of an organised mass-based opposition movement, the depth of the poverty, and the long history of Haiti's failure for over 150 years to create an alternative power-base to the narrow elite-focused one which prevailed even prior to the Duvalier regimes.

There is little to suggest that sustained aid withdrawal would have led to a peasant-initiated revolution or to changes within the elite which would have made a significant impact on development prospects. A central problem, referred to by many analysts, is the absence of local grass-roots organisations and a tradition of local democracy which could provide, and in other circumstances has provided, a catalyst for mass mobilisation of the poor peasantry. What the Haitian case appears to show is that the lack of grass-roots organisation is not only a primary cause of aid failure but a principal reason why aid withdrawal would have been unlikely to lead to a mass political movement resulting in either substantial reformist or revolutionary socio-economic change. In this context, aid withdrawal would most likely have led to the government increasing taxes on the poor to make up the revenue shortfall. As for change initiated at the top, there is little indication both from present political alignments among the elite and also from historical experience that alterations in the power structure at the apex of society would materially help the poor and lead to the fundamental re-orientation of the economy upon which equalising development prospects critically depend.

These conclusions are supported by most analysts of the situation in Haiti. For example, the confidential British NGO report quoted earlier observes that:

> far from producing widespread unrest and rural militancy, deepening poverty is likely to reinforce existing self-interested and opportunistic survival strategies at the expense of collective action unless the latter can offer tangible, large, immediate and comparatively secure prospects of individual benefit.

This outcome was likely to prevail because, as Lundahl explains, there is no group in existence able or capable of initiating the mobilisation of the masses which, in turn, could lead to a change in government. 'No revolutionary change of government is imminent' (1983:274). For his part, English stresses the increased taxation effect of aid withdrawal (1984:31):

> There is certainly ample room to improve the efficiency of domestic resource

mobilization in Haiti. However the historical record and current reality do not recommend isolation as the best way to achieve these changes. Instead, it seems likely that continued international neglect in the 1970s would only have reinforced the tradition of taxing the rural economy for the benefit of the elite without any reciprocal attention to the former's needs.

Lundahl is equally pessimistic about a change at the top leading to a re-orientation away from 'more of the same'. He writes that 'if any opposition exists within the top echelons of the power structure which in the future may form a new government, there is no reason to expect that the latter will be more prone to implement change than any other government Haiti has had since 1820' (1983:278). And in his more recent study, published less than a year before the Duvalier era ended in February 1986, Prince concludes that 'whatever the outcome of the next few years' power struggle in Port-au-Prince, the real problem will remain: the destitute millions of Haitians, for whom no one has any solutions, or offers any hope' (1985:82).

There is, finally, the view that aid withdrawal should have occurred because providing official aid is said, willy-nilly, to have provided international political recognition of the Duvalier regime and implicitly, at least, approval of it and its policies. The case, however, for Haiti, as for most other countries, is less clear-cut because diplomatic arrangements are themselves frequently ambiguous.

Regime approval is characterised by establishing full diplomatic relations between countries, although diplomatic relations do not necessarily imply approval of a regime – Canada has an ambassador in Pretoria, although it is widely known to be opposed to the apartheid government of South Africa. Furthermore, it is not necessary (although in practical terms it is certainly helpful) to have an overt political mission in a country in order to carry out non-political activity. For instance, South Africa flies the flag with a trade mission in Harare, although Zimbabwe is a virulent critic of Pretoria and no political relationship exists between the two countries.

In the world of diplomacy, perceptions of action and inaction are all-important. For Haiti, to the extent that having a bilateral aid programme was widely perceived as providing political legitimacy to the Duvalier regime (and at least indirectly assisting its maintenance), then the case for, first, altering that perception and, if that failed, for aid withdrawal would have been strong. Certainly the US and in the early 1980s Canada were accused of providing political legitimacy, and these accusations did, at least in the case of Canada, play a role in lowering its overt profile in the country. But bilateral aid is not the only means of providing assistance. Official aid channelled multilaterally or through voluntary agencies circumvents the political/diplomatic problems that can arise with bilateral aid. Thus, even in these instances, this particular argument for total aid withdrawal is not convincing. Indeed, in the case of Haiti, there has been an extremely high involvement of multilateral agencies and of voluntary agencies supported by bilateral aid funds precisely because of the diplomatic recognition problems. While figures for voluntary aid are not available, the multilateral share of official aid grants was 55 per cent of all official grants in the period 1969-82, and it exceeded 96 per cent in the years 1971–3 (English, 1983:25).

It is these circumstances which not only question the benefits that would have been achieved by a sustained withdrawal of official aid but which also raise doubts about the positive impact of other, political and military, initiatives that could have been taken to remove the Duvaliers from power. Of course, advocating external destabilisation efforts to dislodge regimes deemed unacceptable is fraught with problems – not that that prevents the superpowers, in particular, from attempting and even succeeding in overthrowing a variety of governments in the Third World. Not only do such initiatives open up the real possibility of greater inter-state instability because they challenge the principle of state sovereignty and, for the West, because they undermine the principle of democratic self-determination, but they are also always highly controversial. Never has it happened that any single Third World regime's behaviour has so incensed the international community that all other governments have advocated and actively sought its elimination by force.[13] Recent examples of international efforts to replace Third World governments, in Afganistan, Angola, Chile, Grenada, Lesotho and Nicaragua, for example, have heightened rather than lessened international tension, while singularly failing to alter domestic policy fundamentally in favour of the poor.

These issues caution against advocacy of internationally-induced interventionism. However, even if the international implications of such action can, for the moment, be set aside, it can still be asked whether external efforts to dislodge the Duvaliers would have solved the essential development problems of the country. At least at one point in time they were attempted. In 1963, the US tried and failed to dislodge the Duvaliers when President Kennedy sided with President Bosch of the Dominican Republic in his initiative to overthrow the Haitian regime. That failure was in no small measure due to the combination of the absence of an alternative government-in-waiting, the lack of any democratic tradition among Haiti's people, and the corruption pervading the government's administration. And it has been the continued absence of these essential pre-conditions for creating a viable alternative to the Duvaliers that has led most analysts to be extremely sceptical of the merits of externally-induced political and military interventionism to establish a quick and clean alternative which would provide hope and material gain for Haiti's poor. While there seems little doubt that the US was involved in the removal of Jean-Claude Duvalier in February 1986 (Washington announced his departure a week early), with its declaration of aid withdrawal in January providing an additional push-factor, the underlying cause of his leaving Haiti had more to do with internal factors – the killing of students and probably church-initiated or supported demonstrations and unrest in the army – than with external pressures.

While, at the time of writing, it is still too soon to judge the effects of the end of Duvalierism, the early signs are that the country's development problems are very far from being addressed, let alone solved.[14] It is true that the abrupt disarming of the *Tontons Macoutes* was a positive step in reducing the prevailing climate of terror; however, the influence of the Duvalierists still remains strong in the country and also in the expanded army, while the administration is still corrupt, incompetent and largely ineffective. Yet some of the country's sternest anti-Duvalierists have concluded that while the new government 'is not the most effective government, there is no immediate alternative'.[15] And the prospects for economic development remain bleak, with poverty likely to continue for years to come and modern-sector expansion constrained by severe balance-of-payments problems and low expectations of export expansion (Burgaud, 1986:53–4). Even acting president General Namphy has stated that Haiti is 'on the brink of anarchy'.[16]

Conclusions

The Haiti case provides an interesting case study for the aid debate because of the extent of widespread and deep poverty in a country whose government has been characterised by extreme corruption and a radical lack of interest in improving the well-being of the poor. The preceding discussion indicates not only that foreign aid has been of extremely limited value but also that the nature of the government and its administration lies at the root of aid's ineffectiveness. Mistakes have certainly been made by donors in different aid projects but it is extremely doubtful that, without these, the overall impact would have been much different. The discussion also reveals the complexity of the aid relationship and the many and different factors which need to be incorporated into an assessment of what aid agencies should or could do in such a hostile environment. There are no easy or quick answers available as historical, social, economic and political elements interwine in an intricate web of cause and effect. Although the discussion has certainly suffered from a lack of information and evidence from which to draw firm conclusions, the analysis of Haiti under the Duvaliers does suggest that the case for aid withdrawal is far from proven: some of the poor would certainly have suffered over the short term with no guarantee of significant medium- or long-term improvements. However, on the political front especially, it does appear that the donors could have done more than they did: by using the joint power they undoubtedly had to better effect, by exposing more clearly the extent of corruption and maladministration that existed under Duvalierism, and by acknowledging the difficulties they continued to experience because of these factors.

What the Haitian case suggests above all else is that *no* general and clear policy on aid presents itself: neither aid insertion nor aid withdrawal (plus or minus non-aid initiatives by the donors) were likely to make a significant and far-reaching difference to either general development prospects or the alleviation of poverty, given the constraints present in the country's political economy. Paradoxically, while aid's critics advocate aid withdrawal when political and institutional factors act to inhibit its effectiveness, the Haitian case tends to suggest that it is precisely these inhibiting factors which would have been likely to frustrate the benefits anticipated from donors adopting a policy of withdrawal or external intervention. And if this conclusion can be drawn from the extreme example of Haiti, there would appear to be grounds for believing that similar conclusions could be drawn in other instances such as Egypt, the Philippines and Pakistan at different stages of their respective histories.[17]

Notes

1. Some also warn about the unique nature of developments in the countries they have analysed. This is particularly striking in the case studies of Taiwan and South Korea where cultural and historical aspects are considered essential to understanding the development process but specific to the countries under consideration. See Steinberg (1984), Scitovsky (1985) and Jacoby (1966).
2. The exception is probably Jacoby's 1966 study of Taiwan, considered in some detail below.
3. It should be stressed again that this discussion of different country experience provides little more than a rapid overview of the highlights of the studies that have been carried out. Those interested in a more thorough analysis should consult the studies referred to in the text and especially the more recent ones prepared for the Cassen (1986) study.
4. Government of India, Seventh Five-Year-Plan, (1986), Vol. I, p.4.
5. World Bank, *World Debt Tables, External Debt of Developing Countries 1984–85, Edition*, The World Bank, Washington, 1985, p.256-7.
6. Most of the figures quoted here and elsewhere on South Korea's economic performance and aid flows are taken from Steinberg, 1984.
7. Of course 'disappointing' is a relative term. A real growth rate of 3 per cent would hardly be

considered disappointing in the African context. It is, in South Korea, the stark contrast with the 1960s and 1970s that makes the early aid-intensive period appear such a disappointment.

8. For a recent discussion of these policy interventions see Leudde-Neurath (1982) and Scitovsky (1985). Reference can also be made to a comment by Sen (1983:13), cited earlier, that no country outside the socialist block ever came near to such a measure of control over its economy's investible resources as South Korea.

9. Not without importance, a draft of the Zuvekas manuscript containing these highly critical comments was submitted to the Haitian Minister of Agriculture and his staff prior to publication, so, one can safely assume, they contain a singularly restrained view and interpretation of the government's development policies.

10. These examples of corruption are taken from English (1984), Prince (1985), Zuvekas (1978) and Plant (1987).

11. It is, of course, not being argued here that food aid has been without substantial problems. For instance, Pietrodangelo quotes a 1983 study suggesting that between 5 and 50 per cent of the food sent to Haiti by the US is illegally sold on the black market (1986:18).

12. *The Economist*, 8 February 1986, p.42.

13. Neither did it happen in the case of Hitler's Germany, although this was, uniquely, an instance of superpower agreement. As for Third World countries, the Non-Aligned Movement of over 100 states has never even come close to approving external policies to remove a fellow Third World government from power, no matter how outrageous its policies. Perhaps the case of South Africa provides an exception here, although South Africa itself is not a member of the Non-Aligned Movement. Yet by no means all Third World states have advocated external military methods to remove the Pretoria regime and, of course, the US's recent policy of 'constructive engagement' has been extremely limited (many would argue ineffective) in pressurising Pretoria into setting in motion substantial political change. See, for instance, *Mission to Southern Africa, The Commonwealth Report*, Report of the Commonwealth Group of Eminent Persons appointed under the Nassau Accord on Southern Africa, London, Commonwealth Secretariat, June 1986.

14. *The Financial Times*, 24 April 1986.

15. A report from the voluntary agency CARE – nearly nine months after the fall of the Duvaliers highlights increasing poverty in the country. *The Independent*, 9 October 1986.

16. *The Guardian*, 6 June 1986.

17. Palmlund draws similar conclusions in arguing against the withdrawal of Swedish aid from Ethiopia (in Frühling 1986:123).

PART IV
Retaking the Middle Ground

18 Retaking the Middle Ground

This has been a long book both to read and to write. Its length reflects in large measure the wide array of issues that need to be considered when judging the merits of providing foreign aid. But even now, there will doubtless be those who consider the treatment of some of these issues an oversimplifacation or that some of the most critical aspects of the debate have been omitted. In this final chapter it is not the intention to go over ground already covered but rather, briefly, to draw some of the main threads together and make some concluding remarks about the role of official aid in today's world.

The case for aid

Two initial sets of conclusions can be drawn from the preceding discussion. The first, singularly unexciting, is that, in spite of efforts to prove otherwise, there is nothing automatic about the link between aid and development: an *a priori* positive or negative relationship between the two cannot be derived theoretically, while the evidence of aid in practice remains at present inadequate to provide a certain guide to the interrelationship. Theoretical debates about aid and development and the analysis of aid in practice have sometimes over-extended themselves or, more commonly, been misused by implying, or attempting to imply, that aid's effects are more predictable in general terms than they are or than we are able to deduce that they are. But this does not mean that they have been without value even if the criticism of them here has at times appeared unduly harsh. Their usefulness has lain in pinpointing and, in practice, extending our understanding of the sub-sets of factors which influence the broad aid and development relationship. Advances that have been made at both the macro- and micro-levels highlight the enormous gaps in knowledge that still exist. The hope is that future work will initially help to isolate better the *range* of factors which affect the relationship and then perhaps eventually clarify the *degree to which* particular factors affect it and the extent to which they themselves are or are not capable of being influenced.

But the fact that there is nothing automatic or pre-ordained about the link between aid and development does not mean that nothing more can be said. Indeed, the thrust of the arguments presented in this book, and *contra* the critics, is that, in spite of all the inadequacies of the debate at the theoretical and practical level, the case for providing official aid can be made, qualified though it has to be.

The second main general conclusion therefore is that there is a role for official aid, based on addressing the needs of the poor in the Third World, and that, while aid is by no means the necessary or even the crucial ingredient for development, it can assist in the alleviation of poverty, directly and indirectly.[1] In part, this conclusion is based on theoretical considerations, with different elements of social science theory indicating that on the basis of not unrealistic assumptions poverty-alleviating development can be achieved. In part, it is based on the evidence that is available which suggests that aid has managed to fulfil this role, although by no means at all times and in all circumstances. In part, too, it is based on the evidence, partial though it is, that failures have led to lessons being learned, resulting in improved performance – although, again, not at all times and in all circumstances. And, finally, it is based on the available evidence which fails to convince that, as a general rule, alternative strategies which exclude aid lead in theory or have led in practice to more rapid improvements in the living standards of the poor than have been achieved with aid. In short, the effort of trying to assist the poor of the Third World by providing official aid is justified, despite its inadequacies and the less than perfect environment in which it is given and received.

Beyond this level of generalisation more specific blanket statements about the role of aid cannot easily be sustained for four interrelated reasons: because of the very different social, political, economic, institutional, ecological, climatic and cultural circumstances and differing internal and external links prevailing in the different regions, countries and societies of the Third World; because of the high degree of ignorance that still exists in theory at both the micro- and macro-levels concerning, at bottom, the dynamics of the process of development and, more specifically, the precise effects of aid in that process; because of the limited knowledge we have in practice of the effects of aid; and, finally, because unpredictable factors external to particular aid projects and programmes, but most commonly tending to disrupt the positive effects expected, can and do change aid's impact. If, however, one more generalisation can be made it would be that, where poverty is at its most acute and the need for help at its greatest, the effects of aid intervention are likely to be the least capable of being predicted, monitored and evaluated.

What this book has set out to show is that attempts to draw firmer and more general radical conclusions about official aid, and to argue, for instance, the general case for no aid, aid withdrawal, aid reduction or, importantly, the case for aid regardless of the circumstances surrounding its insertion or its use, are wrong and misleading. Particular emphasis has been placed on the arguments and conclusions of the critics. The available evidence and the state of theoretical insight reveal that the extreme critics of both left and right are wrong to assert either that aid can never help or that development will proceed better without aid. And it is in the rejection of these views that the moral case for official aid finds its justification.

The moral case is rooted in two elements: the obligation for governments (either directly or through the medium of the multilateral agencies they support) to assist those in extreme need in the Third World, and the weaknesses of alternative moral starting-points which reject needs-based criteria or maintain that the moral order stops at national borders. The moral case is sustained not so much because aid can be proved always to succeed in helping to alleviate Third World poverty but because alternative methods of helping find no general support and because the need to help is so urgent. However, two additional points should be stressed. First, that the moral case for providing aid is only rarely, if ever in practice, an *a priori* non-consequentialist imperative; hence it does depend upon the effects of the funds inserted. Thus to the extent that aid intervention fails to achieve its desired objectives the moral case is itself intricately bound up with ways to improve its poverty-focused impact. Secondly, that because aid constitutes only one element in the wider relationship between donor and recipient, the moral case for providing it (and improving its effectiveness) is complementary to and never a substitute for other non-aid moral-based action which would result in improvements for the poor of the Third World.

Even if these conclusions as a foundation for the case for aid are singularly cautious, their implications for contemporary debate about official aid are important. Historically, proponents of aid for development have been extremely vocal in stating the case for aid rather than in arguing through the reasons for their advocacy. In recent years, criticism first from the radical left and more recently from the radical right has muted if not silenced some of aid's supporters, as the arguments have been presented, become influential and rarely been rigorously challenged. This book has set out to refute these extreme criticisms and, to the extent that it has been successful, has re-established the case for aid more firmly in its intellectually respectable middle-ground position.

As writers and commentators fall over themselves in their eagerness to say dramatic – and more conclusive – things about aid, they continually veer to extremes in maintaining that aid is all-important or, alternatively, that it is of little or no importance. In either case, the reality of the complexity of development issues and the inadequate data-base for arriving at such firm conclusions about the effect of aid in general is lost.

Whereas the analysis of this book points to an array of different factors that have an influence on aid's impact, there continues to be an outpouring of literature that, purporting to be rigorously based, maintains that one or two factors hold the key to progress or, more often, the lack of it. Some pinpoint past colonial relationships, some industrialised country policies, some politics, some ecological factors, some the lack of market forces, and some corruption as the key factor inhibiting aid effectiveness. While all these factors can and frequently do have a bearing on development and aid's impact, and some are clearly of more importance in some countries than in others, evidence is almost entirely lacking to conclude that any one constraint in isolation constitutes such an overwhelming influence that aid cannot assist or that non-aid policies would be preferable, especially across a range of countries.

One sub-theme of the book has been to trace through the different critical approaches to aid which place particular emphasis on the political constraint. The discussion suggests, quite forcefully in places, that political factors, while certainly important, cannot be treated in isolation: some aid can be effective in quite an adverse political environment, while aid can often fail when the political factors are favourable. Similarly, the view popular in some political circles that 'freeing the market' or relying exclusively on market forces will provide *the* answer to development and should constitute the sole or even dominant context in which aid insertion is to be judged is equally misleading. The conclusion is not that political factors or market forces are unimportant; of course they are important but so are ecological factors in dam building, institutional factors in large and complex projects, and prospects for world trade growth in aid associated with structural adjustment initiatives. The essential point is that, while aid would certainly perform best if all constraints were removed, this only applies to cloud-cuckoo-land; the evidence tends to suggest that no single constraint is either immutable or an absolute barrier to progress.

One recent example of such single-factor mystification comes from an article and subsequent correspondence in the London *Times* at the time of the UN Special Session on Africa's economic crisis in May/June 1986. In a feature article, Professor Ayittey proclaimed that *the* cause of Africa's economic and agricultural decline 'can be found in government policies of exploitation of peasant farmers'.[2]

The article drew a response with contributors lauding the writer for having the courage to pinpoint this underlying truth about contemporary Africa. Of course, equally incorrect would have been an article proclaiming that *the* cause of Africa's plight has been the lack of aid that donors have provided to Africa. Both views have elements of the truth (to the extent that we are arrogant enough to believe we know the truth, the former may well be the more important factor, although firm evidence is lacking) but neither view in isolation is either correct or likely to advance attempts to provide a realistic and durable solution to Africa's problems. The fundamental error of both the critics and the supporters is to identify constraints and, especially in the excitement of discovering new constraints, over-emphasise their importance, often to the extent of eclipsing other factors relevant to the development process. Perhaps the most amazing aspect of the aid debate over the past thirty years is the way in which apparently upright and sensible academics, analysts and politicians have led the world to believe or wish to believe that the aid relationship can be simply derived and conclusions simply drawn.

Rejecting the perspectives of the radical critics and retaking the middle ground in the aid debate has equally cutting implications for donors and their supporters. One element concerns aid quantity, the other aid impact. The aid quantity debate has been focused most sharply upon the amounts richer Western nations provide in aid, calculated most commonly as a percentage of GNP or, sometimes, as a proportion of total donor government expenditure. In particular much has been made of whether donor countries have contributed aid amounting to 0.7 per cent of their GNP or agreed to move to this target figure. While there is clearly political merit in using such a device to lobby for an increase in quantitative aid allocations so as to isolate the poor performers on this score, it needs to be recognised that the relationship between this figure and the needs of Third World countries is entirely spurious today, even if its origins can be traced back to heroic if highly questionable attempts to link Western donor aid levels to Third World needs in the early 1960s. Furthermore, it has the added disadvantage of creating the belief among voters that aid flows and the achievement of these targets constitute the principal means available to the donors of improving the welfare of the poor in the Third World. Equally obfuscating is the recent tendency among some donors of playing down the quantitative aspects of aid flows and arguing that it is the quality of aid that is all-important. Besides neatly ignoring the interrelationship that exists between quality and quantity – a trickle of water into a dry hot riverbed will sink without trace into the ground, only a large amount will cause the river to flow – raising the quality issue brings us back to the key issue of aid impact.

There is no doubt that the manner in which most official donors present their aid efforts suggests that the aid they provide is effective in accelerating Third World development and in helping to alleviate poverty, even if problems are more readily acknowledged in the 1980s than they were in previous decades. However, as the previous chapters have indicated, the evidence upon which this predominantly positive impression is based remains largely unproven and in some instances simply does not exist in a reliable form. The view that donors are not being entirely honest in the image they project of their aid efforts is confirmed by the manner in which some large and influential donors (including Britain) keep adverse evaluations very close to their chests.

The present state of knowledge simply does not allow such an uncritical judgement of donor aid intervention to be made. And it is here that the donors face an acute dilemma. The public support that they have for their aid initiatives is built in part upon the belief that the aid they provide *is* effective – and rightly so to the extent that the moral basis for providing aid depends upon its achieving the objectives for which it is given. If donors and aid lobbyists were to reveal the extent of their ignorance and the far from easily predictable outcome of aid's impact, especially the impact beyond project-specific interventions, then they fear that the level of support they would be able to muster for their aid programmes would decline. Even if lack of predictability about aid's lasting impact, the hostile environment, and uncertainty about how best to promote Third World development lie at the root of aid's mixed results, it is easy to see how this less than optimal performance would be picked up by a donor government's political opponents to apportion blame on account of political and technical incompetence.

But there is an added twist to the dilemma. To the extent that donors attempt, on often flimsy evidence, to maintain that on the whole aid does work reasonably well, then ammunition is provided to the critics who, without too much digging around, are able to counter these positive assertions with the evidence of aid projects and programmes that have gone wrong or whose positive outcome can easily be questioned. Thus donor bias supporting the generalisation that aid works not only inaccurately portrays our present state of knowledge, it also indirectly plays into the hands of those who argue that in general aid does not work and who even more misguidedly use this conclusion to maintain that therefore it *cannot* work. One of the things this book has attempted to do is to show that the case for aid and the case against the critics can be sustained without aid's mistakes and uncertainties being concealed. Indeed, to the extent that the argument in the first part of this paragraph is correct, both the case for official aid and wider support for it would be increased by acknowledging more openly the valid criticisms made by aid's opponents.

Strengthening the case for aid

To argue, however, that there is a case for providing aid is not the same as arguing that all is well with official aid. As has been pointed out in different parts of this book, there are still serious problems with official aid at both the general and specific level which reduce its effectiveness. Remedying these inadequacies will certainly improve its impact and, in so doing, will undoubtedly strengthen the case for providing it. We shall end by pointing to some of the areas where improvements need to be made, while recognising that this itself is a vast subject and acknowledging that other recent studies, most particularly Cassen (1986), have addressed this question in detail.

Increasing aid quantities

Based on the needs of the poor in the Third World, there is a strong case for arguing that official aid flows should be increased above their present and projected levels. While this is not the place to provide a detailed justification for this assertion, a few macro-indicators concentrating particularly on low-income countries provide the background context to support this view.

We can begin with the quantitative assessment of living standards. The *per capita* income of all (35) low-income developing countries was $300 a year in 1982 (at 1981 prices, see DAC, 1985:265). The population of these countries amounted to 2,335 million in 1983, some 50 per cent of the total world population (World Bank, 1985:174-5). Of course, not all the people in these countries are equally poor and some are, without a doubt, extremely wealthy; but these figures convey, even if in crude terms, the magnitude of the poverty problem. Contrast them with an average *per capita* income in the OECD countries of $9,740, over 30 times as high. Not without relevance, too, is the fact that in the period 1970–82 average *per capita* income had risen by over $2,000 in real terms in the OECD countries, an increase 25 times as high as that achieved in the low-income countries of the world (DAC, 1985:265).

While the poverty figures establish a *prima facie* case for providing help, and the contrasting figures of OECD wealth at least a strong indication that resources from these countries are available for assistance, it is far from easy to pinpoint with accuracy what level of support should be forthcoming from different donors in the form of concessional aid. However, it is not necessary to be over precise on this score to be able to argue that concessional aid funds should be increased over and above current and projected levels. As all official donors acknowledge that their aid has been provided to help Third World development (and thus directly or indirectly to alleviate poverty), if it can be shown that Third World needs have increased over the recent past and/or are likely to increase in the future, that aid funding has not risen or will not rise to meet these increased needs, and that alternative funding sources will not bridge the gap, then on this basis the case for increasing aid flows can be made.

Sub-Saharan Africa (SSA) is a region which provides the most forceful argument for an increase in official aid. As the 1986 World Bank report, *Financing Adjustment with Growth in Sub-Saharan Africa 1986–90*, pithily puts it, 'low-income Africa is poorer in 1986 than it was a generation ago in 1960'. *Per capita* income of low-income SSA countries (covering 75 per cent of the population of the region) grew by 1.3 per cent a year in the period 1965–73, stagnated in the period 1973–80 and fell by 2.1 per cent a year in the period 1981–4 (World Bank, 1985:148). What is more, future prospects are bleak even on optimistic scenarios. Domestic savings and investment levels have fallen dramatically from 15 per cent and 18 per cent respectively in the mid-1970s to 6 per cent and 11 per cent in 1984 (World Bank 1986:10), while the debt ratio (external debt outstanding over annual export earnings) doubled in the five years to 1983 to some 200 per cent and has stayed at that level ever since (Brau, 1986:2). In the period 1980–85 only 15 out of the 44 SSA countries were able to service their debts promptly; for the low-income countries of the region new commercial borrowings have come to a halt and all have extremely limited creditworthiness. Moreover, debt-servicing commitments are set to rise over the next few years even in the absence of new commercial borrowing contracted.

Contrast this deterioration in living conditions with recent aid disbursement figures for SSA. According to the most recent DAC estimates (although, as discussed exhaustively in Part II above, the accuracy of these figures can be questioned), total net disbursements of official development assistance to SSA rose by only 3.4 per cent between 1981 and 1984 at current prices, suggesting an absolute fall in total disbursements over this most difficult period (DAC, 1986a:20). Looking to the future, over and above current official aid commitments and with favourable assumptions for foreign investment and private capital inflows, the World Bank judges that low-income Africa will need an additional $2.5 billion a year in concessional flows and debt relief in the period 1986–90 merely to restore import capacity *per capita* to 1980–82 levels, let alone raise these levels to previous peaks achieved in the 1960s and 1970s (36–8). This figure is 40 per cent higher than the DAC figures record for total oda disbursed to low-income African countries in 1984.

For other low-income countries outside Africa some indicators provide a more positive picture. For example, average growth rates were 6.4 per cent a year in the period 1980–85, higher than the annual average of 5.2 per cent in the period 1973–80. However, the 1973–80 growth rates were lower than the 6.0 per cent achieved in the period 1960–73 and, more significantly, over the next ten years they are expected to fall to a high of 5.3 per cent and a low of 4.6 per cent, according to World Bank projections (World Bank, 1985:138). And these low figures are themselves based on aid figures 35 per cent higher than DAC projections of likely aid flows to the end of the decade (see Development Committee, 1986:79). Also of importance, the World Bank judges that the current-account deficit of low-income Asian countries will rise from $3.2 billion in 1984 to a high of $15.7 billion or a low of $9.4 billion by 1990 (1985:142). Contrast these figures with a decline in total oda channelled to low-income Asian countries from 34 per cent of all oda in 1960/61 to 24 per cent in 1982/83 (DAC, 1985:121) and a fall in net oda receipts *per capita* in non-African low-income countries of 20 per cent in current prices from 1980 to 1983 (Development Committee, 1986:90). As a proportion of their GNP, official aid disbursements to India constitute 0.9 per cent, and to China 0.2 per cent. These two countries account for 75 per cent of the total population of all low-income countries, yet they currently receive only 9 per cent of all official aid (DAC, 1985:121 and World Bank, 1985:174). While the numbers in absolute poverty in India have hardly declined, gross disbursements of official aid to India have fallen by 20 per cent in real terms in the decade from the early 1970s to the early 1980s (DAC, 1985:124).

The progressive decline in economic performance in most countries of sub-Saharan Africa and the increasing problems facing most other low-income countries in the coming decade contrast sharply with trends in aggregate official aid flows. In the period 1970–71 to 1983–4, total DAC oda grew at an annual rate of 3.5 per cent (101). However, in the latter part of this period the trends of all official aid have been less consistent, with total aid falling by 8 per cent between 1980 and 1983, according to Burki and Ayres (1986:6). The trends in aid to most low-income countries have been even more disturbing. Excluding India and China, net aid disbursements to all low-income countries declined from $6,736m. in 1979 to $5,663m. in 1982 at current prices (a drop of 16 per cent) and, although rising to $6,432m. in 1984, this was still, again at current prices, 4.5 per cent lower than that achieved in 1979 (DAC, 1986:23).

Looking into the future, DAC forecasts point to a significant fall in aggregate aid levels to some 2 per cent over the next few years (DAC, 1985:103). However, even these figures now look optimistic because aid flows from DAC's largest donor, the United States (accounting for 30 per cent of DAC aid in 1983–4), could well decline significantly following Congressional cuts associated with the Gramm-Rudman-Hollings Act. As regards British aid, too, the future will be less rosy than the aggregate DAC forecasts would suggest. Net British official aid was forecast by the Treasury to increase at 0.4 per cent a year in real terms in the 3-year period 1983–4 to 1985–6 (calculated from HM Treasury, 1986, 6 and 48). By the end of 1988 net British aid will have declined substantially in real terms over a 10-year period, having fallen by 6.1 per cent each year from 1978–9 to 1983–4 (DAC, 1985:101). Total aid expansion is also likely to be seriously checked, or even halted, because the fall in the oil price will lead to significant cuts in OPEC aid, which in 1983–4 accounted for 13.5 per cent of all aid and 18 per cent of all DAC aid (DAC, 1985:93). As the cautiously-worded 1985 DAC Chairman's report (written before the Gramm-Rudman-Hollings Act in the US and the 1986 fall in oil prices) explains (1985:170):

Although aid flows are forecast to rise in real terms, this is likely to be at a lower rate than the rather buoyant expansion of the past decade. At the same time, a considerable number of borrowers are in economic and financial trouble, with debt problems that seem likely to continue in many cases . . . The situation, then, is hardly a comfortable one.

There is, of course, no guarantee either that these slower rises in aggregate aid flows will be channelled to the low-income countries or, alternatively, that the aid funds currently channelled to the less deserving upper middle-income developing countries, some 24 per cent of all aid funds in 1982/3 (122), will be diverted to those low-income countries where poverty is deeper and more extensive. That aid is not currently allocated with need as the fundamental criterion has been high-lighted recently by Lipton, who points out (1986:5):

in 1982, 34.1 per cent of allocable aid went to countries containing 2.7 per cent of the population of the developing world – most in middle-income countries; they enjoyed $102 of net aid disbursements per person in that year. The remaining 3.3 billion people of the Third World each received $5.6.

To sum up, trends in economic performance in low-income countries, in aid levels and in allocations and the expected contraction over the next few years in quantitative flows at a time of increasing economic constraint provide the context for arguing the case for both a significant expansion in aggregate aid funds from the donors and for a change in the targeting of allocations more towards those low-income countries that contain so many of the Third World's poor. Indeed, as governments base their moral arguments for providing aid on the needs of Third World countries, then the logic of these arguments is that aid flows should rise when economic circumstances in the Third World worsen. Yet at present, and to the extent that economic recession in the industrialised world leads to recession in the Third World, the linking of donor aid and commitments to a proportion of GNP precisely reverses this relationship: for if donor country GNP actually falls, so, too, on this basis for granting it, will aid flows

Improving effectiveness

Besides quantitative increases there is an additional need for donors to commit aid funds for a far longer time period than has frequently been the practice. There is clearly a stark contrast between a project that can commonly take over six years to proceed from initial approval to completion and aid commitments agreed on an annual or biennial basis. While many donor governments determine overall public expenditure levels on an annual basis, they do place these within longer-term spending and income frameworks. For ongoing aid projects in particular, it would thus seem possible to plan for specific spending programmes to extend to at least a three- or four-year time horizon. This would help planning in recipient countries and contribute to greater aid effectiveness.

Of course, as has been repeatedly stressed, aid is not the exclusive answer to the problems of Third World poverty and increasing quantitative flows is no guarantee, in isolation, that funds allocated will be used productively. We now turn to a series of policy recommendations which, if implemented, should, together with an increased quantity of resources, contribute to improving aid effectiveness.

Both the theoretical discussion in Part II and the analysis of the evidence of aid in practice in Part III pinpoint the nature of recipient-government policies as a fundamental determinant of aid effectiveness at both the micro- and macro-levels. A checklist of all factors playing a role in improving aid effectiveness would be long, and would include the following: a supportive political, institutional, and administrative environment at the local and national levels; socio-economic policies that encourage resource-use efficiency and the greater utilisation of unused or underutilised resources; resource-use co-ordination, especially, in our context, the co-ordination of aid resources; harmonisation of policies that in a consistent manner assist the poor both directly and indirectly through encouraging the expansion of the national economy; outlining both the long-term and specific roles that different forms of aid could be expected to play in the development process and, equally importantly, the short-term and 'fire-fighting' role that aid could play in addressing emergency or unexpected needs and easing crucial bottlenecks; and, finally, detailing a consistent set of policies on the environment, technology use and transfer, and domestic manpower resources (to name just three crucial variables) into which aid resources of donors could be effectively and consistently inserted.

Recognising that each of these different factors plays a role in improving aid effectiveness – although in various ways and with varying intensities in different aid-recipient countries – is an advance but also, if taken in isolation, of limited policy application. It is an advance because it highlights the complexity of the aid relationship and so cautions both against oversimplified solutions and unjustified optimism that, in the absence of a series of favourable recipient-country policies, aid will make a crucial difference. Yet it is of limited policy applicability because pinpointing a host of policy variables does not get us very far in deciding what precisely should be done in particular situations of persistent and widespread aid ineffectiveness.

There are, however, two important policy conclusions to be drawn. The first is that recipient countries have a crucial role to play in drawing up consistent and effectively co-ordinated policies that spell out in some detail the gap-filling role that aid funds are expected to play in promoting development at the national and local levels and in the short and long term. It thus seems appropriate that they should all be encouraged to do so. The second is that donors as a group have a role to play through pooling their experiences in attempting to pinpoint with greater accuracy at the country-specific level those constraints which impede aid effectiveness and, if possible, in quantifying the importance of particular constraints and the scope for eliminating or reducing them.

If these minimal actions were taken, this would be a major advance on present practice which, from the viewpoint of both donors and recipients, still tends to be a very unco-ordinated and hit-or-miss affair. It would also have the added advantage across countries of highlighting those aid recipients where few, if any, attempts are being made to reduce or remove constraints impeding aid effectiveness or to learn with donors the opportunities for increasing effectiveness. If levels of aid flows were then, even in some very general manner, to be related to attempts to remove or reduce major constraints, the greater visibility of recipient-country obduracy would itself have a favourable impact in lessening policy blockages by rewarding those administrations clearly working to alleviate such constraints. Placing emphasis on policy co-ordination and consistency of *recipient*-country policies does not mean that donor countries have no role to play in helping to improve the broad policy environment in aid-recipient countries; indeed donors could well have a crucial role in devising, drawing up and helping to implement such a policy framework. It does suggest, however, that donor-exclusive or donor-dominated initiatives, executed in isolation from the recipient-country decision-making process or attempted in opposition to the recipient's aims and objectives, will tend to have only a limited chance of success, particularly over the longer term.

While a favourable policy environment in recipient countries has rightly been highlighted in recent years as a crucial factor in improving aid effectiveness, donor weaknesses and failings are also important not least because they can exacerbate the problems in recipient countries frustrating aid's greater impact. There is no doubt that one major inhibiting factor here is the manner in which donor self-interest (political, strategic, commercial) influences the direction and destination of aid resources, the quantity of funds allocated to different recipients over time, and the form in which aid is provided. Especially where these interests are dominant they can and do considerably lessen the developmental impact of official aid, either directly through the 'misuse' of aid funds or indirectly through the pursuit of mutually conflicting policies, for instance in the case of trade protectionism. In recent years, the United States, Japan, West Germany and Britain have all increased the impact of their (different) goals of self-interest to the detriment of aid's developmental impact.

There is no doubt, too, that donor unwillingness to co-ordinate their respective aid efforts constitutes a major problem, in spite of increasing recognition and even explicit acknowledgement of this particular problem. This lack of donor co-ordination has a series of adverse effects on aid effectiveness. For instance, it leads to a lack of project or programme harmonisation, resulting in resource-use inefficiency, to inappropriate or inconsistent technological interventions, to project or programme rigidity when changed circumstances would suggest an adaptation or switching of particular initiatives, and to an overloading of aid administrations in the recipient countries.

Exhortation to improve co-ordination and reduce conflicting self-interested policies, while certainly needed, appears to have had little success in leading to improved donor performance in practice. Two more specific suggestions could help. One is to obtain donor agreement for evaluation of all donor projects and aid interventions to be carried out in each recipient country (with recipient-country permission and assistance if desirable) in a manner similar to that attempted in the Intergovernmental Task Force Project for a limited number of aid recipients. Ideally such an initiative should be an ongoing exercise in each country and funded by the donor community, but if an initial country-evaluation study were carried out in each recipient nation then a major advance would have been made. *Inter alia*, other weaknesses of present aid efforts would be likely to be exposed. These would include; the desirability of rehabilitating past aid or state-initiated projects as opposed to new ones; the need to incorporate 'island' projects better into broad national development efforts and to improve sustainability through an examination of recurrent cost funding problems; and, finally, the highlighting of those projects or programmes where particular donors have a comparative advantage over others and where their involvement should therefore be encouraged.

The present lack of donor co-ordination arises in part because donors, while accepting that lack of co-ordination leads to problems for the recipient, fear that increased co-ordination will lead to their individual influences being reduced or their less than fully altruistic motives being exposed. The suggestion of instituting recipient-country evaluations of the impact of all aid interventions in each aid-receiving country will not lessen this fear, but it provides a manner of approach that major donors will find it increasingly difficult continuously to block.

The second suggestion concerns the need to co-ordinate the aid initiatives of donor countries more consistently with those other economically related policies which have a bearing on the development of aid-recipient countries. Problems here are also many and often complex; they would include the over-commercialisation of aid, the dumping of excess food surpluses, and what the Cassen study has termed 'asymmetrical liberalism' – providing aid on the condition that liberal economic policies are implemented in the aid-recipient country, while failing to liberalise donor domestic policies which adversely affect recipient-country development prospects. Policy inconsistency at the donor end could be lessened, or at least made more visible, if the donor institutions responsible for aid matters either widened their concerns to become development agencies as opposed to aid-dispensing agencies or, minimally, if they had separate departments responsible for monitoring the effects on aid-recipient countries of all donor policies affecting their development. Relatedly, increased pressure should be brought to bear upon recalcitrant donors to evaluate their commercially linked aid projects and programmes and to publish the results of these analyses.

Most official agencies set up to dispense aid and monitor aid performance are, in fact, termed 'development' agencies rather than simply 'aid' agencies – the UK's ODA, the US AID, Sweden's SIDA, Canada's CIDA etc. – but their function tends to exclude analysis of the broad development effects of all donor policies. Thus providing them with a specific development analysis role would at least be consistent with their supposed orientation and function. It would be naive to expect that the political, economic and financial forces in donor countries which create conflicts in policy between furthering specific interests at home and the needs of the Third World poor can be eliminated, at least in the foreseeable future. But to have an institution whose function is to monitor these conflicts and inconsistencies in policy would be to promote further open and honest government, on which Western democracies pride themselves and which they wish to export to the Third World.

Moving on to the evaluation process of aid projects and programmes, there are a series of specific recommendations to be made which would help to improve aid effectiveness. First, there is a need to incorporate political, social and institutional factors into both the process of project selection and evaluation. At present, there is a vast gap in knowledge of the effects of these elements on aid effectiveness which requires urgent attention, in the overall context of increasing rather than decreasing efforts to reach the poor directly and indirectly through a variety of projects co-ordinated between bilateral agencies, between bilateral and multi-lateral agencies and, where desirable, through the use of effective NGO networks. There is, too, a need to incorporate an analysis of the effects of aid on the poor into *all* evaluation studies and into the project-appraisal stage. Too little is known of the effects of different types of intervention on the poor and the room for improving effectiveness in this regard. As a first step in improving knowledge here, a poverty-related focus should be incorporated into all appraisals and evaluations. In addition, specific projects need always to be appraised and selected with explicit attention being paid to how they fit into the development objectives of the recipient country and the projects of other donors, and why these particular initiatives have been selected vis-à-vis rejected alternatives.

To reduce the subjective bias in evaluations, consideration should also be given, especially in controversial areas of intervention, to employing at least two evaluators, each with a different perspective, to assess these projects, in part independently and in part together. Of related concern, while it is commendable that outside experts are now employed as a matter of course in evaluating official aid projects, it is surprising that far less use seems to be made of outside expertise in project selection and initial appraisal. There would appear to be great merit, for instance, in incorporating the views of country-specific specialists in determining national priorities for aid intervention as a matter of course.

Much evaluation material is critical of the failure to learn from the lessons of the past. While there is clearly good reason for maintaining an evaluation department distinct and separate from the on-going administrative work of an aid (development!) agency, there is also a need to institutionalise the learning process into all current and future aid initiatives. One particular requirement is for agencies regularly to distribute their evaluation reports to bilateral and multilateral agencies in other countries; at present this appears to be seldom done. Finally, there are convincing arguments to support the recommendation that the results of evaluations should be shared far more widely with the general and interested public than currently is the case in most West European donor nations, including Britain.

There is little doubt that these latter proposals will involve the aid agencies in increased expenditure. This, however, can readily be justified from a number of standpoints. As agreement has already been reached, at least by all DAC donors, that evaluation of aid is important, it follows that resources should be made available to ensure both that it is carried out effectively and that the lessons derived from the evaluations are learned. Perhaps more importantly, however, the process of evaluation is a critical tool in understanding how aid can be made more effective, how the different constraints inhibiting its greater impact can be isolated, and wherein precisely lies the room for manoeuvre. Thus the policy of more widely disseminating the analyses of donor aid impact not only increases public understanding of the complexities of the aid relationship but in so doing undermines the stance of those critics who maintain that as a general rule policies other than aid intervention will more quickly reduce Third World poverty.

These and the other suggestions listed above to improve aid effectiveness do not just happen: ideas may motivate action for change but on their own they remain sterile. In the donor countries, just as in the recipient countries, political pressures and forces are at work: to maintain the *status quo*, to lobby for self-interested policies which conflict with those aimed at increasing aid levels and implementing donor-initiated measures designed to improve aid effectiveness, and, from the left and the right, to argue specifically for a downgrading of the aid effort. Thus if both the quantity of official aid is to rise and its effectiveness be enhanced a crucial requirement is for the aid lobby, both within government and without, to increase its own effectiveness in presenting the case for aid and widening its constituency among other influential groups and the general voting public. One way of doing this is to take seriously the views of the critics and to weave one's way through the different and varied objections they raise to the aid relationship. If at the end of such an exercise, providing and, indeed, increasing official aid to help the world's poor can be justified convincingly, then the pro-aid case will emerge vindicated.

Notes

1. Readers who have followed the course of the argument throughout the book will be ready for me to insert a caveat here to the effect that one could devise a set of constraints whereby, in particular circumstances, aid could provide the crucial ingredient for development to proceed.
2. *The Times*, 27 May 1986, p.12.

References and Bibliography

Achilli, M. and Khaldi, M. (eds) (1984), *The Role of the Arab Development Funds in the World Economy*, London, Croom Helm.

Adelman, I. and Morris, C.T. (1973), *Economic Growth and Social Equity in Developing Countries*, Stanford, Stanford University Press.

Ady, P., 'External factors in the savings propensities of developing countries', (mimeo).

Ahluwalia, M.S. (1975), 'Income Inequality: Some Dimensions of the Problems' in Chenery *et al*.

Aiken W., and Follette H.La. (eds) (1977), *World Hunger and Moral Obligation*, Englewood Cliffs, NJ, Prentice Hall.

Alavi, H. (1972), 'The state in post-colonial societies', *New Left Review*, No. 74, July–August.

All Party Parliamentary Group on Overseas Development (APPGOOD) (1985), *UK Aid to African Agriculture*, London, ODI.

Anand, S. and Kanbur, S. (1981), 'Inequality and development: a critique', paper presented to Symposium on 'From Income Distribution Research to Income Distribution Policy in Ldcs', Paderborn, April.

Apthorpe R. and Krahl A. (eds) (1986), *Development Studies: Critique and Renewal*, Leiden, E.J. Brill.

Areskong, K. (1969), *External Borrowing: Its Role in Economic Development'*, New York, Praeger.

Arnold, W. (1985), 'Aid for Trade debate', *Development Business*, No. 182, 16 September.

Arrighi, G and Saul, J.S. (1979), *Essays on the Political Economy of Africa*, New York, Monthly Review Press.

Arrow K.J. (1978), 'Nozick's Entitlement Theory of Justice', *Philosophia*, No. 7.

Ayres, R.L. (1983), *Banking on the Poor: The World Bank and World Poverty*, Cambridge, MIT Press.

Bachrach, P. (1980), 'Evaluating development programmes: a synthesis of recent experience', in Miller.

Banks, F.E. (1974), 'Economic development, foreign aid and neoclassical growth: a comment', *The Journal of Development Studies*, Vol. 11, No. 1, October.

Barry, B. (1973), *The Liberal Theory of Justice*, Oxford, Clarendon.

Bauer, P.T. (1971), *Dissent on Development*, London, Weidenfeld and Nicolson.

Bauer, P.T. (1974), 'Debt cancellation for development?', *National Westminster Bank Quarterly Review*, November.

Bauer, P.T. (1977), 'Why should the West feel guilty?', *The Daily Telegraph*, 23 and 24 May.

Bauer, P.T. (1979), 'Foreign aid viewed differently', *Aussenwirtschaft*, September.

Bauer, P.T. (1981), *Equality, the Third World and Economic Delusion*, London, Weidenfeld and Nicolson.

Bauer, P.T. (1982), 'Aid and its effects', *Encounter*, November.

Bauer, P.T. (1983), 'Why we should close our purse to the Third World', *The Times*, 11 April.

Bauer, P.T. (1984a), 'Foreign aid: what is at stake?', *The Public Interest*, Summer 1982, reprinted in Meier.

Bauer, P.T. (1984b), *Reality and Rhetoric*, London, Weidenfeld and Nicolson.

Bauer, P.T. (1985), 'Foreign aid: rewarding impoverishment?', *Swiss Review of World Affairs*, October.

Bauer, P.T. and O'Sullivan, J. (1978), 'Foreign aid for what?', *Commentary* 66(6), December.

Bauer, P.T. and Yamey, B. (1981), 'The political economy of foreign aid', *Lloyds Bank Review*, October.

Beard, P.W. and Thompson, B.P. (1983), *Mauritius Electricity Generation Project*, London, ODA EV301.

Beckman, D. (1986), 'The World Bank and Poverty in the 1980s', *Finance and Development*, Vol. 23, No. 3.

Beenstock, M. (1980), 'Political econometry of ODA', *World Development*, Vol. 8, February.

Beitz, C.R. (1975), 'Justice and International Relations', *Philosophy and Public Affairs*, No. 4.

Beitz, C.R. (1979), *Political Theory and International Relations*, Princeton NJ, Princeton University Press.

Beitz, C.R. (1981), 'Economic Rights and Distributive Justice in Developing Societies', *World Politics*, Vol. 33, April.

Bell, C., Hazell, P. and Slade, R. (1982), *Project Evaluation in Regional Perspective: A Study of an Irrigation Project in Northwest Malaysia*, Baltimore, Johns Hopkins University Press.

Bell, C.L.G. (1974), 'The political framework' in Chenery *et al.*

Berg, A. (1985), 'Improving nutrition: the Bank's experience', *Finance and Development*, Vol. 22, No. 3, June.

Bernstein, H. (ed.) (1973), *Underdevelopment and Development*, London, Penguin.

Berry, A. (1985), 'On Trends in the Gap Between Rich and Poor in Less Developed Countries: Why We Know So Little', *Income and Wealth*, Series 13, No. 4, December.

Bertsch G., (ed.) (1982), *Global Policy Studies*, Beverly Hills, Sage in Co-operation with the Center for Global Policy Studies, University of Georgia.

Bhagwati, J.N. (1970), *Amount and Sharing of Aid*, Overseas Development Council, Washington DC, Monograph Series No. 2.

Bhagwati, J.N. and Grinols, E. (1975), 'Foreign capital, dependence, destabilisation and feasibility of transition to socialism', *Journal of Development Economics*, Vol. 2, No. 2, June.

Bienefeld, M. (1980), 'Dependency in the eighties', *IDS Bulletin*, Vol. 12, No. 1, December.

Bienefeld, M. (1981), 'Dependency in the newly industrialising countries (NICS): towards a reappraisal', in Seers.

Bienefeld, M and Godfrey, M. (1982), *The Struggle for Development: National*

Strategies in an International Context, Chichester, J. Wiley.

Billings, M. (1985), *The Recurrent Cost Problem: Or Is There Life After EOPs?*, REDSO/WCO, Abidjan, June.

Bird, G. and Gutman, P. (1981), 'Foreign aid, the issues', *National Westminster Bank Quarterly Review*, August.

Bird, R.M. (1981), 'Exercising policy leverage through aid: a critical study', *Canadian Journal of Development Studies*, Vol. 2, No. 2.

Black L.D. (1968), *The Strategy of Foreign Aid*, Toronto, Van Nostrand.

Blitzer, C.R., Clark, P.B. and Taylor, L. (1980), *Economy-Wide Models and Development Planning*, London, Oxford University Press.

Blomstrom M. and Hettne, B. (1985), *Development Theory in Transition: The Dependency Debate and Beyond – Third World Responses*, London, Zed Press.

Booth, D. (1985), 'Marxism and development sociology: interpreting the impasse', *World Development*, Vol. 13 No. 7, July.

Bornschier, V., Chase-Dunn, C. and Rubinson, R. (1978), 'Cross-national evidence of the effects of foreign investment and aid on economic growth and inequality: a survey of findings and a reanalysis', *The American Journal of Sociology*, Vol. 84, No. 3, November.

Bowles, T.S. (1978), *Survey of Attitudes Towards Overseas Development*, London, HMSO.

Brau, E. (1986), 'African debt: facts and figures on the current situation', Washington, IMF, February (mimeo).

Bridger, G. (1984), 'Are rural development projects failing?', London, Crown Agents, Agricultural Services Unit.

Brittan, L. (1984), 'The moral case for the market economy', Address to the Bow Group, House of Commons, 6 December.

Browning, R.A. (1984), 'The work of the Projects and Evaluations Committee in ODA', in Cracknell.

Bruton, H.J. (1969), 'The two-gap approach to aid and development: comment', *The American Economic Review*, No. 59, June.

Bull, H. (1977), *The Anarchical Society: A Study of Order in World Politics*, New York, Columbia University Press.

Burgaud, J.M. (1986), *The New Caribbean Deal: The Next Five Years*, London, Economist Intelligence Unit, Special Report No. 240, March.

Burki S.J. and Ayres, R. (1986), 'A fresh look at development aid', *Finance and Development*, Vol. 23, No. 1, March.

Burki, S.J. and ul Haq, M., (1981), 'Meeting basic needs: an overview', *World Development* Vol. 9, No. 1, February.

Byres T.J. et al. (1972), *Foreign Resources and Economic Development: A Symposium on the Report of the Pearson Commission*, London, Frank Cass.

Calvocoressi, P., 'Peace, The Security Council and The Individual' in Berridge, G. and Jennings, A. (eds), *Diplomacy At The United Nations*, London, Macmillan (forthcoming).

Cardoso, F.H. and Faletto, E. (1979), *Dependency and Development in Latin America*, Berkeley, University of California Press.

Carty, R. and Smith, V. (1981), *Perpetuating Poverty – The Political Economy of Canadian Foreign Aid*, Toronto, Between the Lines.

Cassen, R.H. (1983), 'North and South – economic links and their implications', Address to the Annual Meeting of the British Association for the Advancement of Science, Brighton, August 1983, (mimeo).

Cassen, R.H. and Associates (1986), *Does Aid Work?*, New York and Oxford, Oxford University Press.

Chambers, R. (1978), 'Project selection for poverty-focused rural development: simple is optimal', *World Development*, Vol. 6, No. 2, February.

Chambers, R. (1983), *Rural Development; Putting the Last First*, London, Longman.

Chambers, R. (1985), 'The market for public office: why the Indian State is not better at development', *World Development*, Vol. 13, No. 4, April.

Chaudhuri, P. (1986), 'Aid and poverty', *IDS Bulletin*, Vol. 17, No. 2, April.

Chenery, H. (1979), *Structural Change and Development Policy*, New York, Oxford University Press.

Chenery, H. (1983), 'Interaction between theory and observation in development', *World Development*, Vol. 11, No. 10, October.

Chenery, H. et al. (1974), *Redistribution With Growth*, London, Oxford University Press.

Chenery, H. and Strout, A.M. (1966), 'Foreign assistance and economic development', *The American Economic Review*, Vol. LVI, September.

Chenery, H. and Syrquin, M. (1975), *Patterns of Development 1950–1970*, London, Oxford University Press.

Chilcote, R.H. (1984), *Theories of Development and Underdevelopment*, Boulder and London, Westview Press.

Christensen, C. et al. (1981), *The Developmental Effectiveness of Food Aid in Africa*, New York, Agricultural Development Council.

Clausen, A.W. (1986), 'Adjustment with growth in the developing countries: a challenge for the international community', address to Commonwealth Secretariat, London, March (mimeo).

Clay, E.J. (1979), 'Food aid and food policy in Bangladesh', *Food Policy*, Vol. 4, No. 2, May.

Clay, E.J. (1985), 'The 1974 and 1984 floods in Bangladesh: from famine to food crisis management', *Food Policy*, Vol. 10, No. 3, August.

Clay E.J. and Schaffer, B.B. (eds) (1984), *Room for Manoeuvre: An Exploration of Public Policy in Agricultural and Rural Development*, London, Heinemann.

Clay, E.J. and Singer, H. (eds) (1983), 'Food aid: food for thought', *IDS Bulletin*, Vol. 14, No. 12, April.

Clay, E.J. and Singer, H. (eds) (1984), 'Food aid and development cooperation: the importance of policy', Paris, OECD, (mimeo).

Clay, E.J. and Singer, H. (1985), *Food Aid and Development Issues and Evidence*, World Food Programme, Rome, Occasional Papers No. 3, September.

Cline, W.R. (1975), 'Distribution and development: a survey of the literature', *Journal of Development Economics* Vol. 1, No. 3.

Cohen, J.M., Grindle, M.S. and Walker, S.T. (1985), 'Foreign aid and conditions precedent: political and bureaucratic dimensions', *World Development*, Vol. 13, No. 12, December.

Colclough, C. (1982), 'Lessons from the development debate for Western economic policy', *International Affairs*, Vol. 58, No. 3, Summer.

Cole, K., Cameron, J. and Edwards, C. (1983), *Why Economists Disagree: The Political Economy of Economics*, London, Longmans.

Commission on International Development (Pearson) (1969), *Partners in Development*, London, Pall Mall Press.

Commission on Security and Economic Assistance (Carlucci) (1983), *A Report To*

The Secretary of State, Washington, House of Foreign Affairs Committee Hearing, 16 February.

Conlin, S. (1984) *The Prodac Project Peru: An Evaluation of ODA Support to the Projecto de Desarrollo Agropecuario de Cajarmarca, 1974–82*, London, ODA EV242, June.

Cracknell, B.E. (1984a), *The Evaluation of Aid Projects and Programmes*, London, ODA.

Cracknell, B.E. (1984b), *Evaluation of ODA's Co-financing Aid with IBRD for Cargo-Handling Equipment at Port Sudan*, London, ODA EV344, October.

Crosswell, M. (1981), *Growth, Poverty Alleviation and Foreign Assistance*, AID Discussion Paper No. 39, Washington DC, Agency for International Development.

Crouch, R.L. (1973), 'Economic development, foreign aid and neoclassical growth', *The Journal of Development Studies*, Vol. IX, No. 3, April.

Cubitt, V.S. and Riddell, R.C. (1974), *The Urban Poverty Datum Line in Rhodesia: A Study of the Minimum Consumption Needs of Families*, Faculty of Social Studies, University of Rhodesia.

Dacy, D.C. (1975), 'Foreign aid, government consumption, saving and growth in less developed countries', *The Economic Journal*, Vol. 85, No. 339, September, pp. 548–561.

Dalton, G. (1976), *British Aid Tractors in India: An Ex-post Evaluation*, London, ODM, EV36.

Daniel, P., Green, R.H. and Lipton, M. (1985), 'A strategy for the rural poor', *Journal of Development Planning*, No. 15, April.

Dasgupta P. and Ray, D. (1985), 'Inequality, Malnutrition and Unemployment: A Critique of The Competitive Market Mechanism', Cambridge, October (mimeo).

Dawson, A. (1985), 'In defence of food aid: some answers to its critics', *International Labour Review*, Vol. 124, No. 1, January–February.

De Kadt, E. (1980), 'Some Basic Questions on Human Rights and Development'. *World Development*, Vol. 8, No. 2, February.

De Silva, L. (1983), *Development Aid: A Guide to Facts and Issues*, Geneva, Third World Forum.

Dervis, K., de Melo, J. and Robinson, S. (1981), 'A general equilibrium analysis of foreign exchange shortages in a developing economy', *The Economic Journal*, Vol. 91, No. 364, December.

Development Assistance Committee (DAC), *Development Cooperation*, Paris, OECD, various years.

Development Assistance Committee (DAC) (1984), *Geographical Distribution of Financial Flows to Developing Countries*, Paris, OECD.

Development Assistance Committee (DAC) (1985), *Twenty Five Years of Development Cooperation, A Review: Efforts and Policies of the Members of the Development Assistance Committee*, Paris, OECD.

Development Assistance Committee (DAC) (1986a), *Geographical Distribution of Financial Flows to Developing Countries 1981–1984*, Paris, OECD.

Development Assistance Committee (DAC) (1986b), *Evaluation Methods and Procedures: A Compendium of Donor Practice*, Paris, OECD.

Development Committee of the World Bank and the International Monetary Fund on The Transfer of Real Resources to Developing Countries, (1986), *Aid for Development: The Key Issues*, Development Committee Pamphlets No. 8, Washington.

Devitt, P. (1978), *The Role of Sociological Factors in Four ODM Projects*, London, ODM EV101, November.

Dower, N. (1983), *World Poverty Challenge and Response*, York, Ebor Press.

Dowling, J.M. and Hiemenz, U. (1983), 'Aid, savings and growth in the Asian region', *The Developing Economies*, Vol. XXI, No. 1, March, pp. 3–13.

Dowling, J.M. and Hiemenz, U. (1985), 'Biases in the allocation of foreign aid: some new evidence', *World Development*, Vol. 13, No. 4 April.

Duncan, A. and Mosley, P. (1985), 'Aid effectiveness: Kenya case study', Study commissioned by the Task Force on Concessional Flows, Oxford and Bath, (draft/mimeo).

Eberstadt, N. (1985), 'The perversion of foreign aid', *Commentary*, Vol. 79, No. 6, June.

Economists Advisory Group (1984), *Evaluation of Selected Appropriate Technology Projects*, London, ODA EV325, February.

Ehrhardt, R. (1983), *Canadian Development Assistance to Bangladesh*, Ottawa, North-South Institute.

Eicher, C.F. (1986), *Transforming African Agriculture*, The Hunger Project Papers No. 4, January.

Elzinga, A. (1981), *Evaluating the Evaluation Game: On the Methodology of Project Evaluation, with Special Reference to Development Cooperation*, Sarec Report, Stockholm, Sarec, RI.

English, E.P. (1984), *Canadian Development Assistance to Haiti*, Ottawa, North-South Institute.

Eshag, E. (1971), 'Foreign capital, domestic savings and economic development: comment', *Bulletin of the Oxford Institute of Economics and Statistics*, Vol. 33, No. 2, May.

Ezechiel, H. (1986), 'Food aid in sub-Saharan Africa', MADIA, Washington, The World Bank, (draft, mimeo).

Faaland, J. (1983), *Does Foreign Aid Reach the Intended Beneficiaries?*, Bergen, DERAP Publications No. 139, April.

Faaland, J. (1984), 'Norwegian aid and reaching the poor', *Development Policy Review*, Vol. 2, No. 1, May.

Faaland, J. (ed.) (1981), *Aid and Influence: The Case of Bangladesh*, London, Macmillan.

Fass, S. (1982), 'Water and politics in Haiti', *Development and Change*, Vol. 13, No. 3, July.

Fei, J.C.H. and Paauw, D.S. (1965), 'Foreign assistance and self-help: a reappraisal of development finance', *Review of Economics and Statistics*, Vol. 47, August.

Ferguson, C.C. (1979), 'Global Human Rights: Challenges and Prospects', *Denver Journal of International Law and Policy*, No. 8, Spring.

Fertado, C. (1971), *Development and Underdevelopment*, Berkeley, University of California Press.

Fishkin, J.S. (1982), *The Limits of Obligation*, New Haven, Yale University Press.

Fishlow, A. (1985), 'The state of Latin American economics' in Inter-American Development Bank, *Economic and Social Progress in Latin American External Debt: Crisis and Adjustment*, Report.

Food and Agricultural Organisation (FAO) (1983), *Fighting Rural Poverty: FAO's Action Programme for Agrarian Reform and Rural Development*, Rome, FAO.

Food and Agricultural Organisation (FAO) (1984), *How Development Strategies Benefit the Rural Poor*, Rome, FAO.

Food and Agricultural Organisation (FAO) (1986), *Food Supply Situation and Crop Prospects in Sub-Saharan Africa: Special Report*, Rome, FAO, April.

Forss, K. (1985), *Planning and Evaluation in Aid Organisations*, Institute of International Business and The Economic Research Institute, Stockholm School of Economics.

Frank, A.G. (1969), *Latin America, Underdevelopment or Revolution*, New York, Monthly Review Press.

Frank, A.G. (1978), *Dependent Accumulation and Underdevelopment*, London, Macmillan.

Frank, A.G. (1981), *Crisis in the Third World*, London, Heinemann.

Freeman, P.D.M. (1985), 'Food aid', in ODA (1985a).

Friedman, M. (1970), 'Foreign economic aid: means and objectives', *Yale Review*, No. 47, 1958, reprinted in J. Bhagwati and R.S. Eckaus (eds), *Foreign Aid*, London, Penguin.

Fruhling, P. (ed) (1986), *Swedish Development Aid in Perspective*, Stockholm, Almqvist and Wiksell International.

Fryer, S. (1981), *Food for Thought: The Use and Abuse of Food Aid in the Fight Against World Hunger*, Geneva, World Council of Churches.

Garcia-Zamor, J.C. (1985), *Public Participation in Development Planning and Management: Cases from Africa and Asia*, Boulder, Westview.

Garcia-Zamor, J.C. and Mayo-Smith, I. (1983), 'Administrative reforms in Haiti: problems, progress and prospects', *Public Administration and Development*, Vol. 3, No. 1, January–March.

Gasper D. (1986), 'Distribution and Development Ethics', in Apthorpe and Krahl.

Girrbach, B. (1986), 'Success and failure of development; German agencies discuss project aid', *Development and Cooperation*, No. 2, March/April.

Gittinger, J.P., Leslie, J. and Hoisington, C. (eds) (1985), *Food Policy: Integrating Supply Distribution and Consumption*, Washington, Economic Development Institute and The World Bank.

Godfrey, M. (1980), 'Editorial: is dependency dead?', *IDS Bulletin*, Vol. 12, No. 1, December.

Goppers, K. et al. (1986), *Elephants Don't Rust: An Evaluation of SIDA-Supported Forestry Development and Forestry Industry in Laos*, Stockholm, SIDA.

Gorgens, E. (1976), 'Development aid – an obstacle to economic growth in developing countries', *The German Economic Review* Vol. 14, Nos. 3–4.

Goulet, D. (1983), 'Obstacles to World Development – An Ethical Reflection', *World Development*, Vol. 11, No. 7.

Goulet, D., and Hudson, M. (1971), *The Myth of Aid: The Hidden Agenda of The Development Reports*, New York, IDOC and Orbis.

Green, R.H. (1986), 'Food, hunger, poverty and famine in sub-Saharan Africa: the inhuman face of failed development', Brighton IDS, (mimeo).

Griffin, K. (1970), 'Foreign capital, domestic savings and economic development', *Bulletin of the Oxford University Institute of Economics and Statistics*, Vol. 32, No. 2, May 1970, and reply in Vol. 33, No. 2, May.

Griffin, K. (1972), 'Pearson and the Political Economy of Aid' in Byres.

Griffin, K. (1978), *International Inequality and National Poverty*, London, Macmillan.

Griffin, K. (1984), 'On misreading development economics', *Third World Quarterly*, Vol. 6, No. 2, April.

Griffin, K. and Enos, J.L. (1970), 'Foreign assistance: objectives and consequences', *Economic Development and Cultural Change*, No. 18, April.

Griffin, K. and Gurley, J. (1985), 'Radical analyses of imperialism, the Third World and the transition to socialism', *Journal of Economic Literature*, Vol. XXIII, No. 3, September.

Griffin, K. and Khan, A.R. (1978), 'Poverty in the Third World: ugly facts and fancy models', *World Development*, Vol. 6, No. 3, March.

Grinols E. and Bhagwati, J. (1976), 'Foreign capital, saving and dependence', *Review of Economics and Statistics*, Vol. 58, November.

Gualti, U. (1978). 'Effects of capital imports on saving and growth in less developed countries', *Economic Inquiry*, Vol. 16.

Gupta, K. (1975), 'Foreign capital inflows, dependency burden and saving rates in developing countries; a simultaneous equation model', *Kyklos*, No. 28.

Gupta, K. and Islam, M.A. (1983), *Foreign Capital, Savings and Growth: An International Cross-Section Study*, Dordrecht-Holland, Reidel Publishing Company.

Gwyer, G.D. and Morris, J.C.H. et al. (1984), 'Some findings from key ODA evaluations in selected sectors: natural resources', in Cracknell.

Haavelmo, T. (1965), Comment on 'The Rates of Long-Run Economic Growth and Capital Transfer from Developed to Underdeveloped Areas' in Study Week on *The Econometric Approach to Development Planning*, Amsterdam, North Holland Publishing Company.

Hahn, F. (1973), 'The winter of our discontent', *Economica*, Vol. XL.

Hahn, F. (1981a), 'Preposterous claims of the monetarists', *The Times*, 28 April.

Hahn, F. (1981b), review of M. Beenstock, *A Neoclassical Theory of Macroeconomic Policy*, in *The Economic Journal*, Vol. 91, No. 364, December.

Hahn, F. (1982), 'Reflections on the invisible hand', *Lloyds Bank Review*, No. 144, April.

Hahn, F. (1984), *Equilibrium and Macroeconomics*, Oxford, Blackwell.

Hahn, F. and Matthews, R.C.O. (1964), 'The theory of economic growth: A Survey', *The Economic Journal*, No. 296, December.

Haig, A. (1981), *Security and Development Assistance*, Statement before Senate Foreign Relations Committee, 19 March, United States Department of State, Bureau of Public Affairs, Washington DC, Current Policy No. 264.

Hart, J. (1975), *Administering an Aid Programme in a Year of Change – A Personal Diary*, Overseas Development Paper No. 3, London, HMSO, February.

Hart, J. (1978), *The Rights of Man*, Overseas Development Paper No. 18, London, HMSO, October.

Hawkins, E.K. (1970), *The Principles of Development Aid*, London, Penguin.

Hayek, F.A. (1976), 'The Mirage of Social Justice', Volume II of *Law, Legislation and Liberty*, London, Routledge and Kegan Paul.

Hayter, T. (1971), *Aid as Imperialism*, London, Penguin.

Hayter, T. (1981), *The Creation of World Poverty: An Alternative View to the Brandt Report*, London, Pluto.

Hayter, T. and Watson, C. (1985), *Aid: Rhetoric and Reality*, London, Pluto.

Healey, J.M. (1971), *The Economics of Aid*, London, Routledge and Kegan Paul.

Healey, J.M. and Clift, C. (1980), 'The development rationale for aid re-examined', *ODI Review*, No. 2.

Helleiner, G.K. (1978), *World Market Imperfections and the Developing Countries*, Washington, Overseas Development Council, Occasional Paper No. 11.

Heller, P.S. (1975), 'A model of public fiscal behaviour in developing countries: aid, investment and taxation', *The American Economic Review*.

Helm, D. (1986), 'The Economic Borders of The State', *Oxford Review of Economic Policy*, Vo.2, No. 2.

H.M. Treasury, (1963), *Aid to Developing Countries*, London, HMSO, Cmnd 2147.

H.M. Treasury (1986), *The Government's Expenditure Plans 1986–87 to 1988–89 Vol. II*, London, HMSO.

Hewitt, A. (1982), 'Aid and growth' in P. Maunder (ed.), *Case Studies in Development Economics*, London, Heinemann.

Hewitt, A and Kydd, J. (1986), 'Malawi: Making Effective use of Aid Resources', *IDS Bulletin*, Vol. 17, No. 2, April.

Hicks, N. (1979), 'Growth and basic needs: is there a trade-off?', *World Development*, Vol. 7 No. 10/11, November/December.

Higgins, B. (1968), *Economic Development*, London, Constable.

Higgott, R. (1983), *Political Development Theory: The Contemporary Debate*, London, Croom Helm.

Higgott, R. (1985), 'The state in Africa: some thoughts on the future drawn from the past', in Shaw and Aluko.

Hill, P.G. (1981), *Synthesis of Rural Road Evaluations*, London, ODA EV311, December.

Hirsch, F. (1977), *Social Limits to Growth*, London, Routledge and Kegan Paul.

Hirschman, A. (1958), *The Strategy of Economic Development*, New Haven, Yale University Press.

Hirschman, A. (1965), 'Obstacles to development: a classification and a quasi-vanishing act', *Economic Development and Cultural Change*, Vol. 13, July.

Hirschman, A. (1967), *Development Projects Observed*, Washington, Brookings Institution.

Hirschman, A. (1982a), 'Rival interpretations of market society: civilising, destructive or feeble?', *Journal of Economic Literature*, December.

Hirschman, A. (1982b), *Shifting Involvements: Private and Public Action*, Princeton, Princeton University Press.

Hirschman, A. (1982c), 'Rise and Decline in Development Economics', in M. Gersovitz *et al.* (eds), *The Theory and Experience of Economic Development*, London, George Allen and Unwin.

Hoare, P. (1984), 'Improving the effectiveness of agricultural development: a case study from North Thailand, *Manchester Papers on Development*, Issue No. 10, November.

Hodson, H.V. (1984), 'Sovereignty Demoted', *The Round Table* No. 290.

Hoffman, S. (1981), *Duties Beyond Borders*, New York, Syracuse University Press.

Hoksbergen, R. (1986), 'Approaches to evaluation of development interventions: the importance of world and life views', *World Development*, Vol. 14, No. 2.

Holtham, G. and Hazlewood, A. (1976), *Aid and Inequality in Kenya: British Development Assistance to Kenya*, London, Croom Helm.

Holzman, F.D. (1971), 'The real economic costs of granting foreign aid', *The Journal of Development Studies*, Vol. 7, No. 3, April.

Hopkins, M. and van der Hoeven, R. (1983), *Basic Needs in Development Planning*, London, Gower.

Hopkins, R.F. (1983), 'Evolution of food aid', *Food Policy*, Vol. 9, No. 4, November 1984 reprinted in Gittinger et al.

Hossain, M. et al. (1984), 'Western European aid to Bangladesh: evaluation of performance and policies', in Stokke, Vol. II.

Houthakker, H.S. (1965), 'On some determinants of saving in developed and underdeveloped countries' in E.A.G. Robinson (ed.), *Problems in Economic Development*, London, Macmillan.

Howe, J. and Richards, P. (1984), *Rural Roads and Poverty Alleviation*, London, Intermediate Technology Publications.

Howell, J. (1982), *UK Aid to Cooperatives in Developing Countries 1977–81, An Evaluation*, London, ODA EV263.

Howell, J. (1984), 'UK aid to the Koshi Hills', Report to ODA, London, ODI, (mimeo).

Howell, J. (ed.) (1985), *Recurrent Costs and Agricultural Development*, London, ODI.

Huizer, G. (1985), 'Peasant participation: Latin American lessons and experience in historical perspective', in Lisk.

Hunter, G. (1981), *A Hard Look at Directing Benefits to the Rural Poor and at 'Participation'*, London, ODI, Agricultural Administration Network Discussion Paper 6, June.

Hunter, S. (1984), *OPEC and the Third World*, London, Croom Helm.

Huntington, S.P. (1972), 'Foreign Aid for What and for Whom', I, *Foreign Policy* No. 1, Winter 1970–71; II, *Foreign Policy*, No. 2, Spring 1971, reprinted in R.E. Hunter and J.E. Reilly (eds), *Development Today: A New Look at US Relations With The Poor Countries*, New York, Praeger and the Overseas Development Council.

Huque K.A. (1985), *Implementation of Aid Projects: A View From the Other Side*, Stockholm, Royal Institute of Technology, Report R3.

Hyden, G. (1980), *Beyond Ujaama in Tanzania: Underdevelopment and an Uncaptured Peasantry*, London, Heinemann.

Hyden, G. (1983), *No Short Cuts to Progress: African Development Management in Perspective*, London, Heinemann.

Hyden, G. (1986), 'Enabling development: insiders and outsiders', *Third World Affairs 1986*, London, Third World Foundation for Social and Economic Studies.

Independent Commission on International Development Issues (Brandt Commission) (1980), *North-South: A Programme For Survival*, London, Pan Books.

Independent Commission on International Development Issues (Brandt Commission) (1983), *Common-Crisis North–South: Co-operation for World Recovery*, London, Pan Books.

Independent Group on British Aid (IGBA), (1982) *Real Aid*, London, IGBA.

International Fund for Agricultural Development (IFAD) (1985), *The Role of Rural Credit Projects in Reaching the Poor*, Oxford, Tycooly Publishing.

International Fund for Agricultural Development (IFAD) (1986), *Africa: Sowing the Seeds of Self-Sufficiency*, Rome, IFAD.

International Labour Office (ILO) (1976), *Employment, Growth and Basic Needs: A One-World Problem*, Geneva, ILO.

International Labour Office (ILO) (1985), *The Participation of the Rural Poor in Development*, Geneva, ILO.

Irvin, G. (1976), *Modern Cost Benefit Methods: Financial, Economic and Social Appraisal*, The Hague, Institute of Social Studies.

Jackson, R.G. (1984), *Report of the Committee to Review the Australian Overseas Aid Program*, Canberra, Australian Government Publishing Service.

Jackson, T. (1982), *Against the Grain: The Dilemma of Project Food Aid*, Oxford, Oxfam.

Jacoby, N.H. (1966), *An Evaluation of US Economic Aid to Free China, 1951-1965*, Washington. AID Discussion Paper No. 11, Bureau for the Far East.

Jacoby, R. (1986), 'Idealism and Economics', in Fruhling.

Jalée, P. (1968), *The Pillage of the Third World*, New York, Monthly Review Press.

Jennings, A. (1984), 'Measuring the success or failure of aid: an experiment in the scoring method for aid evaluation', Leicester, (mimeo).

Johnson, H.G. (1962), *Money, Trade and Economic Growth*, London, George Allen and Unwin.

Johnston, B.F. and Hoben, A. (1986), 'A preliminary assessment of USAID activities to promote agricultural and rural development in Africa', MADIA, The World Bank, (draft, mimeo).

Jones, C. (1985), 'A review of World Bank agricultural assistance to six African countries', Washington, The World Bank, 1985 (mimeo).

Jones, D. (1977), *Aid and Development in Southern Africa*, London, Croom Helm.

Joseph, K. and Sumption, J. (1979), *Equality*, London, John Murray.

Joshi, V. (1970), 'Saving and Foreign Exchange Constraints', in Streeten.

Karmiloff, I.G. (1982), *External Assistance to Least Developed Countries: An Anonymous Country's Case*, Geneva, UNCTAD, Discussion Paper No. 3.

Kay, G. (1975), *Development and Underdevelopment: A Marxist Analysis*, London, Macmillan.

Kennedy C. and Thirlwall, A.P. (1971), 'Foreign capital, domestic savings and economic development: comment', *Bulletin of the Oxford Institute of Economics and Statistics*, Vol. 33, No. 2, May.

Keynes, J.M. (1936) *The General Theory of Employment, Interest and Money*, London, Macmillan.

Killick, T. (1980), 'Trends in development economics and their relevance to Africa', *The Journal of Modern African Studies*, Vol. 18, No. 3.

Killick, T. (1985a), *Balance of Payments Adjustment and Developing Countries*, Overseas Development Institute, London, Working Paper No. 17, June.

Killick, T. (1985b), 'Twenty five years in development: the rise and impending decline of market solutions', address to Overseas Development Institute lunchtime meeting, 21 October.

Kim, S.S. (1984), *The Quest for a Just World Order*, Boulder, Colorado, Westview.

Kirkpatrick, J. (1984), 'The Superpowers: Is There a Moral Difference?', *The World Today*, May.

Kirzner, I.M. (1982), 'Entrepreneurship, Entitlement, and Economic Justice', in Paul.

Kitching, G. (1982), *Development and Underdevelopment in Historical Perspective*, London, Methuen.

Kraska, M. and Taira, K. (1974), 'Foreign capital, aid and growth in Latin America', *The Developing Economies*, Vol. XII, No. 3, September.

Krauss, M. (1983a), *Development Without Aid*, New York, McGraw Hill.

Krauss, M. (1983b), 'Transferring incomes versus transferring prosperity', *Report*, Manhattan Institute for Policy Research, January reprinted in *Economic Impact*, No. 43.

Krueger, A. (1986), 'Aid in the Development Process', *Research Review* (World Bank), Vol. 11., No. 1, January.

Krueger, A. and Ruttan, V.W. (1983a), *The Development Impact of Economic Assistance to Ldcs*, Vols. I and II, University of Minnesota for the Agency for International Development and the Department of State, March.

Krueger, A. and Ruttan, V. (1983b), 'Assistance to Korea', in Krueger and Ruttan, Vol. II.

Kurihara, K.K. (1959), *The Keynesian Theory of Economic Development*, London, Allen and Unwin.

Kuznets, S. (1955), 'Economic growth and income inequality', *The American Economic Review*, June.

Kuznets, S. (1966), *Modern Economic Growth: Rate, Structure and Spread*, New Haven and London, Yale University Press.

Kuznets, S. (1973), 'Modern economic growth: findings and reflections', *The American Economic Review*, Vol. LXII, No. 3, June.

Laclau, E. (1971), 'Feudalism and capitalism in Latin America', *New Left Review*, May–June.

Lacroix, A. (ed.) (1983), 'Dossier: evaluation', *The Courier*, No. 80, July–August.

Lacroix, R.L.J. (1985), *Integrated Rural Development in Latin America*, World Bank Staff Working Papers No. 716, Washington, The World Bank.

Lal, D. (1976), 'Distribution and Development – A Review Article, *World Development*, Vol. 4, No. 9.

Lal, D. (1983), *The Poverty of Development Economics*, London, Institute of Economic Affairs.

Landau, L. (1966), 'Determinants of saving in Latin America', *Project for Quantitative Research on Economic Development*, Cambridge, Mass., Harvard University Press.

Lappé, F.M., Collins, J. and Kinley, D. (1980), *Aid As Obstacle: Twenty Questions About Our Foreign Aid and the Hungry*, San Francisco, Institute for Food and Development Policy.

Lehmann, D. (1979), *Development Theory: Four Critical Studies*, London, Frank Cass.

Leijonhufvud, A. (1981), *Information and Coordination: Essays in Macroeconomic Theory*, Oxford, Oxford University Press.

Lembke, H.H. (1984), *Evaluating Development Assistance Projects*, West Berlin, German Development Institute.

Leudde-Neurath, R. (1982), 'A critical review of existing micro-studies on Korean protection', Brighton, IDS, (mimeo).

Leudde-Neurath, R. (1984), 'State intervention and foreign direct investment in South Korea', *IDS Bulletin*, Vol. 15, No. 2, April.

Lewis, W.A. (1954), 'Economic development with unlimited supplies of labour', *The Manchester School*, Vol. XXII, No. 2, May.

Lewis, W.A. (1984), 'The state of development theory', *The American Economic Review*, Vol. 74, No. 1, March.

Leys, C. (1978), 'Capital accumulation, class formation and dependency – the significance of the Kenyan case', *Socialist Register*, Vol. 15.

Leys, C. (1980), 'Kenya: what does dependency explain?', *Review of African Political Economy*, No. 16.

Leys, C. (1982), 'African development in theory and practice', *Daedalus*, Vol. III, No. 2, Spring.

Lipsey, R.G., and Lancaster, K. (1956-7), 'The general theory of second best', *Review of Economic Studies*, Vol. 24.

Lipton, M. (1972), 'Aid allocation when aid is inadequate: problems of the non-implementation of the Pearson Report' in Byres.

Lipton, M. (1977), *Why Poor People Stay Poor: Urban Bias in World Development*, London, Temple Smith.

Lipton, M. (1983), *Labor and Poverty*, World Bank Staff Working Papers No. 616, Washington, World Bank.

Lipton, M. (1984), 'Aid to agriculture and rural development', in Lipton et al.

Lipton, M. (1985), 'Research and the design of a policy frame for agriculture' in Rose.

Lipton, M. (1985), *Land Assets and Rural Poverty*, World Bank Staff Working Papers No. 744, Washington, The World Bank.

Lipton, M. (1986), 'Aid effectiveness, prisoners' dilemmas and country allocations', *IDS Bulletin*, Vol. 17, No. 2, April.

Lipton, M., Godding, J.P. and Godfrey, M. (1984), *International Perspectives on Rural Development*, IDS Discussion Paper No. 197, Sussex, November.

Lipton, M. and Toye, J. (1984), 'Aid effectiveness: India', Study commissioned by the Task Force on Concessional Flows, London, Brighton and Swansea, (draft/mimeo).

Lisk, F. (1985), *Popular Participation in Planning for Basic Needs, A WEP Study*, London, Gower.

Little, I.M.D. (1982), *Economic Development: Theory Policy and International Relations*, New York, Basic Books.

Little, I.M.D. (1983), 'Distributive Justice and The New International Order' in Oppenheimer, P. (ed.), *Issues in International Economics*, Oxford, Oxford University Press.

Little, I.M.D. and Clifford, J.M. (1965), *International Aid*, London, George Allen and Unwin.

Lloyd, P.C. (1979), *Slums of Hope? Shanty Towns of the Third World*, London, Penguin.

Lundahl, M. (1979), *Peasants and Poverty: A Study of Haiti*, London, Croom Helm.

Lundahl, M. (1983), *The Haitian Economy: Man, Land and Markets*, London, Croom Helm.

Lyons, D. (1965), *The Forms and Limits of Utilitarianism*, London, Oxford University Press.

MacBean, A.I. and Balasubramanyam, V.N. (1976), *Meeting the Third World Challenge*, London, Macmillan.

Mack, E. (1982), 'How to Derive Libertarian Rights', in Paul.

McKinnon, R.I. (1964), 'Foreign exchange constraints in economic development and efficient aid allocation', *The Economic Journal*, Vol. 74.

Marini, R.M. (1972), 'Brazilian sub-Imperialism', *Monthly Review*, No. 9, February.

Marris, R. (1970), 'Can we measure the need for development assistance?', *The Economic Journal*, Vol. 80.

Marsden, K., and Roe, A. (1983), 'The political economy of foreign aid: a World

Bank perspective', *Labour and Society*, Vol. 8, No. 1. January–March.

Marten, N. (1983), 'Britain's Aid Policy', *The Round Table*, No. 286.

Mason, E.S., Je Kim, M. et al. (1980), *The Economic and Social Modernisation of the Republic of Korea*, Cambridge, Mass., Harvard University Press.

Massell, B.F., Pearson, R.S. and Fitch, J.D. (1975), 'Foreign exchange and economic development: an empirical study of selected Latin American countries', *Review of Economics and Statistics*, Vol. 54.

Maxwell, S. (1983), 'From understudy to leading stars: the future role of impact assessment in food aid programmes', in Clay and Singer.

Meier, G.M. (1984), *Leading Issues in Economic Development*, New York, Oxford University Press.

Meier, G.M. and Baldwin, R.E. (1957), *Economic Development: Theory, History, Policy*, New York, John Wiley.

Mende, T. (1973), *From Aid to Recolonisation: Lessons of a Failure*, London, Harrap.

Mettrick, H. (1979), *Oxenisation in The Gambia: An Evaluation*, London, ODA, EV14, April.

Michaely, M. (1981), 'Foreign aid, economic structure and dependence', *Journal of Development Economics*, Vol. 9, December.

Mickesell, R.F. (1968), *The Economics of Foreign Aid*, London, Weidenfeld and Nicolson.

Mickesell, R.F. and Zinser, J.E. (1973), 'The nature of the savings function in developing countries: a survey of the theoretical and empirical literature', *Journal of Economic Literature*, Vol. XI, No. 1, March.

Miliband, R. (1969), *The State in Capitalist Society*, London, Quartet Books.

Miller, D. (1979), *Social Justice*, Oxford, Clarendon.

Miller, D. (1980), 'Justice and Property', *Ratio*, xxii(i), June.

Miller, D. (1980), 'Social Justice and The Principle of Need' in M. Freeman and D. Robertson (eds), *The Frontiers of Political Theory*, Brighton, Harvester.

Miller, D. (1983), 'Constraints on Freedom', *Ethics*, Vol. 94, October.

Miller, Duncan (1980), *Studies on Rural Development Volume I: Studies on Project Design, Implementation and Evaluation*, Development Centre Papers, OECD.

Millikan, M.F. and Rostow, W.W. (1957), *A Proposal: Key to an Effective Foreign Policy*, New York, Harper and Brothers.

Millwood, D. and Gezelius, H. (1985), *Good Aid: A Study of Quality in Small Projects*, Stockholm, SIDA.

Ministry of Overseas Development (1975), *Overseas Development, The Changing Emphasis in British Aid Policies, More Help For The Poorest*, London, HMSO, Cmnd 6270.

Misra, R.P. (1981), 'A critical analysis of the traditional cost benefit approach to economic development', *Development*, Vol. 3, No. 4.

Morawetz, D. (1977), *Twenty Five Years of Economic Development, 1950–1975*, Washington, The World Bank.

Morss, E.R. and Gow, D.D. (eds) (1985), *Implementing Rural Development Projects: Lessons from AID and World Bank Experience*, Boulder, Westview.

Morss, E.R., and Morss, V.A. (1982), *US Foreign Aid: An Assessment of New and Traditional Development Strategies*, Boulder, Westview.

Morton, K. (1975), *Aid and Dependence*, London, Croom Helm.

Mosley, P. (1980), 'Aid, savings and growth revisited', *Oxford Bulletin of Economics and Statistics*, Vol. 42, No. 2, May.

Mosley, P. (1981), 'Aid for the poorest: some early lessons of UK experience', *The Journal of Development Studies*, January.

Mosley, P. (1982), *The Political Economy of Foreign Aid: A Study of the Market for a Public Good*, University of Bath, Papers in Political Economy, Working Paper 1181.

Mosley, P. (1983), 'The politics of evaluation: a comparative study of World Bank and Ukoda evaluation procedures', *Development and Change*, Vol. 14 No. 4, October.

Mosley, P. and Hudson, J. (1984), *Aid, The Public Sector and the Market in Less Developed Countries*, University of Bath, Papers in Political Economy, Working Paper 0184.

Murray, R. (1972), 'Underdevelopment, international firms and the international division of labour' in *Towards A New World Economy*, Rotterdam University Press.

Muscat, R.J. (1986), 'Evaluating technical cooperation: a review of the literature', *Development Policy Review*, Vol. 4, No. 1. March.

Myrdal, G. (1957), *Economic Theory and Underdeveloped Regions*, New York, Harper and Row.

Myrdal, G. (1968), *Asian Drama: An Inquiry Into the Poverty of Nations*, New York, The Twentieth Century Fund.

Myrdal, G. (1970), *The Challenge of World Poverty*, London, Allen Lane, The Penguin Press.

Myrdal, G. (1982), 'Relief Instead of Development Aid', *Scandinavian Journal of Developing Countries*, Vol. 1, No. 4, December.

Nagel, T. (1982), 'Libertarianism Without Foundations' in Paul.

Nelson, G.O. et al. (1981), *Food Aid and Development*, New York, Agricultural Development Council.

Nelson, R.R. (1964), 'Aggregate production functions and medium-range growth projections', *The American Economic Review*, Vol. LIV, No. 5.

Nozick, R. (1974), *Anarchy, State and Utopia*, Oxford, Blackwell.

Nugent, J.B., and Yotopoulos, P.A. (1979), 'What has orthodox development economics learned from recent experience?', *World Development*, Vol. 7, No. 6.

Office of Technology Assessment (1984), *Africa Tomorrow: Issues in Technology, Agriculture and US Foreign Aid*, Washington, Office of Technology, Congress of the United States, December.

Ohlin, G. (1965), *Foreign Aid Policies Reconsidered*, Paris, Development Centre of the OECD.

O'Neill, O. (1982), 'Nozick's Entitlements' in Paul.

O'Neill, O. (1986), *Faces of Hunger: An Essay on Poverty, Justice and Development*, London, Allen and Unwin.

Over, A.M. (1975), 'An example of the simultaneous equations problem: a note on "Foreign assistance: objectives and consequences" ', *Economic Development and Cultural Change*, Vol. 23, July.

Organisation for Economic Co-operation and Development (OECD) (1986), *Financial Resources For Developing Countries: 1985 and Recent Trends*, Paris, OECD, Press/A (86) 27, June.

Overseas Development Administration (ODA) (1980), 'Britain's Overseas Aid Policy, London, ODA (mimeo).

Overseas Development Administration (ODA) (1983), *British Overseas Aid 1982*, London.

Overseas Development Administration (ODA), (1984), 'United Kingdom memorandum to the Development Assistance Committee of the Organisation for Economic Co-operation and Development, 1984', London, ODA, (mimeo).

Overseas Development Administration (ODA) (1985a), *British Overseas Aid 1984*, London.

Overseas Development Administration (ODA) (1985b), *Guidelines for the Preparation of Evaluation Studies*, London, ODA, July.

Overseas Development Council (ODC) (1986), *Policy Focus, The Budget and US Foreign Aid: More Tough Choices?*, Washington.

Overseas Development Institute (ODI) (1964), *French Aid: The Jeanneney Report*, Oxford, Blackwell.

Overseas Development Institute (ODI) (1986a), *The US and International Financial Reform*, Briefing Paper, May.

Overseas Development Institute (ODI), (1986b), *Privatisation: The Developing Country Experience*, Briefing Paper, September.

Palma, G. (1981), 'Dependency and development: a critical overview', in Seers.

Palmlund, T. (1986), 'Altruism and other motives', in Fruhling.

Papanek, G.F. (1972), 'The effect of aid and other resource transfers on savings and growth in less developed countries', *The Economic Journal*, Vol. 82, No. 327, September.

Papanek, G.F. (1973), 'Aid, foreign private investment, saving and growth in less developed countries', *The Journal of Political Economy*, No. 81, 1973.

Papanek, G.F. (1977), 'Economic development theory: the earnest search for a mirage', *Economic Development and Cultural Change*, Vol. 25 (Supplement).

Papanek, G.F. (1978), 'Economic growth, income distribution and the political process in less developed countries', in Z. Griliches, W. Krelle et al. (eds), *Income Distribution and Income Inequality*, New York, Halstead Press.

Papanek, G.F. (1983), 'Aid, equity and growth in South Asia', in J. Parkinson (ed.), *Poverty and Aid*, Oxford, Blackwell.

Parkinson, J.R. (1983), *Poverty and Aid*, Oxford, Blackwell.

Paukert, F. (1973), 'Income distribution at different levels of development: a survey of evidence', *International Labour Review*, Vol. 108, No. 2–3, August–September.

Paul, J. (ed.) (1982), *Reading Nozick: Essays on Anarchy, State and Utopia*, Oxford, Blackwell.

Pietrodangelo, D. (1985), 'Haiti, counting the cost', *The Caribbean and West Indies Chronicle*, June/July.

Pines, J. (1982), 'National nutrition planning: lessons of experience', *Food Policy*, Vol. 7 No. 4, November.

Pinstrup-Anderson, P. and Hazell, B.R. (1985), 'The impact of the Green Revolution and prospects for the future' in Gittinger et al.

Plant, R. (1984), *Equality, Markets and the State*, Fabian Tract 494, London.

Plant, R. (1987), *Sugar and Modern Slavery*, London, Zed Books.

Please, S. (1984), *The Hobbled Giant: Essays on the World Bank*, London and Boulder, Westview Press.

Populorum Progressio (1967), Encyclical Letter of Pope Paul VI, London, Catholic Truth Society.

Poulantzas, N. (1973), *Political Power and Social Classes*, London, Schocken.

Poulantzas, N. (1975), *Classes in Contemporary Capitalism*, London, New Left Books.

President's The, Task Force on International Private Enterprise (1984), *The*

Private Enterprise Guidebook, and *Report to the President*, Washington DC, December.

Prince, R. (1985), *Haiti: Family Business*, London, Latin American Bureau.

Pym, F. (1982), *Britain's Contribution to the Development of The Third World*, Address to the Royal Commonwealth Society, 7 December 1982, London, Foreign and Commonwealth Office.

Quijano, A. (1974), 'The marginal pole of the economy and the marginalised labour force', *Economy and Society*, Vol. 3, No. 4.

Radetski, M. (1973), *Aid and Development: A Handbook for Small Donors*, New York, Praeger.

Radetski, M. (1986), 'Swedish aid to Kenya and Tanzania: its impact on rural development', MADIA, Washington, The World Bank, (draft, mimeo).

Radice, H. (ed.) (1975), *International Firms and Modern Imperialism*, London, Penguin.

Rahman, M.A. (1968), 'Foreign capital and domestic savings: a test of Haavelmo's hypothesis with cross-country data', *Review of Economics and Statistics*, No. 50.

Rahman, S. and McDonnell, N. (1984), 'An analysis of USAID impact evaluation studies; implications for the future', *Scandinavian Journal of Development Alternatives* Vol. 14 Nos.3–4, September and December.

Randall, V, and Theobald, R. (1985), *Political Change and Underdevelopment; A Critical Introduction to Third World Politics*, London, Croom Helm.

Rao, V.K. and Narain, D. (1962), *Foreign Aid and India's Economic Development: A Case Study*, Paris, UNESCO.

Rawls, J. (1973), *A Theory of Justice*, Oxford, Oxford University Press.

Reutlinger, S., and Katona-Apte, J. (1985), 'The nutritional impact of food aid: criteria for selecting cost-effective foods', in Gittinger et al.

Reynolds, L.G. (1983), 'The spread of economic growth to the Third World, 1850–1980', *Journal of Economic Literature*, Vol. XXI, No. 3, September.

Reynolds, L.G. (1985), *Economic Growth in the Third World, 1850–1980*, New Haven, Yale University Press.

Rhodes, R.I. (ed.) (1970), *Imperialism and Underdevelopment: A Reader*, New York, Monthly Review Press.

Riddell, R.C. (1983), *An Economic Evaluation: Zimbabwe's Commodity Import Programs with Special Reference to the United States Programs*, Harare, USAID, August.

Robinson, R. (1971), *Developing the Third World: The Experience of the 1960s*, Cambridge, Cambridge University Press.

Roll, E. (1968), *The World After Keynes*, London, Pall Mall Press.

Rondinelli, D.A. (1985), 'Development administration and American foreign assistance policy: an assessment of theory and practice in aid', *Canadian Journal of Development Studies*, Vol. 6 No. 2.

Rose, T. (ed.) (1985), *Crisis and Recovery in Sub-Saharan Africa*, Paris, OECD.

Rosenau, J.N. (1980), *The Study of Global Interdependence: Essays on the Transnationalisation of World Affairs*, New York, Nichols.

Rosenstein-Rodan, P.N. (1961), 'International aid for underdeveloped countries', *Review of Economics and Statistics*, Vol. 43, No. 2, May.

Rostow, W.W. (ed.) (1963), *The Economics of Take-Off into Sustained Growth*, London, Macmillan.

Rostow, W.W. (1971), *The Stages of Economic Growth*, Cambridge, Cambridge University Press.

Roxborough, I. (1979), *Theories of Underdevelopment*, London, Macmillan.

Ruttan, V.W. (1984), 'Integrated rural development programmes: an historical perspective', *World Development*, Vol. 12, No. 4.

Ruttan, V.W. (1986), 'Assistance to expand agricultural production', *World Development*, Vol. 14, No. 1.

Ryan, C.C. (1982), 'Yours, Mine and Ours: Property Rights and Individual Liberty' in Paul.

Ryrie, W. (1986), 'Managing an aid programme', *IDS Bulletin*, Vol. 17, No. 2, April.

Salazar-Xirinachs, I.M. (1985), 'Reasserting The Case for State Intervention: A Theoretical Critique of Free Market Views on Economic Incentives and Development Strategy', Cambridge, February (mimeo).

Sandbrook, R. (1982), *The Politics of Basic Needs: Urban Aspects of Assaulting Poverty in Africa*, London, Heinemann.

Sautter, H. (1985), 'Underdevelopment through isolationism: dependency theory in retrospect', *Intereconomics*, July/August.

Scanlon, T. (1982), 'Nozick on Rights, Liberty and Property' in Paul.

Schaffer, B. and Lamb, G. (1981), *Can Equality Be Organised?*, Paris, UNESCO.

Scheffler, S. (1982), 'National Rights, Equality and The Minimal State' in Paul.

Scitovsky, T. (1985), 'Economic development in Taiwan and South Korea: 1965–81', *Food Research Institute Studies*, Vol. XIX, No. 3.

Seers, D. (1963), 'The limitations of the special case', *Bulletin of the Oxford Institute of Economics and Statistics*, Vol. 25, No. 2.

Seers, D. (1972), 'What Types of Government should be Refused What Types of Aid?', *IDS Bulletin*, June, 4(2/3).

Seers, D. (ed.) (1981a), *Dependency Theory: A Critical Reassessment*, London, Frances Pinter.

Seers, D. (1981b), 'Development options: the strengths and weaknesses of dependency theories in explaining a government's room to manoeuvre' in Seers.

Seers, D. (1982), 'Wanted – A New Map of The World', *The Guardian*, 28 May.

Seers, D. (1983), 'Time for a Second Look at the Third World', *Development Policy Review*, Vol. 1, No. 1, May.

Seers, D. and Myrdal, G. (1982), 'The withering of aid', *The Guardian*, 2 July.

Sen, A. (1981a), 'Public action and the quality of life in developing countries', *Oxford Bulletin of Economics and Statistics*, Vol. 43, No. 4, November.

Sen, A. (1981b), *Poverty and Famine*, Oxford, Clarendon Press.

Sen, A. (1982a), 'The Right not to be Hungry', *Contemporary Philosophy A New Survey*, Vol. 2, The Hague, M. Nijhoff.

Sen, A. (1982b), 'Just Deserts', *New York Review of Books*, 4 March.

Sen, A. (1983a), 'The profit motive', *Lloyds Bank Review*, No. 147, January.

Sen, A. (1983b), 'Development: which way now?', *The Economic Journal*, Vol. 93, No. 372, December.

Sen, A. (1984), 'Carrots, Sticks and Economics: Perception Problems in Incentives', *Indian Economic Review*, Vol. 18, No. 1.

Sen, A. (1985), 'The new economic gospel', text of talk for 'Opinions', Channel Four, 16 July.

Shand, R.T. and Richter, H.V. (eds) (1979), *International Aid: Some Political, Administrative and Technical Realities*, Canberra, The Australian National University.

Shaw, T.M. and Aluko, O. (1985), *Africa Projected: From Recession to Renaissance by The Year 2000?*, London, Macmillan.

Shultz, G. (1984), *International Security and Development Cooperation Program*, Presented to US Congress, April, United States, Department of State, Washington DC, Special Report No. 116.

Shultz, G. (1986), *Moral Principles and Strategic Interests; The Worldwide Movement Towards Democracy*, Washington, United States, Department of State, Bureau of Public Affairs, Current Policy No. 820, April.

Sibthorp, M.M. and Edwards, G.R. (1984), *Aid to Developing Countries: Improving Its Effectiveness*, London, David Davies Memorial Institute of International Studies.

Siebert, R. (1986), 'The power of the poor: self-help groups in Asia', *Development and Cooperation*, No. 2, March/April.

Sieghart, P. (1983), 'Economic Development, Human Rights and The Omelette Thesis', *Development Policy Review*, Vol. 1, No. 1.

Singer, H. (1970), *Keynesian Models of Economic Development and Their Limitations: An Analysis in the Light of Gunnar Myrdal's 'Asian Drama'*, Communications No. 54, Institute of Development Studies, University of Sussex.

Singer, H, (1984), *The Ethics of Aid*, IDS Discussion Paper No. 195, Brighton, October.

Singer, P. (1971), 'Famine, Affluence and Morality' in P. Laslett and J.S. Fishkin, *Philosophy, Politics and Society*, Fifth Edition, Oxford, Blackwell.

Skeates, R. and Whitlam, G. (1983), 'The role of performance evaluation in the development process', *Asian Development Review*, Vol. 1, No. 2.

Skolka, J. (1983), *Economic Growth, Structure of the Economy and Distribution of Income*, World Employment Programme Research, Working Paper 45, ILO, Geneva, January.

Smith, K. (1984), *The British Economic Crisis*, London, Penguin.

Smith, S. (1980), 'The ideas of Samir Amin: theory or tautology?', *The Journal of Development Studies*, Vol. 17, No. 1, October.

Sobhan, R. (1982), *The Crisis of External Dependence – The Political Economy of Foreign Aid to Bangladesh*, Dhaka.

Social Surveys (Gallup Poll) (1983), 'Overseas Aid 7–11 January 1983' conducted on behalf of Office of Population Censuses and Services, London CQ848/848A *(mimeo)*.

Sommer, J.G. (1977), *Beyond Charity: US Voluntary Aid for a Changing Third World*, Washington, Overseas Development Council.

Steinberg, D.I. (1984), 'On foreign aid and the development of the Republic of Korea: the effectiveness of concessional assistance', Paper prepared for the Task Force on Concessional Flows, Washington, (draft, mimeo).

Sterba, J.P. (1978), 'In Defence of Rawls Against Arrow and Nozick', *Philosphia*, No. 7.

Stern, N. (1974), 'Professor Bauer on development', *Journal of Development Economics*, Vol. 1.

Stevens, C. (1979), *Food Aid and the Developing World: Four African Case Studies*, London, Croom Helm.

Stevens, C. (1983), 'Legal? Decent? Honest?' in Clay and Singer.

Stevens, C. (1985), *Food Aid: An Assessment*, Centre for Development Studies, Universitaire Faculteiten, St. Ignatius, Antwerp, Paper 85/87, January.

Stevens, J.N. and Beard, P.W. (1984), *An Evaluation of Electrification in Bali*, London, ODA, EV330.

Stevens, J.N. and Beard, P.W. (1984), *An Evaluation of Electrification in Tonga*, London, ODA.

Stevens, J.N., and Beard, P.W. (1984), *An Evaluation of Diesel Generators in Nepal*, London, ODA.

Stewart, F. (1971), 'Foreign capital, domestic savings and economic development: comment', *Bulletin of the Oxford Institute of Economics and Statistics*, Vol. 33, No. 2, May.

Stewart, F. (1978), 'Social cost-benefit analysis in practice; some reflections in the light of case studies using Little-Mirrlees techniques', *World Development*, Vol. 6, No. 2, February.

Stewart, F. (1979), 'Country experience in providing basic needs', *Finance and Development*, Vol. 16, No. 4, December.

Stewart, F. (1985), 'Limitations of the neo-classical approach to development: a review of Deepak Lal: "The Poverty of Development Economics" ', SOAS/UCL Development Seminar, Working Paper No. 64, February.

Stokke, O. (ed.) (1984), *European Development Assistance: Volume I, Policies and Performance, Volume II Third World Perspectives on Politics and Performance*, EADI Book Series 4, Oslo, Norwegian Institute of International Affairs.

Stoneman, C. (1975), Foreign capital and economic growth', *World Development*, Vol. 3 No. 1, January.

Streeten, P. (ed.) (1971), *Unfashionable Economics*, London, Weidenfeld and Nicolson.

Streeten, P. (1972), *The Frontiers of Development Studies*, London, Macmillan.

Streeten, P. (ed.) (1978), 'Poverty and inequality', *World Development*, Vol. 6, No. 3, March.

Streeten, P. (1981), *Development Perspectives*, London, Macmillan.

Streeten, P. (1983), 'Why development aid?', *Banca Nazionale del Lavoro Quarterly Review*, No. 47, December.

Streeten, P. (1985), Food Prices as a Reflection of Political Power', *Ceres*, Vol. 16, No. 2, March–April 1983, pp. 16–21, reproduced in Gittinger *et al.*

Sukhatme, V. (1983), 'Assistance to India', in Krueger and Ruttan Vol. II.

Sumberg, T.A. (1973), *Foreign Aid as Moral Obligation?* The Washington Papers 1 (10), Beverly Hills, Sage.

Sunkel, O. (1969), 'National development policy and external dependence in Latin America', *The Journal of Development Studies*, Vol. 6, No. 1, October.

Supple, B. (1972), 'Thinking about economic development', in A.J. Youngson, *Economic Development in the Long Run*, London, George Allen and Unwin.

Swedish International Development Agency (SIDA) (1979–1982), *Report*, various issues.

Swedish International Development Agency (SIDA) (1983), *Sweden and International Development Co-operation*, Stockholm, SIDA.

Swedish National Audit Bureau (SNBA), (1974), *SIDA in Tanzania*, Stockholm.

Swedish National Audit Bureau (SNBA) (1976), *SIDA in India*, Stockholm.

Tendler, J. (1975), *Inside Foreign Aid*, Baltimore, Johns Hopkins University Press.

Tendler, J. (1979a), *New Directions Rural Roads*, AID Program Evaluation Discussion Paper No. 2, Office of Evaluation, Bureau for Program and Policy Co-ordination, USAID, Washington.

Tendler, J. (1979b), *Rural Electrification: Linkages and Justification*, AID Program Evaluation Discussion Paper No. 3, Office of Evaluation, Bureau for Program and Policy Co-ordination, USAID, Washington.

Tendler, J. (1982a), *Turning Private Voluntary Organisations Into Development*

Agencies: Questions for Evaluation, AID Program Evaluation Discussion Paper No. 12, USAID, Washington, April.

Tendler, J. (1982b), *Rural Projects Through Urban Eyes*, World Bank Staff Working Papers No. 532, Washington, The World Bank.

Tendler, J. (1986), 'Captive donors and captivating clients: A Nicaraguan saga', *World Development*, (forthcoming).

Thompson, J.J. (1982), 'Some Rumination on Rights' in Paul.

Thoumi, F.E. (1983), *Social and Political Obstacles to Economic Development in Haiti*, Washington, Inter-American Development Bank, Reprint Series No. 137.

Toye, J.F.J. (1983), 'The Disparaging of Development Economics', *The Journal of Development Studies*, 20(1), October.

Toye, J.F.J. (1984), *A Defence of Development Economics*, Swansea, University College of Swansea.

Toye, J. and Clark, G. (1986), 'The Aid and Trade Provisions (ATP): origins, dimensions and possible reforms', *Development Policy Review*, Vol. 4, No. 4.

Tucker, R.W. (1977), *The Inequality of Nations*, New York, Basic Books.

Twose, N. (1984), *Cultivating Hunger; An Oxfam Study of Food, Power and Politics*, Oxford, Oxfam.

United Nations Development Program (UNDP) (1979), *Rural Development: Issues and Approaches for Technical Co-operation*, Evaluation Study No. 2, New York, UNDP, June.

United Nations Development Program (UNDP) (1982), *International Co-operation Dossier: Haiti*, New York, UNDP.

United Nations Report of the Secretary General (1986), *The Critical Economic Situation in Africa*, New York, UN General Assembly, 20 May.

United Nations ACC Task Force on Rural Development (1984), Panel on Monitoring and Evaluation, *Guiding Principles for the Design and Use of Monitoring and Evaluation in Rural Development Projects and Programmes*, Rome, IFAD, December.

United States Agency for International Development (USAID) (1982), *Recurrent Costs*, AID Policy Paper, Washington, USAID, May.

Van Arkadie, B. and de Wilde, K. (1984), 'Aid effectiveness in Bangladesh', The Hague, ISS Advisory Services, (draft/mimeo).

Van der Laar, A. (1980), *The World Bank and the Poor*, The Hague, Martinus Nijhoff.

Venieris, Y.P. and Gupta, D.K. (1983), 'Sociological and economic dimensions of development: a cross-section model', *Economic Development and Cultural Change*, Vol. 31, No. 4, July.

Wallace, W. (1986), 'What Price Independence? Sovereignty and Independence in British Politics', *International Affairs*, Vol. 62, No. 3, Summer.

Wallerstein, I. (1979), *The Capitalist World Economy*, Cambridge, Cambridge University Press.

Wallis, A. (1983), *Economics and Politics: The Quandary of Foreign Aid*, Address of the Under Secretary for Economic Affairs to the Heritage Foundation, 3 March, United States Department of State, Bureau of Public Affairs, Washington DC, Current Policy No. 461.

Walsh, V. and Gram, H. (1980), *Classical and Neo-classical Theories of General Equilibrium*, Oxford, Oxford University Press.

Ward, B. and Bauer P.T. (1966), *Two Views on Aid to Developing Countries*, London, Institute of Economic Affairs.

Warren, B. (1973), 'Imperialism and capitalist industrialisation', *New Left Review*, No. 81.

Warren, B. (1980), *Imperialism: Pioneer of Capitalism*, London, New Left Books.

Weiner, M.L. (1984), 'The evaluation systems of other governments and institutions: the World Bank' in Cracknell.

Weisskopf, T.E. (1972a), 'An economic test of alternative constraints on the growth of underdeveloped countries', *Review of Economics and Statistics*, Vol. 54, No. 1, Part II.

Weisskopf, T.E. (1972b), 'The impact of foreign capital inflow on domestic savings in under-developed countries', *Journal of International Economics*, Vol. 2.

Weisskopf, T.E. (1983), 'Alternative models of economic development', *Economies et Sociétés*, Vol. 17, No. 2.

Wheatley, C., Arnold, G., Leckscheidt J., and Adade, A. (1985) *Assessment and Interpretation of Development Aid Success: A Proposed Scoring System for Application by the EEC and Other Development Agencies*, Frankfurt, Integration.

White, J. (1974), *The Politics of Foreign Aid*, London, The Bodley Head.

White, J. (1976), 'The evaluation of aid offers', *Development and Change,* Vol. 7 No. 3, July.

Williams, B. (1969), 'The Idea of Equality' in P. Laslett and W.G. Runciman, (eds) *Philosophy, Politics and Society*, Oxford, Blackwell, Second Series.

Williams, P.R.C. (1985), *They Came to Train*, ODA, London, HMSO Books.

Winch, D.M. (1971), *Analytic Welfare Economics*, London, Penguin.

Wolfe, M. (1981), *Elusive Development*, Geneva, UNRISD.

Wood, R.E. (1980), 'Foreign Aid and The Capitalist State in Underdeveloped Society', *Politics and Society* Vol. 10, No. 1.

Wood, R., and Morton, K. (1977), 'Has British aid helped poor countries? – five African cases', *ODI Review*, No. 1.

World Bank (1959), *A Public Development Program for Thailand*, Baltimore, Johns Hopkins University Press.

World Bank (1968), *Economic Growth, Trade and the Balance of Payments in the Developing Countries, 1960–65*, World Bank Staff Paper, Washington, March.

World Bank (Various) *World Development Reports*, London and Washington, Oxford University Press.

World Bank (1981), *Accelerated Development in Sub-Saharan Africa*, Washington, World Bank.

World Bank (1982), *IDA in Retrospect: The First Two Decades of the International Development Association*, Washington, World Bank.

World Bank (1984a), *Institutional Development in Africa: A Review of World Bank Project Experience*, Operations Evaluation Department, Washington, World Bank.

World Bank, (1984b), *Ninth Annual Review of Project Performance Audit Results 1983*, Washington, World Bank.

World Bank (1984c), *Towards Sustained Development in Sub-Saharan Africa: A Joint Program of Action*, Washington, World Bank.

World Bank (1985), *Tenth Annual Review of Project Peformance Audit Results, 1984*, Washington, World Bank.

World Bank (1986a), *Financing Adjustment with Growth in Sub–Saharan Africa 1986-90*, Washington, World Bank.

World Bank (1986b), *Poverty and Hunger: Issues and Options for Food Security in Developing Countries*, Washington, World Bank.

World Food Programme (WFP) (1983), *Food Works: Twenty Years of Food Aid for Development*, 1963–1983, Rome WFP.

Yaser, B. (1980), 'Replication and scaling-up criteria in project design', in Miller.

Yotopoulos, P.A. and Nugent, J.B. (1976), *Economics of Development: Empirical Investigations*, New York, Harper and Row.

Young, R. (1983), *Canadian Development Assistance to Tanzania*, Ottawa, North-South Institute.

Yudelman, M. (1984), 'Agricultural lending by the Bank 1974–84: a retrospective analysis', *Finance and Development*, Vol. 21 No. 4, December.

Zaidi, I.M. (1985), 'Saving, Investment, Fiscal Deficits and The External Indebtedness of Developing Countries', *World Development*, Vol. 13, No. 5, May.

Zeylstra W.G. (1975), *Aid or Development: The Relevance of Development Aid to Problems of Developing Countries*, Leyden, A.W. Sijthoff.

Zinkin, M. (1978), 'Aid and Morals', *The Round Table*, No. 271.

Zuvekas, C. (1978), *Agricultural Development in Haiti*, Washington, USAID.

Index

World Recession & the Food Crisis in Africa
Edited by Peter Lawrence

This book is published in association with the *Review of African Political Economy*

The persistent recession in the world economy has seriously aggravated the crisis of food supply throughout Africa. Assistance from international lending agencies, like the IMF and the World Bank, is an important weapon against famine for countries which cannot feed themselves or which are afflicted by drought. The domination of these institutions by the monetarist orthodoxy makes such aid available only on even tighter conditions.

- This timely and thought-provoking collection examines in Part One the nature of the current depression, places it in historical perspective and highlights the direct and indirect effects on Nigeria and the economies of the Southern Africa Development Coordination Conference (SADCC).

- Part Two describes the nature of aid from the IMF and the World Bank and its conditionality, especially in relation to the analysis of sub-Saharan Africa's problems made in the Berg Report.

- In Part Three, the particular problems of food supply are discussed. How far does aid help to alleviate famine? How far is the crisis of food supply internally or externally generated? How far is the food crisis related to changes in social structures and especially to the disintegration of social systems devastated by labour out-migration? Case studies of Sudan, Nigeria, Zimbabwe, Zaire and southern Africa.

320pp   234 × 156
Bibliography   Index
Cased 0-85255-309-9
Paper 0-85255-304-8

Uganda Now
Edited by Holger Bernt Hansen & Michael Twaddle

The Museveni takeover of power in Uganda has captured the enthusiasm of so many people who have watched the last decade in Uganda with great distress. What does the future hold? These informed assessments of Uganda's quarter century since independence put the present situation in context. They provide up to date material for people to consider whether the country is one of those, in *The Economist*'s words, which is 'on the blink'. Can Museveni's undoubted drive and puritanism bring the country back from the grip of warlords? Can he break the recurring patterns of Ugandan history?

The editors have put the whole consideration of the case of Uganda within the wider context of Africa's development crisis. Uganda has presented in an aggravated form the crisis common to many other African countries; infrastructural breakdown, mounting foreign debt, military and civilian regimes and waves of refugees.

Contents Is Africa decaying? by Ali Mazrui – Contributions on Education, Agriculture, Politics, Human Rights, Refugees, Communications, External and Internal cause of the crisis, etc., by Christopher Wrigley, Aidan Southall, Martin Doornbos, Oliver Furley, D.R.G. Belshaw, Apolo Nsibambi, Nelson Kasfir, Michael Whyte, Keith Edmunds, George Kanyeihamba, Louise Pirouet, Peter Woodward, D.A. Low, Dan Mudoola, John Rowe, Joshua Sempebwa, Christine Obbo, Dan Nabudere, Sentenza Kajubi and others; and a detailed chronology of the years since Amin by Hugh Dinwiddy.

About 256pp   234 × 156
Cased 0-85255-315-3
Paper 0-85255-316-1